The Just and Loving Gaze of God with Us

The Just and Loving Gaze of God with Us

Paul's Apocalyptic Political Theology

HENRY WALTER SPAULDING III

WIPF & STOCK · Eugene, Oregon

THE JUST AND LOVING GAZE OF GOD WITH US
Paul's Apocalyptic Political Theology

Wipf & Stock
An Imprint of Wipf and Stock Publishers
199 W. 8th Ave., Suite 3
Eugene, OR 97401

www.wipfandstock.com

PAPERBACK ISBN: 978-1-5326-6643-8
HARDCOVER ISBN: 978-1-5326-6644-5
EBOOK ISBN: 978-1-5326-6645-2

Manufactured in the U.S.A.   JANUARY 23, 2019

For my parents, Henry and Sharon Spaulding

All I am is because of you. Every single day I try to be a person worthy of the countless gifts you have given me.

Contents

Acknowledgements

The process of converting a dissertation into a book is not a venture taken without companions. In my educational journey, I have relied upon the goodness of others for wisdom, guidance, encouragement, and hope. I am grateful first and foremost for my parents, Henry and Sharon, who have been my biggest supporters and encouragers throughout this process. Undoubtedly, I would not have finished without them and their many gifts. My father read through many drafts of each chapter and gave invaluable feedback. My father is my first and greatest teacher of theology, and he is also the greatest man I have ever known. My mother also spent many days blessing me with gifts that made the darker days of the journey not as rough. My mother's grace, generosity, and love are evident in these pages. This project is dedicated to them.

I am also grateful for my soon-to-be wife, Michaela Bruce, who was very patient and understanding in my need to be secluded and type this dissertation. She too has read and listened to me speak about my dissertation more than most people would tolerate. I do not know how to repay this patience.

I would also like to thank my good friends Patrick John Taylor, Luke Harbaugh, and Jerry Romasco, who encouraged me not to quit my calling.

I would like to thank all the many people who helped me edit the dissertation while also giving valuable feedback: Krista Armstrong, Jeanne Bruce, Hallie Logan, Zac Sherman, Brett Wiley, Andy Johnson, and Nathan Figueroa.

No acknowledgement would be completed without a hearty thank you to all the professors who were instrumental in my educational process. This first includes those who taught me as an undergraduate at Trevecca Nazarene University, where I first fell in love with theology: Nate

Kerr, Brent McMillian, Steve Hoskins, Tim Green, Dan Spross, and Kathy Mowry.

Second are my many influences during my time at Duke Divinity School: Warren Smith, C. Kavin Rowe, Anathea Portier-Young, Richard Hays, Stanley Hauerwas, Randy Maddox, and Amy Laura Hall. I wish to single out J. Kameron Carter and Willie James Jennings, who guided my Master's thesis and endured many hours of probing questions about it.

Third, I wish to thank personally the few professors with whom I worked at Garrett-Evangelical Theological Seminary. First, Jim Papandrea, who gave me many directed studies and allowed me the opportunity to be his teaching assistant. Second, to Nancy Bedford, who challenged my understanding of many figures crucial to this project, specifically Karl Barth.

Special thanks are due to Brent Waters, who guided me gracefully through my doctorate. Dr. Waters is not only an advisor, but a mentor and friend. His influence and humor made the dissertation not only bearable, but fun. I cannot thank him enough for the opportunity to study with him. I also wish to thank the other two members of my committee, Charles Cosgrove and William Cavanaugh. Dr. Cosgrove tirelessly worked with me on the vexed and complicated discipline of New Testament and apocalyptic. Without his patient and wise clarifications, I would not have come to the full appreciation of apocalyptic theology that I now have. Dr. Cavanaugh was a tireless inspiration and his questions helped form the best work possible.

Finally, I would like to thank the good people at Wipf and Stock Publishers—specifically Matthew Wimer, Daniel Lanning, Caleb Shupe, George Callihan, and the editors, who tirelessly worked with me on making this dream a reality.

As this work matured, I directed it at two communities.

First, my students and colleagues at Mount Vernon Nazarene University. All theological academia should consider the minds of the new generation of students who develop the necessary tools to confront new threats and challenges. The university slogan of Mount Vernon is "To Seek to Learn is to Seek to Serve." My hope is that the students and faculty who seek to learn from this text will recognize the profound call to serve.

Second, I had in mind my own congregation, Shepherd's House Church of the Nazarene, while writing this dissertation. All theology is ultimately for the church. I hope this document helps engage a new century of problems that now confront her.

HENRY WALTER SPAULDING III
Advent 2018

Introduction
The "Political" Paul

THE WRITINGS OF THE apostle Paul have long held a prominent place in both New Testament studies and the Christian faith. Recently, however, a new philosophical approach to Paul's writings has appropriated the apostle's words for nontheistic, modern political ends. These philosophers approach Paul, Peter Frick writes, in order to find "an ally in their attempt to deconstruct a world that accords with neoliberal political and economic policies," which in turn leads to a "world [that] is dominated, exploited, and threatened by power structures that breed injustice, inequality, poverty, and reinforce many of the 'isms' that devalue human lives individually and collectively."[1] Frick raises questions concerning the new approach to Paul and this project. What is the "liberal" problem that the new approach disdains? To what school of thought does this use of Paul most appeal? Why does Paul solve a problem raised by liberalism? These terms and questions must be examined in order to identify the purpose this study undertakes.

LIBERALISM: THE MODERN POLITICAL PROBLEM

Liberalism is the dominant political doctrine arising from the Enlightenment. Philosopher John Rawls defines *liberalism* as the traditional "conception of justice for specifying the fair terms of social cooperating members of society over a complete life, from one generation to the next."[2] Liberalism is the modern form of government attempting to

1. Frick, "Paul in the Grip," 4–5.
2. Rawls, *Political Liberalism*, 3.

1

establish lasting political structures that can serve to create a fair and equitable society for the highest number of people.

An example of such a liberalism is found in the work of Thomas Hobbes. According to Hobbes, liberalism takes the form of a contract where individuals cede some of their rights so that others might cede some of theirs. The mediator of this social contract is not the individual, but the sovereign state. Without this, warnings would not be heeded in regard to the limits of the contract. This form of government seems egalitarian, but fails to acknowledge its complex and dominating history.[3]

Despite its good intentions, modern and late–modern philosophers, theologians, and social theorists note that problems are inherent in liberalism. For example, one of the historical struggles of liberal governments was recognition of individual rights not only inside the nation-state, but outside it as well, such as colonial holdings. In such cases, colonies were not equals to the colonizing nation, but existed in servitude to them. This failure to recognize a multitude of people who exist inside a supposed egalitarian politics is a clear abuse of the rights inherent to liberalism and a consistent historical problem of liberalism.

Though liberalism was originally an attempt to overcome the religious barbarity of the early Middle Ages, it became an inadequate, abusive governmental system. Lisa Lowe, a professor of American studies, suggests that the same historical and philosophical trajectory of liberalism toward equality also creates the economic and political conditions of imperial sovereignty and colonialism.[4] Liberalism excludes as much as it includes. Lowe acknowledges that the positive power of liberalism is reflected in Rawls's understanding. However, this same liberalism comes with a "negative power to seize, capture, occupy and subjugate."[5] The power of the sovereign guarantees that the social contract possesses the power to do violence beyond its prescribed purpose. This forms the "metacrisis of liberalism," which, due to the problems inherent to liberalism and abuses of liberalism, "cannot be transcended, whether for good or ill, in a purely liberal way."[6] In other words, liberalism cannot solve the problems of liberalism.

---

3. See Milbank and Pabst, *Politics of Virtue*, 14–15.

4. Lowe, *Intimacies of Four Continents*, 104.

5. Lowe, *Intimacies of Four Continents*, 133.

6. Milbank and Pabst, *Politics of Virtue*, 58.

In the eyes of the figures engaging Paul as described in this work, liberalism has resulted in the rise of biopolitics. As Judith Butler writes, biopolitics signifies "those powers that organize life, even the powers that differentially dispose lives to precarity as part of a broader management of populations through governmental and non-governmental means, and that establish a set of measures for the differential valuation of life itself."[7] Liberalism begets biopolitics by its desire to present a universal political organism capable of guaranteeing rights for all. The social contract, as the practitioners of liberalism historically recognize, is often revoked for certain people. This ability to revoke and to give people a certain status apart from their natural state shows that the social contract is not inherently neutral. Liberalism is interested in giving life a meaning in addition to biological data. Despite the fact that this crisis in liberalism leads to biopolitics, liberalism appears to be the only viable form of government active in the world today.

THE "LEFT": NEW INTERPRETERS OF PAUL

The historical group that has been committed to a thorough dismantling of liberalism is the philosophical Left. Philosopher Roger Scruton writes, "The modern use of the term 'left' derives from the French Estates General of 1789, when the nobility sat on the king's right, and the 'third estate' on his left."[8] The dichotomy between philosophical motives is clear. Scruton clarifies, "Leftists believe, with the Jacobins of the French Revolution, that the goods of this world are unjustly distributed, and that the fault lies not in human nature but in usurpations practiced by a dominant class."[9] If this is the belief that drives the Left, then their two main occupations are social justice and liberation.[10]

Social justice is, Scruton writes, the "comprehensive rearrangement of society, so that privileges, hierarchies, and even the unequal distribution of goods are either overcome or challenged."[11] Equality, the original intention of liberalism, is the single virtue of politics. However, a crucial distinction is that the Left's equality is not a legal equality. The

7. Butler, "Can One Lead a Good Life," 10.

8. Scruton, *Fools, Frauds, and Firebrands*, 1.

9. Scruton, *Fools, Frauds, and Firebrands*, 3.

10. Scruton, *Fools, Frauds, and Firebrands*, 3.

11. Scruton, *Fools, Frauds, and Firebrands*, 4.

legal apparatus that was established in the rise of liberalism is part of an old, inequitable social order filled with "existing custom, institution, law [and] hierarchy . . . [that] must be pulled down and built again."[12] The goal of the left leads away from old ways, which have brought about inequitable politics such as liberalism. In order for a true equality to emerge, a new order must arise that exists outside the realm of *law*. However, if liberalism is the only remaining viable form of politics—despite the best efforts of leftist intellectuals—then in order to critique liberalism, the new approach needs a figure who can help "unthink" this deeply modern and Western tradition that resulted in liberalism. Paul represents a new source for the critique of law and liberalism from a leftist perspective.

WHY THE APOSTLE? PAULINE POLITICAL RESOURCES

The apostle Paul already has a political message. Most clearly, this appears in Paul's letter to the Romans when Paul urges believers to "be subject to governing authorities" (Rom 13:1, NRSV). Much of Paul's "political" message arises from the small portion of the book of Romans, namely Romans 13:1–7. This text assists Christianity's understanding of Paul's political world and his political prescription to Christians. Historically, theologians and biblical scholars focus on this text, but this is not the text explored by the new approach. Rather, Paul has become an ally of the left, philosopher Alain Badiou identifies, because of Paul's "antiphilosophy," which is not necessarily tied to one specific text, but to Paul's general gospel message.[13] According to Badiou, the writings of Paul are antiphilosophy in that they predate the modern world and, more importantly, actively resist established philosophical categories.[14] Take, for example, Paul's words to the Corinthians: "For Jews demand signs and Greeks desire wisdom, but we proclaim Christ crucified, a stumbling block to Jews and foolishness to Gentiles" (1 Cor 1:22–23, NRSV). Paul suggests a radically new way of thinking and perceiving that is not bound to any earthly philosophical categories. Creston Davis, John Milbank, and Slavoj Žižek summarize the importance of Paul's antiphilosophical approach in the introduction to their book on Paul's new political use. They write that the new political approach to Paul

12. Scruton, *Fools, Frauds, and Firebrands*, 4.
13. Badiou, *Saint Paul*, 17, 58.
14. See Harink, "From Apocalypse to Philosophy," 1.

matches well with Christianity's claim to the Incarnational
Event, inasmuch as its truth-claim is not determined by a set
of predetermined *a priori* coordinates but is an unabashedly
positive event not capable of being absorbed into the domesti-
cated ideological fabric of our world. In short, and siding with
Paul, we propose that Christian theology contains within it an
irreducible revolutionary possibility that ruptures with the predetermined coordinates of the world and offers an entirely new
kind of political subject altogether.[15]

The value in this Pauline disregard for other established epistemological
norms reveals the Left's entrenched desire for a new type of politics not
previously found in modernity.

This Pauline emphasis is coordinate with the rise in "political
theology" as a critical discourse outside of the Christian academy and
dominated by the philosophical Left. Elizabeth Castelli writes, "The philosopher's turn to Paul has itself generated a massive cottage industry
of commentary, and 'political theology' has emerged as a preeminent
theoretical category of the twenty-first century."[16] This rise in political
theology is not confessional, meaning that the academy has not suddenly
returned to the church for answers to modernity. Rather, political theology is a critical category constructed for the sake of new language about
the ailments of politics and its resulting paradigms: liberalism, biopolitics, etc.

This move to political theology avoids the confessional elements of
theology, politics, and Paul. This new political theology, William Cavanaugh writes, attempts to remove confessional theology as a "respectable
discourse."[17] This is because confessional theology commits an error,
according to late-modernity in an appeal to transcendence. An "appeal
to any transcendent realm beyond the immanent is an ideological ploy
that must be contrary to any truly progressive politics."[18] The political
theology of the new approach, in order to combat this ideological ploy,
embarks on a twofold task: to end transcendence and to begin a new
leftist, progressive politics, which fuels the turn to Paul.

The return to Paul, coupled with the rise of political theology, Castelli continues, is "unencumbered by the customary practices of the field

15. Davis et al., "Introduction," 2.
16. Castelli, "Philosopher's Paul," 653.
17. Cavanaugh, "Mystical and Real," 112.
18. Cavanaugh, "Mystical and Real," 112.

of biblical studies," which should not surprise anyone.[19] As such, there is no commitment to the God Paul proclaims. According to Peter Frick, these thinkers "have their own ideological structures and therefore employ Paul in service of those structures."[20] These ideological structures often displace the exegetical practices normally associated with those who study Paul. Philosophers of the new approach use Paul as a tool to sharpen the ideas of their already-developed leftist ideology.[21] They need not commit to a comprehensive exegesis of Paul's entire corpus. They prioritize certain texts that speak to legal structures which revitalize the leftist dream of egalitarian politics.

A brief critique must be leveled at this point. I agree with Scruton that there is a danger embedded within this leftist approach. Though I am inclined to sympathize with many of their deployments of Paul, I recognize a fundamental flaw in their approach, namely their concept of reality. The issue of reality in the new approach is evident in their troubled relationship to the individual. Scruton writes that the world of the thinkers of the left "is a world of abstract forces, in which individuals are local embodiments of the 'isms' that are revealed in them."[22] The challenge here is that much of the left relies on abstract concepts of reality that struggle to translate into concrete political action. Their view of reality, in a variety of shapes and forms, relies on a materialist philosophy. Materialism as a practice, Scruton suggests, is that the localized is lost in favor of the universal "ism." By relying on a variety of "isms," it ontologizes errant political structures and takes an indefinite posture of revolution toward liberalism in all its errors. As such, the materialism *alone* of the new approach is insufficient toward the ends they expect.

Alternatively, Paul assumes a very different version of reality than that of naked materialism. Theologian David Bentley Hart writes that Paul is concerned with "bad angels."[23] Traditionally, these bad angels are what New Testament scholars refer to as the powers in Paul's writings. These fallen powers influence and sway humanity away from God's good purposes in creation. They are the reason for violent political structures. The new approach does not take this as their starting point. In fact, it

---

19. Castelli, "Philosopher's Paul," 654.

20. Frick, "Paul in the Grip," 7.

21. Frick, "Paul in the Grip," 7.

22. Scruton, *Fools, Frauds, and Firebrands*, 9.

23. Hart, "Everything You Know," para. 4.

is mostly rejected and, as Alain Badiou understands, considered nothing more than fable.[24] Badiou defines "fable" as "that part of a narrative that . . . fails to touch on any Real, unless it be by virtue of that invisible and indirectly accessible residue sticking to every obvious imaginary."[25] This is Badiou's appeal to a universal, which is capable of doing great damage to liberalism. This is a modern gesture bound to a general project of demythologization we find in modernity. However, this move cannot be rejected outright. The project of demythologization assumes that the myths of Christian Scripture conceal the truth they depict. Hart writes, "It would surely be a category error to assume that the story of Christ's overthrow of death and sin cannot express a truth that transcends the historical and cultural conditions in which it was first told."[26] However, it would be equally erroneous to assume that this means the original picture of the world described by Paul can be so easily dismissed as fable. Rather, it might be possible that certain idioms of the gospel are told in such a way that the gospel cannot be described outside those idioms. Hart continues,

> Paul's voice, I hasten to add, is hardly an eccentric one . . . And yet it would be foolish to try to judge the gospel's spiritual claims by how plausible we find the cosmology that accompanies them. For one thing, the ancient picture of reality might be in many significant respects more accurate than ours . . . But, before we decide anything at all about that story, we must first recover it from the very different stories that we so frequently tell in its place.[27]

Hart's point reveals a crucially neglected element by the new approach: politics is not the reordering of material realities, but is fundamentally about worship. Paul's account of reality, one under siege by fallen powers, suggests that we either worship fallen powers or God. The revelation of God over and against these powers is what I define as the essence of Paul's apocalyptic theology. It is through this gospel that the distinction between fallen powers and God's goodness becomes clear. Depending on whether we worship God or the powers, our political structures are impacted. Paul's political theology must be recovered from certain stories

24. Badiou, *Saint Paul*, 4–5.
25. Badiou, *Saint Paul*, 4.
26. Hart, "Everything You Know," para. 9.
27. Hart, "Everything You Know," para. 8.

moderns now tell for the sake of seeing how he might give a more-accurate account of our political situation.

ILLUSTRATING THE PROBLEM: THE LEFT, PAULINE THEOLOGY, AND MODERN POLITICS

I now must illustrate the problems of modern politics, the response of the new approach, and the possible theological alternative. The new approach has in its sights the liberal and neoliberal politics of modernity. The embodiment of such politics is evident in John Locke's seemingly axiomatic political insight—the right to life, liberty, and the pursuit of property. For Locke, the nature of the human person is solitary. Individuals come together in order to form society. Liberty and personal property go hand in hand. The one thing that brings society together, according to Locke, is purely materialistic: the preservation and maintenance of one's ability to produce for oneself. He writes that the purpose of society is "for the safety and security of the commonwealth and of every particular man's goods and person."[28] The point that Locke makes is that citizens do not come together to discuss and discern the nature of the common good; they come together to secure personal material possessions against their neighbor. Montesquieu writes of the error in this formation of the state: "We see that in countries where the people move only by the spirit of commerce, they make a traffic of all the humane, all the moral virtues; the most trifling things, those which humanity would demand are there done, or there given, only for money."[29] Montesquieu shows that private interests or goods, despite Locke's best intentions, cannot serve as an organizing principle for political life. In this foundation of politics, the common good is no longer operative.

The common good is essential for political life. Thomas Aquinas makes this point in his magisterial *Summa Theologica*. Aquinas is clear: human life is oriented toward beatitude. The laws erected in politics must share that end. Aquinas writes, "Since every part is ordained to the whole, as imperfect to perfect; and since one man is a part of the perfect community, the law must regard properly the relationship to universal

---

28. Locke, *Letter Concerning Toleration*, quoted in Storck, *From Christendom to Americanism*, 50.

29. Montesquieu, *Spirit of Laws*, 146.

happiness."[30] Aquinas, as is his custom, develops this theme from Aristotle, who argues that laws must produce happiness for the whole political community. Aquinas continues,

> Now in every genus, that which belongs to it chiefly is the principle of the others, and the others belong to that genus in subordination to that this: thus fire, which is chief among hot things, is the cause of heat in mixed bodies, and these are said to be hot in so far as they have a share of fire. Consequently, since the law is chiefly ordained to the common good, any other precept in regard to some individual work must needs be devoid of the nature of a law, save in so far as it regards the common good. Therefore every law is ordained to the common good.[31]

Human community exists for the sake of happiness. The chief end of every law that establishes human community is for the common good, which serves as a helpful tool to analyze the errors of liberalism. Aquinas understands the common good as that which orients human community away from selfish ends. He clarifies that each command of the law is applicable to particular ends, but is ordered toward the common good.[32]

The liberalism detested by the new approach yields a society oriented toward individual gain, not the common good. The highest virtue in such a society is freedom from interference, including the interference of shared ends, which already moves diagonally from common good. Liberalism, theologian William Cavanaugh writes, "was not democratic in origin, but an attempt to protect and enlarge the liberties first of nobles and then of a merchant middle class."[33] According to Locke and others, once one is free to seek individual ends and the accumulation of private interests and goods, politics is equal. One should note that this is a freedom merely to pursue private goods and interests toward private ends. No longer do shared ends or the common good play a role in political life. Cavanaugh continues, "Despite the claim to equality, however, liberal democratic theorists accepted class division."[34] For example, political philosopher John Stewart Mill "thought that participation in the competitive market would allow the working class to develop its own human

30. Aquinas, *Summa Theologica* I-II.90.2.
31. Aquinas, *Summa Theologica* I-II.90.2.
32. Aquinas, *Summa Theologica* I-II.90.2.
33. Cavanaugh, "Are Corporations People," 24.
34. Cavanaugh, "Are Corporations People," 24.

potential, but in the meantime, the elite should be given a dispropor-
tionate share of votes, since in their present debased condition the lower
classes could not be trusted to vote in the interest of the common good."[35]
Here, the common good is mutated by private interests, specifically the
interests of a certain class of individuals over and against others.

In addition to this mutation, there is a further problem in liberalism. Locke's understanding of liberalism allowed for the justified own-
ing of humans as private property.[36] Such a basic failure of the original
intent of liberalism, even if it is a misunderstanding or misappropriation,
warrants a critique.[37] This is the critique offered by the left and the new
approach. As Scruton noted, the leftist critique is a move for a radical
social justice of reorientation and destruction of the private interests that
yield such inequality. Therefore, the Left and the new approach critique
most heavily a central apparatus of liberalism: the market that creates
such inequalities. Badiou writes,

> Capital demands a permanent creation of subjective and ter-
> ritorial identities in order for its principle of movement to
> homogenize its space of action; identities, moreover, that never
> demand anything but the right to be exposed in the same way as
> others to the uniform prerogative is the market.[38]

The market is a false universal because it cannot sustain a multitude of
narratives, only its own empty abstraction. It cannot secure equality. It
only favors its own logic, so lends itself to unjust classes and slavery, as
illustrated above by Locke and Mills.

In its place, the Left and the new approach offer Paul's gospel as a
possible alternative to liberalism's capitalistic politic. Paul writes, "There
is neither Jew nor Greek, there is neither slave nor free, there is neither
male nor female" (Gal 3:28, NRSV). The proclamation of Christ is a true
universal because it provides an "unprecedented gesture [that] consists in
subtracting truth from the communitarian grasp, be it that of a people, a
city, an empire, a territory, or a social class."[39] The power of Paul's proclamation is not in its transcendent appeal to the reality enabled by God, but

---

35. Cavanaugh, "Are Corporations People," 24–25.

36. Lowe, *Intimacies of Four Continents*, 10–11.

37. The only reason I give pause here is that many political philosophies were once
complicit in slavery, including natural law.

38. Badiou, *Saint Paul*, 10–11.

39. Badiou, *Saint Paul*, 5.

its "subjective gesture grasped in its founding power with respect to the generic conditions of universality."[40] The universal is that which moves beyond the liberal, market-based ideology toward a more equitable understanding of identity. The identities created by liberal, market-based ideology (i.e., Jew, Greek, etc.), according to Badiou, is only overcome in the subjective fidelity to the universal that makes individuals uninterested in the difference created by the homogenization of the market. The universal, or what Badiou calls the "truth event," enables a politics decentered from market-based liberalism.

Despite the attractiveness, this approach suffers from an obvious failure. The philosophers of the new approach assume the same basic Western narrative of philosophy.[41] As such, they all assume a certain commitment to the abstract seizure of subjectivity embedded within the West itself. The problem with this capture is that not all forms of humanity neatly fit within the universal categories assumed by the new approach. For example, critic Alexander Weheliye shows that this transcendental capture of subjectivity by Western discourse has yet to fully account for the violence of the slave trade and colonialism, which is, consequently, the mired legacy of liberalism. Weheliye argues that the capture of subjectivity is insufficient to account for the "indeterminability" of what he identifies as the flesh, which is the very particularity of the subject that has been excluded from modern politics. He writes, "the flesh is not an abject zone of exclusion that culminates in death but an alternate instantiation of humanity that does not rest on the mirage of [W]estern man as the mirror image of human life as such."[42] Implicit within the new approach is a failure to account for the private ideology and interests that motivate their fundamentally Western thought, which are just as private as liberalism's economic ideology. The contingency of human identity can never be properly accounted for by the leftist new approach. This does not mean that their inclination about modern politics is misplaced, but that their method ultimately troubles their aims.

To summarize, the above example serves as a means to understand the new approach and the modern turn to Paul. Liberalism and its mired legacy presents modern politics with its own failure to provide a truly equitable politics. By way of the new approach, proponents of the left

40. Badiou, *Saint Paul*, 6.

41. See Frick, "Paul in the Grip," 3–13.

42. Weheliye, *Habeas Viscus*, 43.

attempt a philosophical critique of liberalism for the sake of proposing new universals that overcome the market-driven ideologies of liberalism. The goal is the interruption of private interests that guide inequitable politics. However, under their new approach, they cannot escape their own private, ideological commitments and account for the contingency of individuals in political communities. Therefore, it is from this place that a theological alternative to the new approach should begin, taking the best of their instinctual rejection of the mired history of modern politics and supplementing their mistakes with the revealed truth of Paul's apocalyptic gospel. Paul's gospel is so wed to the revelation of the incarnation of Israel's messiah that it is only within this context that his political critique can emerge, without which one does violence to the apostle. Such an engagement overcomes the violent ideology of modern politics and the tyranny of private interests that prevents the common good.

SUMMARY OF ARGUMENT

The turn to Paul by late modern philosophy is worth a theological exploration. Theological engagements with this new approach already exist.[43] However, this project considers the intersections of Paul's apocalypticism, the new approach, and modern politics. The ailment of modern politics, as illustrated by liberalism and the new approach, lies in private interests and violent ideology. Paul, when read apocalyptically, provides a more-accurate account of modern politics than the new approach because apocalyptic thought endures through the fretful currents of modern thought. Though I do appropriate the helpful elements of the new approach, I ultimately rely on a theologically rooted engagement with Paul's political insights. Only a gospel with such a weighty hope can penetrate the deep-seated political malaise of the late modern period.

At this point, I must define what is at stake in Paul's apocalyptic that critically re-situates the philosophical new approach. This begins with a definition. "Paul's apocalyptic theology," as Pauline scholar Beverly Roberts Gaventa understands,

> has to do with the conviction that in the death and resurrection of Jesus Christ, God has invaded the world as it is, thereby revealing the world's utter distortion and foolishness, reclaiming the world, and inaugurating a battle that will doubtless culminate in

---

43. See the many essays in Harink, *Paul, Philosophy and the Theopolitical Vision.*

the triumph of God over all God's enemies (including the captors Sin and Death). This means that the gospel is first, last, and always about God's powerful and gracious initiative.[44]

Therefore, Paul's apocalyptic theology is iconoclastic and proclaims a different sovereignty operating in the world. This includes both what Christ has done and the work Christ will do in the future. This is the classic tension between the *already* and the *not yet* in Paul's theology. Paul's apocalyptic theology spans beyond the political space to the entire created order liberated for God.[45] The fundamental reality through which Paul understands public space is not liberalism or leftist politics. Rather, it is the created order liberated for God's own self. Expanding the political vocabulary to include a creation-wide scope and God's reign places politics firmly beyond humanity's private interests and constructed ideology. Paul's apocalyptic theology resembles William Cavanaugh's statement that through God's radical liberation of the cosmos, humanity is "thrown into . . . pure contingency, and [they must respond] as an enfleshed being to another being of the same flesh."[46] This is Paul's apocalyptic politics in its most basic form, achieved through Christ's incursion into the cosmos and our habitual participation into that reality, which unseats private interests guided by ideology.

Paul's main object of inquiry is not errant political systems, but the whole created order liberated for God's purpose. He proposes certain practices that attest to this reality and make the efficacy of such a reality visually apparent in the face of the world of private interests. This is how Paul throws humanity into the contingency of one another. The shape of Paul's practices resembles what philosopher Iris Murdoch calls the "just and loving gaze."[47] The just and loving gaze is opposed to private interests and ideology. When considering Paul's emphasis on God's salvific invasion of the cosmos and the *not yet* return of Christ, one notes that this is not just an ideological supplanting of liberalism. Rather, it is a new vision, a set of habits and convictions arising from Christ's saving work. The just and loving gaze is neither self-centered nor interested in constructing a

44. Gaventa, *Our Mother Saint Paul*, 81.

45. By "created order" I refer to the work of Oliver O'Donovan. He claims that to speak of creation is not to speak of "undifferentiated energy." Rather, creation has an order to it that is shaped by God. See O'Donovan, *Resurrection and the Moral Order*, 31.

46. Cavanaugh, "Mystical and Real," 118.

47. Murdoch, *Sovereignty of the Good*, 33.

social space around a political ideal. It understands public interactions in a context of loving attention to the neighbor. In our conversion to Christ, harmful, private, selfish ambitions must be crucified with Christ in order that humanity might "unself" to the point of just and loving interactions with the neighbor. Paul's apocalyptic places the just and loving gaze in the tension between the *already* and the *not yet*. The just and loving gaze is a means to see and practice God's reign over the world now, and it provides a persistent hope in the face of errant political orders that tempers and empowers the repetition of apocalyptic vision and practice. It is in this tension that Paul's political theology emerges.

My central argument is that the just and loving gaze, enabled by Pauline apocalyptic, overcomes the errant and harmful politics of our day. By defeating sinful powers in the cosmos that prevent just and equitable life together, Christ places a new center of intimacy and formal equality before all people for the sake of just and loving actions. Christ's centrality enables the just and loving gaze by requiring the moral agent to become selfless in moral activity, love Christ who is the good, and investigate the needs and particularity of the neighbor. This is a politics that focuses on the inner dispositions and moral formation of the community. The advantage of the just and loving gaze is that it does not make the individual the local embodiment of "isms." It is a way to love individuals in their particularity while also seeking the common good.

OUTLINE OF PROJECT

Chapter 1 begins with a critical description of modern politics followed by an examination and interpretation of three of the philosophers of the new approach: Jacob Taubes, Alain Badiou, and Giorgio Agamben. In order to understand these thinkers, one must understand modern politics. We turn our attention away from liberalism and the left in order to examine, in simple terms, the ailments of modern politics. I do not intend to critique both liberalism and the left, but rather I clarify the exact ailments manifest in modern politics. I interpret modern politics through the philosophy of Hannah Arendt, which provides three important emphases for my study. First, she characterizes politics as a second life in addition to the life one has in private. This second life exhibits the qualities of good actions and bad actions that yield different forms of political community. This helps to clarify the ailments of modern self-centering of the public space. Second, she defines modernity as a world-alienating turn to the self that overplays the will.[48] The turn to the self is a part of modern politics, but Arendt's emphasis on world-alienation and the will provide a helpful addition to the description of modern politics. Third, closely related to the two previous points, modern politics has become dominated by private interests.

These three emphases help Arendt determine the particular form of modern politics as the creation of a self-sufficient humanity. This presents humanity with a particular *telos*—an ideal, private state of humanity that has to be guarded and preserved against all threat. The self-sufficient human is the political form that life must take. Arendt, along with an important critical biopolitical framework offered by Michel Foucault, provides a historical example of the ailments of modernity that yields the politicization of life. The rubric against which this self-sufficient, privately interested life is preserved is a politics of death. This is one that attempts to define its populace in such a way that some are naturally excluded. This underside of liberalism is biopolitics.

I conclude the chapter by describing the positions of the three philosophers of the new approach: Taubes, Badiou, and Agamben. I offer the materialist, nihilistic hermeneutics that inform their particular deployments of Paul. Each figure has a distinctive agenda in utilizing Paul and accompanying politics. Each figure attacks the underside of liberalism— biopolitics. I will show how each possesses strengths and weaknesses, such as a failure to account for contingency (gnosticism). In the end, the weaknesses are too great to overcome biopolitics, and they neglect crucial elements of Paul.

In chapter 2, I seek to remedy the deficient elements of the new approach by arguing for an alternative reading of Paul's theology that is more familiar to the Christian tradition: Paul's theology as apocalyptic theology. The word "apocalyptic" refers to Paul's insistence on the invasive revelation of God over and against the powers of sin and death in Christ's incarnation, crucifixion, and resurrection, as well as in the return of Christ, the new creation, and resurrection of the dead. Locating Paul's work within this context deeply interrogates the priority of self-sufficiency, private interests, and ideology in modern politics by recognizing the powers of sin and death as the powers responsible for these political ailments. The apocalyptic interpretation takes seriously the cosmology

48. Arendt, *Human Condition*, 260–64.

of the apostle Paul and how this cosmology, not modernity's, is vital to Paul's theology.

To perform this interpretation of Paul, I argue that one must read the Bible as Scripture, which is a dogmatic approach. To read the Bible specifically as Scripture requires locating it within its purpose in the overall economy of the grace of God. This approach comes from theologian John Webster, who argues that in modernity, the reading and interpretation of Scripture has been subjected to less-than-fruitful endeavors. Webster argues that reading the Bible as Scripture locates its ontology in the revelation of the triune God. Scripture exists to bear witness to the triune God's self-presentation. The new approach fundamentally reorients Scripture's and Paul's rightful gravitational center away from this ontological home and toward an ideological home. Though one certainly can engage in a conversation between Paul and modern philosophy/politics, the reality that Paul unpacks is perpetually alien to the concerns of modernity and must be treated as such.

I argue that Paul must be reread within Scriptural context: the apocalyptic gospel that communicates the saving activity of God. In the words of Karl Barth, this means "to carry on theology, and only theology, now as previously, and as if nothing had happened."[49] This approach allows one to read Paul's documents without assuming any allegiances to modernity or cultural presuppositions; we can read the Bible as an introduction to the triune God and to the shaping and forming of our actions in response to this inescapably good God. Only through this lens can Paul help modern politics rid itself of its demons.

After establishing the necessity to read Paul as Scripture, I posit that Paul's theological language is apocalyptic. I offer a brief narrative and definition of the term "apocalyptic" by utilizing some work of contemporary theologians and New Testament scholars. Central to apocalyptic language is what Paul understands as the apocalyptic "powers." These powers are those spiritual entities that could be angels on one hand, or harmful ideologies on the other. Both understandings of these powers know them to be fallen with humanity. In turn, these fallen powers influence and drive humanity away from the purposes of God and the *summum bonum*. They cultivate inhospitable private interest. This definition leads to a brief history of the modern rediscovery of the apocalyptic. The primary historical figures that initiate this rediscovery are Rudolf

49. Barth, *Theological Existence To-Day*, 9.

Bultmann and his student Ernst Käsemann. These two figures help orient the discussion of apocalyptic around Paul's emphasis on the righteousness of God and the *already/not yet* in Paul's theology.

From Bultmann's perspective, one must emphasize the *already* as an individual, existential theology. From Käsemann's perspective, one must emphasize the *not yet* as a creation-wide reign of God. Here, creation enters as an element of Paul's theology that is essential to understanding the material space as redeemed and summoned by God to righteousness. This understanding opens up a broader sociopolitical critique of politics, which reframes humanity's relationship to the world by recognizing the world as something that awaits its final redemption. For Käsemann, it is not enough to be content with an existential translation of the gospel. Christ must be Lord even now *and* must be expected to come.

Paul's language of the *already* includes a language of the *not yet*. The *not yet* takes new perspective with biblical scholar and student of Käsemann, J. Christiaan Beker. He agrees with the early Käsemann thought that there must be some realistic new creation to redeem from suffering and injustice. The tension between the *already* and *not yet* focuses on how the apocalyptic event, which is yet to come, informs our present condition. What difference does Christ's resurrection make to us at this moment? What is the context and content for our hope in the future? Beker's position helps answer these questions and highlights a salvation, historical approach that spans from the act of creation to the story of the people of Israel to the life, death, and resurrection of Christ, and points forward to the new creation.

I am sympathetic with Beker's position, but his position is not the last word on Pauline apocalyptic; e.g., four recent insights of J. Louis Martyn, David Congdon, Michael Gorman, and Neil Elliott. I come to a middle ground between the *already* and the *not yet*, which is more traditional to Pauline studies. My synthesis of the *already* and *not yet* assumes a Wesleyan hermeneutic. Unlike many of the apocalyptic interpreters of Paul, I do not assume a Lutheran theological commitment. Luther is helpful toward the end of unseating self-sufficient, private interest, but lacks a coherent account of human healing from the pathos of the powers. On the contrary, while Wesley assumes Luther's "unselfing" in faith, he also posits the positive account of healing, or santification, from the powers of sin and death. For Wesley, justification by faith moves toward a therapeutic, sanctification of the image of God in humanity, which culminates in God's redemption of creation. Therefore, Wesley helps synthesize the apocalyptic *already* and *not yet*.

I conclude, in chapters 3 and 4, with an account of how the apocalyptic Paul is the political Paul. In chapter 3, I argue that by living into the reality of Jesus's lordship through faithful Christian practices, not a fabricated social ideology, Paul can confront modernity and its politics. I return to Hannah Arendt, who provides a constructive politics in response to the anti-Semitism and totalitarianism of her day. Arendt offers two complimentary points in her work. In a time of deeply entrenched anti-Semitism, Arendt uses her own Jewish identity as a point of departure from the politics of her day. Unlike Badiou, she finds value in identity politics. Arendt's particularity serves as a new means to rehabilitate her own persecuted subjectivity, and is an optic toward seeing just political activity. Arendt argues that politics must value the deep particularity of an individual in order for politics to be an exercise of freedom. Arendt's emphasis on identity is coupled with her emphasis on speech. Speech in a definable public sphere is a political act that leads to the construction of a lasting reality greater than labor and work. Arendt has in mind the reality of constitutions and constitutional orders. These orders are passed down from generation to generation, ensuring freedom as a fundamental feature of political life. Though she does not connect her identity politics with her emphasis on speech, I argue that bringing these two themes of her work together offers a new type of politic where individuals can come together in appreciation of their particularity toward the common good.

Though Arendt brings together identity and speech *for* the common good, she lacks a clear understanding *of* the common good. It is unclear in her work what makes identity valued and speech impactful. To correct this weakness, I bring the work of philosopher and novelist Iris Murdoch into conversation with Arendt's key insights. The advantage Murdoch brings to Arendt is a focus on what she terms the just and loving gaze, a realist position that attempts to look lovingly and compassionately on human realities in themselves. According to Murdoch, the just and loving gaze is a way of close, intimate attention to one's neighbor arising from love of the Good. Attention to the neighbor forces one's inner, private interests to change based on love of the Good, justice, and love due the neighbor. Arendt's politics do not provide a means to overcome private interests in a way that makes speech possible. However, by implementing the just and loving gaze, one is forced beyond the interior of self and to a compassionate attention toward neighbor. Only in this gaze can the neighbor's identity come to change the inner dispositions of the moral agent. One must become exterior to oneself to listen to and love the neighbor, and thus to form a just politic. One must be good "for nothing."

I conclude my discussion of the just and loving gaze with a brief theological segue between Murdoch and Paul, using the theology of *already* in Galatians. The Pauline *already* highlights the need for a new type of vision in order to practice the just and loving gaze, which the apocalyptic incursion of Christ provides. The incarnation draws humanity into a desire to love the triune God who calls us to love of neighbor. Therefore, Murdoch's philosophy provides a helpful theological tool to envision Paul's political theology.

Before turning back to Paul, I offer my dissatisfaction with the new approach and how their political interpretation of Paul fails to escape the politics of the coercion they detest. The main issue is the fundamental inability to see neighbors as fellow humans. They ignore the particularity in favor of a false universal/antirealist ideology that requires all people to conform to its constructed reality. This political position can never be free from the errors of coercion. I use Agamben's depiction of the *Muselmann* in the death camps to illustrate this issue and briefly show how this approach is not exclusive to Agamben, but is featured by Badiou and Taubes, as well.

After adopting the theological interpretation of Arendt and Murdoch, I show how the just and loving gaze moves beyond idea to practice. The great weakness of the new approach is its inability to do this. Paul's apocalyptic political theology engenders a way of knowing fellow humans inside the love of God. In order to illustrate this, I briefly engage two of Paul's moral exhortations, the instruction on eating the Lord's Supper (1 Cor 10–12) and the prohibition on eating idol meat (1 Cor 8, Rom 14). Both exhortations set the works of Christ as a center of intimacy on which the congregation's social lives are centered. In the context of these practices, the broader apocalyptic appeal of Paul becomes tangible. This shows that Paul's politics does not yield to powers, but creates a new community centered on concrete practices that promote neighbor love. Paul's political theology is a body politic of the just and loving gaze enabled by the apocalyptic invasion of Christ.

In chapter 4, I argue that the *not yet* serves as an object of hope that provides a type of *telos* for our worldly activities. I first explore the hope of the *not yet* expressed in Paul's famous text, 1 Corinthians 15. I argue that this text points to a bodily resurrection that is the hope and fulfillment of bodily human life. This establishes a tenor for bodily life that is peculiar to the Corinthian congregation. This places humanity in disruptive continuity with Christ's own body. The purpose of Christ's parousia is to defeat death and draw all of creation into the relationship between Father and Son. This procession and recession of the Son is mirrored in the drawing and transformation of human bodies by the Spirit into the triune life. In 1 Corinthians 15, we have a divine dance in which the entire cosmos is brought into the very life of God, so much so that God is proclaimed to be all in all.

Next, I return to the political thought of Hannah Arendt. She proposes that "natality," the ability to perform new actions without being hopelessly bound to the past, is an essential political posture. Without natality, Arendt argues, humanity is trapped in a vicious cycle of violence. This posture is essential to the just and loving gaze, for the essence of the just and loving gaze is predicated on the ability to make new judgements in light of past prejudice. Through an exploration of Murdoch's novel *The Nice and the Good*, I show the necessity of natality for the just and loving gaze: good choice.

Though natality is crucially important for politics, I argue that political theology would do well to translate it into theological language. I utilize the work of John Webster in order to discuss how natality serves a political, apocalyptic purpose by ontologically grounding human agency in the realization and fulfillment of divine purpose in creation. First, I connect human agency to the realization of divine purpose in Christ. Webster argues that this is the ontological well from which human agency springs. Second, since human action is ontologically grounded in the new reality of Christ, it follows that action is directed toward its fulfillment in Christ's return. This will form the theological, political critique of realized eschatological politics. I argue that the just and loving gaze needs an eschatological outlook to encourage a continual practice of newness that relates to a need to continually "unself."

As with chapter 3, the Pauline politics arising from apocalyptic is practiced, but this time in the *not yet*. I propose the practice of forgiveness. In forgiveness, Paul offers a practice that places us fully within the natality of the *not yet*. Utilizing 2 Corinthians 5, I argue that forgiveness is properly understood as a means to locate our agency within the reconciling work of God in Christ. As with Webster, human agency arises from the unfolding of God's purpose within creation in order to fulfill it. God, who "reconciles everything to himself" (2 Cor 5:19), gives humans the "ministry of reconciliation" (2 Cor 5:19) to participate in that agency of God in order to find our agency. I will turn to the political importance of this practice as it arises from Paul.

I then offer a Pauline apocalyptic political theology of the *not yet*. If forgiveness is a central practice of the *not yet*, then the apocalyptic political theology of Paul cannot succumb to a discourse of coercion. Primarily utilizing Philippians 3, I argue that the Pauline apocalyptic political theology of the *not yet* lies in heavenly citizenship. I contrast the political theology of Carl Schmitt with an exegesis of Philippians 3 in order to highlight the difference apocalyptic will make. The apocalyptic political activity is an activity of faithfulness to the life of the cross, which is logic through which we understand heavenly citizenship. The time that remains is fraught with activity—but an activity centered on the cry of the church, "Come, Lord Jesus."

The argument of this work is that Paul's apocalyptic overcomes harmful ideology and private interests for the sake of a new political theology. At the conclusion of this work, I offer a few theses that emerge from this central conviction as a result of my findings. A politics enabled by the reality of Christ and practiced concretely in the community celebrates the common good and embodies the just and loving gaze. This project has implications not only for politics, but also Paul's theology and the nature of eschatology itself.

1

Whose Paul, Which Politics?
Modern (Bio)Politics and the Apostle Paul

PAUL'S APOCALYPTIC THEOLOGY PROFESSES the invasion of Christ into the cosmos inaugurating a present Lordship over the powers and setting creation on a course to final consummation. This *already/not yet* tension of the salvation of the cosmos endures the shifts in political culture throughout time and calls humanity out into the world for just and loving interaction with each other. The political life arising from apocalypticism is already apparent within the Pauline corpus. However, in recent years Paul has been stripped of his apocalyptic core for the sake of a purely materialist appropriation of Paul for the sake of engaging modern political orders.

This chapter will first outline modernity's biopolitical problems and the Pauline philosophical responses to these problems. My own construction of Paul's political theology is a response to both. I begin with Hannah Arendt, who helpfully interprets these modern political ailments. Arendt illustrates that the problem inherent in modern politics is a tension between a free public space and private interests. Private interests complicate public space, but private interests beget a political ideology. This ideology most correlates to the contemporary political philosophy of Michel Foucault. It is Foucault who forms the language of sovereignty and biopolitics to which the new approach to Paul responds. There are two issues arising from Arendt and Foucault: the private interests that lead to self-sufficiency and the private interests worked out in public in the form of a biopolitical ideology. In both, private interests are the key.

A possible political alternative to private interests is proposed by the new approach. To begin, I briefly describe the discrete hermeneutical strategy at the heart of the new approach. The new approach appeals to a univocal, materialist philosophy that shapes their reading of Paul. Materialism serves as a hermeneutical device for a possible interpretation of Paul. After unpacking the hermeneutic of the new approach, the deployment of Paul against contemporary political philosophy is revealed as a way to maintain individuality and universality within a less-violent politic. This is the answer to the tyranny of private interests. The weaknesses and strengths become apparent, such as the materialist's inability to account for contingency (Gnosticism). It is from the vantage point of seeing modern political philosophy, its problems, and the response of the new approach that my own response comes into focus.

HANNAH ARENDT ON MODERNITY: PRIVATE INTERESTS AND SELF-SUFFICIENCY

Hannah Arendt helpfully critiques modern politics in a way not encumbered by the discussion of liberalism or the left. Though her political thought is oriented toward human, individual freedom—a classic tenant of liberalism—her work recognizes the historic problems of such a system. She posits that modernity arises when humans abandon the Archimedean understanding of the universe and begin to "turn to the self."[1] Arendt writes that this turn to the self "reduce[s] all experiences, with the world as well as with human beings, to experiences between man and himself."[2] This emphasis is not just the preference for human creation versus nonhuman creation; it is a deep mistrust of anything not founded in the human will.

This distrust of anything outside the human will leads to the founding of the self through thought alone. Arendt claims this modern emphasis comes from a reduction of science to mathematics.

> At the beginning of the modern age . . . is the entirely un-Platonic subjection of geometry to algebraic treatment, which discloses the modern ideal of reducing terrestrial sense data

1. Arendt, *Human Condition*, 254.
2. Arendt, *Human Condition*, 254.

and movements to mathematical symbols . . . .In the experiment man realized his newly won freedom from the shackles of earth-bound experience; instead of observing natural phenomena as they were given to him, he placed nature under the conditions of his own mind, that is, under the conditions won from a universal, astrophysical viewpoint, a cosmic standpoint outside nature itself.[3]

In Arendt's summary, humanity wins freedom from its captivity to worldliness through force of will. Humanity creates its new existence, becoming autonomous from the world. This is the foundational thought of modernity famously proposed by Rene Descartes: *Cogito ergo sum*, "I think, therefore I am." The result of this position lies in an anthropocentric politics where any reality external to the self is deemed questionable, thus nonessential. Arendt labels this position "Cartesian doubt." Furthermore, Arendt calls the subsequent suspicion and separation from the world "world-alienation." The error of Cartesian doubt is that it tricks humanity into conceiving of the world as a product of the human mind. In modernity, only a constructed world is the "real" world. Such a conceiving of the world forms the essence of ideology, namely replacing physical-sense data with a constructed picture. When constructed ideologically, the world is flattened.

Ideology: A Brief Excursus

Ideology, as a constructed picture of the world arising from our modern world alienation, must be explored. According to Terry Eagleton, the word *ideology* is impossible to define. Depending on where one stands, liberalism and socialism could both be called ideological. When one calls something ideological, usually it designates that which supports a ruling class.[4] Despite this, ideology represents something far more innocuous. Eagleton writes that, in many cases, ideology can mean a "medium in which social actors make sense of their world."[5] However, if we were to define it in light of the modern proclivity to world-alienation and the *Cogito*, then the closest definition we can offer is "false consciousness."[6]

---

3. Arendt, *Human Condition*, 265.

4. Eagleton, *Ideology*, 5–6.

5. Eagleton, *Ideology*, 2.

6. Eagleton, *Ideology*, 7.

Ideology, as a concept, is crucial for the philosophical Left and the new approach to Paul. To begin, the Left uses Paul as a means to critique structural ideologies as they present themselves in modernity. Philosopher Slavoj Žižek argues just this point. For example, one of the main ideological structures under critique by the Left, as illustrated in the introduction, is capitalism. As Žižek points out,

> nobody seriously considers possible alternatives to capitalism any longer, whereas popular imagination is persecuted by the visions of the forthcoming 'breakdown of nature', of the stopping of all life on earth—it seems easier to imagine the 'end of the world' than a far more modest change in the mode of production.[7]

Žižek offers this analysis in order to reveal a very strange contrast in modernity. As such, he argues that ideology has three distinct yet interconnected moments: in-itself, for-itself, and in-and-for-itself.

First, ideology is in-itself. This is ideology as doctrine, namely as "a composite of ideas, beliefs, concepts, and so on, destined to convince us of its 'truth', yet actually serving some unavowed particular power interest."[8] Ideology, then, has an evangelical posture that seeks to convert the masses to its own interior rationality. As Žižek understands, the implicit assumption of ideology as in-itself lies in a "naturalization" of its "symbolic order . . . that reifies the results of discursive procedures into properties of the 'thing itself.'"[9] This much is clear from Arendt's analysis of Descartes, namely that the self becomes the most real when it eliminates any prior assumptions about the nature of reality in favor of its chosen construct of reality.

Second, in-itself is followed by for-itself. This is ideology as belief *and* ritual. As Louis Althusser argues, this is ideology as state apparatus. As Althusser argues, "[t]he ultimate condition of production is therefore the reproduction of the conditions of production."[10] This is the way that ideology is itself perpetuated, namely by being taken up into the very life of the modern subject. As Althusser argues, "in order to exist, every social formation must reproduce the conditions of its production at the same time as it produces, and in order to be able to produce. It must

7. Žižek, "Spectre of Ideology," 1.
8. Žižek, "Spectre of Ideology," 10.
9. Žižek, "Spectre of Ideology," 11.
10. Althusser, "Ideology and Ideological State Apparatuses," 100.

therefore reproduce: 1. the productive forces; 2. the existing relations of production."[11] In short, ideology as for-itself, as both Althusser and Žižek argue, stands for "*the very mechanisms that generate it.*"[12]

Finally, there is ideology as in-and-for-itself. Here ideology becomes more than a doctrinal statement or a practice, but rather a "Wittgensteinian 'family'" resemblance.[13] In the leftist critical optic, capitalist ideology forms the familial structures by which meaning itself is recognizable. This enables ideology to "penetrate every pore of the social body."[14] This is the form of ideology grown from the ingraining of the two prior moments of ideology. As Žižek writes, ideology thus ceases to be doctrine or material practices, but "the elusive network of implicit, quasi-'spontaneous' presuppositions and attitudes that form an irreducible moment of the reproduction of 'non-ideological' (economic, legal, political, sexual . . .) practices."[15] Ideology that travels to this third phase becomes, in other words, the house we live in.

Obviously, this new house is precarious. Despite the rather pessimistic occasion this brings about, one thing is clear: ideology is still only a constructed state of being arising first from the self-positing *cogito*. As such, the central practice of the Left seeks to subvert and displace ideologies such as capitalism. However, the Left is well aware of the conditions by which ideology is displaced. As Žižek writes, "When some procedure is denounced as 'ideological *par excellence*', one can be sure that its inversion is no less ideological."[16] Therefore, the Left is at least aware of the ideological nature of their own critique, even though they claim a return to a real and better way of making sense of the world.

If the problem is that ideology is simultaneously something false and a way to make sense of the world, then Eagleton is correct to say that our "routine sense making" is "depressing."[17] The modern tendency, when confronted with undesirable ideology, is to construct a new and more attractive ideology. Such a tendency is problematic. However, for the sake of brevity, the definition of *ideology* assumed in this work is

11. Althusser, "Ideology and Ideological State Apparatuses," 101.

12. Žižek, "Spectre of Ideology," 12. Emphasis original.

13. Žižek, "Spectre of Ideology," 14.

14. Žižek, "Spectre of Ideology," 14.

15. Žižek, "Spectre of Ideology," 15.

16. Žižek, "Spectre of Ideology," 4.

17. Eagleton, *Ideology*, 2.

false consciousness, which is a direct result of Cartesian foundations of modernity.

The Ideological World: Arendt on Modernity

This Cartesian foundation of modern thought leads to a general world alienation and preference for complete human autonomy. According to Arendt, this modern turn "demonstrates no more than that man can always apply the results of his mind, that no matter which system he uses for the explanation of natural phenomena he will always be able to adopt it as a guiding principle for making and acting."[18] The concept of the self's autonomy is foundational to modernity and, therefore, distances the human from the material world in order to produce a product of its mind—a new world where autonomy and selfhood can thrive. Modernity, as Arendt suggests, is characterized by humanity's need to create the world in its own image.[19] The impact of this need yields an undue reliance upon the self as the harbinger of all meaning and throws doubt upon all exterior reality, alienating each "self" from both the world and other "selves."

The turning to the self and away from the world places a heavy burden on the will. Both modern turns reveal that the will must play an overcompensated role due to the rise of the self-interested individual and world alienation. Arendt believed willing was synonymous with being.[20] According to this calculus, one cannot exist within the world naturally. Instead, the world must be produced in a form more appropriate to the self. The will, as liberated by modernity, plays this dizzying role, Arendt writes, whereby "we are *doomed* to be free."[21] In this sense, Arendt correctly analyzes her modern situation as a product of the history of the will.

Here we pause to clarify the form of the modern self Arendt describes. She argues that humans in modernity turn to the self and away from the world. Such a construction of the self is what I call the attempt to create self-sufficient, privately interested humans. When the individual rejects the world, thereby alienating oneself from it, then the self relies on something else as its source of *being*. In modernity, the self's source lies

---

18. Arendt, *Human Condition*, 287.
19. Arendt, *Human Condition*, 295.
20. Arendt, *Life of the Mind*, 20.
21. Arendt, *Life of the Mind*, 217.

interior to the self. Self-sufficiency, then, is understood in relation to the world and others. In other words, self-sufficiency understands itself over and against the world and others.

Arendt's analysis of modernity underscores a momentous shift in our understanding of the human condition. The turn toward a self-sufficient human away from the social human—who is radically dependent on creation, the neighbor, and God for meaning—signals a loss of self who could potentially be interested in true political life. Rather than a social creature, Arendt shows that humanity has become, in modernity, a private creature. As a result, reality proceeds from the self outward and is independent of physical data. Humanity exists in private from the world.

To be clear, the private is not altogether wrong, as it represents a place that one can rest from public life. However, when the private becomes the exclusive preoccupation of the individual, the possibility of public life is lost. Furthermore, when self-sufficiency becomes the primary motivation of the individual, then the positive role that the will and individuality play in private are corrupted and ultimately lost.

Despite the potentially dangerous role the private plays in forming the self-sufficient human, the will, free from exclusively private concerns, can take on a positive role in forming a public space. Arendt argues that humanity, when organizing a free public space, moves toward true permanence, not toward perpetuation of self-sufficiency. Arendt argues that life must exist beyond the private so that humanity can experience true permanence. She argues that power and will are essential to create this permanent space.[22] Arendt writes, "Wherever people gather together, [there] is potentiality . . . Power is what keeps the public realm, the potential space of appearance . . . in existence."[23] Therefore, when people gather together, a space of permanence potentially exists, but it is the power of the will that must actualize that space.[24]

This discovery of the will's power brings to light the ability of individuals to band together and create the public, political realm.[25] It is the goal of all politics to create a public space free from private interests. However, self-sufficiency makes the concerns of the private, modern self focused primarily on its own perpetuation. The only public space that

22. Arendt, *Human Condition*, 200.

23. Arendt, *Human Condition*, 199–200.

24. Arendt, *Human Condition*, 200.

25. Arendt, *Human Condition*, 204.

emerges in modernity is that which proceeds from the self. The will is not necessarily the root cause of private interests, but when the will becomes self-sufficient, it strays into error. If the will was in error *in se*, then the positive existence of the public would be a fiction. Only when the will becomes committed to world-alienating and self-interested activity does it slip into private interests and self-sufficiency. This does not mean that one should have no private interests, only that private interests should not play a central role in the construction of a free, public space. Without the power of the will, the public realm disappears.

Private Interests: A Brief Excursus

Briefly, I wish to define Arendt's concept of private interests. Arendt understands that all life is divided into the political and private. This is a classic Greek division that Arendt brings into modernity. Therefore, private interests are in opposition to the political. As she writes,

> It is with respect . . . [in relation to the political] . . . that the term 'private,' in its original privative sense, has meaning. To live an entirely private life means above all to be deprived of things essential to a truly human life: to be deprived of the reality that comes from being seen and heard by others, to be deprived of an 'objective' relationship with them that comes from being related to and separated from them through the intermediary of a common world of things, to be deprived of the possibility of achieving something more permanent than life itself.[26]

Arendt, here, clearly sets up her understanding of private interests. There is a common world assumed in the political. A world where something lasting can exist, and where individuals get to exist among equals. Private interests inhibit this political end, namely they prevent individuals from having equitable, public relationships with other humans. In short, private interests are anything in opposition to the political, and thus the common good.

With this basic definition in mind, private interests arise in three distinct forms. First, private interests include that which is private to the individual self. This includes what Arendt most properly points to, namely any racist, fetishizing of the neighbor that prevents their full humanity from participating in political life.

26. Arendt, *Human Condition*, 58.

Second, private interests also signify any organization of a group within a nation that prevent the common good. Yale law professor Amy Chua terms this form of private-interests tribalism. She writes, "Humans are tribal. We need to belong to the group. We crave bonds and attachments, which is why we love clubs, teams, fraternities, family. Almost no one is a hermit. Even monks and friars belong to orders. But the tribal instinct is not just an instinct to belong. It is also an instinct to exclude."[27] Chua's understanding of tribalism couples well with that of private interests. Even though one's private interests can be shared, such as racist ideologies, the sheer existence of a group does not guarantee true political goods and ends. Tribalism is private in that it excludes and prevents individuals from, as Arendt already stated, "an 'objective' relationship with [others] that comes from being related to and separated from them through the intermediary of a common world of things."[28] Examples of tribalism include the racism that begat Jim Crow laws, the internment of Japanese citizens following Pearl Harbor, and the racism inherent in national socialism. These are private interests, though shared and seized by a public group, that prevent equitable political life. In tribalism, there is no objective good, relationship, or life made possibly by its perpetuation, but only prevents full access to true political ends.

Thirdly, there are private interests accorded to nationalist tendencies that prevent global discernment of the political. Chua's description of tribalism fits within nationalist tendencies, though the main purpose of her work lies in unmasking how tribalism impacts the nation alone. Tribalism is that which prevents the common, political good of the nation. To be clear, the political is understood most often within a nation. To seek a common good means seeking the good of the city or nation-state. However, in an increasingly globalized world, one cannot neglect the tribalist narratives of nationalism that prevent truly international political goods. Theologian Karl Barth comments on the nationalism of his day. He writes,

> The French, the English, and the Austrians feel the same way. *A feeling of ecstasy* has possessed all these nations. This intoxication of spirit is not a pretense but is something that we must acknowledge as absolutely genuine. External, material, and private interest have largely given way to great thoughts and common

27. Chua, *Political Tribes*, 1.
28. Arendt, *Human Condition*, 58.

ideals, and for me that is the greatest thing about this awakening of the nations.[29]

For Barth, nationalism at least inhibits purely individual thinking. However, like Chua, Barth recognizes that here too is not a common, political good, but that which is "against."[30] In short, nationalism, in Barth's definition, is against other nations, and thus excludes others from political goods that might extend beyond the nation state.

This troubling definition of nationalism ascends to the level of intuitive political rationality in modernity. In short, the first and primary goal of all nations is selfish. However, this nationalist tribalism comes against a theological problematic, which I think most appropriately fits Arendt's understanding of the political. Nationalism ultimately prevents the political because it excludes humans from a desired creaturely relationship with those that Barth calls distant neighbors.[31] A distant neighbor, as Barth describes, consists of

> different . . . peoples . . . which have a different natural and historical basis and form, to which he does not belong and is not directly bound and committed, and which individually and in their totality form the outer circle by which he and his people are surrounded, so that indirectly and perhaps very directly he, too, stands in a relationship with it.[32]

Here Barth gestures toward the sheer plurality of humanity under the theological rubric of creation. Though there are different people with different national histories, this does not dismiss the need to be in creaturely relationship with them. Furthermore, God commands that national boundaries not limit fellowship with other creatures. This "command," as Barth continues,

> affects and embraces the whole man and his whole being and activity, since there is no sphere of human existence which escapes it or is neutral in relation to it, and since it also belongs to man to stand in these relationships to near and distant neighbors, it inevitably calls him to obedience and sanctifies him to the extent that he stands in these relationships.[33]

29. Barth, "October 18, 1914," 146. Emphasis original.

30. Barth, "October 18, 1914," 149.

31. Barth, *CD* III.4 §54.3.

32. Barth, *CD* III.4 §54.3.

33. Barth, *CD* III.4 §54.3.

The political dimension of this is clear when considering private interests. The command of God to be in fellowship with one's distant neighbors is simultaneously to locate distant neighbors within objective relationship to the political, but more importantly to God. It requires a political rationality that recognizes other nations do not compete for the common good but partner in it. Therefore, nationalism, like tribalism and individual interests, ultimately resists the full potential of the political and is in essence private.

In sum, private interests are opposed to the political in Arendt's philosophy. They take shape in individual interests, tribalism, and nationalism. Though the latter two do offer a social element, their ultimate concern lies in exclusion and are, thus, private in nature. The true, equitable political relationships that are the goal of Arendt's political philosophy depends on the will of individuals to come together and form something lasting beyond private interests. Therefore, despite private interests, one can recognize with Arendt the positive role of the will. In short, without the power of the will, the public realm disappears.

What Is a "Second Life" in Politics?

Because the will has the power to bring people together to build a public space, Arendt states that the will *can* be a positive force. However, she misses an important detail in her critique: in modernity, the will does not have the common good, or the good of the public space, as its gravitational center. Rather, the good of the will is the self. Here we must distinguish between the will as organically bound up with the human being and the will captivated by its own self-sufficiency and private interests. Plato, along with all the ancients, would have been suspicious of will that moved free of the Good as its central desire. However, Arendt is not a Platonist, nor does she make a Platonist argument to counteract private interests and self-sufficiency. In fact, she rejects the political structure put forward in *The Republic*.[34] Rather, she is more sympathetic toward an Aristotelian approach. Even so, she fails to recognize Aristotle's equally important emphasis on friendship as affection, common ends, and the common good that guides much of *The Nicomachean Ethics*.[35] In either Platonic or Aristotelian moral philosophy, the will is not an end in and

34. See Arendt, "Socrates," 5–39.
35. See Aristotle, *Nicomachean Ethics*, §8–9.

of itself. Rather, the end of the will is the Good. Only when this is central can the will be instrumental in the creation of a free public space. Without affection for the Good, Arendt is left with the naked will in its abyss of freedom, detached from a true *political*, common good.

Arendt argues that public life is a creation of the will, but in order for that public space to be free, it must avoid centralizing private interest. Private interests limit what can be held in common, such as shared ends and the common good that are necessary ingredients of a free political space.[36] What needs to be recovered is a proper understanding of a truly public realm and a truly private realm as distinct, good realms of human affairs. According to Arendt, a truly public realm is the free space where individuals create something lasting alongside fellow humans. Arendt offers a crucial distinction between the public and private spheres. The private is the interest of the home. Private interests are permissible as long as they do not transcend to the public realm. Private interests are those that one should have at home in an attempt to find rest from one's labors in reasonable comfort and stability. The public, on the other hand, is the realm that should be free from private interests because it is the place humans inhabit to be among equals. Politics is the act of creating and maintaining a public realm that exists apart from the self's private interests. Arendt shows that politics should be a second, yet primary, life in addition to the one we have in private.

Arendt claims that politics is the attempt to create a "second life."[37] This approach attempts to hold together two important aspects of modernity: the intrinsic worth of the individual and the general space of political equality. Arendt argues that because politics is a "second life," it offers a

> reality that comes from being seen and heard by others . . . [to have] an 'objective' relationship with them that comes from being related to and separated from them through the intermediary of a common world of things, to be deprived of the possible of achieving something more permanent than life itself.[38]

Arendt suggests, contrary to Cartesian philosophy, one's meaning can be found not only in oneself, but also in and among others. Individuals live not only a selfish private life, but also a corporate public life. There is the

36. Arendt, *Human Condition*, 35, 50–67.

37. Arendt, *Human Condition*, 24.

38. Arendt, *Human Condition*, 58.

life of the private, which rests from public life, and the second life offered by the public space, which finds meaning in an outward manner, establishing a permanent space for humanity. In this way, Arendt suggests that politics helps transcend "mere life," which is a life devoid of the public and exists only in private.[39]

In modernity, the second life of politics lacks freedom because it is subject to private interests of mere life. Private interests bleed into public space and, as a result, the public is, Rowan Williams writes, "enslaved to idolatrous objectifications, fetishes and slogans."[40] This is what is at stake in subjecting the public to private interests: the loss of individual freedom in favor of a fetishized social space where no equitable relation is possible. The neighbor exists only to fulfill my own fetishes; they must conform to my perception of the good.

Private interests go against the very meaning of politics. Arendt writes, "The meaning of politics is freedom."[41] Politics is freedom in its desire to create a space where individuals can meet each other as equals, to speak and be heard by others. Such a freedom suggests that the political realm must be capable of sustaining multiple narratives from the speech arising from such a diverse set of narratives. The radically egalitarian nature of this political space gives voice to a variety of differences for the sake of a community where individuals can be free to act in their differences and speak into the differences of others.

Speech and action make people equal to one another and are necessary for what Arendt qualifies as "the truly human life."[42] She writes, "A life without speech and without action . . . is literally dead to the world; it has ceased to be a human life because it is no longer lived among men."[43] Speech is essential in the creation of a public space where individuals can construct permanent structures, such as constitutional orders for the human artifice. The free political being is one who can speak and act in the political sphere without the need for violence. Arendt writes, "To be political, to live in a *polis*, meant that everything was decided through words and persuasion and not through force and violence."[44] Only free

39. Arendt, *Human Condition*, 11.
40. Williams, "Politics and the Soul," 108.
41. Arendt, "Introduction *into* Politics," 108.
42. Arendt, *Human Condition*, 58.
43. Arendt, *Human Condition*, 176.
44. Arendt, *Human Condition*, 26.

men and women capable of persuasion and speech can perform political actions.

Arendt claims that public space capable of sustaining practices of speech is the ideal free, political realm. However, modernity lacks such space because politics does not perpetuate the creation of permanent structures for the human artifice. Rather, modernity is committed to actions that sustain the basic functions of life. Such a political community is not free in the fullest sense, according to Arendt. They are, in essence, private. The private as the political realm enables political actions that perpetuate the basic functions of life and is not oriented toward the common good or shared ends with the neighbor. As such, the primary activity in politics is not speech for persuasion, but coercion for the sake of security. If citizens are bound together with mutually exclusive private interests, then the goal of political life is to secure one's interests against the neighbor. Rather than a true public space where people can be free and among equals, modernity has subjected the public to the competition of private interests.

Subjecting the public to the private realizes specific forms of life. Arendt proposes two: *animal laborans* (the form of life associated with actions concerning animality and labor) and *homo faber* (the form of life associated with actions unnatural to human life and defined as work). Both labor and work name specific types of private interests that form the basis of private political communities where one's activity is to accumulate and secure against the neighbor. These forms of life prove inadequate, either explicitly or implicitly, to structure a public realm, free from the private.

Arendt's first form of life is the *animal laborans*, which is primarily concerned with maintaining the biological processes of life. To the *animal laborans*, life is the highest good. This good is explicitly concerned with the private. Labor, the chief action of the *animal laborans*, achieves the necessary product to maintain the life processes of private life. Arendt writes, the "human condition of labor is life itself."[45] In labor, one consumes and leaves nothing behind for public benefit; it only serves the basic life processes of the individuals in the home.

Arendt's preference for something lasting leads to her rejection of labor. This is due to the fact that labor does not make anything lasting for the human artifice. Therefore, subjecting politics to the mere task of labor

---

45. Arendt, *Human Condition*, 7.

robs it of the chance to perform any meaningful, public action. It allows "private interests [to] assume public significance."[46] Arendt continues, labor "everywhere uses up durability, wears it down, makes it disappear, until eventually dead matter, the result of small single, cyclical, life processes, returns into the over-all gigantic circle of nature herself, where no beginning and no end exist."[47] This cycle of labor turns the dealings of humans in society to an indistinct mass of people who consume.

Such a mass is what Arendt calls "society."[48] Arendt continues, "Society is the form in which the fact of mutual dependence for the sake of life and nothing else assumes public significance and where the activities connected with sheer survival are permitted to appear in public."[49] In the socialization of humanity, self-interest guides the laborer's social life, but self-interest is the one interest of the whole. What remains is a "'natural force,' the force of the life process itself, to which all men and all human activities were equally submitted . . . and whose basic aim, if it had an aim at all, was survival of the animal species man."[50] With survival as the only intention, the laborer fails to make anything lasting for the human artifice, which is victory of the *animal laborans*.[51] The modern world has seen a shift where one's labor is synonymous with one's public work.

The public realm offered by labor is no public realm. Arendt writes, "As long as the *animal laborans* remains in possession of [the public realm], there can be no true public realm, but only private activities displayed in the open."[52] In the modern era, there is a victory of private interest over the political, which signals the end of a free public realm. This devolves the political realm to the point that "the only thing people have in common is their private interests."[53] This is problematic because the claims of private interests are difficult, if not impossible, to negotiate. Theologian Oliver O'Donovan writes that this tendency to "set up political authority, as a device to secure our own essentially private, local and unpolitical purposes, has left the Western democracies in a state of

---

46. Arendt, *Human Condition*, 35.

47. Arendt, *Human Condition*, 96.

48. Arendt, *Human Condition*, 321.

49. Arendt, *Human Condition*, 47.

50. Arendt, *Human Condition*, 321.

51. Arendt, *Human Condition*, 320.

52. Arendt, *Human Condition*, 320.

53. Arendt, *Human Condition*, 69.

pervasive moral debilitation, which, from time to time, inevitably throws up idolatrous and authoritarian reaction."[54] The inability to negotiate these private interests, O'Donovan argues, leads to the establishment of legal apparatuses that secure individual private interests over and against the neighbor. These apparatuses are not lasting, unlike constitutional orders, because they, too, participate in the consumption of nature. Their only role is to preserve our consumption in the name of private interests.

One of the private interests that guides this political order of laborious society is happiness. The highest goal of happiness is to maintain life processes, but to do so without pain. Pleasure is the new calculus of social achievement.[55] This calculation has no beginning and no end. In labor, all life is subjected to the value of its own consumption and happiness, which is a strictly private interest.

Arendt juxtaposes labor with another action: work, which at least creates something for public benefit.[56] Work, though somewhat lasting, does not create something permanent, as does speech. Contrary to labor, work is concerned with the semipermanent nature of one's productivity and provides a public realm that is not primarily concerned with private interests. Work, as opposed to labor, attempts to "work upon" nature and thus fabricate something semipermanent in the material.[57] Again, this is different from speech, which creates something fundamentally lasting, such as constitutions and institutional politics.

Work reflects the modern turn to the self, as outlined by Arendt, where the self-sufficient individual seeks to produce and fabricate a world of one's own rather than live in the world exterior to the self. This is the height of world alienation. The *homo faber*, the person of work, constructs an objective world between humanity and nature. It creates a second world in addition to the world of the private. This is still not Arendt's public space, but something fabricated by the *homo faber* in which individuals must continually produce and fabricate in order to be valued.

The world of work is the world of commerce. The *homo faber*'s "public realm is the exchange market, where he can show the products of his hand and receive the esteem which is due him."[58] When the *homo*

54. O'Donovan, *Desire of the Nations*, 49.

55. Arendt, *Human Condition*, 308–9.

56. Arendt, *Human Condition*, 88–89.

57. Arendt, *Human Condition*, 136.

58. Arendt, *Human Condition*, 160.

faber constructs the public, it does so toward its own material gain. The creation and accumulation of products become a central feature of work. One's ability to fabricate the world and material into personal gain becomes central.

Similar to *animal laborans*, the peril of the *homo faber* is the degradation of the created order. The *animal laborans* "consumes" nature. As a master worker, nature is "used" as a means to the *homo faber*'s own end. This leads to the degradation of created things and the loss of "intrinsic worth."[59] This causes an inability to create a true public realm. Means and ends are an economic register measurable by greater fabrication and, thus, capital. The issue is not the good or evil of capital, but the inability of capital to sustain public life. Arendt writes, "Only when wealth became capital, whose chief function was to generate more capital, did private property equal or come close to the permanence inherent in the commonly shared world."[60] Work gives meaning to a person based on the products of his or her own hands and signals the coordinate loss of intrinsic worth prior to production and exchange. This means the *homo faber* does have a public space an individual can distinguish oneself, but it only values individuals insofar as it benefits and serves the interests of fellow producers. Here the clear virtues are freedom from external influence toward this fabrication and protection of one's personal property. Even though a public space now exists for the *homo faber*, it is free of private interests. Arendt writes that the public sphere "has become a function of the private . . . [it is] the only concern left."[61] The *homo faber* values life only in light of this economic, private calculus. Therefore, the public realm created by the *homo faber* is not a true public realm.

Labor and work have overtaken political space. This means that public space is controlled by private interests and private commodities. The success of private interests and commodities lead to the malformation of political philosophy, which transcends subjective dispositions into a legal, legislative apparatus that thrives on the success of these private desires.

An example of such a legal structure, according to Arendt, is totalitarianism. For Arendt, totalitarianism is the legal, political structure of Nazi Germany that is capable of sustaining labor and work as exclusive

59. Arendt, *Human Condition*, 156.
60. Arendt, *Human Condition*, 68.
61. Arendt, *Human Condition*, 69.

ends of political life. Arendt offers an excellent definition of the tactics of a totalitarian regime. She writes,

> Totalitarian politics—far from being simply anti-Semitic or racist or imperialist or communist—use and abuse their own ideological and political elements until the basis of factual reality, from which the ideologies originally derive their strength and their propaganda value—the reality of class struggle, for instance, or the *interest* conflicts between Jews and their neighbors—have all but disappeared.[62]

When the political realm loses all capability to discern the common good, regimes emerge to prey on a variety of private interests that make the real world disappear. This is the function of the modern: to construct a world that does not rely on objective physical-sense data. Again, this is ideology. Note that Arendt places conflicting private interests at the center of the totalitarian regime. The totalitarian regime draws its strength and propaganda from the realm of private interests. The heart of labor and work easily couples with the totalitarian regime. The totalitarian regime is one, through its ideological interests, that captures the imagination of a nation and succeeds in appealing to the private interests of citizens and, thus, mobilizes them for political ends. The totalitarian regime subtly and explicitly appeals to fears associated with class interests and racism toward Jews in order to call citizens beyond legal and moral constraints toward different ends. Fear and racism are private interests devoid of the common good because they arise from a desire to preserve basic life functions (i.e., labor). Although Germany was in crisis, this does not dismiss the fact that German citizens were exclusively concerned with perpetuating their own life functions. The totalitarian regime seized on this by assimilating these fears into a fabricated, ideological account of reality. As a result, everything else—competing goods, alternative forms of humanity, etc.—falls away in light of the private made political. In this way, readers can discern in Arendt's description of totalitarianism similar themes to her critique of modern politics in general.

To summarize, Arendt theorizes the political is a second, primary life in addition to the private. However, due to the modern disposition toward self-sufficiency and private interests, this second life has diminished. In modernity, it is increasingly more evident that political structures are dictated by private interests rather than the common good. A

---

62. Arendt, *Origins of Totalitarianism*, xv. Emphasis mine.

free political realm would enable citizens to speak and act among equals for the sake of constructing something permanent for the human artifice. However, because private interests rule, speech and persuasion cannot work. Coercion and violence replace persuasion because neighbors do not pursue common ends or goods, each seeking to secure private interests against the other.

SOVEREIGNTY AND DEATH: ARENDT, FOUCAULT, AND THE BIOPOLITICS

Arendt illustrates through her analysis of labor and work that the historical structuring of politics is directed toward less fruitful endeavors. For Arendt, labor and work are not abstract ideals, but are testament to historical horrors that must be critiqued. Arendt does not make this connection explicitly, but it is clear that if private interests (i.e., the perpetuation of one's bodily life) dominate the political realm, some benefit while others suffer. Arendt's totalitarian example illustrates that when life (the continuation of basic life functions) is the greatest political virtue, death becomes an obsession to be avoided at all costs. Legally, this takes shape in governing apparatuses. In these apparatuses, death is used as an instrument of fear toward those who embody a threat to the basic functions and property of life and work. Arendt's political analysis then sets up a late modern critical approach to politics. Arendt, more than anyone before her, recognizes the way that horror grows from the anthropological errors of modernity. Arendt gives us the historical and theoretical tools to note how and why some lives have greater meaning in politics than others, pointing beyond her own political analysis toward biopolitics.

In order to fully unpack Arendt's political analysis, I utilize aspects of the philosophical framework of biopolitics. In two ways, biopolitics explains the political themes Arendt establishes. First, biopolitics places the biological life of citizens as the central concern of politics, namely life preserved against death. In Arendt's analysis, labor places life, as an end in itself, at the top of the political sphere. The central concern of life, as political good, is death. This is a central theme of modernity itself. Theologian John Milbank writes that the objective in modernity is "to *secure* life against death: this is 'morality.'"[63] Not only is this a task of morality in modernity, but also of politics. The very meaning of politics,

63. Milbank, "Can Morality Be Christian," 223. Emphasis original.

then, becomes the securing of life against death. Theologian Catherine Pickstock writes, politics keeps "death and life apart in order to preserve life immune from death in pure sterility."[64] Taken together, Milbank and Pickstock clarify the political ramifications of biopolitics. When one structures political community around life, the greatest political concern becomes bracketing life from death. This necessarily excludes some, who embody the threat of death, from this very sterile politics of life.

Second, biopolitics locates political structures within Arendt's emphasis on private interests and commodities. For Arendt, private citizens already possess private interests. Foucault shows how these private interests are the subject of training by political bodies. If life and the desire to live occupy the center of private interests, then these desires, according to Foucault, can be trained. Much like the ideological capture of private interests by the totalitarian regime, as illustrated in Arendt, hospitals, prisons, and other structures that publicly preserve life against death equally seize upon and train private human interests. The apparatuses of this training are called technologies of the self. In such structures, it is clear which forms of life are privileged (the healthy, the law-abiding, etc.) and which are discouraged (the sick, the prisoner, etc.). Absent shared ends for the common good, private interests become unrestricted in public space; figures present in hospitals and prisons become the living embodiment of death. This provides a clear spectrum of desirable and undesirable life made public and internalized in the life of the subject.

With these two elements in mind, I must define biopolitics. Though biopolitics is made popular by Michel Foucault, the term actually predates him first appearing in the early twentieth century. Biopolitics denotes the simultaneous rise of the sciences, specifically biology, and the liberal state. Therefore, biopolitics, in essence, is the combination of *bios* (biological life) and politics. To be clear, premodern political bodies have been concerned with life in the past through segregation, internment, etc. However, in modernity, with the rise of the science, biopolitics assumes that political relations can be perfected through biological means.[65] Therefore the goal of biopolitics in modernity, through legal and medical means, is the optimization humanity.[66]

---

64. Pickstock, *After Writing*, 104.

65. See Lemke, *Bio-Politics*, 11.

66. Lemke, *Bio-Politics*, 15.

Foucault advances these aspects of biopolitics. For Foucault, bio-politics is actively concerned with "making live and letting die."[67] The theme of "life" should immediately recall Arendt's emphasis on labor in politics and intensify the biological element central to her analysis. For Arendt, labor is the continuation of biological processes that use up all material it creates. For late moderns after Arendt and Foucault, biopoli-tics denotes that "life [namely biological life] occup[ies] the very center of the political scene of modernity."[68] When biological life becomes the center of politics, then the immediate concern is the perfectibility, steril-ization, and the form life takes. In short, it is concerned with making live and letting die.

These definitions are not without history. Foucault implicitly builds upon Arendt, but provides a helpful distinction that compliments Arendt. For Arendt, the totalitarian despot seizes upon social fears and anxieties for the sake of controlling society. To restate, totalitarian politics is racial: it plays on the fears of society by casting its fear in biological terms. For example, the Jew was not just posed as a political threat in Nazi Germany, but also a biological (namely viral) threat. Foucault extends this biologi-cal parsing to political sovereignty, a concept central to liberalism. For Foucault, the rise of biopolitics is commensurate with the rise of liberal-ism.[69] As Foucault writes,

> I think an essential characteristic of this new art of government is this organization of numerous and complex internal mecha-nisms whose function—and this is what distinguishes them from *raison d'Etat*—is not so much to ensure the growth of the state's forces, wealth, and strength, to ensure its unlimited growth, as to limit the exercise of government power internally.[70]

To be clear the regulation of the form life takes is a concern that pre-dates the eighteenth century. For example, Agamben argues that this is a monastic concern that dates back to the foundation of the first as-cetic orders.[71] However, this general concern for forms of life, which does

67. Foucault, *Society Must Be Defended*, 241.

68. Agamben, *Homo Sacer*, 3.

69. This is evident in the fact that Foucault's original title for his famous "Birth of Biopolitics" lectures was the "Birth of Liberalism."

70. Foucault, *Birth of Biopolitics*, 27.

71. See Agamben, *Highest Poverty*, 91–146.

show up in premodern political bodies, is distinct from the radical and exclusive concern for biological life in modernity.

The preservation of life is not an overtly coercive politics, but embodied within the life of the masses, namely a naked will to live.[72] Foucault writes,

> Sovereignty is, therefore, constituted on the basis of a radical form of will, but it counts for little. That will is bound up with fear, and sovereignty is never shaped from above, or in other words, on the basis of a decision taken by the strong . . . Sovereignty is always shaped from below, and by those who are afraid.[73]

The will, as Arendt has already stated, creates political space. Therefore, the will, as illustrated by Arendt, is central even to totalitarian politics. Foucault furthers Arendt's understanding of totalitarianism under a different name: sovereignty. Sovereignty arises from the will of the self, which in turn becomes the will of the mass, and this will orients political space toward private interests through the fear of death.[74] Like any private interest, fear can be seized upon. An example of this lies, for Arendt, in the plight of the Jews in Germany, in which Jews took on the form of the enemy—not of the state, but of life. Furthermore, Arendt laments this will of life as the negative use of power that corrupts any positive understanding of the will.[75] Therefore, from an Arendtian perspective, Foucault argues that the political space mobilized by labor and work is sovereignty.

Sovereignty preserves life for the masses as a way to perpetuate its own rule by dispersing sovereignty into the masses. Foucault shows that sovereignty does not come from the powerful above, but from below. Sovereignty is not an abstract sovereign over and against the masses. Instead, it works through the freedom of the masses. Sovereignty, then, is the general will of the masses toward the end of "making live and letting die."[76] Our collaboration with sovereign ideology serves as the perpetuation of the dichotomy between what is allowed to live and to die. This dichotomy reorganizes bodies around a new center of visibility, which represents a technological achievement to indirectly influence bodies in

---

72. Foucault, *Society Must Be Defended*, 96.

73. Foucault, *Society Must Be Defended*, 96.

74. Foucault, *Society Must Be Defended*, 96.

75. Arendt, *Human Condition*, 204.

76. Foucault, *Society Must Be Defended*, 241.

space. It is a politics of fear against which the politics of life (biopolitics) itself is constructed. If biopolitics is truly that which makes live and die, then it presents the masses with a global value of desirable interests that can be taken up in the self through technologies of the self. Foucault writes,

> The new technology that is being established is addressed to a multiplicity of men, not to the extent that they are nothing more than their individual bodies, but to the extent that they form, on the contrary, a global mass that is affected by overall processes characteristic of birth, death, production, illness, and so on.[77]

By focusing the attention of the masses upon the variety of life processes surrounding them and how those processes impact the masses locally, the sovereign regime makes the whole world the enemy of the masses. This is much akin to the totalitarian insistence that the Jews are a "threat" to the law of nature, to the German lived existence.

If sovereignty concerns itself with the preservation of life, there always exists a negative, unhealthy, death-bound life that is continually weaned out of the population. This is the power of the sovereign. Those who live in death-bound subjectivity, as Abdul JanMohamed argues, bear the ontological threat of death in their very humanity and exist under the constant threat of death.[78] This is the essence of making life and letting die, which divides the population between healthy life and unhealthy life.[79] The death-boundness of some is embodied in the masses in order that those who are death-bound might remain so. The boundary between life and death must be collaborated in technologies of the self or else it would lose its meaning. Foucault's example of this collaboration is racism. Racism is not just the prejudice against certain pigmentations of skin, but prejudice against the life that must be removed in order to "make life in general healthier: healthier and purer."[80] For Foucault, racism always takes this shape. Foucault elaborates on the Arendtian way that private interests inhibit a free public space. Politics is no longer an activity of shared ends or the common good. Rather, it is a sterilizing of particular life against other forms of life. Life as the end of the political life is not a

77. Foucault, *Society Must Be Defended*, 243.
78. JanMohamed, *Death-Bound-Subject*, 13–15.
79. Foucault, *Society Must Be Defended*, 255.
80. Foucault, *Society Must Be Defended*,255.

common good, only a private interest made public in which each citizen is responsible in paradoxical isolation.

With the help of Foucault, we see that private interests are twofold. First, there are the private interests themselves that arise from self-sufficiency. These are the personal concerns, such as labor and work, that intensify private, isolated existence. Since self-sufficiency is remote of any common good or end, then private interests become the way humans interpret their world and construct politics. Second, since this is the plight of humanity, private interests beget ideology. Ideology is any form of constructed reality that does not require or manipulates physical-sense data. This is a broader symptom of the Cartesian subject, but one that has political ramifications. If life is defined by self-sufficiency and motivated by private interests, such as the preservation of life processes and property, then the neighbor is most concretely a threat. Therefore, humans come together in a politic to preserve the self against neighbor. This works against the possibility of the common good and the important possibility that the neighbor is not a threat. Therefore, a constructed form of reality must replace both the common good and factual data about the neighbor. This constructed reality is the ideological center of biopolitics and totalitarianism. Recognizing this twofold definition is important to the further development of Arendt's political insight.

Arendt's helpful analysis of the ailments of modern political philosophy and political space reveals three key struggles. First, Arendt shows that modernity has done damage to our understanding of the basic nature of the human. In modernity, there is a categorical shift toward the self-enclosed, self-sufficient human that constructs the world for self. This individual is divorced from shared narratives or physical space in favor of purely individual ones. This understanding is anemic because it leads humanity away from the possibility of community and the common good as an objective.

Second, Arendt argues cogently that the political realm lacks a space where humans can come together in equality and create something lasting for the human artifice. Such a creation would enable people of vast differences to come together for the sake of speech and action that help improve upon the political space. Such a space is very valuable to Arendt because it possesses the potential to rescue humanity from mere existence.

Third, private interests inhibit this free political space. Private interests consist of the desire to live and accumulate private property divorced from the common good or shared ends. Private interests are twofold. First, there is the private interest itself, which is the concern for life processes or private property. Second, there is the ideological structures that emerge from private interests. Private interests create the condition for ideology, and ideology perpetuates and encourages private interests. Here, politics only consumes life. As such, the only meaning the neighbor can possess is either a threat or an opportunity to advance the individual's private interests. When private interests become the motivating factor in organizing the political, then the space created by such intentions is inherently biopolitical. Politics takes the posture of promoting "valuable" versus "invaluable" life. When the masses come together to preserve private interests, it creates structures that discard various people for the sake of preserving the majority. Arendt sets up the modern political problem as a failure to preserve individuality and universality.

These central reflections precede the Pauline political response by the new approach. Modernity suffers from an inability to make citizens equal in political space and honor individuality. The figures of the left attempt to overcome this difficulty by turning to the apostle Paul. However, as do many moderns, they presuppose that much of biopolitics is propped up by theology and theological reflection. Therefore, they subtract God and confessional theology from Paul's writings in favor of a more materialist depiction of reality. They deploy a specific hermeneutic toward the double effect of answering the unique political problems of modernity, emptying Paul of his theological center. Ultimately, I believe this is a mistake and argue that Paul's own apocalyptic theology is the answer to modernity's ailments. However, I wish to engage the insight of these thinkers before providing my own constructive alternative. Such an engagement is essential because it provides a rhetorical center from which my engagement can emerge.

The Hermeneutics of Materialist Nihilism: Politics after the Death of God

The movement of private interests into the political sphere that leads to sovereignty, biopolitics, and totalitarianism must be undone. In order to do this, the philosophers of the new approach reach for alternative political sources that critique modern biopolitics and envision a different form of politics. This different form envisioned is materialism, a form of politics that focuses on material realities and causes. There are many forms of materialism: new materialism, dialectical materialism, historical materialism, naturalistic materialism, discursive materialism, etc. The inner disagreement and dispute about what constitutes true materialism is problematic for the new approach because each possess its own implicit assumptions about materialism. What is central, however, is the emphasis on material change in the political realm and the banishment of classical metaphysics from consideration of the ailments of politics. Some believe this is logically warranted because if one is critical of the sovereign and totalitarian biopolitics of modernity, then it is expected that the focus of an alternative material community will be on the good of material realities neglected by sovereignty and totalitarianism.

Despite the emphasis on material realities to secure a better politic outside of sovereignty and totalitarianism, a new source for materialism has emerged: Christian theology. Materialist philosophers have begun, since the early twentieth century, to plunder the resources of Christianity to clarify their philosophy. This does not represent a renaissance of Christian theology. In approaching the texts of Christianity, their materialism serves a hermeneutical commitment, namely nihilism. As a hermeneutic, nihilism attacks the very meaning-making process inherent in the world. This is an appeal to foundational nihilist Friedrich Nietzsche, whose nihilism is not only an exorbitant refusal of all meaning, but also the one placed over humanity by God, the state, and culture. As commentator Michael Lackey writes,

> In killing God and His crown of creation [namely the subject], Nietzsche does not become the quintessential nihilist; rather, he becomes, to his mind, the first sane voice crying in the intellectual wilderness: make way the coming of a new human, a 'subject' which can only become a 'self' when it paradoxically learns to overcome its very constructed 'self' . . . so long as God exists, a subject which overcomes itself cannot come into being.[81]

The death of the subject provides the destruction of present, available meaning, such as private interests and the self, in order to insert new meanings into political life. The death of the sovereign, either in God or the state, begets the death of the projection of another's private interests over the self and ideological perpetuation of meaning in modernity.[82]

---

81. Lackey, "Killing God, Liberating the 'Subject,'" 737.

82. See Foucault, *Order of Things*, 385.

This political commitment in late modernity, in the wake of Arendt and Foucault, eliminates the ideological value inherent to biopolitics. Christianity, and specifically Paul, is used in order to enact a type of nihilist revolution as a prolegomenon to a materialist politic.

A chief example of this nihilistic use of Christianity is the historical materialist politics of Walter Benjamin. Even though materialism generally resists the transcendent categories of classical metaphysics and places heavy confidence in the natural, many forms of materialism are open to theological categories. For example, Slavoj Žižek's description of the new materialism is inspired by the world of Giles Deleuze. Žižek writes that new materialism is a depiction of reality "as an enchanted world full of magic forces, good and evil spirits, etc., but strangely *without gods*—there are no transcendent divine entities . . . all magic is immanent to matter, as a spiritual power that dwells in our terrestrial world."[83] This form of materialism is distinct from other more naturalistic forms of materialism. The magic and spiritual forces envisioned by Žižek suggests that materialism can allow for more than just mere matter, but does not need the transcendence of classical metaphysics. Even though the materialists kill God, they still desire an enchanted reality.

Self-professed materialists help humanity reorient reality as it is experienced naturally. In general materialist terms, as Terry Eagleton defines it, reality is a set of "sense-impressions stem[ming] from one's environment." Materialists hope "that if this environment could be so refashioned as to generate the 'right' kinds of sense data, human behaviour could be dramatically changed for the better."[84] One should note the modern themes parallel to Arendt's insights. If materialism is about manipulating sense data, then it is equally liable for constructing reality. Paul assists materialists toward this end. Specifically, Paul helps unmask how the material commitments of distinct individuals prevent the proliferation of private interests.

Now that we have defined what materialism is and what it does, I approach Benjamin's nihilistic hermeneutic that arises from his historical materialism. Historical materialism differs slightly from the materialism of Deleuze and Žižek. Eagleton defines historical materialism as

> a far more modest proposal [than that of general materialism]—
> one which views class struggle, along with a conflict between

83. Žižek, *Absolute Recoil*, 12. Emphasis original.
84. Eagleton, *Materialism*, 2.

the forces and relations of production, as the dynamic of ep-
ochal historical change. It also regards the material activities of
men and women as lying at the source of their social existence,
a view which is not confined to Marxism.[85]

Historical materialism looks for the material means to produce humanity's freedom from certain struggles against private interests by placing
their concern outside of themselves to a broader humane narrative.
Historical materialism is very open to theological categories. Eagleton
specifically states that one who prays and exercises faith in God would be
comfortable as a materialist.[86] This aside, historical materialism arises as
a peculiar form of materialism to overcome the "economic" hierarchies
between life that must live (bourgeois) and life that must die (proletariat).
Historical materialism, in an attempt to recover a common humanity,
focuses on the commonality that all humans share, their human bodies.
Benjamin's work attempts to empty biopolitical values of private interests.
This occasions the need for his nihilism. The particular way that nihilism
functions in this hermeneutic is that biopolitics and private interests are
emptied of meaning for the sake of reordering material realities.

Benjamin's materialistic hermeneutic, therefore, is a type of constructive nihilism. Scruton recognizes the left and the new approach
work toward the destruction of all privileged hierarchies, and nihilism is
the tool toward that destruction. Historical materialism, though attempting to remain enchanted by reality, has already removed any classically
understood transcendent meaning so as to construct a material account
of reality from below. Benjamin's constructive nihilism does not just re-
lieve one specific manifestation of hierarchies, but attempts at a lasting
shift away from hierarchies. Historical materialism removes the meaning
associated with private interests. Benjamin's nihilism questions how certain forms of life have become the highest value due to the dehumanizing
effect in creating hierarchies.

Benjamin's nihilism arises from his messianism. He writes, "Only
the Messiah himself consummates all history, in the sense that he alone
redeems, completes, creates its relation to the Messianic."[87] For Benjamin, as a Jewish thinker, the Messiah signals something important about
history and politics: its end. This includes biopolitics. Benjamin assumes

---

85. Eagleton, *Materialism*, 8.

86. Eagleton, *Materialism*, 8.

87. Benjamin, "Theologico-Political Fragment," 312.

an apocalyptic interpretation, one in which history does not progress to a conclusion. Rather, history is interrupted. This is the nihilism of messianism. "Nothing historical can relate to itself on its own account to the Messianic."[88] The messianic brings an end to history, not teleologically, but nihilistically, the end of its existence and meaning.

Benjamin's materialist nihilism arising from his messianism can alter sense perceptions for the sake of reorienting material life. The messianic brings an end to every meaning constructed in the human edifice. The messianic plunders theological and Pauline theological resources for the sake of a messianic politic. Benjamin is messianic in his Jewish convictions, but he augments his messianic with Paul.[89] Paul's messianic confesses that Christ, at the end, turns over all things to the Father in order to bring creation to a close (1 Cor 15:20–28) and the captivity of nature to futility (Rom 8:28). Understood in this light, the messianic is that which signals an end, not only the end of the world but also the futility of creation.

Messianic, as described by Benjamin, destroys the order of the "profane" that founds modern politics by revealing the modern futility to found politics of such a limited end. The profane is established out of private interests where the preservation of life, happiness/pleasure, and private property is crucial. Benjamin writes, "The rhythm of this eternally transient worldly existence . . . [is] transient in its totality."[90] Since the Messiah signals the end of history, the Messiah also unmasks the very impermanent nature of private interests. The life that is secured by private interests, Arendt notes, is based on a happiness that is fleeting. In labor, all that is preserved and created is consumed. Benjamin recognizes that to place the foundation of politics on this is futility. True to Nietzsche, the order of the profane is nihilism. The messianic must inform this understanding. For Benjamin, the messianic signifies this passing transience of nature and the end to any order based on the profane.[91]

In order to leave profane politics behind, the messianic must "violate" the very order of the profane, every private interest that locates politics within the impermanent. This violation is nihilistic because it empties the private interest of meaning and also opens the way for new meanings. In

88. Benjamin, "Theologico-Political Fragment," 312.

89. For more on the reliance of Benjamin on Paul see Poettcker, "Messiah's Quiet Approach," 95.

90. Benjamin, "Theologico-Political Fragment," 312.

91. Benjamin, "Theologico-Political Fragment," 313.

Judaism, the coming of the Messiah brings to an end the current political order. This is true for ancient Judaism, but Benjamin brings this into his understanding of historical materialism. Messianic's "divine violence" is how the messianic dislocates the meaning of the profane.

In order for Benjamin's materialism not to collapse back into an abstract political theory, it must concretely dislocate the profane in practice. For Benjamin, the messianic is imbued with divine violence, which is "law-destroying."[92] This debilitates profane politics because divine violence erupts from within the profane order itself in order to reorder the fundamental presuppositions of an individual.[93] Benjamin's example is the Mosaic command, "Thou shalt not kill." This command arises from divine law and comes against the profane law not to kill. Profane and divine laws can coordinate on such an issue in principle, but not, Benjamin notes, through enforcement. The profane enforces the law not to kill through "striking at the life of the perpetrator."[94] This has the effect of driving the perpetrator into a deeper love of his or her own life, which is the source of the perpetrator's happiness and private interests. While the profane order maintains its monopoly on the transience of happiness through striking at the life of the perpetrator, the divine law confronts the individual from without. The individual who adheres to the divine law not to kill refuses to murder out of a tangential obedience rather than out of the will to preserve his or her own life or transience. Put another way, divine violence destroys private interests by becoming out of sync with the aims of private interests. This is the messianic power in the immanent world. Through the power of the theological concepts of the messianic and divine violence, private interests (i.e., desires for that which is passing away) are reordered. In this way, humanity escapes its captivity to mere life (i.e., the life that is passing away) and sense data is reordered outside profane politics.

A reading of Paul can emerge from Benjamin's historical materialism with two unique materialist commitments.[95] First, Benjamin proposes a severely contingent rendering of reality, one that resists totalizing universal forms of reality. As envisioned in his description of divine violence, the messianic undercuts all teleological developments rendered by ideal-

92. Benjamin, "Critique of Violence," 297.

93. Benjamin, "Critique of Violence," 297.

94. Poettcker, "Messiah's Quiet Approach," 107.

95. I am utilizing Benjamin and theologian Nate Kerr's own summary of Benjamin. See Kerr, *Christ, History, and Apocalyptic,* 57–60.

ized, private interests. This is essential in its ability to resist biopolitical forms of governing. It is not the universal regulation of a profane human that matters, but the sheer contingency and difference of humanity inside politics.

The ability to live in genuine relation to difference leads to a second crucial implication of the messianic: embodiment. Briefly, this is the great struggle of the modern, postcritical approach to political theology. Contemporary philosophers have a great many things to say about ideology but often surrender in their philosophical musings the ability to articulate the most basic practices essential to sustaining a political life contrary to biopolitics. Theologian Nate Kerr summarizes this point: the messianic "is nothing less than the revolutionary critique and subversion of the real and material institutions that secure the appearance of assumed universality of 'historical continuity.'"[96] Drawing again on the example of divine violence, only the concrete refusal and embodiment of the command "do not murder" actually displaces private interests inherent in biopolitics. Divine violence secures new practices and embodiment not captivated by technologies of the self. Through the refashioning of Paul's theology, the messianic achieves a faithful action of the messianic event that is contingent and resistant to totalizing norms.

Benjamin describes the refashioning of Paul's theology through a dwarf who is a grand puppeteer. Benjamin argues that this theological construct is like the dwarf, in the sense that it guides the historical materialist puppet from behind the scenes. The imagery comes from the story of an eighteenth-century chess-playing Turkish mechanism. Chess players would come from all over the world to play this miraculous autonomous machine that could best any chess player. It was revealed, however, that the Turk actually contained a dwarf who guided it by its strings.

The Turk is the historical materialist puppet and the dwarf is theology. The Turk is imbued with new abilities that are attributed to the Turk itself, and no one knows of its true source of power. Benjamin writes, "The puppet called 'historical materialism' is to win all the time. It can easily be a match for anyone if it enlists the services of theology, which today, as we know, is wizened and has to keep out of sight."[97] Historical materialism, thus, utilizes theology in order to critique modern politics.

96. Kerr, *Christ, History, and Apocalyptic*, 59.
97. Benjamin, "Theses on the Philosophy of History," 253.

Theology serves as a greater ideological tool to displace meaning in modern politics that philosophy can do alone.

Benjamin's messianic, apocalyptic, historical materialism is very provocative. The strength of his position is the unique description of the material aliments of the profane with an eye toward nonmaterial origins. In short, Benjamin's analysis suggests that there is more than material causes at work in the order of the profane and the ailments of late modern politics. Furthermore, Benjamin's philosophy does not remain abstract but dwells within concrete, material actions. Such a concentration on material causes and solutions leads to a robust materialism lacking in much of Christian history. It is not just enough to analyze the problem, but one must provide a means and practice to engage it. To this end, Benjamin highlights the resources available in his Jewish tradition, namely divine violence. This provides a means for individuals to resist the material manifestation of these powers that guide history. Benjamin's nihilism is an exercised, albeit constructive, nihilism rather than a vague rejection so apparent in late modernity. It is a nihilism that refuses to live in a world guided by the profane and a flat refusal of its meaning-making enterprise. It is this nihilism that is fundamentally instructive for Paul's apocalyptic, political theology.

Any problem I have with Benjamin arises not from his material expression of Paul's theology, but rather that the puppet stays out of sight. Theology remains an ideological whetstone instrumentally ordered toward the success of a materialist agenda. Benjamin is crucial toward developing a political interpretation of Paul's apocalyptic messianism, but ultimately Paul, through moral exhortation, draws God liturgically to the center of communal life.

Though Benjamin cannot finally make the Kierkegaardian leap of faith he provides the best political interpretation of Paul's writings. The weakness present in the new approach is most drastically apparent in those who follow Benjamin because their ideological commitments are more evident. This is because Benjamin assumes a messianic-Judaism that resists corrupted projects of universality, progress, and political autonomy. This clarity does not exist among his followers. Rather, the ideological funding of materialism by those who follow embrace the corruptions as essential to a late modern political project. Though they still provide provocative insights into late modernity and raise new questions about Paul's continued relevance for politics, the new approach will misstep into these errors in ways not evident in Benjamin.

I wish to log a peevish criticism of materialism and the hermeneutic deployed by the new approach. It is unclear why there is an abandonment of the transcendence of Paul's God and classical metaphysics. New materialism, as Žižek depicts, emphasizes that reality is magical and full of powers that guide and motivate human life. However, there is no transcendence of classical metaphysics, there are no gods. David Bentley Hart's analysis of Paul offers a more accurate account of reality than our modern one. As P. Travis Kroeker writes,

> only if one may reintroduce the distinction between the sphere
> of immanence and the sphere of transcendence will one be able
> to discern Paul's apostolic message—it is a revelation not a phil-
> osophical teaching; it is rooted in divine, not human authority;
> it cannot be rationally penetrated, only spiritually discerned in
> complete submission to the *logos* of the *stauros*.[98]

Therefore, there lies a lacuna in materialism. Žižek, Benjamin, and the materialists friendly to theological categories recognize the need of Paul because they deploy a world of powers very similar to Paul's world. However, they leave God behind. Benjamin recognizes that when the profane comes up against the puppet guided by the dwarf, it is no match. Based on these insights, I am left to believe that the value of the Pauline critique of modernity is abundantly clear to materialists and is desirable for the sake of sharpening *their* ideological categories. I believe this is the reason for Paul's new moment in the academy. The desire to use Paul absent his confessional elements is for the purpose of granting a higher authority to the ideological structures they deploy.

Benjamin helps identify the materialist, nihilist hermeneutic of the new approach. This hermeneutic resists the influence of private interests by undercutting the meaning it creates. Divine violence removes competing private interests for the sake of encouraging a shared humanity. As such, Paul's political message is that all are one in Christ Jesus (Gal 3:28). This message appears to answer the warning sounded by Arendt's emphasis on private interests by expanding human interest beyond self-interest. Though each member of the new approach will work with themes of materialism toward individual ends, the basic rhythm of an appeal to materialism, a concrete motivation to reorient sense data (such as divine violence), and a political philosophy of an Arendtian free space will remain.

98. Kroeker, "Living 'As If Not,'" 23.

To summarize, Benjamin correctly diagnoses that the situation plaguing modernity is an alien sovereignty. Furthermore, Benjamin rightly judges that the only counter is a messianic sovereignty that challenges the basic presuppositions and normativity of sovereignty and the biopolitical order. In this way, Benjamin's political alternative to biopolitics is apocalyptic because he settles for nothing less than an interruption of this orders. Benjamin helpfully mobilizes Paul against such orders, but ultimately mutes Paul's broader theological confession. Ultimately, the dwarf must stay out of sight and only speak through the puppet. For Paul, the messiah must be worshiped. Worship, not mere materialism, is what animates Paul's apocalyptic. This central conviction cannot move into the background but must remain firmly in the foreground.

PAUL'S NEW MOMENT[99]

The revival of Paul does not have one figure to thank. There are many figures at the heart of this new movement, both living and dead: Friedrich Nietzsche, Martin Heidegger, Jacob Taubes, Walter Benjamin, Giorgio Agamben, Alain Badiou, Slavoj Žižek, Ted Jennings, Ward Blanton, Ben Dunning, and Daniel Boyarin. This new group of scholars has adopted theological language to assist in the displacing of modern politics' elevation of private interests. Unlike Benjamin, they use Paul explicitly, in some cases exclusively, to solve this riddle. They see in Paul a companion in their construction of new communities of meaning beyond the structures of biopolitics. Timothy Luckritz Marquis writes that, according to the new approach, "Paul's rhetoric and the social composition of his communities resonates with contemporary analysis of the role of marginality with respect to communal truth."[100] Paul's message is a welcome alternative to the exclusive nature of biopolitics. The continuity between the new approach and the historical Paul, Marquis recognizes, is that "Paul lived in an environment of Roman imperial oppression."[101] As such, this connects Paul to the new approach's leftist political task to undo oppressive, *modern* structures, such as biopolitics. The very task of the new approach mirrors Paul by summoning, structuring, and motivating a new commu-

---

99. The section heading refers to a book about Paul with similar views as Taubes, Badiou, and Agamben. See Davis et al., *Paul's New Moment*.

100. Marquis, *Transient Apostle*, 15.

101. Marquis, *Transient Apostle*, 11.

nity. For the new approach, Paul's new community confronts biopolitical structures of modern politics and works with the rhythm set in place by Benjamin. This means that the new approach does not seek a nihilistic erasure of the world, but the positive construction of a new community. To illustrate the new approach to Paul, I utilize three of its proponents: Jacob Taubes, Alain Badiou, and Giorgio Agamben. Each will offer a unique use of the hermeneutic developed by Benjamin, but ultimately toward the individual's own end.

Jacob Taubes

Jacob Taubes (1923–87) was one of the twentieth century's greatest Jewish intellectuals. Though holding many chairs in Jewish and religious thought, Taubes does not attempt to engage Paul from a strictly Christian perspective.[102] Taubes explicitly states in his work, "Now I of course am a Paulinist, not a Christian, but a Paulinist."[103] Paul assists Taubes in answering the political situation articulated by Arendt and Foucault by arguing that Paul's potential response to sovereignty and biopolitics is a new community arising from a different sovereignty.

Before turning to Taubes's use of Paul, I need to identify his political commitments, which ultimately shape his use of Paul.[104] In the only book Taubes published when he was alive, *Occidental Eschatology*, he outlines his apocalyptic, political commitments. In this work, Taubes resonates, like Benjamin, with Jewish apocalyptic convictions. "Apocalypticism," he writes, "negates this world in its fullness. It brackets the entire world negatively."[105] Taubes resonates with apocalyptic because it yearns for a different world. In his own experience, as a Jewish intellectual operating in the streams of twentieth-century thought, nothing short of an overturning of the world will do. However, this does not mean that Taubes is troubled by the delay in the apocalyptic appearance of God that displaces the world. Rather, he embraces the immanent task of the apocalyptic, namely the material, realizable ideal. In the place of an advent of a divine kingdom, Taubes focuses on an apocalyptic revolution. Theologian Da-

---

102. Taubes, *Political Theology of Paul*, 2.

103. Taubes, *Political Theology of Paul*, 88.

104. A detailed account of Taubes's political commitment can be found in David Congdon's work, "Eschatologizing Apocalyptic," 128–31.

105. Taubes, *Occidental Eschatology*, 9.

vid Congdon summarizes: "[Taubes] understands apocalypticism to be a response to a sociopolitical crisis whose purpose is then fulfilled through revolutionary action."[106] Taubes is a materialist in the vein of Marx and Benjamin. The revolutionary act is comparable to the apocalyptic vision of a new heaven and a new earth where an equitable form of politics is realized through an overthrow of political powers. This revolution is "singular" in its purpose to enact a variation of a Marxist revolution that rules out the possibility of a transcendent God.[107] This resonates deeply with Pauline theology, but narrows it to an exclusive material purpose. Rather than wait for a realization, Taubes argues that this apocalyptic vision names a political ideal that humanity must achieve through revolution.[108] Taubes's concern, then, is the immanent sphere of liberation, which is only achieved through a radical overturning of the structures that haunt modernity. It is through this means that Taubes realizes a space beyond private interests and biopolitics, which begets his reading of Paul.

Taubes's lectures on Paul are, Castelli writes, "heirs to a particular narrative about the Western political canon."[109] These are heirs of the political left, and Taubes delivers these lectures for the sake of a revitalization of the left. Taubes gives these lectures amid what he calls "apocalyptic time pressure," which not only signals the pressure of the end times as witnessed to by Paul, but also the pressure of Taubes's own terminal illness.[110] Therefore, Taubes's book, *The Political Theology of Paul*, should be read with such pregnant political urgency because Taubes speaks as one who is terminally ill.

Taubes's lectures focus on Jewish messianic thought, which reclaims Paul's Jewish roots from centuries of Christian history. Emphasizing Paul's Jewishness is not altogether different from the approach of many modern biblical scholars, specifically N. T. Wright, E. P. Sanders, etc. Taubes combines Jewish messianic hope with the emphasis developed by Benjamin. For Judaism, the messianic is the culmination of Jewish history, whereby they expected the Messiah to restore political sovereignty

---

106. Congdon, "Eschatologizing Apocalyptic," 129.

107. Congdon, "Eschatologizing Apocalyptic," 129, 136.

108. Congdon, "Eschatologizing Apocalyptic," 128–29.

109. Castelli, "Philosopher's Paul," 658.

110. Taubes, *Political Theology of Paul*, 1.

after the destruction of the Jewish temple in 580 BCE.[111] Messianic hope replaces and brings to an end the history of Jewish political sovereignty.

Within this sovereign description, Taubes utilizes Benjamin's messianic politics of nihilism.[112] Benjamin argues that, in the messianic, all profane orders meet their downfall.[113] Benjamin, in his nihilism, is crucial for Taubes's Jewish interpretation of Paul. For Taubes, the messianic signals the end of the political sovereignty of Judaism, changing Judaism's meaning, history, and trajectory. Taubes writes,

> Paul comes and says: Here is the Messiah . . . the son of David hanging on the cross! Now try to think from the center in a Jewish Way: expelled from the community he hangs here, accursed . . . This is a total and monstrous inversion of the values of Roman and Jewish thought.[114]

The messianic inverts the political virtues of both Judaism and the Roman Empire by proclaiming a new sovereignty. Both orders are disrupted. The Messiah denies the theocratic grounds of Jewish and Roman politics. Taubes's messianic is the political subversion of sovereignty as Jews understand it, but also sovereignty in general. Taubes's sovereignty is neither an abstract category nor exclusively Jewish. Rather, the Messiah presents a problem for all politics.

Taubes's critique of sovereignty arises from his primary interlocutor, Carl Schmitt. For Schmitt, political theology concerned itself with sovereignty for the sake of a new order centered on constitutional law, which serves as the standard of social order. Each individual can appeal to the law. However, this is not a freedom in the absolute sense. Freedom only absolutely exists with the sovereign. Schmitt specifies that sovereignty is "he who decides on the exception."[115] For example, in Arendt's life, the sovereign had the power to assign citizenship and take it away. Citizens only have freedom insofar as they are granted citizenship, which is on loan from the sovereign.

Taubes recognizes that sovereignty understood in this way must be destroyed by Paul's messianism. Taubes uses Paul, like Benjamin, to show how messianism destroys sovereignty and its meaning. One must recall

---

111. See Hartwich et al., "Afterword," 80.

112. Benjamin, "Theologico-Political Fragment," 312.

113. Benjamin, "Theologico-Political Fragment," 312–13.

114. Taubes, *Political Theology of Paul*, 10.

115. Schmitt, *Political Theology*, 5.

the divine violence proposed by Benjamin that brings an end to the order of the profane and robs sovereignty of its staying power. Rather than establishing a new order of sovereignty, Taubes uses the messianic to end it.

Taubes appropriates Paul's theological critique of the law in the book of Romans for a messianic elimination of sovereignty. This is Taubes's political reading of Paul. He writes, "My thesis is that . . . the Epistle to the Romans is a political theology, a *political* declaration of war on the Caesar."[116] Paul declares war on all law. The law creates the division (or in Schmitt's terms, the "exception") that exceeds the law's parameters. For example, the Mosaic law created such a division between Jew and gentile. Paul's declaration of war happens materially at these sites. Taubes broadens Paul from the Mosaic law and critiques any constitutional order that props up sovereignty. This is Paul's *nomos* theology.[117] Paul, according to Taubes, reinterprets the law in order to pose a threat to Roman rule, and most explicitly the Caesar cult.[118] The war that Paul declares must alter the values of not only Judaism (i.e., the allowance of gentiles in the Jewish community), but of the laws of the Mediterranean as well. There is no longer Jew nor gentile, slave nor free (Gal 3:28). Taubes provides a crucial insight for Pauline theology, namely thatPaul presents a new sovereignty and it must be obeyed in all arenas. This is a liberation for community that establishes itself in the face of political sovereignty. Though the Jewish law and Roman rule appear as mutually exclusive sovereignties, they express the single sovereignty that would divide based on the exception of who is acceptable and who is not. For Taubes, when Paul attacks one, he attacks the other. In attacking the law, Taubes argues for a new community beyond the law. This is a possibility to get beyond the divisions created by private interests.

In order to ground the political beyond law, Taubes appeals to Nietzsche. In Nietzschean terms, the law is the embodiment of God, who must be killed. In Nietzsche's great work *Thus Spake Zarathustra*, the main character Zarathustra recognizes the law as the great "thou shalt not."[119] These "thou shalt nots" create the subject, which must be slain or brought to an end. According to Taubes, the subject created by law is

116. Taubes, *Political Theology of Paul*, 658. Emphasis original.

117. Taubes, *Political Theology of Paul*, 14–19.

118. Taubes, *Political Theology of Paul*, 23.

119. In *Thus Spake Zarathustra*, Nietzsche depicts law and value as a dragon that must be slain in order for new values to take its place. See Nietzsche, "Thus Spake Zarathustra," 138–39.

what Paul transvalues through his emphasis on the crucifixion. The law, or *nomos*, is that which ended in the crucifixion. Therefore, to place the "crucified" at the center of worship undercuts the entire legal system of Paul's day. Taubes writes, "This is nothing like *nomos* as *summum bonum*. This is why this carries a political charge; it's explosive to the highest degree."[120] Paul's emphasis on the crucified is explosive to the entire value system of the Mediterranean, where neither Jew nor gentile is safe. This political demolition ends in the destruction of political community as it formerly existed. This makes room for Taubes's central insight to this study, a *new* community centered on something other than law, which is both profoundly Pauline and devastating to biopolitical regimes.

This new Pauline community is centered on the love command. This is not shocking to exegetes and theologians, but Taubes makes a problematic detour. The Pauline love command in Taubes is in competition with the Gospels. After the law of the "thou shalt not" is destroyed and God is killed, the community encounters itself with a new law: love one another. The absence of the need to love God in Paul's command is curious. Taubes draws upon this in his own new orientation of the community. Taubes illustrates this difference between Jesus's command in the Gospel of Matthew, "He said to him, 'You shall love the Lord your God with all your heart, and with all your soul, and with all your mind.' This is the greatest and first commandment. And a second is like it: 'You shall love your neighbor as yourself.' On these two commandments hang all the law and the prophets" (22:37–40, NRSV), and Paul's re-narration in Galatians, "For the whole law is summed up in a single commandment, 'You shall love your neighbor as yourself'" (5:14, NRSV). Whereas Jews were formerly called to love God and one another, they now are no longer bound by the law Jesus references in Matthew. Formerly, the Jewish community's social bond was centered on law, but now it is centered on the command to love neighbors. This is how the new community can exist in spite of the sovereign exception and biopolitical orders. Gentiles formerly couldn't fulfill the requirements of the law, but now they are only required to love.[121] This is something clearly displayed in Paul's reinterpretation of Jesus's word, and Taubes puts a lot of interpretive weight on Paul's simplification of the twofold command to love.

---

120. Taubes, *Political Theology of Paul*, 24.
121. Taubes, *Political Theology of Paul*, 52.

Despite the attractiveness of this political appropriation of Paul's critique of the law, it misses some of the important elements Paul maintains about the law. The collapse of the love command does not mean that the law has been destroyed, but that the law has been fulfilled (Rom 8:3–4). This fulfillment does mean, however, that the gentiles are invited into the Jewish story through the Jewish Messiah.

Even so, Taubes argues that the end of law also brings an end to guilt. Paul's revolutionary new community of both Jew and gentile fulfills a "nihilistic" politic in the new time signaled by Paul. Nihilism enables those under the guilt of the law (Romans 7) to escape such debilitating emotions. This resembles Benjamin's insistence on messianic nihilism and flows from Nietzsche's call to kill God in order to liberate the subject. Taubes argues that Benjamin's nihilism is the correct interpretation of Paul's *hos me* (as if not yet possessing) as the time of now in which we live.[122] It is the now time of the will, liberated from the guilt and strain of the law, that can find new objects of love. The will free of constraint can love as it pleases, including those who exceed the sovereign exceptions. According to Taubes, Paul overcomes the sacrificial and guilty consciousness normally attributed to Paul's lament of his sin in Romans 7 by ending the order that causes such guilt. For Taubes, it is only when the community can abolish guilt that it can discover the neighbor and thus love.

In order to heal this cruelty of guilt, Taubes argues for a Freudian recasting of Paul after the law's death in Nietzsche. All historically available exegesis of Paul is "trivial" to Taubes.[123] The whole purpose of Taubes's study is to "Begin anew to interpret Paul!"[124] Paul is a launching point into something else, or rather someone else; a gateway into the psychoanalytics of Sigmund Freud. Taubes writes:

> I believe that Freud, so to speak, enters into the role of Paul, of the Paul who supposedly brings redemption only phantasmatically, while Freud realizes it through this new method of healing [from guilt], which is not only an individual method, but also a theory of culture. Freud is not only a doctor of the individual, but a doctor of culture.[125]

122. Taubes, *Political Theology of Paul*, 72–73.
123. Taubes, *Political Theology of Paul*, 95.
124. Taubes, *Political Theology of Paul*, 95.
125. Taubes, *Political Theology of Paul*, 95.

Therefore, Taubes interprets Paul through Nietzsche, leading to the liberation of Paul for Freud, who then liberates culture from guilt (Rom 7). All of this leads the new community from guilt into freedom of the will.

At this point, Taubes's use of the materialist hermeneutic of nihilism is clear. Paul's *nomos* theology serves as a dwarf that guides his puppet. Paul sharpens the ideological structures that Taubes wishes to deploy, while emptying the biopolitical divisions of meaning. In turn, this calls an individual into a community of universal love free from guilt—a tool that lends itself, in his mind, to technologies of the self. He thinks that Paul provides an accurate account of the cosmos and uses his theology to describe the world, proposing a type of divine violence to biopolitical structures in the new love command. Therefore, like Benjamin, he provides an ideological construct driven by Paul, a new concrete practice, and reorients the material-sense data (removal of guilt) of citizens.

The communal nature of love beyond biopolitics and private interests is promising, but I find the removal of guilt and remorse from the moral conscience to be a dangerous and, ultimately, unloving mistake. If Paul's gospel is a liberation of the self from guilt, then the only reality in which Taubes remains confident is the self-sufficient human. Anything else is radically suspect. When Taubes sees guilt, he sees gross self-flagellation that holds the self captive. This is a problem created by Christianity, and one that is healed by the great doctor Freud. Those who are predisposed to agree with Taubes should consider the warning of theologian Rowan Williams: "[A] culture which tolerates the loss of a sense of damage to the moral identity, the loss of shame and remorse, is bound to be one that dangerously overplays the role of the will in the constitution of human persons."[126] Williams reminds readers that the theological problem in losing guilt and remorse is a failure to recognize the sheer terror of the uninhibited will. In a world created by the will alone, Williams argues, "there are no tragedies," so no real suffering as a result of tragedy.[127] Guilt and remorse suggest that there are things about one's existence unable to be controlled.[128] As such, to borrow a phrase from theologian Philip Ziegler, Taubes's account of the will is "soteriologically anemic."[129] Private interests and self-sufficiency do not require the need to recognize suffer-

126. Williams, *Lost Icons*, 102.

127. Williams, "Trinity and Ontology," 155.

128. Williams, *Lost Icons*, 106.

129. Ziegler, "Final Triumph of Grace," 98.

ing, and the loss of guilt only encourages this. Taubes does not provide a strong enough account of conversion, material or otherwise, that does more than merely authorize a perpetual authorization to believe in as well as an instrumentally ordered will enabled to continually advance itself.[130] Furthermore, Taubes is captive to an understanding of time in which humans progress toward their desired end.

In spite of this modern tendency, suffering, specifically the suffering caused by the tyranny of the will, must be the site not of the abolition of guilt, but the practice of forgiveness and reconciliation. The failure to forgive also fails to recognize suffering *as* suffering, which tragedy brings. A failure to see another's suffering in favor of one's freedom from guilt is certainly false consciousness. The people impacted the most by this sudden loss of remorse are specifically those who bear the burden of suffering.[131] One then must ask Taubes's question: How can one love their neighbor if one cannot afford to recognize their neighbor's suffering?

In summary, Taubes shows that a community of love overcomes private interests and biopolitics by overcoming the divisions essential to both. Taubes turns to materialism in his critique of sovereignty. His motivating political rationality is messianism, and his universal political community and space is love. This, in Taubes's view, removes the biopolitical formation of politics. As noted above in Arendt and Foucault, the problem in modern politics lies in the way it places private interests at its center. Taubes utilizes Paul in order to describe how this order is overcome in the Messiah for the sake of a new community. Paul transvalues modern political systems and founds a new reality centered around love of neighbor and not of God. Though I disagree with his overexaggeration on the collapse of the love commandment and the insistence of love without guilt, this new community is essential to politics on the other side of private interests.

Alain Badiou

Alain Badiou (b. 1937) is one of the most original and significant living philosophers today. Like Taubes, Badiou is a strict materialist. Badiou, as a materialist, presents a post-metaphysical reading of Paul. Rather than

---

130. Ziegler, "Final Triumph of Grace," 98. This is Ziegler's critique of Kant, but fits Taubes. I borrow his terminology here.

131. Williams, "Trinity and Ontology," 155.

dealing with sovereignty and political theology, Badiou's subject of critique is the sovereignty of capital. For Badiou, the sovereignty of capital yields to private interests as much as political sovereignty. The errors of capital and modern political philosophy are confronted by Paul's proclamation of the event of Christ's resurrection. Such an event ruptures all previous contingent meanings and reorganizes the community around a new gravitational center. Badiou's concept of the event has many theological ramifications and helps deploy Paul in service of a more equitable politics. However, like Taubes, my appreciation of Badiou is not without critique.

To begin, Badiou's philosophy proposes a mathematical ontology, which replaces the metaphysics of classical thought. Badiou argues in his mathematical ontology that all reality is tied to "set theory," which is a form of algebraic theory that deals with the formal properties, not of an individual factor, but as it appears in a set.[132] This is to say that the value of every individual piece of a set lies exclusively in the way that it belongs in the set, not on its own terms. For example, a puzzle piece is of no value on its own; in order to be of any value, the piece must "belong" or fit as part of a larger set. To Badiou, the individual (the puzzle piece) alone is irrelevant—only the establishment of a generic multiplicity (puzzle) matters.[133] The only form of "predication," or logical affirmation, of the individual within the set is "belonging."[134] This is the ontological truth of the world. Badiou's insistence on this universal set theory attempts to critique the ways that capital (i.e., monetary value) has come to dissolve universality and perpetuate a world without truth.

It is important to note that Badiou's adherence to algebraic set theory fits within Arendt's critique of modernity's "ideal of reducing terrestrial sense data and movements to mathematical symbols."[135] According to Arendt, this results in "man realiz[ing] his newly won freedom from the shackles of earth-bound experience," where "he placed nature under the conditions of his own mind."[136] This mathematical ontology, though convincing, is ideology. One should consider Arendt's critique alongside a statement made by Badiou: "It is when you decide what exists that you

132. See Hallward, "Badiou's Ontology," 82–90.

133. Hallward, "Badiou's Ontology," 84.

134. Hallward, "Badiou's Ontology," 85.

135. Arendt, *Human Condition*, 265.

136. Arendt, *Human Condition*, 265.

tie your thought to being."[137] Badiou sees reality as ontologically structured around generic, multiple sets, and this perspective directly affects how he interprets Paul.

Badiou's mathematical ontology influences his interpretation of Paul and his critique of biopolitics. Badiou asks the question of what it means "to live?"[138] Badiou's answer is that life is more than just material accidents of the body or commodities.[139] To live means to be caught up in the eternal forms of mathematics, namely the ideal. This places mathematics as the concrete universal into which humanity must live. For Badiou, this is the only way out of the biopolitical trap of modernity. One does not seek happiness or life in the profane, but in the universal.

Badiou's universal is organized by the "event." The event is detailed in set theory as that which disrupts the contingent in favor of the universal by creating the set itself. Christopher Norris summarizes Badiou's "event" as

> that which occurs unpredictably, has the potential to effect a momentous change in some given situation, state of knowledge, or state of affairs, and—above all—has consequences such as require unswerving fidelity or a fixed resolve to carry them through on the part of those who acknowledge its binding force.[140]

Paul, for Badiou, signals such an event: the resurrection of Jesus of Nazareth. However, the theological trappings of this event (the Christian God, general resurrection of the dead, etc.) are dismissed as "fable," namely those contingencies that are discarded in favor of the universal significance of such an event.[141] Badiou goes so far as to say that Paul rejects the contingencies of Christ's life, like the crucifixion.[142] Paul's *proclamation* of the resurrection is the dwarf that drives the new material puppet of the event.

Paul's event, as described by Badiou, offers a new "subjective gesture grasped in [the event's] founding power with respect to the generic

---

137. Hallward, "Generic or Specific," 275.

138. Badiou, "What Is It to Live," 412–20.

139. Badiou, "What Is It to Live," 413, 419.

140. Norris, "Event," 115–16.

141. Badiou, *Saint Paul*, 4–5.

142. Badiou, *Saint Paul*, 60.

conditions of universality."[143] The event shapes the subject, not only in its particularity but also according to universality.[144] This presents an interesting parallel between Badiou and Arendt. Both maintain the tension between intrinsic particularity and general universality. For both Arendt and Badiou, there must be a space of freedom where all individuals can act and speak as equals. The event provides such an opportunity for this free universality. The event is what one swears fidelity to, not identity. It would appear that the event also empties private interests of its fetishizing function by downplaying identity and particularity. The event is the rupture of identity in any form. When identity no longer has weight, one can speak unhindered by both self-identity and neighbor's identity. Badiou takes a radical departure from Arendt's approach, with which she would ultimately be uncomfortable.[145] For Badiou, it is not one's identity that is the site of revolution, but the event, which is always the universal, generic multiple set.

Badiou's event, Arendt would recognize, provides a universal space that potentially establishes a free public space. However, it moves too far in two distinct ways that are beginning to emerge. First, though identity politics limits the potential of a free public space, Badiou suggests that difference and identity only play a secondary role in political life. Such a move is risky. Arendt's goal is a space where difference is appreciated to the extent that it informs an equitable politic. Thus, it is not that one is indifferent to identity, but that another's identity shapes one's own.

Second, stripping Paul of the theological core of the resurrection and the narrative continuity between this event and the whole gospel ultimately robs Paul of his ability to be universal. By insisting on a radical rejection of Christian theology and even Jewish particularity, Badiou has ceased to be universal. One is not indifferent to the Christian and Jewish message, but one must reject it in order to be universal. This is a weakness in his argument. For Paul, Christ is the concrete universal. Redemption occurs in and through the incarnation of God as this Jewish man.[146] This universality is not achieved by means of Badiou's, as Daniel Bell argues,

143. Badiou, *Saint Paul*, 6.

144. Badiou believes that truth is the real content of philosophy. There is not only one truth, but various manifestations of truth. It is the "thingness" within thinking. Badiou outlines four areas for truth: art, politics, science, and love. See Badiou, *Logics of Worlds*, 1–40.

145. See chapter 3 for more on Arendt's identity politics.

146. Bell, *Divinations*, 67.

"transcendental capture but entering into relation with this concrete, particular one."[147] Thus, the universal Paul proposes is much more radical than Badiou because it, as theologian Hans Urs von Balthasar writes, "outside our most elementary forms of thought."[148] Christ is not an individual among other individuals because he is God, but is not universal in the way that Badiou describes because he is this one particular human.[149] For Paul it is only inside these particular confessions that the concrete universal emerges.[150]

Despite these critiques, one has to recognize Badiou's description of universality. For Badiou, universality arises from his coordinate concern with the relativist nature of politics. Though not at odds with the essence of identity politics, he notes that identity politics has limited human appeal to truth and universality. Politics has lost its ability to talk about political truths in an objective sense.[151] As a materialist, Badiou recognizes that capital is the reason for such limitation:

> Capital demands a permanent creation of subjective and territorial identities in order for its principle of movement to homogenize its space of action; identities, moreover, that never demand anything but the right to be exposed in the same way as others to the uniform prerogatives of the market.[152]

Capital, through the logic of a market-state, makes identity a commodity to be bought and sold. This economic structure leads to fragmentation between different co-modified identities that are necessarily in competition. Badiou writes that in the logic of capital "there is a process of fragmentation into closed identities, and the culturist and relativist ideology that accompanies this fragmentation."[153] According to Badiou, capital offers a homogenous whole, with only a relative universality in each person's ability to buy and sell. Thus, capital is unable to sustain a

---

147. Bell, *Divinations*, 67.

148. Balthasar, "Characteristics of Christianity," 170.

149. Balthasar, "Characteristics of Christianity," 170.

150. These insights emerged from my reading and engagement with Bell, *Divinations*, 1–73. I regret that Bell's book came out too late in the process of my own project to be a major conversation partner.

151. See also on the topic of political truths Badiou, *Metapolitics*, 10–25

152. Badiou, *Saint Paul*, 10–11.

153. Badiou, *Saint Paul*, 10.

community because there is no truth outside a mere "general equivalent" to each contingent truth of identity.[154]

A true universal event "erupts as singular, [and] its singularity is immediately universalizable, [which] . . . breaks with identitarian singularity."[155] According to Badiou, the universal event is clearly expressed in Paul, which presents his readers with an entirely new discourse. Badiou illustrates this in Paul's statement to the Galatians: "There is no longer Jew or Greek, there is no longer slave or free, there is no longer male and female; for all of you are one in Christ Jesus" (Gal 3:28, NRSV). Timothy Marquis writes that "a truly 'new' discourse contrasts itself not to one, dominant discourse (say, the totalizing 'wisdom' of Greek philosophy), nor to a discourse defined as an exception to the dominant (for Badiou, the Jewish discourse of prophetic 'signs'), but to all prevailing discursive regimes."[156] Badiou's interpretation of Paul suggests that universality lies in contrast to a variety of privileges and exceptions in order to realize a true universality, one without identity. Badiou's rejection of identity politics should be read as a rejection of private interests, for such interests serve as a roadblock to Arendt's universal account of politics. In the baptismal formula, as well as Jewish and Greek expectations in 1 Corinthians 1:17–29, a universality emerges that can adequately confront the errors of capital as a false universality.

Through the baptismal formula, Paul guides Badiou's readers to the philosophy of event. In the event, truth and truth procedures are outside a particularistic understanding. Badiou writes, "To sharply separate each truth procedure from the cultural historicity wherein opinion presumes to dissolve it: such is the operation in which Paul is our guide."[157] The need to resist each discursive regime by not privileging one against another is crucial; there is no longer a privilege between Jew and Greek.

Despite this departure from discursive regimes, the universality of event in Paul does not ignore difference. Rather, it is indifferent to difference. Difference no longer operates as an obstacle in political life; there is only the universal. Badiou summons Paul's concern over circumcision and the Jew/gentile relation to his defense on this matter. At the center of this controversy is communitarian identity. Paul himself struggles with

154. Badiou, *Saint Paul*, 10.
155. Badiou, *Saint Paul*, 10.
156. Marquis, *Transient Apostle*, 126.
157. Badiou, *Saint Paul*, 6.

the privileged status of Judaism. Badiou recognizes this, too. However, instead of retaining Jewish particularity like Taubes, Badiou argues that Paul makes identity indifferent. As Badiou writes,

> It is not that communitarian marking (circumcision, rites, the meticulous observance of the Law) is indefensible or erroneous. It is that the postevental imperative of truth renders the latter *indifferent* (which is worse). It has no signification, whether positive or negative. Paul is not opposed to circumcision. His rigorous assertion is 'Circumcision is nothing and uncircumcision is nothing' (I Cor. 7:19).[158]

The event makes truth procedures "indifferent to difference" because it makes difference nothing in light of the universal. Badiou uses this to invert the "value" system of the existing order. This system becomes inverted in the strongest sense by disrupting the ways that communitarian and identitarian politics prevent universality. In materialist terms, these are the ways that classes come to define and stigmatize each other. Therefore, in light of the universality of event, one can truly become indifferent to difference because each is not identified by class, but by event. This does not mean that difference has no purpose. On the contrary, Badiou argues that the universal "is organically bound to contingency."[159] This is not conformity.[160] Rather, differences become opportunities to attest to universality.[161]

Badiou's indifference to difference is problematic. Theologian Rowan Williams suggests that a system that passes over differences—and negates, in some cases—is radically incoherent because it lacks the ability to stand outside of contingency.[162] The system, and thus the event, is always bound to historical contingency and cannot exist outside of it, only in opposition to it, which goes against Badiou's claim that contingency and universality coincide organically. This requires, then, that humanity swears fidelity to a reality that logically stands opposed to contingency. Badiou's interpretation of Paul does not fit, even at the level of fable, because the logical appeal to Paul's theology is incoherent. Badiou's honest intention robs the way that identity politics prevents discussion

158. Badiou, *Saint Paul*, 23.
159. Badiou, *Saint Paul*, 81.
160. Badiou, *Saint Paul*, 111.
161. Badiou, *Saint Paul*, 105–06.
162. Williams, "Trinity and Ontology," 155–56.

on truth and politics. However, I suggest that there are more options than indifference and capitalistic privatization. One must learn a way to love difference and let that difference form and shape individuals and communities.

Badiou's indifference to particularity—such as the crucifixion—also poses a problem not only to Paul's political message, but also to his gospel message. This further complicated Badiou's own indifference to difference as a deep rejection of contingency. Without contingency as an abiding and necessary element central to any political gesture, what is left to Badiou? P. Travis Kroeker suggests that "Paul himself, however, would have refused Badiou's account of the messianic event. This new gnostic politics of fabulation divides what Paul's messianism unities: the cross and resurrection."[163] Paul's ethics and politics resists what Kroeker calls Badiou's gnostic universalism because Paul does not celebrate the transcendental capture of contingency. Rather, the contingent is that which is loved and embraced by divine agency in its contingency.[164] The resurrection of the dead in 1 Corinthians 15 provides such a lens to see how Paul critiques gnosticism (vv. 12–29), God's embrace of contingency (vv. 35–41). For Paul, especially in 1 Corinthians, the cross and resurrection are one.[165]

Despite a possible alternative to the fetishizing of private interests, Badiou's emphasis on indifference to difference as a result of the universal event cannot be sustained in a world of private interests. As Arendt's life and works show, it is problematic to take away identity for the sake of a universal political structure. Furthermore, Badiou's indifference to Paul's Jewishness utilizes some of the worst possible tendencies of Christianity, namely supersessionism.[166] The danger in this reading of Paul is that it fails to see the reality that the resurrection signals. The opening up of the Jewish narrative to the gentiles is not an erasure of Jewishness, but a reorientation of Jewishness to now include the gentiles, and for gentiles to accept salvation from this Jewish Messiah. Badiou is half right when he argues that Jews and gentiles no longer possess exclusive identities that require the exclusion of others. However, the differences that remain after the event of Christ are not erased, nor are they the cause of indiffer-

---

163. Kroeker, "Living 'As If Not,'" 18.

164. Kroeker, "Living 'As If Not,'" 18.

165. For more, see my exploration of 1 Corinthians 15 in chapter 4.

166. See Castelli, "Philosopher's Paul," 660–63.

ence. Rather, they are reconciled and reoriented within the very life and teachings of Jesus as a new site of social happening.

Badiou provides a provocative and original read of Paul, but ultimately Badiou's philosophy is wanting. Badiou suffers from a philosophical problem that has haunted philosophy since Immanuel Kant. Badiou requires a complex ideology that allows him to disregard the basic, fundamental reality of the world we inhabit. Set theory is a closed system of thought that performs an essential function for the self-sufficient will. Badiou casts the event of set theory in Paul's language of resurrection, even though he dismisses its content as fable. Like Taubes, Benjamin, and Žižek, Badiou agrees that Paul provides an accurate account of reality but denies his fundamental convictions in order to sharpen and authorize his own ideological structures. Badiou's interpretation of Paul arises from his mathematical ontology, which suggests that any singularities are determined in their generic universal sense, rather than in relationship with any other singularities. Thus, the singularity's relation to the universal overrides the singularity in relation to a social group.[167]

Badiou must be critiqued in light of Arendt's claim that all reality is subject mathematics. In light of Arendt's claim, I argue that this ultimately distorts reality in the same way that she describes. The reason Badiou argues for this mathematical ontology lies in the purpose that it serves his philosophical system. Roger Scruton writes, Badiou's mathematical ontology "will not prove to be translatable into any idiom but [its] own . . . [It] teaches a new way of thinking, which is guaranteed to turn any subject in the required direction, regardless of whether they cast any light on it."[168] Badiou falls into false consciousness and, when considering also his critique of the cross, gnosticism. Badiou transposes all reality into a mathematically based, modern system of necessities for the sake of bending reality to his own philosophical outcomes. Ultimately, this is to appeal to materialism, and his theory of the event is the ideological motivation of his politics. Finally, the universal constructed by the event is *his* political philosophy. Obviously, Badiou translates Paul into this system as well, which has the effect of adding Paul to an echo chamber in Badiou's work, only reproducing his own thoughts and motives. I argue that Paul's depiction of reality resists assimilation. Rather, Paul, as Balthasar writes, "starts from Christ who, as this individual is universal,

167. See Hallward, *Badiou*, 275.

168. Scruton, *Fools, Frauds, and Firebrands*, 248.

because embodying the absolute norm, and who, as this contingent being within history is the necessary being above all history and nature: he it is to whom, as Head, all things in heaven and earth must be brought back."[169] The Christian vision of reality is intelligible, but escapes Badiou's universal systemization.

Giorgio Agamben

Giorgio Agamben (b. 1942) is an Italian philosopher whose work, more so than Taubes and Badiou, focuses on the situation of severe oppression in modern politics, which is his materialist gesture. He shares many concerns with Arendt, Foucault, Taubes, and Badiou. Agamben, too, attempts a messianic interpretation of Paul that critiques sovereign life and biopolitics. The central concept of his system is "bare life." Bare life denotes the political reality of a human existence that has become so defined by politics as to be viewed as inhuman and no longer under the protection of the law that is normally afforded *to* humans.[170] The bare life subject needs liberation from this inhuman state, and Paul provides the logic of liberation for Agamben.

Bare life, as the inhuman one, is excluded from the law. According to Badiou, this is the central, modern, political problem. Agamben, like Arendt, recalls the ancient definition of life as the distinction between *bios* and *zoe*. Both words translate to *life*, but are distinctly different. *Bios* is the political definition of life, namely life that is given meaning in the political arena. *Zoe* is bare life, namely animal life. The connection to Arendt is clear: the *animal laborans* is closely related to the *zoe*, and the *bios* is one that has a second life in politics. As Arendt notes, this is the ancient definition between two aspects of life. One had a political life in public life, and mere life in private life. The law, therefore, does not serve as a blanket protection. Rather, it gives life meaning.

An example of bare life is the Roman legal figure: the *homo sacer* (i.e., the sacred human). The *homo sacer* was permissibly allowed to be killed by anyone but not ritually sacrificed. The rights and protections of the law of a normal citizen no longer apply to him; his *bios* is removed. The *homo sacer* and *zoe* are distinct in that the latter is a form of life for

169. Balthasar, "Characteristics of Christianity," 170–71.

170. See Agamben's description of bare life as werewolf in Agamben, *Homo Sacer*, 107.

all people with *bios*. The *homo sacer*, contrarily, has been forcibly reduced to *zoe*.

There is a very interesting parallel between Agamben and Arendt on the *homo sacer*. The *homo sacer* is another form of political life alongside the *animal laborens* and *homo faber*. Like Arendt's *homo faber* and *animal laborens*, the presence of the *homo sacer* prevents a free political space. It is the opposite of the *vita activa* in that the *homo sacer* is only acted upon and never acts. Alongside its forcible reduction to bare life, i.e., *zoe*, the *homo sacer* is sacred. Sacred is always that which is in excess of the profane society (Benjamin). The excess of society must exist in order to maintain certain biopolitical balance that moves the mass of society forward. Therefore, Agamben's work is an addendum to the work of Arendt, but whether it is ultimately faithful is another question.

The similarity between Agamben, Arendt, and Foucault is clear in this definition of the *homo sacer*. By having a clear excess of the political order, the sovereign is able to maintain the distinction between what is allowed to live and die. The *homo sacer*, as an embodied form of life, permits a participation on behalf of the masses. By allowing, encouraging, and actively recognizing the exile of the *homo sacer*—such as the terrorist, the death-row inmate, and the werewolf—society can participate in the sovereign decision. Furthermore, the preservation of private interests of the masses, life itself, coincides with these figures in that they serve as a threat to the private interests of the individuals. The sovereign, by creating the *homo sacer*, enables the conditions in which the synthesis of the sovereign will and private interests is able to take place.

Agamben argues that sovereignty arises from Christianity itself and is not necessarily tied to Paul. This is something granted to politics by the rise of Christianity and trinitarian doctrine.[171] This is not a Pauline innovation, and Agamben claims that Christianity went wrong when it departed from Paul.[172] Like Taubes, Agamben attempts to recover Paul as the founder of messianism in the Western tradition in order to destroy sovereignty and, thus, bare life.[173] The messianic, as in Benjamin, overcomes the divisions created by the law. Agamben's target, again like Taubes, is the juridical regime of sovereignty, which begets bare life.

171. For a full description in Agamben's own words, see Agamben, *Kingdom and the Glory*, 17–52.

172. He notes the historical trajectory from Paul's economy of mystery to the trinitarian mystery of economy. See Agamben, *Kingdom and the Glory*, 35.

173. Agamben, *Time That Remains*, 1.

The juridical-legal division of humanity must be undone. This is a central concern of Agamben's larger project, and Paul offers a tentative solution. Agamben recognizes that law is the mediating reality that trains individuals in political identity. Therefore, the actualization of law upon citizens must be revoked. Agamben believes, along with philosopher Martin Heidegger, that beings are invested with potentiality. Like Aristotle, Agamben holds that law actualizes potentiality. What must be reclaimed is a pure state of potentiality.

The obstacle to potentiality is the actuality of the law. The law, as instrument of sovereignty, actualizes political identity in the individual and creates a division between those inside the profane order and those exterior to it. According to Agamben, Mosaic law actualizes the identities of Jew and gentile. The law divides the people among Jew and gentile. Therefore, the law must somehow be rendered unable to actualize this division in the life of political communities, which would simultaneously undo the biopolitical gesture of modern politics in its foundational anti-legal moment. Agamben believes Paul's messianic philosophy does this. He writes, "The Mosaic law . . . is . . . rendered inoperative by the Messiah."[174] In Romans 7:5–6, Paul, according to Agamben, suggests that our transference from under the law into the new life of the Spirit as a work of Christ signals that the law is inoperative in its ability to divide between Jew and gentile. Each person becomes "re-potentialized" under the new life in the Spirit, though Agamben is not upholding trinitarian doctrine. Paul helps Agamben articulate how the Messiah not only attacks the law itself, but also the divisions made *by* the law.[175] Like Taubes, Agamben argues that this pertains to all law, not just the Mosaic law.

By making the law inoperative, Agamben believes "the divisions of the law themselves . . . [are rendered] . . . inoperative, without ever reaching any final ground."[176] The victory over the law recovers a community based in a natural, prepolitical state (potentiality). A community of potentiality arises in place of the community actualized in a juridical regime. Agamben's new community is in excess of the political community founded on sovereignty and is called a remnant by existing as a remainder to the sovereign community.

174. Agamben, *Time That Remains*, 121.

175. Agamben, *Time That Remains*, 52.

176. Agamben, *Time That Remains*, 52.

According to Agamben, the remnant is not just a remainder. Rather, the remnant is in a particular relationship to the formation of modern politics. The remnant will be a community where these semantic codes lose their weight and form a culture in contradiction to the wider culture. "The remnant is what prevents divisions [such as sovereign life and bare life, Jew and Gentile, etc.] from being exhaustive and excludes the parts and the all from the possibility of coinciding with themselves."[177] The goal of Agamben's Pauline political theology is to achieve the "re-potentializ-ing" of every individual in opposition to the way law has created social divisions and influenced individual identity for the sake of a subversive community beyond actualized semantic codes.

The inoperative law eliminates the old designators by allowing the remnant to exceed the law's ability to divide. In this sense, the remnant is eschatological for Agamben because it anticipates the *telos* of God, "when God will be 'all in all,' [and] the messianic remnant will not harbor any particular privilege and will have exhausted its meaning in losing itself in the *pleroma*."[178] The remnant is all there is, and the right-now time is the only time. Agamben asserts this is a ceaseless revocation of all vocation.

Revocation of vocation is coupled with Agamben's understanding of time, which is, like Benjamin and Taubes, messianic. As Agamben writes,

> *The messianic vocation is the revocation of every vocation.* In this way, it defines what to me seems to be the only acceptable voca-tion. What is a vocation, but the revocation of each and every concrete factual vocation? This obviously does not entail substi-tuting a less authentic vocation with a truer vocation. Accord-ing to what norm would one be chosen over the other? No, the vocation calls the vocation itself, as though it were an urgency that works it from within and hollows it out, nullifying it in the very gesture of maintaining and dwelling in it. This, and nothing less than this, is what it means to have a vocation, what it means to live in messianic *klesis*.[179]

This revocation is essential to Paul's own messianic theology and the life of the remnant. As Agamben illustrates, the messianic revocation brings to an end every vocation, namely every vocation that attempts to seize the sovereign power that forms the biopolitical nature of Western society. Rather, it is required that the remnant not be witnesses to the power and

177. Agamben, *Time That Remains*, 56.
178. Agamben, *Time That Remains*, 56.
179. Agamben, *Time That Remains*, 23–24. Emphasis original.

wisdom of human beings, but to the power of God, a foolish wisdom
displayed in a servanthood that possesses nothing but acts as if all things
are given to it as God's gift.[180] This treats the world ontologically within
its place as "passing away" (Benjamin). Therefore, by nullifying vocation, one embodies the Pauline *hos me*, namely dispossessively as one
who does not seek to hold onto that which increases sovereignty. This
revocation appears as a failure, but is actually a conforming to the mind
of the Messiah "that," as P. Travis Kroeker writes, "willingly empties itself
in order to serve the other, a pattern of radical humility and suffering
servanthood."[181] The remnant, as the community where revocation and
dispossessive habitus exists, serves as the means of salvation in modern
politics by instantiating a communal life outside the logic of bare life,
indeed in excess of modern politics, because it refuses to embody technologies of self and private interest.

Agamben, though indebted to Arendt, digresses in a crucial manner. Agamben's new community is one of pure potentiality; Arendt's
community is one of activity and speech. Arendt's political philosophy
is shot through with practical acts that are disregarded in Agamben's
philosophy. For Agamben, the new community does not exist by way
of reminiscence, present idleness, or future expectation of fulfillment.[182]
Rather, this new community is "coming" but never arrives to fulfill what
Agamben depicts as Paul's emphasis on the messianic now, or Paul's *hos
me* (as if not yet possessing; i.e., 1 Cor 7:2). The *hos me* enables a dispossessed activity where we love and act without seeking possession of the
neighbor. In this way, as P. Travis Kroecker writes, one can "use without
possessing."[183] This raises a question in his Arendtian foundation: How
does one create something lasting? Arendt would not deny that individuals should not possess other individuals, but surely the public space is not
radically dispossessed.

Despite these questions, Agamben remains committed to a dispossessed activity. According to Agamben, this activity is what humans do in
the time that remains, which

> is the time that time takes to come to an end, or, more precisely,
> the time we take to bring to an end, to achieve our representation

180. See Kroeker, "Messianic Ethics and Diaspora Communities," 77.

181. Kroeker, "Messianic Ethics and Diaspora Communities," 78.

182. Agamben, *Time That Remains*, 62, 76.

183. Kroeker, "Living 'As If Not,'" 31.

of time . . . It is operational time pressing within the chronological time, working and transforming it from within; it is the time we need to make time end: *the time that is left to us* . . . [It] is the time *that* we ourselves are, and for this very reason, is the only real time, the only time we have.[184]

The activity of the "coming" community is not action, as it is for Arendt's new, free political space. The goal of the coming community is not to act or bring about history's end. Rather, it is a "peculiar sort of sabbatical vacation."[185] It is the ability to say, "I'd prefer not to."[186] This ceasing to act, or act upon, is a process by which the coming community resists the temptation to move individuals toward actuality, instead allowing them to remain in their potentiality. It is a politics to will not-to-will.[187]

The central witness of the coming community subverts the cultural ideologies of private interests and biopolitics. Agamben's own use of the materialist hermeneutic operates at the site of the will. By resisting the temptation to actualize one's will on any individual, Agamben removes the ability of private interests and technologies of the self to form biopolitical divisions of society. In this way, he is able to simultaneously empty the biopolitical division of meaning and reorganize material life. Agamben writes, "Seeing something simply in its being-thus—irreparable, but not for that reason necessary; thus, but not for that reason contingent—is love."[188] "Being-thus" for Agamben is the state before actualization, a state before the will. Such is the role of the coming community: to love in their being-thus.

In order to achieve the Pauline community, as interpreted by Agamben, it must be a weak community of potentiality, free from law.

> This is the remnant of potentiality that is not consumed in the act, but is conserved in it each time and dwells there. If this remnant of potentiality is thus weak, if it cannot be accumulated in any form of knowledge or dogma, and if it cannot impose itself as a law, it does not follow that it is passive or inert. To the contrary, it acts in its own weakness rendering the work of

184. Agamben, *Time That Remains*, 67–68.

185. Agamben, *La Comunitàcheviene*, 92.

186. Agamben, *Potentialities*, 254–71.

187. This is a description of a Heideggerian category developed by Agamben that helps organize Agamben on the coming community. See Arendt, *Life of the Mind*, 172–94.

188. Agamben, *Coming Community*, 106.

law inoperative, in de-creating and dismantling the states of fact or of law, making them freely available for use. *Katargein* and *chresthai* are the act of a potentiality that fulfills itself in weakness. That this potentiality finds its *telos* in weakness means that it does not simply remain suspended in infinite deferral; rather, turning back toward itself, it fulfills and deactivates the very excess of signification over every signified, it extinguishes languages (1 Cor. 13:8). In this way, it bears witness to what, unexpressed and insignificant, remains in use forever near the word.[189]

This passage from Agamben is related to his juridical-legal concept of sovereignty. By living in weakness without possessing, the community has a relationship to the law that exceeds it by remaining in potentiality. Here he returns to a presovereign state where true potentiality can emerge. However, he is clear that potentiality is not just nonaction. Rather, "potentiality . . . conserves itself and saves itself in actuality. Here potentiality . . . survives actuality and, in this way, gives itself to itself."[190] By living "as if not possessing" and returning to a state of potentiality, the community can live exterior to the law.

Through his *homo sacer*, Agamben articulates what Charles Cosgrove would call a hermeneutic of "counter-cultural witness," which is a hermeneutical rule that affords greater weight in Scripture to counter cultural tendencies.[191] Agamben's approach to Paul resembles this definition. However, Agamben is not just reading the Bible. Rather this hermeneutic is for culture. In this way, Agamben's entire political theology serves the purpose of striking at the heart of private interests and the victims of private interests.

Addressing victimization requires listening and respecting victims' descriptions of their victimization, without attempting to appeal to a universal category of human experience. This is essential, though Agamben's insistence on re-potentiality goes against this emphasis. Agamben's system attempts to recreate life categorically, in the vein of Immanuel

189. Agamben, *Time That Remains*, 137.

190. Agamben, *Potentialities*, 184.

191. This phrase comes specifically from New Testament scholar Charles Cosgrove's analysis of biblical hermeneutics for moral debates. I find this to be the most fitting because it is not just a means to read scripture. Cosgrove's analysis could be read as indicative of Agamben's entire political theology. See Cosgrove, *Appealing to Scripture in Moral Debate*, 90–115.

Kant, as a transcendental phylum in which one's experience either fits or is discarded.

Critical theorist Alexander Weheliye states that Agamben's weakness is his failure to see that bare life is "not an abject zone of exclusion that culminates in death but an alternate instantiation of humanity that does not rest on the mirage of western Man as the mirror image of human life as such."[192] Western man is the form of life that Agamben, as Weheliye critiques, implicitly assumes. It then functions as a type of private interest that forms biopolitical antinomies. Agamben's "being-thus" as "not . . . necessary" runs counter to Weheliye's assessment.[193] For Weheliye, Agamben's potentiality is dangerous because "I'd prefer not to" is an impossible option for those who are subject to colonial and racial violence. Weheliye deserves to be quoted at length in order to fully unpack his critique of Agamben's potentiality.

> 'I'd prefer not to' is simply not an option—how do privation, impotentiality, non-Being, lack, and darkness (Agamben uses all these terms to describe the 'abyss of potentiality') encounter the flesh and rest in the unfree? Freedom stands at the juncture of the flesh's privation and potentiality: the flesh carries the potential for manumission, although not the actual freedom to undergo and suffer (paschein) Man's liberty. Put simply, the world of Man denies the flesh its opulent and hieroglyphic freedom by relegating it to a terrain of utter abjection outside the iron grip of humanity, thereby disavowing how the ether of the flesh represents both a perpetual potentiality and actuality in Man's kingdom, only enveloping some subjects more than others . . . Agamben's theorization of bare life leaves no room for alternate forms of life that elude the law's violent embrace. What seems to have vanished from this description is the life in the bare life compound; hence the *homo sacer* remains a thing, whose happening slumbers in bare life without journeying through the rivulets of liberations elsewhere. The potential of bare life as a concept falls victim to a legal dogmatism that equates humanity and personhood with a status bequeathed or revoked by juridical sovereignty in much the same way as human rights discourse and habeas corpus do. Because alternatives do not exist in Agamben's generalized sphere of exception that constitutes bare life, the law denotes the only constituent power in the definition and adjudication of what it means to be

192. Weheliye, *Habeas Viscus*, 43.

193. Agamben, *Coming Community*, 106.

human or dehumanized in the contemporary world. If alternate forms of life, what Wynter dubs genres of the human beyond the world of Man, can flourish only after the complete obliteration of the law, then it would follow that our existence, whether it is bare or not, stands and falls with the extant laws in the current codification of Man.[194]

This passage refers directly to what is at stake in Agamben's reading of Paul: an inability to envision *life* in bare life. Potentiality cannot achieve the ends of eliminating biopolitics for it still stands in need of judicial sovereignty. For Weheliye, the flesh in its opulence articulates a world beyond that of the world of man. Weheliye then rejects the one thing that Agamben, Badiou, and most members of the new approach cannot, namely, the Western, biopolitical narrative of modernity. This includes a recognition that Agamben cannot envision a life of contingency beyond a legal apparatus and, thus, cannot finally escape biopolitics.

With this critique in mind, I return to this quote by Agamben: "Seeing something simply in its being-thus—irreparable, but not for that reason necessary; thus, but not for that reason contingent—is love." [195] Agamben does not develop what he means by "contingent," but if Weheliye is correct, this failure to love in contingency is a critical misstep. Agamben slips into a false consciousness and fails to see the *life* of bare life. Much like Badiou, his account of reality resists contingent embodiment and, like Badiou, falls into gnosticism. In so doing, Agamben fails to let sufferers narrate their own suffering and rejects even the most practical activity to escape the violence of biopolitics. Therefore, bare life "slumbers . . . without journeying through the rivulets of liberations elsewhere."[196]

In sum, Agamben's work is filled with promise and peril. I appreciate Agamben's intense effort to materially improve the lives of those who experience the most extreme forms of political violence. His community of the remnant provides an interpretive lens to understand how Paul's community exceeds the semantic codes of biopolitics. In so doing, it subverts the meaning of biopolitical community by the very nature of the remnant's existence. Agamben, like the rest of the highlighted authors, recognizes the accuracy of Paul's description of reality, but Paul sharpens

194. Weheliye, *Habeas Viscus*, 130–31.

195. Agamben, *Coming Community*, 106.

196. Weheliye, *Habeas Viscus*, 131.

Agamben's ideological categories. Paul is the theological dwarf that drives Agamben's Heideggerian-Aristotelian materialism. It is unclear whether the sabbatical vacation finally achieves the ends Agamben desires. Chief among these concerns is whether he escapes the legal traps he himself describes. Agamben's bare life is an ideological construction that depends on a transcendental capture of subjectivity. Agamben's concern for victims is finally undercut by his construction of the ideological, gnostic category of victimhood where victims must fit, rather than allowing the contingencies to be confronted in their contingency.

MOVING TO APOCALYPTIC: THE LIMITS OF MATERIALISM

As mentioned in the introduction, the thinkers of the new approach help reorient Paul toward new political ends. Each figure attempts, as Timothy Marquis writes, a "thick, materialist description of Paul's social (and especially political) world as a launching point for examining the trajectories of his thought and practice," in order to critique the biopolitical legacy of Western politics.[197] I am not offering a general critique of materialism, but rather the specific way materialism is deployed in the new approach. The materialist description of Paul serves the material lives of people, but some elements of this description relies heavily on Paul's account of reality and ultimately must betray a strict materialism. Though materialism makes a valiant effort to truncate Paul's theology to fit materialistic cosmology, Paul ultimately assumes a reality that exceeds and undercuts a purely materialist lens. Without Paul's theological account of reality that each member explicitly assents to, all that can be sustained in their materialist description is, as theologian John Milbank remarks, "a nihilistic revolution."[198]

The new approach, Milbank continues, "crucially recognizes . . . that human histories of apparent peace are really histories of hidden conflict and opposition."[199] This is the world of powers—even as they are materially deployed in sovereignty, capital, and political violence—described by Paul as complex material realities and ideologies. Rather than the powers resembling bad angels, as Hart purports in the introduction,

197. Marquis, *Transient Apostle*, 11.

198. Milbank, "Materialism and Transcendence," 423.

199. Milbank, "Materialism and Transcendence," 423.

the new approach argues the various political ideologies supported by private interests are the powers. The new approach, through eliminating God but keeping the powers, unwittingly *"ontologize[s]* this prevailing circumstance."[200] This appears to be Agamben's failure in his account of bare life. By removing God, the powers—even ideologically—are the only remaining "thing." Milbank points out that they should "instead insist on [their] contingency."[201] One can see how the nihilistic revolution is intended to mitigate the meanings created by these ideological "powers." In so doing, the new approach believes they can show the sheer contingency of the supposed universality projected onto the bodies of historical victims. Though I argue that they ultimately fail to account for these bodies, I still recognize their attempt. However, I also argue that there is a far more radical argument for the contingency of biopolitics.

The alternative I propose is a Pauline, apocalyptic historicity that unmasks the radical nature of the gospel account of bodies under the weight of biopolitical tyranny. This historicity takes the form of an anti-essentialism that arises from the good news that, as David Bentley Hart writes, "Christ . . . abides with and in the poor, the godforsaken, the forgotten, and the lowly . . . because Christ—who is the truth of being—in dwelling among and embracing these 'slaves,' shows them to be luminously beautiful."[202] There is no "more radical anti-essentialism" than this fundamental truth of the gospel "that noting in the world so essentially determines the nature of humanity or the scope of the human soul that there is no possibility of being reborn."[203] Therefore, the new approach makes too much of the powers and cannot make biopolitics any more contingent than "a God who goes about in the dust of exodus for love of a race intransigent in its particularity."[204] It is from this place that liberative politics can emerge. To borrow from Augustine, the biopolitical orders must appear as privations of the good rather than realities that truly possess ontological purchase.

Paul's gospel challenge to biopolitical orders, then, arises from his theological convictions. It is my assumption that Paul gives a more accurate account of reality than the new approach and truncated materialism.

---

200. Milbank, "Materialism and Transcendence," 423.

201. Milbank, "Materialism and Transcendence," 423.

202. Hart, *Beauty of the Infinite*, 123–24.

203. Hart, *Beauty of the Infinite*, 124.

204. Hart, *Beauty of the Infinite*, 126.

Paul's theology requires more than a strict materialism or post-meta-physical theology can allow. Either would limit Paul's theological challenge. The clearest example of Paul's challenge to a strict materialism is his statement in his first letter to the Corinthians,

> For what human being knows what is truly human except the human spirit that is within? So also no one comprehends what is truly God's except the Spirit of God. Now we have received not the spirit of the world, but the Spirit that is from God, so that we may understand the gifts bestowed on us by God. And we speak of these things in words not taught by human wisdom but taught by the Spirit, interpreting spiritual things to those who are spiritual. (2:11–13)

Paul argues that there is a hidden spiritual reality behind the material that orders and orients the material toward proper ends. This does not mean that Paul betrays the thick material descriptions of the new approach for an escapist spirituality. Rather the spiritually ordered person (*pneumatikos*) is embedded in the trials of this world. Yet, the *pneumatikos* recognizes the indescribably spiritual source of life beyond the material. To fail to recognize this source of being is a crucial error. As P. Travis Kroeker writes,

> Such human beings live according to the flesh by trying to construct their own meaning in the world, make their own mark, take their own measure independent of the divine and invisible source of life. Such a life is sinful not because it is embodied but because it cannot see and embrace the spiritual meaning of bodily life – it ends up in strife (political, intellectual, ecclesial, and indeed with itself, as Romans 7 shows), a strife that by its very nature *negates* what is good, the power to affirm and celebrate life.[205]

The spiritually mature person is not negligent of materiality, but rather does not seek a perpetual revolution against that which is already passing away. A deep resonance between Benjamin and Paul is apparent at this juncture, namely the futility and passing nature of this world. Paul's apocalyptic theology too recognizes that the world is passing away. To fail to recognize the futility of the world passing away means living a life in the flesh, which, as Paul adds, is foolishness (1 Cor 2:14). The answer to this foolishness is the revelation of the hidden spiritual reality that orders

205. Kroeker, "War of the Lamb," 142.

and orients bodily life.[206] This hidden spirituality that reveals the wisdom of God, which cannot finally be guaranteed by any visible, material form of reality, is essential to Paul. To ignore this consideration would be to censor Paul beyond recognition.

It is essential to recognize that Paul assumes a hidden spiritual reality that orients and shapes bodily life to the recognition of the true for of the world, namely that which is passing away. A nihilism is helpful to end the meanings of such a world, but Paul gives a more spiritually constructive answer. A revolution against this would be to commit the same error as sovereignty and biopolitics. In other words, a permanent revolution is futile when the revolution has been won.

I am grateful to the work of the new approach to initiate the conversation on Paul's political potential against biopolitics and private interests. However, I now depart from them. I take the gifts of new community, event, and countercultural witness and now engage the apocalyptic Paul in order to show how these gifts are enlivened, not by the triune Lord's subtraction, but by God's apocalyptic fullness. Here the biopolitical orders and our own private interests are not the positive political realities to which we are fatefully victims. Rather, they are sinful orders disrupted by the invasion of Christ into the cosmos. I explore these critiques of modern politics, not by a thick description of materialism, but by a thick description of the apocalyptic invasion of Christ who defeats the powers of sin and death while promising a new creation. In this invasion, creatures are called into the life of God's infinite plentitude, "unselfing" from their private interests and seeing with the just and loving gaze, which does not rely on ideological constructions but on the fullness of creaturely reality.

CONCLUSION

In conclusion, though the philosophers of the new approach to Paul offer some positive new avenues of political interpretation, they struggle to recognize all the issues at stake in modern politics and the apostle Paul's writings. In modern politics, they fail to recognize Hannah Arendt's astute diagnoses of modern politics arising from private interests. Such a politic results in biopolitical orders that preserve our private interests rather than challenge them.

---

206. Kroeker, "War of the Lamb," 142.

The new approach provides many provocative reflections to counter these biopolitical tendencies arising from close readings of the apostle Paul and materialist hermeneutics. While providing helpful rhetorical devices to counter hegemonic structures of biopolitics, I move beyond their insight due to their inability to transcend private interests. While they only confront ideology with ideology, I turn to Paul's apocalyptic theology that celebrates God's defeat of such orders and the path of the just and loving gaze.

2

You Have the Words of Life

Pauline Apocalyptic and the
Ontology of Scripture

I NOW ATTEMPT AN interpretation of Paul for the sake of unpacking the political implications of his apocalyptic theology. Paul's writings serve as a means to instruct faithfulness to God within the modern problematic of biopolitics. Certain practices, postures, and visions emerge as a means to inhabit this reality. Only when the community engages these practices in public can it be called political. It is not Paul's exclusive intent to be political, but rather to form a community according to the gospel of justice and love that confronts a wider political culture.

I begin this chapter by offering my general hermeneutic for reading Paul. The new approach relies on a materialist, nihilist hermeneutic for reading Paul against the biopolitical orders. I argued in the previous chapter that, though attractive, the new approach actually hinders their intended aim by deploying such a hermeneutic. Alternatively, I take on that which is rejected: a harmonious order through the divine activity of God to save the cosmos that names the sheer contingency of biopolitical orders. I assume that Paul is correct not only about the description of the cosmos, but also its salvation by God. Therefore, my hermeneutical presupposition is that Paul should be read as ontologically located within that order of salvation. In this hermeneutic, one reads Scripture dogmatically within the saving event of the triune Lord. Paul, as an author of Scripture, must be read within the communication of this saving event as well. I argue that it is within this context that Paul's message has political implications.

After outlining this hermeneutic, I briefly define and unpack Paul's apocalyptic theology. This includes describing the powers of sin and death that beget private interests. Sin is twofold in its apocalyptic context. First, sin and death are fallen powers in the cosmos. Second, the powers of sin and death lead to self-interest. I conclude that apocalyptic includes the revelation of God's righteousness to the cosmos, which defeats the powers of sin and death, and the *not yet* consummation of the cosmos according to the work of Christ.

In order to fully deal with the powers, and thus provide a faithful political theology despite the persistence of the powers, Paul's political theology needs the *already* and the *not yet*. New Testament scholars and theologians dispute the *already* and *not yet* character of Paul's apocalyptic theology. Therefore, in order to fully account for a thick description of Pauline apocalyptic, I provide a historical account of Paul's apocalyptic gospel, which shows why there is a divergence. This account describes how scholars converge and diverge on what is completed in Christ's invasion and what is yet to happen. Ultimately, they must be treated together, though this is not a conclusive opinion in the academy because of various influences of the great reformer Martin Luther. Nevertheless, I maintain they must remain together. By assuming this synthesis, I deploy a Wesleyan hermeneutic that brings together the *already* and the *not yet*. For Wesley, salvation, sanctification, and eschatology are inextricably bound together.

BIBLE AS SCRIPTURE: DOGMATICS AS HERMENEUTICS

Paul's letters are a peculiar set of documents located within Christian Holy Scripture. As Scripture, Paul's writings assist in communicating divine speech. This does not limit the insights of modern biblical scholarship, but rather emphasizes that Scripture has a place in the event of salvation that escapes modern biblical scholarship alone. Scripture is by no means the saving agent in this event. Rather, it is the record of God's self-disclosure to humanity, and so it plays a role in continued witness to this self-disclosure. Scripture can be read in light of modern biblical scholarship, but it cannot lose its place within the unfolding grace of God and humanity's growth into that grace. Reading the Bible as Scripture illuminates the error in the new approach to Paul, which locates the Bible away from its dogmatic, ontological center. Reading Paul's letters as Scripture allows one to see how the meaning of the text is truncated when taken away from its intended center.

Theologian John Webster gives the clearest account of the Bible as Scripture by positioning Scripture in the light of the saving activity of God. According to Webster, "both the texts and the processes surrounding their reception are subservient to the self-presentation of the triune God . . . by which readers are accosted."[1] Scripture is a created reality used for divine purposes.[2] This is a way of both talking about the text itself and what the text does. By attesting to the self-presentation of the triune God, Scripture also speaks to a saving fellowship with God.[3] Therefore, to read Scripture outside of this saving fellowship, which Webster identifies as the "economy of grace," means to lose the significance of that text's purpose.[4]

Webster's analysis of Scripture's content could be summarized as follows: God saves. This is a simple summary of the entire narrative of Scripture. By qualifying Scripture within the economy of grace, Webster argues that Scripture is read in light of the triune God, which creates a new reality not bound by previous assumptions about the nature of reality. One such new creation of God's self-presentation is the new community—the community of the saved. Salvation is not a spiritual exchange, but the positing of a new communion between God and humankind. John Webster writes, "Salvation is reconciliation, and as such includes the healing and restoration of communicative fellowship between God and humankind, broken by the creature's defiance and ignorance."[5] The possibilities of such a community are revealed in the light of the revelation of God's self-presentation. The agent of revelation is not Scripture, but God. However, the Scriptures, Paul's writings included, witness to this self-presentation of the triune God and the positing of new community. Thus, Scripture provides a type of theological poetic in response to the self-presentation and revelation of the triune God, a new way of

1. Webster, *Holy Scripture*, 6.
2. Webster, *Holy Scripture*, 8–9.
3. Webster, *Holy Scripture*, 13.
4. Webster, *Holy Scripture*, 68–106.
5. Webster, *Holy Scripture*, 70.

being in the world that makes a new community. Scripture reveals the divine speech about how God saves and how this yields new creaturely possibilities.

This begs the following question: Exactly where does Scripture fit in this formation of new creaturely possibilities? In this "dogmatic" approach to Scripture, the purpose is not primarily philological or philosophical, but a submission to the text's unique ability to attest to this self-presentation of God. This type of reading resists private calculations because one must submit to that which is outside of the individual. Thus, reading Scripture is essential in order for the community to surrender its own priority and private interests. To read Scripture in the economy of grace means to become a certain kind of *reader*.[6] The church consists of readers who are submitting to this text and are confronted with divine speech, and so must be bound to others in community.

Reading Scripture as a document within its attestation to the revelation of the triune God subordinates all other creaturely concerns to this task. For example, the work of reading Scripture is not to unleash the will, but rather the submission of the will to Scripture. In so doing, this revelation centralizes the divine overcoming of human estrangement from God, but also estrangement from one another.[7] The church is not grounded in human will or individual self, but in the divine speech of the voice of the self-presentation of the triune God.[8] God, through divine speech, as Webster cites, continually accosts humanity and reorients away from the dangers of the will toward a reality that cannot be controlled: the reality of God. This is not a turn to the self, but to God and God's self-presentation, which confronts us on every page of the Scripture. Webster proposes that, when one reads the Bible as Scripture—as created reality that attests to the self-presentation of God—one is "slain and made alive."[9]

> The rectitude of the will, its conformity to the matter of the gospel, is crucial, so that reading can only occur as a kind of brokenness, a relinquishment of willed mastery of the text, and

6. Webster, *Holy Scripture*, 88.

7. Webster, *Holy Scripture*, 87–88.

8. Webster, *Holy Scripture*, 83.

9. Webster, *Holy Scripture*, 88.

through exegetical reading's guidance towards that encounter with God of which the text is an instrument.[10]

Reading the Bible as Scripture is an antimodernist stand against the ways that the self attempts to give the text meaning according to private interests, instead looking to the text for the saving self-presentation of the triune God.

The value of Webster's ontology of Scripture is its insistence that the Bible's intelligibility rests in the triune God. Thus, it resists the equally problematic tendency of fundamentalism. Furthermore, anything other than God's own triune nature posited into Scripture is ideology. The point of the scriptural narrative found within the text is simply to point to this revelation and the resulting consequences of this revelation. Rowan Williams writes,

> The point is surely this: we cannot say what God is in himself; all we have is the narrative of God with us. And that is a narrative of a 'journey into a far country' . . . a story of God's Son as a creature and a mortal and defeated creature: The unity of God and his Son in this story is not, in the actual detail, moment by moment, of the story . . . It emerges at last, when Christ goes to his Father risen and glorified . . . In other words it is a story of 'risk'; and only at Easter are we able to say, 'he comes *from* God, just as he goes *to* God', and to see in the contingent fact of the resurrection . . . that which is not contingent, the life of God as Father and Son together.[11]

Scripture bears witness to these contingent details as an indispensable means to point to God as triune and, thus, reality itself. Williams declares that Scripture not only tells the story of "risk and consummation," but also that Scripture points to the triune nature of God. As such, this is the gravitational, coherent center of Scripture. Scripture, therefore, is a witness to the crucified and resurrected Lord, who is proclaimed to be the second person of the Trinity. To be sure, it is the God who is revealed that is the center, not Scripture itself. However, to dismiss this central narrative as fable and still attempt to work with the text means working into an ontological void.

If we commit to Webster's ontology of Scripture located within the self-presentation of the triune God, then the path forward for the human

10. Webster, *Holy Scripture*, 88.
11. Williams, "Trinity and Ontology," 159.

centered on private interests becomes closed. Scripture does not point to the self-enclosed human, but beyond this human to the triune Lord. It does not respect ideological structures that attempt to define humanity apart from this ontological center. Furthermore, the self-presentation of the triune God in Christ is nothing less than a radical rupture of this enclave of humanity in order to open the cosmos to God's own triune self. In short, it is an apocalypse. Therefore, humanity must place itself under the internal logic of this apocalyptic disruption and be bound into the community it posits.

THE POWERS OF SIN AND DEATH: PAULINE
APOCALYPTIC AND PRIVATE INTERESTS

The term "apocalyptic" comes from the Greek ἀποκάλυψις, which in English most closely means revelation. Apocalyptic interpretations of Paul have recently increased in popularity. This is due in part to popular media hyping a catastrophic end of the world, playfully called "apocalyptic." The popular form of apocalyptic as catastrophe comes from the Judeo-Christian literature, which often depicts the battle between heaven and hell and the cataclysmic end of the world. Therefore, apocalyptic, through the popular genre about the cataclysmic end of the world, is commonly associated with a particular type of eschatology.

Despite this clear association with eschatology, the subject of apocalyptic theology is not self-evident. Rather, it is the subject of intense debate and escapes simplistic definition. According to New Testament scholar John G. M. Barclay,

> the term "apocalyptic" [is] used in at least six ways: i) for the revelation of mysteries; ii) for a strong sense of newness (compatible with the "new covenant"), perhaps accompanied by shock or surprise; iii) for eschatology of a particular kind; iv) for the expectation of an imminent end; v) for an epistemological stance whereby truth is ascertained, first and foremost, through the Christ-event; vi) for a three-actor drama (involving God, humanity, and evil forces), in which God saves by invading the world.[12]

Barclay's summary highlights the slippery nature of the word in light of its popular understanding. A few of Barclay's definitions of apocalyptic

12. Barclay, "Apocalyptic Allegiance and Divestment," 257.

gesture to God's self-presentation or revelation. This is the theme of Paul's gospel and why he must be read as Scripture, as prescribed by Webster. The connection between Paul and apocalyptic is a natural correspondence.

Paul's apocalyptic focuses on the invasion of Christ in history. However, if Christ invades or goes into a far country, he goes into enemy territory, namely a territory occupied by other powers. This invasion is against fallen powers. These "powers" are deemed hostile to God and thus dangerous. Defining the powers proves, like the very nature of apocalyptic itself, to be difficult. Take one such definition of the powers offered by New Testament scholar Victor Paul Furnish:

> The present age is viewed as being held captive by powers which are alien to God and hostile to his purpose . . . The hostility of these alien powers is expressed not only in their attempt to enslave [humanity] to their own purposes (Gal. 4:3), but also in their blinding [them] to the gospel of Christ and thus to the true God himself (II Cor. 4:4) and, ultimately, in their crucifixion of "the Lord of glory" (I Cor. 2:8).[13]

In Furnish's analysis, the powers are hostile forces that work against the purpose of God and enslave humanity. Despite this clear analysis, the role these powers play and how Paul deals with them remains unclear. As theologian David Bentley Hart has written, Paul's theology of Christ's saving event is mostly concerned with "bad angels."[14] The forces that hold humanity captive, based on Hart's account, come from that which is beyond human reach. For example, theologian Walter Wink writes that the fall of the sons of God in Genesis 6:1–4

> was enlisted to explain the presence of an evil that emanates not from humanity alone but from something higher as well; not divine, but transcendent, suprahuman, that persists through time, is opposed to God and human faithfulness, and seeks our destruction, damnation, illness and death.[15]

Powers, then, are those forces that stand beyond mere human life and in opposition to God. These powers, as John Howard Yoder writes, are *mostly* "fallen."[16] Yoder goes on to state that if the powers are fallen, then

---

13. Furnish, *Theology and Ethics in Paul*, 115–16.

14. Hart, "Everything You Know," para. 4.

15. Wink, *Naming the Powers*, 23.

16. Yoder, *Politics of Jesus*, 141.

their intention in God's creation was originally *for* goodness.[17] Like humanity and creation, the powers were among those realities originally called good by God. Along with humanity, the powers fell. Old Testament scholar Gerhard von Rad understands the consequences of the fall as creation-wide, especially in the Yahwistic tradition.[18] The fall of humanity results in the fall of angels and powers. Again, recalling the sons of God in Genesis 6:1–4, Rad writes, "The Yahwist wanted to show man's general corruption. He wanted to represent the mixing of superhuman spiritual powers with man, a kind of 'demonic' invasion and thus point out a further disturbance caused by sin."[19] The fall leads to human disobedience, fratricide, and even the fall of heavenly powers in the midst of creation. In short, the fall and the entrance of sin and death into the world is nothing short of a creation-wide crisis and occupation.

Despite the connection between the heavenly host and the fall, angels are not the exclusive way Scripture understands powers. Within Paul's own narrative, you see another understanding of powers. The Greek *exousia* also denotes power. For Paul, as Oscar Cullman writes, *exousia* means "angelic powers."[20] However, *exousia* has a larger meaning in the New Testament canon: "not spiritual beings but ideological justifications, political or religious legitimations, and delegated permissions."[21] This understanding of power has a profound modern implication by showcasing the ancient perspective. For the ancients, there was a richer account of political authority, one a mere materialist optic cannot witness. Rather, Wink writes,

> [the ancients] seem to have taken [supernatural forces] for granted and to have been much more preoccupied with that more amorphous, intangible, indefinable something that makes it possible for a king to command subjects to voluntary death in war or for a priest to utter words that send a king to his knees . . . they must have been in touch with dimensions of power which our more materialistic point of view scarcely glimpses.[22]

---

17. Yoder, *Politics of Jesus*, 141.

18. Rad, *Genesis*, 109–10.

19. Rad, *Genesis*, 112.

20. Cullmann, *Christ and Time*, 194. Quoted in Wink, *Naming the Powers*, 16.

21. Wink, *Naming the Powers*, 16.

22. Wink, *Naming the Powers*, 16.

This layered understanding of powers reveals the deeper motivation be-hind the activities of humanity, that humans are not individuals acting alone but within a framework of powers. One can see why Žižek and the new approach all appreciate Paul's account of reality. Paul's understand-ing of power and ideology shows that there is some "magical" way that biopolitical ideology can hold captive an entire people. Therefore, *exou-sia* is extremely helpful toward the end of the new approach.

An example that illustrates this *exousia* understanding of powers is offered by the erudite analysis of the Holocaust by historian Timothy Snyder.

> [The Holocaust] cannot be explained by stereotypes of passive or communist Jews, of orderly or preprogrammed Germans, of beastly or anti-Semitic locals, or indeed by any other cliché, no matter how powerful at the time, no matter how convenient today. This unprecedented mass murder would have been im-possible without a special kind of politics.[23]

Snyder, in an implicit way, illustrates *exousia* as ideology offered by Wink. The mass murder of the Holocaust cannot be explained by quantitative or qualitative analysis, but a power *politics* that motivates a nation into action. Once *exousic* ideology takes shape alongside human experience, it provides the potential for a local performance of Nazi ideology by "rec-onciling [local] interests and hopes with the perceived ideas of those who now held power."[24] Snyder gives a historical account of the ideologies that support the totalitarianism and biopolitics of Arendt and Foucault. *Exou-sia* as ideology is the power to capture and seize upon private interests for the sake of rule. This power, this ideology, works against God's intended purpose in the world. Therefore, *exousia* denotes ideology that is just as powerful to the ancients as spiritual *beings*. Both are fallen and, for Paul, both are commingled.[25] Therefore, in Paul's apocalyptic understanding, the fallen powers operate outside God's original ordering intention. They obey a sovereignty foreign to God.

The powers exist under the sovereignty of sin and death. The pow-ers of sin and death—and by extension humanity—are hostile to God.[26] Furnish writes,

23. Snyder, *Black Earth*, 150.

24. Snyder, *Black Earth*, 151, 154.

25. Wink, *Naming the Powers*, 46.

26. Furnish, *Theology and Ethics in Paul*, 116.

Sin is not an original part of the world but "infiltrates" itself
into the world (Rom. 5:12) . . . to take it captive and subject
[humanity] to its reign . . . Sin "deceives" [humans] (Rom. 7:11);
it demands [their] obedience and, then enslaves [them] (Rom.
6:16–17, 20; 7:14, 25), and it finally "kills" [them] (Rom. 7:11;
8:10).[27]

This pattern of sin and death is an extension of the drama depicted at
the fall. Sin as the seductive possibility of not following the command
of God enslaves humanity to another, fallen way of being in the world.
Theologian Dietrich Bonhoeffer writes that by disobeying, "humankind
must live in the fallen world, that humankind gets what it wants, that as
the being who is [like God] it must live in its [like God] world—that is
the *curse*."[28] This curse leads to the death of human creaturehood. Not
only is this the death of the creature's status before God, but the entrance
of death itself into creation.

The fall has massive ramifications for humanity and the world. The
sin committed—the possibility of life without God—is birthed by human selfishness. The curse of sin leads to death. The powers, according to
New Testament scholar J. Christiaan Beker, are allied "under the sovereign rule of death."[29] Death for Paul, as New Testament scholar C. Kavin
Rowe understands, is "the condition of our humanity and the power that
reduces us to being dead."[30] Sin leads to death, but death is the power
that ceases control of the cosmos. Furnish writes, "Death, like sin, is a
demonic power which "reigns" in this age . . . and is in fact the manifestation of sin's reign (Rom. 5:21), the "enemy" power which still holds out
when all others have been conquered (1 Cor. 15:26)."[31] Paul can say with
confidence that he still feels the power of death exercising dominion in
his body (Rom 7:23–24). The infiltration of sin and death (Rom 5:12)
into the world corrupts the good purposes of creation.

The powers distort and corrupt creaturely existence and work
against God's intentions in the cosmos. Paul understands that the chief
example of this corruption lies in traded "the glory of the immortal
God for images resembling mortal human beings . . . [and] the truth
about God for a lie and worshiped and served the creature rather than

27. Furnish, *Theology and Ethics in Paul*, 116.

28. Bonhoeffer, *Creation and Fall*, 132.

29. Beker, *Paul the Apostle*, 189.

30. Rowe, *One True Life*, 99.

31. Furnish, *Theology and Ethics in Paul*, 117.

the Creator" (Rom 1:23, 25).[32] New Testament scholar Ernst Käsemann writes that this "rebellion is seen as the signature of human reality before and apart from Christ."[33] This rebellion results in the fall of the powers (*exousia*) and leads to political problems. This is why the new approach of recognizing Paul's account of reality is correct, but also wrong in that it can be answered without God. The new approach witnesses to the powers in their material organization, but argues that the answer lies in an equally materially organized ideological scheme. This plays into the trap of *exousia*, because these material schemes can always be seized for the interests of the powers. The entire history, therefore, of biopolitics and totalitarianism, is the ideological seizing of experience for the sake of power. The powers are beyond the tangibility of these schemes. The issue is not the lack of ideological structures, but false worship. Because the spiritual and ideological powers that undergird creation are fallen, humanity is then left with poor political goods.

Conflicted political goods and the fallen powers are illustrated well in Augustine's depiction of the *summum bonum* in *City of God*. Augustine describes the *summum bonum* in his engagement with the conflicting loves of the two cities, the heavenly city and the earthly city. Each city possesses its own love: the heavenly city the *amor Dei* (Love of God), and the earthly city *amor sui* (love of self). As Augustine depicts, "Love of self, even to the point of contempt for God, made the earthly city, and love of God, even to the point of contempt for self, made the heavenly city. Thus, the former glories in itself and the latter glories in the Lord."[34] The *amor sui* is a selfish, *privately* interested love that inhibits a truly public realm, exemplified in Augustine's understanding of the human turned inward upon itself (*voluntas incurvatus*). The *summum bonum* lies in love of God (*amor Dei*), which is not selfish but truly public in its celebration of the common good. Therefore, one cannot discount the individual participation against God's good purposes. It is the love turned inward against God that leads to a political community contrary to the *summum bonum*. Furthermore, as Gregory Lee recently argued, Augustine's definition of *summum bonum* is apocalyptic. The difference, according to Lee, between

---

32. The argument that Paul's critique of idolatry is about the ideology of modern man is best exemplified in Karl Barth. Barth's *Epistle to the Romans* marks a stance on Romans 1 different from what had previously been offered. See Barth, *Epistle to the Romans*, 49–52.

33. Käsemann, *Commentary on Romans*, 42.

34. Augustine, *City of God* 14.28, 136.

the two loves is not between heaven and earth, but rather "the difference between heaven and hell."[35] This is classic apocalyptic language. Heaven and hell, exemplified in Augustine's two cities, are powers competing for the love of humanity. As such, the chief political good is vulnerable to fallen powers at the site of our loves. The *amor sui*, the love of self, is associated with the earthly realm. This is a love performed in service of the self for the sake of the self and constructs the earthly city.[36] This love is inherently private. If self-love is located in the tension of apocalyptic powers, then private self-love is drawn away from God's good purposes.

Powers, sin, and death provide a matrix of signifiers in Paul's gospel and the history of theology. Sin is the resulting condition of the fall that infringes upon the powers and human ability to partner with God's purposes for the world. Under the sovereignty of death, sin leads away from life with God. This is a creation-wide condition that groans with humanity for its redemption (Rom 8:22). Sin is an influence, as well as a selfish inhabiting of its influence. Both are contrary to God, both attempt sovereignty apart from God, and both must be engaged with the truth of the gospel.

I pause here and draw a connection between the apocalyptic Paul and the Paul of the new approach. The powers, in apocalyptic, are fallen as a result of the fall of humanity. Therefore, human selfishness leads to a fallen cosmos with powers that in turn influence further selfish behavior. This is also the way that private interests and ideology work. According to Arendt, private interests cannot create a truly political realm. Private interests, namely labor and work, only promote private actions in public. She continues that the will creates the public realm, but when the will is focused on private interest it lacks the ability to be free. This matches Augustine's and Paul's own understanding of the powers. Humanity's original sin causes the powers to fall, but when humanity attempts to act in public, they are confronted with their own will turned inward, their *voluntas incurvatas*. The powers that influence and seduce, like *exousia*, encourage and seize upon this state in humanity for the sake of warped political power. There is a fundamental connection between the new approach and the apocalyptic because both recognize the relevance of this interpretation of reality in their respective depiction of Paul. However,

35. Lee, "Republics and Their Loves," 7, 46–63.

36. The deployment of the "self" here does not mean that Augustine recognizes a self-enclosed subject. Rather, Augustine understands the self to be a complex set of desires that remains unfixed and capable of conversion.

the means by which they use Paul to fix the problem that he himself diagnoses is vastly different. This is ultimately where we depart.

Central to my argument is that Pauline apocalyptic provides a better critique of private interests and powers than the new approach. In order to fully grapple with private interests, one must recognize not only their root in prideful humanity, but also their potential seduction by the powers which transcend the human potential to grasp it. The ailments of modernity lie in its acceptance of the powers of sin and death that form sinful private interests. The value of Paul's theology lies in his proposal of an apocalyptic response in Christ's incarnation where "the power of God . . . [and] righteousness of God is revealed (ἀποκαλύπτεται)" (Rom 1:16–17, NRSV). God's righteousness is revealed against self-sufficiency, private interests, and fallen powers. Therefore, the immediacy of private interests is not just one's private concerns, but when one's activities mirror ungodliness and wickedness (Rom 1:18, NRSV). This is a result of the fallen angelic and ideological powers (*exousia*) that continually lure humanity away from God's good purposes and the *summum bonum*. Theologian Nathan Kerr writes, in apocalyptic terms, that "Jesus is uniquely the *apostolos*, the one who is *sent* into the world, in order that he might *give* himself to the world's own *transformation*—the world's own *freedom* from the powers."[37] Christ invades the cosmos in order to bring the sovereignty of the powers to an end. Apocalyptic, as I now take it to mean, signifies Paul's theology of Christ's interruption of these powers and the transformation of the world through *his* lordship. In so doing, apocalyptic is a means to deal with the twofold cause of private interests, human self-love and the fallen powers. The revelation, or apocalypse, of Christ interrupts the powers of sin and death that materially manifest in self-sufficient, idolatrous humanity.

Apocalyptic confronts the sovereignty of sin and death exercised in private interests with the reality of God. Paul's apocalyptic theology, as Kerr stipulates, calls into question any "sovereignty which itself requires . . . nothing beyond or outside its own immanent circulation."[38] In order to do this, "apocalyptic . . . stresses that, in a singular historical event, God has acted to inaugurate the reign of God by making real and present an eschatologically perfect love in the middle of history."[39] This

---

37. Kerr, *Christ, History, and Apocalyptic*, 3. Emphasis mine.

38. Kerr, *Christ, History, and Apocalyptic*, 4.

39. Kerr, *Christ, History, and Apocalyptic*, 4.

singular event interrupts and, as John Howard Yoder writes, breaks the sovereignty of the powers.[40] This event inserts into history a new way of being that usurps the sovereignty of sin and death that manifests in the self-sufficient, self-loved, and privately interested human.

Christ's interruption of history transforms the very structure of human existence. Kerr continues, apocalyptic recognizes "the in-breaking of God's reign . . . made real and available only as a way of *life*, a concrete *practice*, a mode of historic *action*, which 'way of life,' 'practice,' and 'action' constitutively and fundamentally concur as this world's *conversion*."[41] This means that in Christ a new way of being in the world, not tethered to self-love, has emerged. The apocalyptic Christian mission proclaims the gospel of God's action within history to all political realities. It is the sovereignty of *this* action in Christ that is the first moment of a faithful Christian political theology.

Despite the breaking of sinful sovereignty that enables a new life not formed in self-love and private interests, the powers must be removed. Political theology, then, assumes the eschatological. Talk of apocalyptic eschatology is problematic to modernity, but it cannot be removed from our contemporary readings of Paul. I contend that it is because humanity has become an idol to itself that a different configuration of the human must be considered. Under the powers of sin and death, humanity becomes self-sufficient and takes on a politics of private interests. This is sinful, unrighteous behavior, which makes politics not an issue of ideology but fundamentally an issue of righteousness. Such a statement is an affront to the political organization of the privately interested and self-sufficient human. Humans would rather, as Arendt illustrates, think of themselves as operating an exclusive place in the universe that previously was reserved for God. Such a description helps identify the alternative understanding of humanity offered by Paul. Theologian Karl Barth writes in his famed *Epistle to the Romans*,

> Thinking of ourselves what can be thought only of God, we are unable to think of Him more highly than we think of ourselves. Being to ourselves what God ought to be to us, He is no more to us than we are to ourselves. This secret identification of ourselves with God carries with it our isolation from Him . . . If mankind be itself God, the appearance of the idol is then inevitable.[42]

40. Yoder, *Politics of Jesus*, 144.

41. Kerr, *Christ, History, and Apocalyptic*, 2.

42. Barth, *Epistle to the Romans*, 45.

If this is the case, then a fundamental shift to materialism alone will not do. Rather, an exorcism and an iconoclasm must occur that fundamentally reorients humanity's understanding of itself. In the in-breaking of Christ, one does not merely materially reorganize life, but crucifies it and the old biopolitical divisions of the world in order to unmask their sheer contingency.

Though the in-breaking of Christ brings an end to the reign of sin and death, the resurrection of Christ signals something different. The resurrection of Christ, so central to Paul, is not only apocalyptic in its disruption of the powers, but also in its wider context of the resurrection of the dead. For Paul, Christ's resurrection is the "first fruit" (1 Cor 15:23) of all who have died, meaning that, like Christ, those who have died will be resurrected from the dead. Apocalyptic, therefore, is essential not only because it represents the best interpretation of Christ's interruption in history, but also in its emphasis on the resurrection of the dead as an incursion of a different kind. Not only does God disrupt the world in Christ, but God also provides the world with its *telos*, its shared end.

The consummation of creation in the apocalyptic return of Christ cannot be abandoned in Paul's theology. Beker writes, "Paul expects the future to be an apocalyptic closure-event in time and space embracing the whole of God's created order."[43] In the incarnation and resurrection, Christ embraces the created order and promises our future resurrection. In the event of the resurrection of the dead, bodies are remade into the likeness of the resurrected body of Jesus and, thus, capable of the triune life. One must have the resurrection of Christ, or else faith is in vain (1 Cor 15:17). However, if Christ is raised, then an even deeper scandal is true, namely the resurrection of the dead. Apocalyptic, therefore, names Christ's resurrection as the objective content of hope not only in exercising lordship over the powers, but also as the content of Paul's eschatology—a resurrection of the dead similar to Christ's resurrection.

In sum, I argue that apocalyptic is the best reading of Paul. I believe that Paul's apocalyptic theology should be read as Scripture much in the vein of Webster's analysis. Paul's apocalyptic theology centers on the revelation and self-presentation of God against the powers, and forms a new community. Webster notes that reading Scripture in this manner posits a new kind of community. This community is saved from the powers of sin and death. If I am correct in locating the modern manifestation of this

43. Beker, *Paul's Apocalyptic Gospel*, 14.

sin as idolatrous, self-sufficient, privately interested humanity, then it is a community not bound by the ailments of modern politics. The freedom arises from its appeal to a different order where human exchange is not only possible, but the norm, in contrast to the fallen nature of the powers. In being saved from the present order into a new communal life and the possession of shared ends, the community of faith is not wed to private interests.

PAUL'S APOCALYPTIC THEOLOGY: THE *ALREADY* AND THE *NOT YET*

Before analyzing the *already/not yet* division, it is important to set the scene for how apocalyptic even became a topic of debate in modern biblical scholarship. The origin of apocalyptic in the twentieth century begins at least as early as the work of theologian Albert Schweitzer. However, the current conversation is most indebted to the debate between Rudolf Bultmann and his student Ernst Käsemann. For Bultmann, the apocalyptic expectation of the immanent end of the world represents a myth that must be demythologized.

> By "demythologizing" I understand a hermeneutical procedure that inquires about the reality referred to by mythological statements or texts. This presupposes that myth indeed talks about a reality, but in an inadequate way. It also presupposes a specific understanding of reality.[44]

Demythologization preserves the saving action of God, but without the premodern myth of an imminent end of the world. Bultmann believes the New Testament authors (Paul included) speak of reality, but their mythological world must be demythologized in order to address modernity. By demythologizing Paul, Bultmann attempts to preserve the reality of God spoken of in myth against objectification in any one *Weltbild*. Bultmann does not think God can be captured and owned by any one system of theology or philosophy, but must be understood dialectically.

Bultmann's most famous student, Ernst Käsemann, engages with Bultmann on how to interpret the New Testament. Contrary to Bultmann, Käsemann maintains that the apocalyptic expectation of the final

---

44. Bultmann, "On the Problem of Demythologizing," 155.

defeat of the powers of sin and death through the lordship of Christ is essential to Paul.

> Christian apocalyptic . . . was released on the Church by the experience of the Spirit in the time after Easter, preserved as a living phenomenon by those endowed with the Spirit, nourished theologically from the tradition of Jewish apocalyptic, and finally accompanied by enthusiastic hopes and manifestations . . . of advancing post-Easter enthusiasm.[45]

Here Käsemann locates apocalyptic as the early Christian enthusiasm for God's reign made possible by the events of the incarnation, crucifixion, resurrection, and ascension of Jesus of Nazareth, which provides the clearest revelation of God.[46] This enthusiasm is accompanied with "the expectation of an imminent Parousia," or rather the coming reign of God, which is *not yet*, but provides hope to the individual and all of creation still trapped within the powers of sin and death.[47] In his exploration of historical Christianity, Käsemann notes the disappointment arising from the fact that the imminent parousia did not occur in the timeframe envisioned by early Christians. In light of this perceived failure, as Käsemann notes, apocalyptic begins to wane. In its place, Christianity developed a grammar of Jesus's divinity somewhat divorced, in Käsemann's mind, from the original apocalyptic hope of early Christianity.[48] Käsemann asks "whether Christian theology can survive in any legitimate form without this [apocalyptic expectation], which sprang from the Easter experience and determined Easter faith."[49] In other words, he asks this question: without apocalyptic, can Christian theology survive?

---

45. Käsemann, "On the Subject," 109n1.

46. It should be clear at this point that I do not have a problem with using the word "event" to signal the life, death, and resurrection of Christ. Therefore, I am sympathetic to Badiou's read of Paul's theology. However, I differ from Badiou in that the event of Christ does not posit an identity indifferent to difference, but rather one wrapped up in the opening of the story of Israel to the gentiles. In this social reality, one is not indifferent to difference. An example of this embrace is found in a possible apocalyptic interpretation of the covenant to Israel. Apocalyptic embraces difference as genuinely different manifestations of bearers of the covenant, which was first promised to Israel and now, through Christ, to the gentiles. This is a radically unforeseen occurrence that nevertheless results in the acceptance of a radically plural account of humanity.

47. Käsemann, "On the Subject," 109n1.

48. Käsemann, "On the Subject," 115.

49. Käsemann, "Beginnings of Christian Theology," 107.

Bultmann would answer Käsemann's query with a resounding yes. For Bultmann, apocalyptic is a mythology of the ancient world of the prophets and apostles.[50] Though it is a myth, Bultmann argues that there is an integrity in the myth that must be preserved existentially. Bultmann succinctly refers to this myth, and all mythology of this sort, as a thing of the past.[51] The apocalyptic must be demythologized in order for the Christian message to remain authentically eschatological, and thus not rely on the mythological *Weltbild* of Paul predicated on an apocalyptic, imminent end. By eschatological, Bultmann means "not . . . that God's Reign is already here; but . . . that it is dawning."[52] The weakness of apocalyptic, according to Bultmann, is that it expects an end within chronological history. "Eschatology," on the other hand, "is the notion of the end of the world; it is a notion which as such does not intend to include a concrete picture of the end-occurrence, which does not even think of the end as chronologically fixed."[53] Such a claim would betray the non-objective nature of his dialectical theology. As a dialectical theologian, Bultmann expresses God's activity outside the realm of observable fact. God's acts can only be preserved by faith in the moral response of the individual. Bultmann argues,

> If the lordship of Christ and the subjection of the cosmic forces are understood only as apocalyptic statements, then, although they occur in the relation of the already and the not-yet, they are not in a dialectical relation. They do this only if they are oriented toward the individual.[54]

Bultmann emphasizes, over and against the apocalyptic, that fixed end-times hopes for the saving event of Christ is capable of being responded to in the realized eschatological. In this reading, eschatology ceases to be a concept and is opened up to the advent of grace, in which the individual responds in obedience to the demand of God. This is firmly Lutheran,

50. My engagement with Bultmann is primarily through the enlightening work of theologian David Congdon, who has opened up Bultmann beyond traditional theological caricatures of him. For Congdon's summary and interpretation of Bultmann's engagement with apocalyptic, see Congdon, "Bonhoeffer and Bultmann," 172–95.

51. Bultmann, "New Testament and Mythology," 2.

52. Bultmann, *Theology of the New Testament*, 7.

53. Bultmann, "Ist die Apokalyptik die Mutter der Chrislichen Theologie?" 476. Quoted in Congdon, "Bonhoeffer and Bultmann," 182.

54. Bultmann, "Ist die Apokalyptik die Mutter," 480–81. Quoted in Congdon, "Bonhoeffer and Bultmann," 184.

namely that one must respond to the demand of God in faith. Only by this faith is one justified and one's self-love and private interest put off. This is how God delivers humanity from captivity to sin and death.

Though both Bultmann and Käsemann are deeply committed Lutherans, they disagree on the cosmic scope of the deliverance from sin and death. Bultmann's theology is commonly associated with the individual, but he is open to a broader self-presentation of God in creation. Bultmann states in a sermon at Marburg on December 16, 1931, "[The Lord's Coming] . . . is not something which the soul ever and again experiences . . . Rather it is the coming of the Lord into the world."[55] Where Bultmann speaks about the salvation of the entire created order as experienced through the salvation of the individual, Käsemann emphasizes the apocalyptic coming of God as "Christ's seizure of power as the Cosmocrator."[56] Therefore, according to Käsemann, apocalyptic answers the question: "To whom does the sovereignty of the world belong?"[57] The answer lies in the tension between what Christ has done in his resurrection and the expectation of the imminent parousia in the resurrection of the dead. Käsemann writes, "The Resurrection of Christ is therefore, even while it counts as the beginning of the general resurrection, still for the time being the great exception, in which we can participate by hope alone."[58] Käsemann strongly emphasizes that Paul's apocalyptic gospel must include the resurrection of the dead.

Käsemann, through the resurrection of the dead, argues that the human individual is only part of a broader world and cannot be understood in isolation. Creation, like humanity, is captive to powers of sin and death (Rom 8:19–22). Käsemann argues that, in Romans 8:22, the Greek word for creation (κτίσις) "is all creation including mankind, with no sharp line of differentiation."[59] To emphasize the individual as proof of the salvation of the whole world misses this crucial aspect of Paul's theology, in that Paul sets an "indissoluble interrelation of mankind and world."[60] Therefore, the powers of sin and death possess both human and

---

55. Quoted in Congdon, "Bonhoeffer and Bultmann," 188–89.

56. Käsemann, "New Testament Questions of Today," 14.

57. Käsemann, "On the Subject," 135.

58. Käsemann, "On the Subject," 134.

59. Käsemann, *Commentary on Romans*, 233.

60. Käsemann, *Commentary on Romans*, 233.

nonhuman creation. This matrix of possession determines humanity. Käsemann writes,

> Man, for Paul, is never just on his own. He is always a specific piece of world and therefore becomes what in the last resort he is by determination from outside, i.e., by the power which takes possession of him and the lordship to which he surrenders himself. His life is from the beginning a stake in the confrontation between God and the principalities of this world. In other words, it mirrors the cosmic contention for the lordship of the world and is its concretion. As such, man's life can only be understood apocalyptically.[61]

Human life is, like creation, possessed by the powers of sin and death. There is no human exemption from this reality. Therefore, humanity must be understood apocalyptically, because it exists in the tension between its liberation from the powers of sin and death and its final salvation.

Modern Apocalyptic and the *Already* Potentiality of Political Thought

The work of Käsemann and Bultmann are modern interpretations of Paul's theology that have important political implications. Despite the gap between Bultmann's realized eschatology of Paul and Käsemann's cosmic apocalyptic theology, both figures overlap in their understanding of the already-present saving action of Christ. Such a description of the *already* is imbued with pregnant political implications. This overlap yields two crucial insights for Paul's political theology not realized by the new approach.

First, both emphasize ethical fidelity in response to God's saving event in Christ. For Bultmann, this fidelity is found at the moment of epistemological crisis before the saving event of God. This is traditionally known as the indicative and imperative distinction.[62] In the saving event of Christ, Bultmann argues that we are presented with a reorientation of ourselves by faith to the world through the indicative of grace. This indicative implies an imperative that guides Christians to just and moral actions toward one's neighbor. The themes of grace and faith operate differently for Bultmann. He asserts that this is manifest in one's experience

---

61. Käsemann, "On the Subject," 136.
62. See Bultmann, "Problem of Ethics in Paul," 195–216.

of God alone. The believer is sent into crisis while surrounded by sinful powers.

Similarly, Käsemann believes that the inauguration of the lordship of Christ requires a response of obedience. Those to whom Christ lays claim are now responsible for the whole of creation. This is Käsemann's *nova obedientia*, the "new obedience."[63] Equally for both, there is a coordinate action bound up with the self-presentation of God in the economy of grace. This emphasis helps readers tend to the moral exhortations of Paul, not just as his own prescription but as the Christians' "bound-upness" to this self-presentation and to the ones whom this self-presentation claims. Käsemann includes all human and nonhuman creation. This is how Paul's theology is political. When confronted by the interrupting presence of Christ's lordship, all worldly claims to sovereignty are upended. Therefore, Käsemann provides an avenue to explore the political implications of Paul's apocalyptic theology, even for the contemporary world.

Bultmann and Käsemann both deploy demythologization, though differently, in order to clarify Paul's message for the contemporary world. Both Bultmann and Käsemann are committed Lutherans. For Bultmann specifically, demythologization is for the purpose of maintaining a Lutheran nonobjectifying hermeneutic that prevents self-sufficient, privately interested capture of the gospel. Rather, according to Bultmann, the gospel always confronts the believer as a gift that must be responded to in faith. Käsemann, in his later years, became a proponent of demythologization arising from his similar Lutheran commitments. One then must posit that there is a distinction between the early and late Käsemann if one wants to argue that this emphasis on demythologization softens the ideal of an imminent parousia.[64] Käsemann's later demythologization is much more radical than Bultmann. This is a shift that reflects his own deep conviction that the text is not the only thing to be demythologized.[65] Rather, the modern world must be demythologized as well.

> Today, demythologizing must be more radical than in the days
> of Enlightenment, more critical toward its faith in progress and

63. Käsemann, "On the Subject," 136.

64. See, for example, Congdon, "Eschatologizing Apocalyptic," 132.

65. It should also be noted that Käsemann's daughter was murdered during this later period of his life. Her death was a result of the military dictatorship in Argentina. Käsemann believed that it was the failure of the church to obey the command of God that led to his daughter's death.

science . . . No texts are to be demythologized respecting their
ideological wrappings. In the evangelical sense demythologizing occurs as a battle and resistance against superstition. And
superstition, at least according to Luther's explanation of the
first commandment, is everything that does not allow us most
deeply and without compromise to fear, love, and trust God
"above all things."[66]

The world must be demythologized by removing cultural ideologies that
prevent fidelity to God's command. Luther's commitment to the first
commandment, as sighted by Käsemann, is a commitment to God by
faith and against worldly disobedience and unfaithfulness. These ideologies (*exousia*) are things that demand our fear, trust, or love apart from
Christian fear, trust, and love of God. They are not God, which includes,
but is not limited to, the loyalty to private interests and righteousness.

Käsemann's demythologization includes a mythological project
that juxtaposes the righteousness of God with the ideological (*exousia*),
which he calls the demonic. What is at stake for Käsemann is not just
conflicting ideologies, but false worship. The goal in apocalyptic is the
reintroduction of the possibility of participation in the righteousness of
God into the human sphere. This possibility is an already-potential for
righteousness in the present.

Käsemann develops his emphasis on the righteousness of God from
theologian Karl Barth's own emphasis on the righteousness of God.[67]
Barth's early career is dominated by his study of Pauline apocalyptic
themes against his German ideologically charged culture. Barth's Pauline
critique of ideology lies mostly in his *Epistle to the Romans*. The righteousness of God serves as a means to unseat the ideology and private
interests of modernity in favor of the ultimate concern that is God. Barth
responds to this problem through the apocalyptic text of Romans 1:16:
"The power of God is not the most exalted of observable forces, nor is it
either their sum or their fount. Being completely different, it is the *krisis*
(judgment) of all power, that by which all power is measured."[68] Sin is, as
Barth understands, any elevation of a human, private interest over God.
Therefore, Rome is like Barth's Europe because it is possessed by sin that
needs healing from the righteousness of God. This is also Arendt's world,

66. Käsemann, "Healing the Possessed," 199–200.

67. Käsemann is the first to admit that the early Barth greatly influenced his
work. See Käsemann, *On Being a Disciple of the Crucified*, xv.

68. Barth, *Epistle to the Romans*, 36. Emphasis mine.

namely a world turned toward self-sufficiency and private interest against God. In a sermon preached October 18, 1914, Barth speaks directly to this human grasping at its own private interests and self-sufficiency, which he calls human unrighteousness. The inability of the West to transcend its self-interested, private disposition is evident in the adamant conviction of "rightness" over and against others.[69] God's righteousness is revealed, or "apocalypsed," against all unrighteousness.

The apocalyptic origin of this human unrighteousness is a mixture of the human attempt to save itself and, what Barth calls, "hidden powers and spirits."[70] Barth adopts apocalyptic language in order to express this false righteousness not only in human origins, but also within the Pauline powers and principalities evident in the modern world. Barth modernizes apocalyptic by partially blaming the modern horrors of war and his bourgeois society on the powers.[71] The powers seize upon love of earthly things (home, nation, homeland) and turn them into "devilry."[72] The powers are "now at work" to corrupt humanity into thinking its self-sufficiency and privately interested politics were the "greatest achievement of human beings."[73]

Private interests, namely righteousness as self-possession, emerges against God's righteousness. Käsemann takes this central emphasis from Barth and expands upon it with his own emphasis on the righteousness

69. Barth, "October 18, 1914," 147.

70. Barth, "October 18, 1914," 147.

71. Barth writes, "[The powers] are the 'angels, principalities, and powers' of which Paul has spoken. On another occasion he called them the 'spirits that rule in the air' (see Eph 2:2) . . . There are evil powers in the world between heaven and earth, between God and human beings. They are powers of folly, darkness, and destruction. They exert a powerful influence upon humanity that we experience daily in our hearts and lives. They are permitted to exert this influence because God has given them the freedom to do so. In the difficult struggle against them, God's kingdom will be established. We know nothing about them except that we have to struggle with them and overcome them. For they obstruct the access of men and women to God. They are the enemies of love and truth. They will not the kingdom of God but the kingdom of folly and malice. They sow lies, injustice, and violence. Their great strength is to work under the guise of good. They rarely present themselves as they really are; they are disguised almost always as messengers of God. They whisper in the ear, 'People must do evil, so that good will come out of it.' They inspire people to do good, and thereby they use them for their evil purposes. And when they triumph over them, they then end up deep in the night of sin and error, deep in a hell that they create for themselves" ("October 18, 1914," 152).

72. Barth, "October 18, 1914," 152. Emphasis mine.

73. Barth, "October 18, 1914," 152.

of God. Käsemann argues that the present significance of Christ's saving act is the coordinate righteousness bestowed on the believer.[74] Here,
Käsemann argues that the righteousness of God is the power of God, but
it is also a gift bestowed upon humanity.[75] The righteousness bestowed
upon humanity is the righteousness that we receive in our baptism and
that is realized in the moral life.[76] Humanity's God-given righteousness
is under constant assault from the powers of sin and death. It is only
perfected in the final parousia of God. The righteousness of God is not
human autonomy apart from God, but the eschatological ability, much
like Bultmann's existential emphasis, to choose between the "kingdom of
Christ and the kingdom of Satan."[77] The kingdom of Satan is the personification of those powers that cause humanity to stray away from obedience to God. The freedom to choose is not a liberation of the will, as in
Taubes, but a freedom for the good (Rom 7:19). However, being able to
choose also demands that the Christian make this decision anew. It is not
autonomy, but an ever-new walking by faith in which believers receive
grace to realize their faith in action.[78] The righteousness of God posits
a coordinate righteous reality in humanity within creation, where the
power of grace enables Christians to act in obedience to God.[79]

The righteousness of God in Paul, then, unmasks the demonic and
idolatrous powers that possess believers and prevent them from following
the first commandment. Käsemann continues, "The one who is possessed
is the person . . . turned in upon the self, concerned only with the self."[80]
Here the *amor sui* and *voluntas incurvatas* are at work in Käsemann's theology. Furthermore, the one who is bound up in self-love is synonymous
with one possessed by the demonic. The divide between demonic possession and righteousness is an apocalyptic division. The demonic is not
abstract for Käsemann, but embodied through very specific biopolitical

74. Käsemann, "'Righteousness of God' in Paul," 169.

75. Käsemann, through his emphasis on the righteousness of God, is again at
odds with Bultmann, who argues that the biblical witness attests to the righteousness
of God and is the subjective righteousness of God. Käsemann argues it is both the subjective righteousness of God and also the gift God gives to humanity. See Käsemann,
"'Righteousness of God' in Paul," 173n4.

76. Käsemann, "'Righteousness of God' in Paul," 175.

77. Käsemann, "'Righteousness of God' in Paul," 176.

78. Käsemann, "'Righteousness of God' in Paul," 175.

79. Käsemann, "'Righteousness of God' in Paul," 177.

80. Käsemann, "Healing the Possessed," 204.

antinomies of the world. As Käsemann writes, the demonic lies today in "the cries of a humanity for centuries exploited by the white race, herded into the misery of slums and starved there, plagued by epidemic, and for the most part treated worse than cattle."[81] Käsemann's description of racial oppression should recall the construction of racism by Foucault in chapter 1, which is a biopolitical division. The righteousness of God provides an important apocalyptic critique of modernity: In the revelation of the righteousness of God in Christ, the biopolitical powers of modernity, including racism, are unmasked as demonic.

These demonic powers prevent believers from following the *nova obedientia*, particularly when believers fail to obey God in acting justly and lovingly toward God's creatures. Käsemann writes that humans "too often deny the radical fellowship with all creatures of their Lord and his righteousness. Yet creatures have no privileges that exempt them from earthly society."[82] Käsemann asserts that since the apocalyptic incursion of Christ into the cosmos establishes God as the *Cosmocrator*, failing to obey God in the face of the fellow creature is a failure of righteousness. The righteousness of God is a power and a gift that calls believers to abandon the demonic powers that prevents equitable treatment of the neighbor. Käsemann writes,

> The world is delivered over to demonic forces when we ignore the justification of the godless occurring in Christ, when we measure the neighbor or stranger by our worldview and morality instead of by God's mercy, when we reserve the Crucified for ourselves.[83]

These demonic forces, which are inherently private, namely reserving the crucified for ourselves, and self-sufficient, must be interrupted, disturbed, and exorcised in order for the righteousness of God to operate in modern political culture. The righteousness of God, which is revealed (apocalypsed) against ungodliness, posits the possibility of choosing the reign of Christ in a world dominated by sinful, private, and demonic interests. This provides an optic to distinguish between the kingdom of Christ and the kingdom of Satan. The believer is then called to resist the demons unmasked in the revelation of the righteousness of God. The apocalyptic saving event of Christ leads to a demythologization of culture

81. Käsemann, "Healing the Possessed," 201.
82. Käsemann, "Healing the Possessed," 201.
83. Käsemann, "Righteousness of God," 184.

by unmasking cultural demons and calling Christians to a radical obedience to God.

The already-present, revealed righteousness of God in Paul places before believers the radical obedience that is the common good of the church. The righteousness of God serves as that gift that displaces all other meanings, political or otherwise. The righteousness of God is the gift and power of God in the world as the Cosmocrator. It is this reign that is placed before us. The responsibility of obedience to this rule is crucial, especially to those that God is Lord over: fellow creatures. This obedience to the reign of God practically works against the biopolitical organization of political communities by refusing to accept the boundaries and meanings placed in society by the pseudo-sovereign will. The beginning of apocalyptic theology is the already-efficacious righteousness of God made manifest in the apocalyptic incursion of Christ into the cosmos that places before believers the common good of obedience to God's reign.

Though the *already* of the righteousness of God places before the community the common good, I believe the abandonment of a future apocalyptic-eschatological event limits the hope in the lordship of Christ. This returns to Käsemann's earlier question: Can Christian theology exist without such a future hope? I argue that the answer is no, for two main reasons.

First, the obedience suggested by Bultmann and Käsemann, if we follow the thesis that Käsemann softened his *not yet* approach, lacks a clear narrative of how the actions of believers find rest. In Käsemann's own moral theology, the obedient actions of believers are under constant assault from the powers of sin and death. They are only perfected in the *parousia* of Christ. Believers are only left with either a continual tension in obedience or a perpetual revolution where one must achieve the ends of their actions (Taubes). Furthermore, obedience, without the *not yet*, lacks shared ends of political action.

This brings up the question of martyrdom, which further begs the question: do the actions of the martyrs make sense in a world without resurrection of the dead? Käsemann presents a Christian potentiality for righteousness that is tested in obedience. Käsemann states early in his career, "Righteousness is only to be had on earth as a pledged gift, always subject to attack, always to be authenticated in practice—a matter of promise and expectation."[84] Moral and political action, which is correctly called righteousness before God anticipates an end or *telos*, which is not realized by human means but instead realized into humanity from without. Therefore, righteousness is always received as a gift and perpetuated by means of expectation. Even the righteousness that works against the biopolitical righteousness of modernity is always subject to attack. The purpose of perpetual expectation that finds rest in another agency's *telos* is to give new moral and political energies against the ever-new presence of imposed coerciveness found in biopolitical structures.

Second, without a new creation that undoes the deeds of victimization, the hope of apocalyptic theology is incomplete. Paul's hope in Christ's resurrection is not for an "attitude" of hope, but hope in a specific object, namely the resurrection of the dead promised in the resurrection of Christ. Without the undoing of victimization by raising victims of horrendous evil, all the believer is left with is the actions of earthly life. Thus, the victim and the martyr are left somewhat under the meaning-making enterprise of the orders of violence that persecute and execute them. Rather, Christian hope lies in the cry of the faithful in Revelation 6:10 (NRSV): "When will our blood be avenged?" Believers need not only an open future, but also a new creation.

In sum, the *already* of Pauline apocalyptic presents the believer with the current lordship of Christ realized in his apocalyptic incursion into the cosmos. As such, a new righteousness is opened to the world from the place of the crucified and resurrected Lord. Christians are invited into this righteousness through their obedience as authorized through the present lordship of Christ. The activity takes the form of obedience to God which mimics the apocalyptic disruption of the powers by living under a new sovereignty outside the logic and pretension of biopolitics. Here the meanings exercised by biopolitics over individuals is revealed to be radically contingent and false. Rather, as God's creation-wide reign emerges, creatures are reestablished in their creaturely relation to one another. This is not a hierarchical relationship of bodies that matter to ones that do not, but creatures united in equal fellowship under God's sovereign rule. This rule cannot be represented in any creaturely institution and, thus, calls every institution to judgement. The authorization of human righteousness is open to and includes the *not yet*. Without the *not yet*, Christian hope lacks the ability to proclaim good news before the

---

84. Käsemann, "'Righteousness of God' in Paul," 170.

nations and to the oppressed. As such, the *not yet* places before Christians
the fulfillment of their actions and the hope of those long departed.

The *Not Yet* of the Resurrection of the Dead and New Creation

A description of the *not yet* and new creation is best exemplified in the
work of Käsemann's student J. Christiaan Beker. He, like Käsemann before him, insists on the importance of the *not yet* in Paul's apocalyptic
theology. Biblical scholar J. Louis Martyn notes concerning the work of
Käsemann and Beker, "Paul's theology is thoroughly apocalyptic . . . in its
insistence (a) that the world is not yet fully subject to God, even though
(b) the eschatological subjection of the world has already begun, causing
its end to be in sight."[85] Beker remains committed to an apocalyptic *not
yet* because of his concern for theodicy. Only a new creation that restores
victims of evil and sustains certain patterns of habituation offers a coherent political rationality that overcomes powers and biopolitics. The new
creation, therefore, possesses political implications by stating that the
world is not brought to closure by human effort but by God alone.

Beker's insistence on the *not yet* of new creation arises from Paul's
distinct hermeneutics. In Beker's analysis, Paul, in his letters, "relates
the universal truth claim of the gospel directly to the particular situation to which it addressed. His hermeneutic consists in the constant
interaction between the coherent center of the gospel and its contingent
interpretation."[86] Beker states the obvious about Paul's letters: They are
not a fully worked-out systematic theology. Rather, they are specific cor-
respondences addressed to an array of issues in early Christian churches.
Thus, Paul's letters all have an important contextual element that must
be understood. Paul, according to Beker, possesses a *coherent* center that
is nourished by his "primordial experience" of the Christ-event, which
shapes his language and orients him to the not-yet consummated future.
As stated above, and echoed by Beker, the theological structure that informs Paul's language is Jewish apocalyptic.[87] This structure is augmented
by Paul's experience of the Christ-event. This event "nourishes, intensifies, and modifies" Paul's apocalyptic thought, but its christological
reinterpretation makes his apocalyptic almost unrecognizable to Jew-

85. Martyn, "Apocalyptic Antinomies," 113.

86. Beker, *Paul the Apostle*, 11.

87. Beker, *Paul the Apostle*, 15–16.

ish apocalyptic thought. God is presented to Paul apocalyptically in the Christ-event. Therefore, like Webster, Beker reads Paul's coherent center within the self-presentation of God in the Christ-event.

The Christ-event modifies Paul's apocalyptic in a twofold manner. First, it is the revelation of God in Christ's crucifixion and resurrection that inaugurates the triumph of God. Second, the main thrust of Paul's apocalyptic theology is the future immanent fulfillment of God's reign, which results in the resurrection of the dead and the new creation. In the Jewish apocalyptic tradition, there is a clear engagement with powers, but these powers are celestial bodies fighting for the control of creation. In Paul's apocalyptic, Christ engages with the powers of sin and death. Sin and death are not abstract forces lacking the clear personification of demons and heavenly hosts battling for the end-time. Rather, the powers of sin and death are "those ontological powers that determine the human situation within the context of God's created order and comprise the 'field' of death, sin, the law, and the flesh."[88] This understanding of power is exemplified as *exousia*. Christ's death and resurrection inaugurate the victory against these powers, and his return will see this victory's completion.

In Beker's thought, salvation from this present and evil age is not just a distant new creation, but also a new creation in the midst of the present creation.

> The resurrection of Christ has a clear historical-ontological referent in Paul . . . the believer is "a new creation" in Christian (2 Cor. 5:17; Gal. 6:15) and participates in the life of Christ in such a way that his Christian status is visible in the world; nonbelievers confess to the presence of Christ in the church (1 Cor. 14:25) and believers can resist the "deeds of the body" (Rom. 8:13) and can live like "shining lights in the world" (Phil. 3:15).[89]

The lordship of Christ over all creation makes possible the visible life of the believer over and against the ontological historical powers that structure human life against the lordship of Christ. Beker emphasizes the present as an important aspect of apocalyptic and should not be read as idealistically focused on the future. The present sits within a historical continuity between Israel, the resurrection of Christ, and the future

---

88. Beker, *Paul the Apostle*, 145.
89. Beker, *Paul the Apostle*, 151.

apocalyptic in-breaking at the resurrection of the dead even as it is unforeseen from those who initially experienced. Beker writes,

> For Paul, the death and resurrection of Christ are cosmic-ontological events. The resurrection has inaugurated a new ontological reality, that is, the reality of resurrected life as "the new creation" that—however proleptic—has changed the nature of historical reality.[90]

Beker does not place an exclusive emphasis on the *not yet* of Paul's thought. Rather, something has happened in the resurrection of Christ that impacts the believer now.

In order to express this necessary connection between Christ's resurrection and the general resurrection, which fully appreciates the *already* and *not yet* of the Christ-event in Paul, Beker draws upon the theology of 1 Corinthians 15. Beker's use of contingency and coherence is on display in his interpretation of this passage. For Beker, this text is a central marker of Paul's apocalyptic gospel and forms our understanding of the coherent center of apocalyptic.

The internal logic of 1 Corinthians 15 lies in the bodily, future-orientated resurrection of the dead. Beker writes, "When the resurrection of Christ is isolated from its linguistic apocalyptic environment and from the reality of future apocalyptic renewal, it may well retain its traditional nomenclature in exposition of Paul's thought, but it becomes something radically different."[91] According to Beker, understanding the resurrection becomes "docetic" when it fails to impact the transformation of historical processes.[92] The resurrection is not only futurity, but also bodily. Beker continues, "The 'bodily' character of the resurrection manifests the resurrection as an event that not only occur in time but also signals the 'bodily' ontological transformation of the created order in the kingdom of God."[93] The body, namely its materiality, connects it to the rest of the created order as humanity's solidarity with all the created, material order. Thus, the resurrection of the dead is essential to 1 Corinthians 15 and the formation of the coherent center of Paul's apocalyptic gospel.

The resurrection of Christ and the resurrection of the dead are joined together in 1 Corinthians 15. As Beker writes, "It cannot be too strongly

---

90. Beker, *Paul the Apostle*, 196.
91. Beker, *Paul the Apostle*, 155.
92. Beker, *Paul the Apostle*, 155.
93. Beker, *Paul the Apostle*, 159.

emphasized that Paul's thought is motivated by the future consummation as God's goal with history and creation."[94] The final consummation is a part of a historical trajectory that includes all that has come before. It is the gathering together of those who have gone (Eccl 3:15) and deals with historical evil. This is of great significance for Beker.

> The historicity of the resurrection of Christ and its "bodily" character are crucial. The historicity of the resurrection signifies it's eschatological-temporal significance, that is, it is a proleptic event that inaugurates the new creation. The "bodily" character of the resurrection manifests the resurrection as an event that not only occurs in time but also signals the "bodily" ontological transformation of the created order in the kingdom of God. Therefore, the resurrection of Christ is both crucial and yet provisional. It is crucial because it marks the beginning of the new creation; it is provisional because it looks forward to the consummation of that beginning.[95]

The resurrection of Christ and the general resurrection are understood together, not apart. Beker argues that, in 1 Corinthians 15, Paul's theology of Christ's resurrection gestures toward the promise of the future resurrection of the dead. Without both Christ's resurrection and the future general resurrection of the dead, "we are to be most pitied" (1 Cor 15:19, NRSV). Yet the resurrection of Christ already inaugurates the new creation. Beker draws from A. M. Hunter's description of the resurrection as allusion to D-Day and V-Day in World War II.[96] History after D-Day continued, but the Axis Powers were dealt a blow from which there was no recovery, and V-Day was assured. D-Day and V-Day taken together illustrate the connection between Christ's resurrection and creation's own resurrection. In Christ's resurrection, the powers were dealt a blow from which they cannot recover and the resurrection of the dead is assured. The decisive nature of Christian existence in the *already* is one of hope.

Hope is the intelligibility under which Paul places all actions. For example, the martyrs who committed faithful actions in response to the righteousness of God must have an intelligible fulfillment of their actions. God has a responsibility to undo the evil done in history. As Käsemann established, the righteousness of God must be fulfilled, and those under constant assault by the powers of sin and death must find their rest. The

---

94. Beker, *Paul the Apostle*, 176.

95. Beker, *Paul the Apostle*, 159.

96. Beker, *Paul the Apostle*, 159.

martyr faces death out of a love for a world that is promised, despite the
evil committed against them, and in full knowledge that the kingdom of
God does not come through their actions. Neither the martyrs nor any
believer can bring about the resurrection of the dead. They can only, as
the Greek meaning of martyr (μαρτυρέω) indicates, "bear witness." The
martyrs are not venerated in order to become moral exemplars. Rather,
they are venerated because they are witness to the new creation and
Christ's lordship, namely the resurrection of the dead and the new creation. If the dead are not raised and the general resurrection is false, then
they are to be most pitied because they have tragically perished (1 Cor
15:16–19). The resurrection of the dead is not only a necessary element
to understand Christ's resurrection, but also the actions of the faithful.

It is not just the actions and lives of the martyrs that find fulfillment in the new creation and the resurrection of the dead, but also all
righteous actions taken up by the believers. Paul writes, "I am sure that
he who began a good work in you will bring it to completion at the day of
Jesus Christ" (Phil 1:6, NRSV). This recalls Käsemann's statement on the
righteousness of God, that "even the gift of divine righteousness does not
bring us to the goal, but only sets our feet upon the road . . . and has to
be continually appropriated anew . . . as the reflection of the fact that the
ultimate righteousness of God is still to be realized."[97] Righteousness is
not completed, but must be continually practiced and put to the test. The
juxtaposition here of "began" and "completion" fits within Beker's understanding of Paul's apocalyptic theology. Commentator John Reumann
writes that this represents "God's activity all the way, in the gospel process
of bringing the Philippians to faith and sustaining them until God's work
with them is completed."[98] Faith exists in eschatological tension, where
God works together with believers in their work.[99] Good actions must
have a fulfillment or completion in God, according to Paul.

The logic of completed actions in God's coming reign is central to
Paul's apocalyptic theology. However, there is another equally important
aspect of Beker's analysis of Paul's apocalyptic: justice for victims that
are not martyrs per se. It is a new creation that finally realizes justice for
victims of violence and horrors. Käsemann interprets the righteousness
of God not only as the justifying gift and power of God, but also the later

97. Käsemann, "'Righteousness of God' in Paul," 170.

98. Reumann, *Philippians*, 151.

99. Reumann, *Philippians*, 151.

Käsemann understands righteousness to include God's command to care for the ones Christ has been given as Lord, and especially to those who are history's victims. Beker, as well as Käsemann, include new creation as the fulfillment of righteousness. For example, Beker references the cry of the martyrs in the book of Revelation: "O Sovereign Lord, holy and true, how long before you will judge and avenge our blood on those who dwell on the earth?" (Rev 6:10, NRSV) According to Beker, this reflects a Pauline concern for those who have died as witnesses to Christ, who have enacted, as it were, the ultimate command to righteousness.[100] It would be unjust for their deaths not to be set right.

Justice for the martyrs extends, I argue, to victims of injustice. If, as Käsemann argues, God is given to the victims of violence in this way and shows the utmost concern for them to the extent that it is a command to serve them, then in the fulfillment of righteousness—which Beker already affirms in the lives of the martyrs—these too must be set right, given justice, and raised up from their graves. The coming reign of God must include justice for victims. If it is God's prerogative to fulfill the righteousness of our actions and our actions directed toward those in whom God has given himself as Lord, then God affirms these whom history has victimized and realizes their justice in the new creation. This does not mean that it is less of a command to seek out victims and pursue their justice in the *already*. Quite the contrary; doing so is a means of witness (μαρτυρέω), much like the martyrs, to a coming new creation that fulfills all righteousness, including the righteousness due to victims. The insistence of justice for martyrs and victims of historical violence helps locate the radical independence of God's agency against the powers and rulers of this age showing that no part of creation is or will be lost to God. The powers, in the biopolitical form, cannot claim for itself the bodies of its victims. Instead, to quote the author of the Ecclesiastes, "God seeks out what has gone by" (Eccl 3:15, NRSV). Thus, I conclude that Beker's interpretation of Paul's vision of fulfilled righteousness realizes the goodness God intends by creating a community established by righteousness for those who are victims.

If Beker is correct about the necessity of God to bring to completion good works, then this means confronting what faithful actions are and rejecting a narrative of what theologian John Howard Yoder calls

---

100. Beker, *Paul's Apocalyptic Gospel*, 47.

"effectiveness."[101] The fact that God, not humanity, must finally fulfill the righteousness of God revealed into our bodies means questioning whether "we are adequately informed to be able to set for ourselves and for all society the goal toward which we seek to move it."[102] Humans are not equipped to determine or fulfill human ends. Yoder recognizes that this narrative of "effectiveness" is often what prevents the contemporary world from recognizing the normativity of Christ's ethical pronouncements.

To cure this ailment of effectiveness, Yoder himself turns to apocalyptic. Yoder recognizes that there are things yet to be revealed that cannot be weighed by the individual and can only come to us by way of apocalypse.[103] Apocalyptic troubles empirical moral claims, but this is not an excuse for quietism. Though believers don't know all that will be revealed, they are given clues in Christ's life. The intimacy between Christ's resurrection and the coming reign of God cannot be understated. Yoder writes, "the crucified Jesus is a more adequate key to understanding what God is about in the real world of empires and armies and markets."[104] This well summarizes Paul's emphasis on completing a good work. The believer is always, according to Beker, "regress[ing] to the foot of the cross" in order to perform faithful good works, which only find "confirmation in God's coming glory."[105] Beker's understanding of human agency in response to God's coming triumph is a constant appeal to what will be.

The necessity of a persistent hope outside the grasp of humanity is an affront to private interest and self-sufficiency. Reflecting the apocalyptic expectations of the early Käsemann, the apocalyptic gift of righteousness is beyond our grasp.[106] The bodily resurrection of the dead, as understood by Beker, places before each human a shared end in which all activities, political or otherwise, find their rest and end. As such, the political activity of the church cannot be subject to the private interests of a few because the entire created order in the resurrection of the dead is subject to God's reign. Our political activities must be coordinate to that end in faithfulness, rather than what might be effective toward the

101. Yoder, *Politics of Jesus*, 230, 246.

102. Yoder, *Politics of Jesus*, 229–30.

103. Yoder, *Politics of Jesus*, 245.

104. Yoder, *Politics of Jesus*, 246.

105. Beker, *Paul the Apostle*, 290. This is also the optic through which Agamben's economy of glory must be critiqued.

106. Käsemann, "'Righteousness of God' in Paul," 170.

end of our political, self-sufficient power such as technologies of the self, biopolitics, private interest, and sovereignty.

Beker provides an understanding of Paul's apocalyptic theology as grounded in not just what Christ has done, but in a thorough ongoing expectation for a future new creation and resurrection of the dead. Though Beker wants to augment this message to fit our contemporary time, he does so with a persistent emphasis that to remove a future expectation of God's completed reign would strip Paul of his message. The new creation is helpful in that it provides a tangible fulfillment of creation not bound with the private interests of humanity. One of the strengths of Beker's argument is that he insists that apocalyptic celebrates the interruption of the self-sufficient human. The new creation must be something that happens independent of human willing. Rather, it arises from God's saving action alone. Beker provides a trenchant analysis of Paul's theology in his insistence on God's coming reign.

Apocalyptic in the Academy Today: Congdon, Martyn, and Gorman

Though Beker comes after the work of Käsemann and Bultmann, he is not the last to engage the apocalyptic Paul. In the last several decades since Beker's work, new figures have emerged to develop new trajectories of Paul's apocalyptic theology. These figures have their own commitments to apocalyptic and biblical interpretation. It must be noted that, for the most part, the main interpreters of the apocalyptic Paul are almost exclusively interested in the *already*. This does not mean that the *not yet* is absent or unimportant. Rather, it is that the apocalyptic of the *already* is much more popular in today's academy.

David Congdon is one who argues that the *already* is more popular. For Congdon, there are two clear schools of apocalyptic. First, we have Apocalyptic A, which is primarily the early Käsemann and Beker. This group defines apocalyptic as "something literal, immanent, and directly observable."[107] This is contrasted with Apocalyptic B, which is comprised of figures such as Martyn, the later Käsemann, Kerr, and Morse. This group defines apocalyptic "as something nonliteral, transcendent, and indirectly or paradoxically present."[108] Congdon's distinctions are his own,

107. Congdon, "Eschatologizing Apocalyptic," 132.
108. Congdon, "Eschatologizing Apocalyptic," 132.

but they help show, for the most part in the academy, that a line has been drawn in apocalyptic scholarship.

The reason for maintaining this division in apocalyptic lies in Congdon's rediscovery of Bultmann. What this acknowledges is that each theologian, even when interpreting Paul, relies on certain theological figures and perspectives. For example, Bultmann relies on Luther. This names his theological commitments. Likewise, Congdon makes a decisive turn back to Bultmann with some apocalyptic resituating. Congdon levies a Bultmannian critique against Beker's apocalyptic interpretation of Paul. Congdon argues that the resounding shift to the *already*, the expectation of a literal imminent end, has no future in the academy.[109] According to Congdon, Bultmann's original hesitation in accepting apocalyptic lies in its mythical understanding of the end of the world. Congdon argues that Bultmann's objection is that apocalyptic "fixes the *telos* of history at a particular point in chronological time . . . and claims to describe the specific form that this chronological *telos* will take."[110] The objection lies in a linear picture of history, to which Beker appeals, that progress to a predetermined conclusion is the subject of objective inquiry.

Congdon, utilizing Bultmann, denies Apocalyptic A where the present is qualified by the future. He reverses the claim by Beker that the immanent end of the world is what gives the present meaning. Quoting Bultmann, Congdon writes, "As true as it is today—that is, against the enthusiastic pneumatics—that present eschatology is 'anchored and qualified' [*verankert und eingeschränkt*] by apocalyptic, it is, in my opinion, also true to say, conversely, that apocalyptic eschatology is anchored and qualified by the present."[111] Instead of an objective view of the end of history, which Bultmann claims inevitably falls into speculation, Congdon argues that Bultmann only makes more intelligible the original apocalyptic position of Käsemann: to clarify Christ's lordship. Rather than speculation, Congdon argues that apocalyptic is best understood under an originally Bultmannian position that "Christ's reign is understood as his lordship over me."[112] Congdon argues that, by locating apocalyptic away from Beker and the early Käsemann to Bultmann, one no longer has to accept a literal end as the central theme of apocalyptic.

109. See Congdon, "Eschatologizing Apocalyptic," 118–27.

110. Congdon, "Eschatologizing Apocalyptic," 122.

111. Bultmann, "Ist die Apokalyptik die Mutter," quoted in Congdon, "Eschatologizing Apocalyptic," 122.

112. Congdon, "Eschatologizing Apocalyptic," 122.

To the contrary, by celebrating Christ as continually at hand, one can appreciate the present saving power of the Christ-event. Congdon writes that the "Christ-event transfigures history for the one who faithfully participates in it."[113] Apocalyptic as a means to interpret Christ's lordship over creation is existential and eschatological, always coming in a nonliteral fashion. Therefore, Congdon advocates for an apocalyptic not concerned with "when and what."[114] Rather, it is solely focused on the "who, namely, the crucified Christ, who is the wholly other in our midst, the transcendent one who continually breaks anew into our immanent situation. The 'when' is always *now*, and the 'what' is always *new*."[115] Therefore, Congdon advocates an existential interpretation of the apocalyptic message more fitting to modern culture for the sake of engaging in a missional work to modern culture.[116]

In addition to Congdon, J. Louis Martyn is a central figure credited with transitioning Beker's emphasis on the *not yet* back to the *already*. To be fair, Martyn does make a place for the *not yet*, but he attempts a more cosmic interpretation of the *already* not expressed in terms of pure obedience. Martyn shifts the cosmic scope of Beker and the early Käsemann onto Galatians as Paul's central apocalyptic text. Beker argued that the apocalyptic immanent end of the world is repressed in Galatians and instead focuses on an eschatological present.[117] Beker's thesis (to his detriment, according to Martyn) relegates Galatians to a "hermeneutical supplement to Romans," thus repressing the apocalyptic gospel of Paul.[118] Martyn overturns this assumption, placing Galatians at the center of Paul's apocalyptic gospel through its constant depiction that the "gospel is a matter of apocalypse (1:12, 16; 2:2, 5, 14)."[119] Through the implementation of Galatians as central to Paul's apocalyptic, Martyn argues that Christ's victory over the powers is a radical incursion into a fallen world, rather than the salvation-historical approach offered by Beker. The crucifixion of Christ means "the death of . . . the cosmos . . . in which all

---

113. Congdon, "Eschatologizing Apocalyptic," 125.

114. Congdon, "Eschatologizing Apocalyptic," 135.

115. Congdon, "Eschatologizing Apocalyptic," 135. Emphasis original.

116. For more, see Congdon, *Mission of Demythologizing*, 247–438.

117. Beker, *Paul the Apostle*, 37–58.

118. Beker, *Paul the Apostle*, 35.

119. Martyn, "Review of *Paul the Apostle*," 196.

human beings live."[120] Christ's advent is a present victory in which believers struggle against a new set of antinomies. Rather than the antinomy between the present age and the age to come in traditional apocalyptic language, Martyn shows that in Christ's death and resurrection the new antinomy is between the flesh and the Spirit (Gal 5). There is a present new creation in Christ that is more than a proleptic promise.

Though Martyn argues for the present significance of Christ's lordship, it would be a misreading of Martyn's critique of Beker and early Käsemann to conclude that he only sees the present significance of Paul's apocalyptic. "Paul's apocalyptic perspective . . . has, in fact, three foci: Christ's future coming, Christ's past advent (his death and resurrection), and the present war against the powers of evil, inaugurated by his Spirit and taking place between these two events."[121] Clearly, Martyn was not closed off to an apocalyptic future, but attempts to reorient how one speaks of the apocalyptic *already*. Martyn's work, then, must be read as an attempt to correct the inequitable emphasis on the *not yet*, through the opening of the present to a cosmic *already*. This trifold depiction of Paul's apocalyptic flows from his previous critique of Beker and Käsemann: apocalyptic must focus on the present change that the resurrection has enacted as the final defeat of his enemies (1 Cor 15). Martyn writes,

> If Paul is sure that Christ's Parousia will bring the final victory of God over all his enemies (1 Cor. 15), he is no less sure that Christ's advent has commenced the way that will lead to that victory. Thus, in an anticipatory but altogether real sense, Christ's advent is that victory, even if its victorious character can be seen only in the bifocal vision of apocalyptic. Christ's advent has already changed the world, commending God's war of liberation in a way that can be celebrated in "enthusiastic" terms, without forgetting the future of Christ (Gal. 5:5). Specifically, both God's sending of Christ to suffer death on behalf of humanity (the cross) and Christ's future coming (the Parousia) are invasive acts of God. And their being invasive acts—into a space that has temporarily fallen out of God's hands—points to the liberating war that is crucial to Paul's apocalyptic theology.[122]

Martyn shows that the *already* and *not yet* do not have to be isolated from one another. Both are invasive acts of God, which confirms Beker and

120. Martyn, "Apocalyptic Antinomies," 119.
121. Martyn, *Galatians*, 105.
122. Martyn, *Galatians*, 105. Emphasis original.

describes the *already* in a cosmic way. Both point to the same liberative activity of God to free creation from powers foreign to it. Christ saves creation in the present from the powers of sin and death. Here, history is not a linear timeline culminating in the eschaton; it has been invaded. Christ has brought the world under God's own lordship. This intensity of invasion must be read inside the tension of the covenant to Israel. These are not mutually contradictory aspects that confess exclusive understandings of the Christ event. Rather, the means by which God achieves the fulfillment of the covenant to Israel is an unforeseen incursion. As such, this already-present lordship of Christ must be given not only its eschatological consummation, but also its Jewish roots. There is a present liberation that must be acknowledged as attested to in the Galatian correspondence, even as one awaits the final invasion of God into the cosmos.

Martyn's work intensifies my claim that the *already* provides believers with an understanding of the common good. By emphasizing the cosmic war between Spirit and flesh, the believer is called to resist forms of this world that are passing away, namely those political norms which do not fit the righteousness of God. Thus, Martyn helps clarify and expand Käsemann's original intention and implicitly entrenches the political response Paul offers to biopolitics and private interests.

In addition to Martyn, Michael Gorman reintroduces covenant as a central apocalyptic concept. Gorman's argument agrees with the critiques of Martyn, but extends beyond Martyn by reintroducing Israel as central to Paul's apocalyptic theology. Drawing on the prophetic words of Jeremiah and Ezekiel, Gorman argues, along with Martyn, that Paul's apocalyptic takes on the form of a new covenant. The language of a new covenant comes from Jeremiah: "But this is the covenant that I will make with the house of Israel after those days, says the Lord: I will put my law within them, and I will write it on their hearts; and I will be their God, and they shall be my people" (31:33, NRSV). The language of covenant and heart is not limited to this passage; it extends to Ezekiel's emphasis on a new spirit (Ezek 11:19; 18:31; 36:26). Covenant language, for Gorman, helpfully locates "the new covenant . . . [as] a powerful act of divine grace entailing the people's receipt of the Law or the Spirit within, their inner transformation, and their consequent faithfulness to the covenant."[123] The language envisioned by Ezekiel and Jeremiah yields an image of humanity cleansed, forgiven, and restored. Ezekiel 36–37 also speaks to a

123. Gorman, "Apocalyptic New Covenant," 321.

resurrection and new creation, but of "restored land and the abundant living."[124] The language of prophetic speech is a holistic picture of living, according to Jeremiah: "they shall be my people and I will be their God" (24:7, NRSV). As Gorman writes, the prophets display "sort of a divine incursion—in other words, as an apocalyptic event" in their description of the new covenant.[125] Gorman suggests that this Jewish theological imagination informs Paul's apocalyptic theology.

Gorman, utilizing Martyn, argues that this Jewish covenantal theology is central to understanding Paul's apocalyptic language. Like Martyn, Gorman works with Galatians as centrally insightful. Gorman understands this language of new covenant as a divine incursion, expressed first in Paul's conversion at Damascus in Galatians 2:15–21. Gorman writes that Paul's crucifixion with Christ signals his "nomistically determined self was ended and a new life begun."[126] Gorman notices two uses of ἐνέμοί ("to me") in Galatians 1:15–16a and 2:20. Echoing New Testament scholar Martinus de Boer, Gorman suggests that, in Galatians 1:15–16a, "ἀποκαλύψαι τὸν Υἱὸν αὐτοῦ ἐνέμοί" ("to reveal his Son to me"), the "ἐνέμοί" ("to me") takes a locative meaning, signifying that the location of the Son's apocalypse is not just in Paul as a subjective experience, but in Paul's former manner of life.[127] Therefore, Paul represents the turn of the ages in his own person. He once lived a life to the law; now he lives only to Christ. The event of Christ has begun a new age not determined in nomistic fashion, but christologically. Paul is the chief example.

The second use of ἐνέμοί ("to me") comes in Galatians 2:20. Gorman argues this second usage differs because Paul is referring to his apostolic ministry.[128] Gorman asserts de Boer understands this apostolicity to include the inner disposition of God's dwelling in the believer, which is in line with Galatians 4:6 (NRSV): "And because you are children, God has sent the Spirit of his Son into our hearts crying 'Abba! Father!'" Paul's apostolic ministry highlights, Gorman writes, "the public domain of human affairs and interpersonal relationships."[129] This holds together an existential experience of God sending the Son into our hearts and pos-

124. Gorman, "Apocalyptic New Covenant," 321–22.
125. Gorman, "Apocalyptic New Covenant," 322.
126. Gorman, "Apocalyptic New Covenant," 323.
127. Gorman, "Apocalyptic New Covenant," 322–23.
128. Gorman, "Apocalyptic New Covenant," 324.
129. Gorman, "Apocalyptic New Covenant," 324.

sesses a wider inclusion of all people, a new community of both Jew and
gentile, concerned with a new center of gravity and in which humans
recognize each other as fellow children of God. Gorman recognizes this
Pauline language as covenantal language. Galatians 4:6 and its language
of kinship to God and God's sending of the Spirit of Christ echoes themes
in Jeremiah and Ezekiel. Extending beyond de Boer, Gorman proposes

> that Paul's self-portrayal as the apocalyptically "invaded" perse-
> cutor, crucified (and raised) with the Messiah, is simultaneously
> a self-portrayal as the recipient of the surprising Spirit of the
> new covenant that enables him, and all believers, to embody the
> cruciform patter of the Messiah's self-giving love.[130]

Paul's self-witness to an apocalyptic new covenant in his own being, liberated by the invasive actions of Christ and the Spirit, reveals a new possibility of life in community conforming to a particular cruciform lifestyle.
Therefore, apocalyptic includes a covenantal language whereby believers
are given the Spirit of Christ and a new law is etched on their hearts. It
is invasive because it intrudes upon the old, nomistically ordered world,
and centers the world on the crucified and resurrected Lord.

Gorman's study also yields a more robust drama unfolding at the
center of what he calls the new "intimate bond between God and the
people."[131] Returning to Galatians 4, Gorman notes a particular unity of
persons that apocalyptically intrudes on humanity. Gorman recognizes
the apocalyptic language that begins Galatians 4:4–6, namely "in the fullness of time" (4:4a). Gorman recognizes this preface as a very apocalyptic
statement, showing a coming to close one age and beginning of another.
However, the intruding, saving event of Christ occurs amid our enslave-
ment to powers of sin in the world (Gal 4:3). The liberation of humanity
occurs in two steps. First God sends the Son into the world and, second,
sends the Spirit of the Son into believers' hearts.[132] The close tie between
the sending of the Son and the Spirit is not accidental. Here, three members are qualified by each other. The Son is qualified by the Father in being sent to impact the adoption or sonship of all children. It is by this that
believers can call God Abba, Father. Furthermore, it is by the Spirit that
this adoption is "existentially" realized.[133] Gorman concludes, "So what

---

130. Gorman, "Apocalyptic New Covenant," 324.

131. Gorman, "Apocalyptic New Covenant," 326.

132. Gorman, "Apocalyptic New Covenant," 325.

133. Gorman, "Apocalyptic New Covenant," 325.

we have, finally, is an apocalyptic new covenant in which, at the initiative of God the Father, Christ affects humanity's liberation and redemption, and the Spirit establishes and maintains a residential new-covenant relationship between God the Father and God's adopted children."[134]

Gorman writes that the trinitarian identification of God is "impossible to resist."[135] The proposed Pauline relationship between humanity and God mirrors a prophetic covenantal relationship between our ability to intimately call God "Abba" and God's prophetic being with God's people so that they might be with God (Jer 31:33). This is a new place of intimacy with God at the center. Humans are gathered around this site as children, no longer divided according to Jew or gentile (Gal 3:28). Though connected to the past, Jewish theology of the apocalyptic new covenant is a "disruptive continuity," which locates the new center of intimacy within the triune God rather than the law.[136] The community that bears the meaning of this apocalypse must reveal a new level of intimacy to the world.

Gorman offers an expansion on a political theme important to Pauline apocalyptic, namely the place of difference in political theology. As noted in chapter 1, the new approach struggles to depict how Paul understands his Jewish heritage in relation to the apocalyptic invasion into the cosmos. Badiou suggests that the event Paul signals is a third universal category beyond the designation of Jew and gentile. Yet, Pauline apocalyptic, as depicted by Gorman, is covenantal in nature. This suggests that Paul is not superseding Judaism; rather, he is opening up Judaism for the gentiles. The invasion of Christ into the cosmos fulfills Old Testament prophecy by not ending Judaism, but inviting gentiles into Israel's covenant through its Messiah. According to theologian Willie Jennings,

> Jesus's election . . . becomes the stage on which Israel's God will make known the intensity and depth of the Holy One's journey with Israel and God's great love for the elect people. From the womb of a virgin, God will announce a reality of newness placed in the midst of Israel's conventional cultural realities. The scandal of this claim is bound tightly to the scandal of Israel's existence as the people of God. Jesus's election is not an election next to or in competition with the election of Israel, but an election in the heart of Israel's space, displaying the trajectory

134. Gorman, "Apocalyptic New Covenant," 327.

135. Gorman, "Apocalyptic New Covenant," 327.

136. Gorman, "Apocalyptic New Covenant," 337.

of the Holy One toward communion with the elect. Just as Israel's election ruptures Gentile space (and time), breaking open knowledge and reorientating truth, so does Jesus's election bring to Israel a rupture. This rupture, however, is not the destruction or eradication of Israel's knowledge, its theological truth. This rupture breaks open their story and reveals a deeper layer for how Israel should understand birth, family, and lineage. Jesus is both Son of David and Son of God. The God who created the first family of Israel is now in Israel recreating the family.[137]

Jennings helps narrate the way that difference is accommodated in Pauline apocalyptic. The apocalyptic invasion of Christ attested to in Paul gives the definitive posture for how Christianity relates to that which is different. At the heart of Pauline political theology is a deep filiation of difference—the coexistence of two very different identities within a singular event. This is not far from Badiou's own philosophy, but Paul's apocalyptic theology differs from Badiou by not leaving difference to indifference. The opening of Judaism to the gentiles signals that the apocalyptic political objective is not to void the political meaning of identity. It is an invitation to be shaped and formed by another's identity within this one family of God around the new center of intimacy that is the triune life. Therefore, the apocalyptic-covenantal theology of Paul allows for both a synthesis of the *already* and *not yet* and a political posture toward the neighbor not bound to modern problems.

In sum, these contemporary discussions of Pauline theology by Congdon, Gorman, and Martyn recapitulates and clarifies the positions of the *already* and *not yet* as bound together. Both are central to Paul's apocalyptic theology. The history of interpretation offered in this chapter reveals an oscillation to varying degrees between emphasizing the *not yet* to the *already* and back since the beginning of the twentieth century. The purpose of this display is to show the ways that the *already* and *not yet* need each other. Each critic insists that there must be a real change in the life of the world and believer as a result of the life, crucifixion, and resurrection of Jesus that exceeds a proleptic hope. This change confronts all realities already immanent to political forces. As such, the apocalyptic gospel challenges what type of political life define believers.

137. Jennings, *Christian Imagination*, 264–65.

THE *ALREADY* AND *NOT YET*: A WESLEYAN SYNTHESIS OF PAUL'S APOCALYPTIC THEOLOGY

Paul's apocalyptic theology is the subject of serious conversation. There is a debate, as Congdon illustrates, whether the *already* or the *not yet* is individually efficacious, but historically they belong together. Therefore, this dichotomy is misplaced. Christ is lord over the powers now, but it is also correct to insist on "the objective reality of the coming kingdom, and . . . that Paul's theology of hope does not center in the *attitude* of hope, but especially in the *object* of hope . . . [the apocalyptic] coming triumph of God."[138] One must recognize how intimately Christ's resurrection is tied to the general resurrection of the dead. There must be a new creation and a resurrection of the dead in order to complete a believer's faith in Christ's resurrection.

This synthesis is possible due to a Wesleyan hermeneutic. Most figures who approach Paul with an apocalyptic interpretation are Lutherans. These Lutherans have a specific orientation to apocalyptic as a means to describe justification by faith alone, that the righteousness of God is a means to overcome the self-centered, prideful human in the face of sin. However, John Wesley holds a slightly different view, which does not exclude Luther but rather extends the necessity of the *already* and *not yet* in Paul.

> Who has wrote more ably than Martin Luther on justification by faith alone? And who was more ignorant of the doctrine of sanctification, or more confused in his conceptions of it? In order to be thoroughly convinced of this, of his total ignorance with regard to sanctification, there needs no more than to read over, without prejudice, his celebrated comment on the Epistle to the Galatians.[139]

Wesley offers a hermeneutic of sanctification as a critical response to Luther's hermeneutic of justification by faith. Despite Wesley's criticism, he was very much appreciative of Luther's work. Wesley's praise of Luther comes from personal experience. It was during a reading of Luther's commentary of Romans on May 24, 1738, that Wesley experienced an assurance of his salvation. Wesley upholds much of Luther's understanding

---

138. Beker, *Paul the Apostle*, xix.
139. Wesley, "On God's Vineyard," 204.

of justification by faith, but with some minor augmentations.[140] Most notably, and apparent in the above quote, is Wesley's emphasis on sanctification. For Wesley, justification is not only a matter of faith, but proved in good works. Wesley believes that justification is fundamentally a gift by grace and agrees with Luther that justification by faith speaks directly against the self-sufficient, privately interested humanity that was produced in the fall. But Wesley extends this to sanctification in order to move the focus from sheer obedience to gracious transformation to enabling the willing of the will of God.

To illustrate the difference between a Wesleyan interpretation of apocalyptic and the Lutheran standard interpretation, I return to Bultmann's Lutheran commitments. Bultmann's demythologizing project is a result of a Lutheran hermeneutical commitment to justification by faith alone.[141] Bultmann's main critique of apocalyptic is its objectifying capture of the future. Rather than the believer objectifying the future, Bultmann writes,

> For [the believer] who is open to all that is future as the future of the coming God, death has lost its terror. He will refrain from painting in the future which God bestows in death, for all pictures of a glory after death can only be the wishful images of imagination and to forego all wishful images is part of the radical openness of faith in God's future.[142]

This eschatological posture is an act of faith, which does not seek a literal picture but walks into death faithfully.

Faith in Bultmann's interpretation of Luther is an act of obedience.[143] This is clear in Bultmann's de-objectified, demythologized eschatological faith, which calls for radical obedience. Wesley's account of eschatology, justification by faith, and the interim between differs. Wesley faulted Luther in his lack of theology of sanctification. This is Wesley's alternative to demythologization for the sake of obedience. Wesley believes that the Holy Spirit's therapeutic presence heals our damaged humanity. Like the

---

140. For a concise description of Wesley's view on justification by faith, see Maddox, *Responsible Grace*, 148–51.

141. I thank Charles Cosgrove for his assistance in helping me recognize this Lutheran element of Bultmann.

142. Bultmann, "Christian Hope," 278.

143. Consequently, this is also a key element of Käsemann's demythologization, that all ideology and mythology is demythologized for the sake of radical obedience in faith.

apocalyptic Paul, Wesley argues that, as a result of the fall, humanity is now subject to an alien power, though Wesley understands this more as an infirmity in our nature. The consistency between the two, however, is that something infringes on our ability to obey God. Rather than a hermeneutic demythologization and justification by faith, Wesley argues, through a hermeneutic of sanctification, that the presence of the Holy Spirit enables a renewing of the human condition itself through its death. This is the difference between Luther and Wesley. Wesleyan scholar and theologian Randy Maddox writes,

> If fallen humanity were left to respond to God's initiative from our own resources we would never overcome our spiritual infirmity, because our faculties are debilitated. For this reason God has graciously provided not only pardon but also a renewed empowering presence in our lives.[144]

This is crucial because such a presence creates a "habitual disposition of soul . . . [which] is termed holiness."[145] The Holy Spirit encourages love in the believer that enables love of God, but this love of God must be taken up in the believer in practice or, as Wesley argues, in the means of grace. This is the process of sanctification whereby fallen powers are overcome in concrete practice and the therapy of the Holy Spirit. Maddox contends that Wesley "became convinced that we *can* love God only in response to our awareness of God's salvific love for us."[146]

The importance of this for Wesley's apocalyptic cannot be understated. Here emerges a deep affinity between Augustine, apocalyptic, and Wesley. The *amor sui* is overcome only by the enticing love of the Holy Spirit which transforms bent, unholy tempers into the *amor Dei*. Wesley's account of sanctification is a means to overcome the influence of the powers, private interests, and self-love that prevents the *summum bonum*. If the powers are at work, according to Wesley so is grace, which is nonetheless a power.[147]

Wesley's account of sanctification is apocalyptic in its ability to resist the powers through an ever-increasing love of God in the present. This mirrors Gorman's trinitarian account of apocalyptic. The Spirit of the Son is sent into the hearts of believers so that we might cry "Abba Father!"

---

144. Maddox, *Responsible Grace*, 119.

145. Wesley, "Circumcision of the Heart," 25.

146. Maddox, *Responsible Grace*, 174.

147. For more on grace as "power," see Boer, "Paul's Mythologizing Program," 20.

(Gal 4:6). This is already an apocalyptic disruption of the sinful order of the world that enables the love of God and the *summum bonum*. In addition to the Spirit's apocalyptic disruption, Wesley also emphasizes the *not yet* eschatological transformation of the cosmos through a hermeneutic of sanctification. Wesley articulates a therapeutic recuperating of damaged sinful humanity that sanctifies the believer for the *amor Dei* that does not just pardon or justify the sinner. One can be free of sin in the present as one grows in love.

One is called to obey and put off selfishness in faith and will grow in grace in sanctification. However, this does not mean that Wesley has no use of eschatology. Wesley also argues that sanctification is incomplete without the new creation and the resurrection of the dead.

> It will not always be thus: these things are only permitted for a season by the great Governor of the world, that he may draw immense, eternal good out of this temporary evil ... It is enough we are assured of this one point, that all these transient evils will issue well, will have a happy conclusion, and that "Mercy first and last will reign"
>
> ... And we have strong reason to hope that the work he hath begun he will carry on unto the day of his Lord Jesus; that he will never intermit this blessed work of his Spirit until he has fulfilled all his promises; until he hath put a period to sin and misery, and infirmity, and death; and reestablished universal holiness and happiness, and caused all the inhabitants of the earth to sing together, "Hallelujah! The Lord God omnipotent reigneth!" "Blessing, and glory, and wisdom, and honour, and power, and might be unto God for ever and ever!"[148]

Wesley is clear: the work of sanctification progresses and culminates in a new creation. This new creation is determined by God's reign and frees creation from sin and death. Wesley operates with an apocalyptic eschatology where three things are assured. First, evil is temporary. Second, God reigns. Third, all things will be fulfilled in the new creation. Wesley believes that God will remove that which impinges upon the created order, that which prevents universal holiness and happiness.

This Wesleyan hermeneutic operates by connecting the apocalyptic *already* to the *not yet* in a way I assume to be present in the rest of this work. Though Bultmann and Käsemann offer a more demythologized picture centered on justification by faith, and Beker's answer to theodicy

---

148. Wesley, "General Spread," 499.

includes the removal of the powers, both cohere in Wesley. In the *already*, the Holy Spirit sheds the love of God abroad in our hearts and makes love of God (*amor Dei*) possible. It is not obedience, but the actual rehabilitation of our capacity to love God. This is sanctification. Wesley places sanctification as a unique work of the Holy Spirit and ontologically locates our action within the action of another. In other words, the Holy Spirit is now the active power of God's eschatological reign.[149] Our activity comes to completion not in our work, but from the God who draws creation to its completion. Wesley describes it in a manner much akin to the apocalyptic thinkers of the *not yet*. He writes, "And to crown it all, there will be a deep, an intimate, an uninterrupted union with God; a constant communion with the Father and his Son Jesus Christ, through the Spirit; a continual enjoyment of the Three-One God, and of all the creatures in him!"[150] For Wesley, the entirety of the Christian life is a slow drawing of creation into the very triune life. First, as the Spirit renews the human heart for love of God and, second, when the entire created order is drawn into the life of the trinity, a new uninterrupted intimate center between God and creation. God is apocalyptic.[151]

POLITICAL THEOLOGY AS APOCALYPTIC THEOLOGY: TRANSITIONING TO THE POLITICAL PAUL

The apocalyptic interpreters of Paul recognize the political implications of Paul's apocalyptic. The explicit political challenge to modern politics posed by Paul's apocalyptic gospel is that the world does not belong to the

149. See Ziegler, "Not Without the Spirit," 72.

150. Wesley, "New Creation," 500.

151. To state that God is apocalyptic could mean potentially two different things. First, it could mean, as Congdon writes, "The God who saves is the apocalyptic trinity whose being is ontologically located in the event of salvation, in the existential interruption of the apocalypse" (*God Who Saves*, 254). Congdon argues that election is ontologically prior to triunity. However, I believe a second understanding of this phrase is apparent. Summarizing the work of John Webster, the holy realized and infinitely lively Being of God is the anchor of his loving, creative, redemptive relation to creatures. As such, God's infinite perfections are not self-enclosed. Rather, they repeat externally the internal being of God. God's election is not ontologically prior to triunity, but it is anticipated by God's triunity. God is apocalyptic in that God's triune life is charged with limitless economic potency and enacts God's completeness as the very basis of creaturely life. God is revealed as the ground of creaturely being over and against the sinful fallen powers of the world. For more, see John Webster's Kantzer Lectures, "God's Perfect Life."

human but to God. Along with the philosophers of the new approach, a strong political appropriation of Paul has occurred by Pauline Christian scholars. As I transition into chapters 3 and 4, I offer a brief segue that clarifies the political potential of Paul's apocalyptic gospel. It is possible to wed political theology and Paul's apocalyptic in a clear and visible way. This "theological turn" will provide the optic that will guide the remaining chapters on Paul's apocalyptic critique of modernity.

Talk of apocalyptic eschatology is problematic in modernity, especially for talk of politics. However, it cannot be removed from our contemporary readings of Paul precisely because humanity has become an idol to itself in modernity. As Catholic theologian Henri de Lubac writes,

> Man sacralizes, "absolutizes" persons, objects and events which should not be treated in that way; and after a period of enthusiasm he finds himself alone, disappointed, with his broken idols in his hands. The real question, then, is not whether the sense of the sacred has diminished of disappeared but rather what makes man transform a reality of this world into something sacred for him, something which he places ahead of everything else, on which he spends his time and to which he even devotes himself wholly.[152]

As Lubac illustrates, modernity, through its emphasis on self-sufficiency, has made humanity an idol to itself. As such, it participates in the very powers of sin and death that give birth to biopolitical modernity. I believe that a turn back to an apocalyptic, ancient picture of humanity as embedded within a world enslaved by powers will help liberate humanity from itself. This turn takes shape in three distinct features: the reignition of the form of the world that is passing away, apocalyptic realism in the tension of *already* and *not yet*, and the metaphysics of apocalypse.

First, modernity struggles with this ancient picture of humanity precisely because it resists the liberation it offers by way of the form of the world that is passing. Recently theologian Christopher Morse argues that if biblical scholars remove all references to heaven and the return of Christ, our New Testament would look like "a very censored document indeed."[153] That being said, Morse does recognize the need to understand the difference between the New Testament world and our own. Morse proposes an interpretation of apocalyptic eschatology which recognizes

152. Lubac, *Brief Catechesis*, 297.
153. Morse, *Difference Heaven Makes*, 2.

this difference. In so doing, he understands apocalyptic as the return of Christ in "the form (σχῆμα, "schema") of this world [that] is passing away" (7:31, NRSV). Morse is in sympathy with the philosophy of Walter Benjamin, who argues precisely this point. However, Morse, unlike Benjamin, argues that the "form" of the world possessed by the powers of sin and death is passing away.

Morse's theological definition of apocalyptic centers on the return of Christ as an at-handedness manifested in the form of the world that is passing away. The "at-handedness" of Christ is contrasted with an in-handedness of Christ, namely the possession of God. Rather, Christ is always breaking into the present in the form of the world that is passing away. Christ's incarnation, resurrection, ascension, and return is heard as good news that makes history a new form of the world emerging in the midst of the old.[154] Only as Christology weds itself to eschatology in this particular way can this sovereignty of the self-sufficient human be broken today.

In this apocalyptic theology, the self-sufficiency of humanity is directionally broken from the future. Here, Morse contrasts two aspects of the future described by theologian Jürgen Moltmann, namely *futurum* and *adventus*. *Futurum* denotes an understanding of the future as that "idea of becoming that emerges from the potentialities of the past."[155] *Adventus* is the future that comes to us from beyond ourselves. Morse writes, an "eschatological and apocalyptic sense of the future, in contrast, is of an *advent* in which a new reality comes into the present that is not accounted for as an extrapolation from any available residue of what has gone before."[156] Thus, Paul's apocalyptic eschatology is "the promised future that ultimately determines what becomes of the past and present, and not the other way around."[157] The future thus breaks in upon the present. Therefore, a Pauline apocalyptic theology emerges, namely an in-breaking that has at once occurred in Christ's incarnation, exhausting the sovereignty of sin and death, and again in the future at-handedness where the form of this world is passing away.

The apocalyptic designation of the world's own passing away is essential for political theology. The implications of such a project runs

---

154. Morse, *Difference Heaven Makes*, 7.

155. Morse, *Difference Heaven Makes*, 46.

156. Morse, *Difference Heaven Makes*, 46.

157. Morse, *Difference Heaven Makes*, 46.

counter to the sovereign politics of modernity so aptly illustrated in Arendt, Foucault, Benjamin, Taubes, Badiou, and Agamben. For apocalyptic theology, there is a loving service implied in discipleship in which the community gives itself to loving service of the world. There is a particular kind of making use of the world that treats it in a manner appropriate to its "passing away," a use not proprietarily related to human sovereignty or juridical ownership that dwells in the world.[158] Only when the Christian recognizes that the world is passing away can one love the world's true form.[159] Furthermore, the political posture of such a recognition is a kenotic self-giving to the world from below rather than a sovereign rule from above. This is the means by which apocalyptic finds a "loophole of retreat" from modernity's self-sufficient sovereignty.[160]

Second, such a political theology does not merely operate inside the powers of sin and death through harmful ideology. Rather, it operates in a different register, namely a different realism that refuses ideological politics. Neil Elliott was a student of Beker and recognizes the connection between ideology and apocalyptic realism. Elliot's work argues that Paul has been deeply depoliticized in his original apocalyptic intentions. Elliott places Paul's political context, Roman imperial ideology, within the contemporary world more than any other figure discussed in this chapter. Elliott writes, "In Paul's day, as in ours, creation is a fundamentally *political* and *ideological*, not simply a *theological* topic . . . [which] requires moving beyond the customary boundaries of 'theology' to a critical understanding of the ideological currents at work in our own world—and a creative opposition to them."[161] Paul's apocalyptic serves as a helpful theological optic to see not only Paul's time but also our own.

The clearest example of this apocalyptic optic that Elliott asserts is the realism of citizens under first-century Roman imperialism. According to Elliott, the Pharisees of Paul's day operated with a sense of this realism.[162] In order to secure Israel's political future, Pharisees understood the Roman imperial ideology as a power ordained by God over the Jews. Elliott writes, "Pharisees affirmed the biblical teaching that God's

158. Kroeker, "Messianic Ethics and Diaspora Communities," 78.

159. Kroeker, "Living 'As If Not,'" 26.

160. A loophole of retreat is a space of freedom described by Harriet Jacobs in *Incidents in the Life*, 128–31.

161. Elliot, "Creation, Cosmos, and Conflict in Romans 8–9," 131. Emphasis original.

162. Elliot, *Liberating Paul*, 159–67.

sovereignty could be exercised through foreign rulers."[163] Elliott clarifies that there were Pharisees who were revolutionaries, but a large number sought "to withdraw from the idea of a Jewish state and to cleave to the recognition of the advantage and necessity of Roman rule in Judea."[164] This is a realistic shift in that the Pharisees moved away from covenantal hope in favor of what could be realized by Rome. This realism grew out of a "prophetic-apocalyptic rationale" that proposed that the movements of kings and empires was enacted by the will of God.[165] The result led to a submission to the ideologies and purposes of Rome.[166] However, this realism became a trap for the Pharisees that bound them to an unapocalyptic submission to powers.

The pre-converted Paul persecuted the early preachers of Christ because of the threat to the Jewish community by Roman power.[167] Elliott recognizes that this is a political assumption Paul makes about the gospel of Jesus Christ that he continues to hold after his conversion. Elliott writes, "Given the political dimension of Paul's own 'conversion,' it is reasonable to suggest that what Paul finds 'wrong' in Israel's conduct is the persistence in an endeavor he has abandoned—namely, striving to secure Judea's future through the precarious balance of power vis-à-vis Rome."[168] Paul is not anti-Jewish in his theology, even after his conversion. His persecution of Christians before his conversion is a result of his hope that Israel will be saved. After Paul's conversion, his strategy changes, though this political hope for Israel remains. Elliot writes that Paul

> never surrendered his hope for his people, but he became convinced that that hope would find fulfillment in a way many of his contemporaries in Judea had failed to recognize. Paul's work among the Gentiles was driven by the conviction that he was participating in God's liberative purposes *for Israel*. He continued to pursue as an apostle of Jesus Christ the same goal that he had served as a Pharisee and a persecutor of the church, namely, "the revelation of the liberation of the children of God" (Rom. 8:21). His "conversion" changed not his goal but the strategy he

163. Elliot, *Liberating Paul*, 161.

164. Elliot, *Liberating Paul*, 163.

165. Elliot, *Liberating Paul*, 161.

166. Elliot, *Liberating Paul*, 164–65.

167. Elliot, *Liberating Paul*, 148–49.

168. Elliot, *Liberating Paul*, 178.

would now adopt to reach that goal; the apocalypse of the crucified Messiah convinced Paul that God did not work through
the balance of terror through which successive empires exacted
their will.[169]

The apocalyptic that buttressed Roman ideology and subsequent realisms comes into conflict with a Jewish, christologically refined apocalyptic that confronts ideology with the power of the gospel to open up the
story of Israel for the world through its Messiah.

Paul's apocalyptic, in Elliott's interpretation, provides a Pauline
theological politic that is dependent upon the crucified Nazarene. If it
is apocalyptic, it must be *already* and *not yet*. Following Elliot, then, the
Pauline politics of apocalyptic has a twofold character that will unfold in
the final two chapters.

The *already* of Elliott's political interpretation of Paul's apocalyptic
lies in confronting Roman ideologies (*exousia*). Drawing on the work of
Ernst Käsemann, Elliott notes the political nature of Paul's emphasis on
the righteousness of God. This is "God's integrity, faithfulness to God's
own being and purposes. Those purposes, according to the broad sweep
of the biblical tradition, are the redemption of the creation and the fulfillment of the covenant with Israel (which has the redemption of creation
as its horizon)."[170] Elliott notes that this directly corresponds to Roman
ius (justice), which was part of the "lifeblood of Augustan propaganda."[171]
Elliot argues that Paul's use of righteousness and justice in Romans
1:18–32 mobilizes God's righteousness against the justice of Rome. The
strong sexual message of this passage is due to the well-known sexual
abuses by Emperors Tiberius and Caligula.[172] As such, that Paul says
"the righteousness of God is reveal through faith for faith" (Rom 1:17,
NRSV) is directly lobbed against "the moral bankruptcy of the imperial
house itself."[173] The righteousness revealed by God is revealed against *this*
ungodliness (Rom 1:18). The Roman imperial "pretension to justice" is
under Paul's apocalyptic critique. Paul's main message is that those "baptized into Christ" already know that "the justice of God is not what the

169. Elliot, *Liberating Paul*, 179.

170. Elliot, *Liberating Paul*, 191.

171. Elliot, *Liberating Paul*, 191.

172. Elliot, *Liberating Paul*, 194.

173. Elliot, *Liberating Paul*, 195.

empire calls justice."[174] Thus, Paul tells the Roman congregation that they have been demobilized from the Roman order by the apocalyptic revelation of God's righteousness, which teaches Christians to love God, and consequently, the *summum bonum*.

In addition to this apocalyptic unmasking of the imperial ideology, Elliott also provides a political interpretation of the *not yet*. Paul's politics lie in solidarity with the crucified Messiah for the sake of solidarity with the crucified of the world. His apocalyptic politics comes against the Pharisaic realism of his day, and his rejection of the Pharisees is the rejection of "striving to secure Judea's *future* through the precarious balance of power vis-à-vis Rome."[175] Pharisaic realism is a rejection of God's future in favor of one made apart from God. Paul is convinced of God's future consummation of the cosmos.[176] The political activity, as is apparent in Paul's own converted understanding of his mission, is that which participates in the future coming of God. Paul does not see the delay in the parousia as a problem. Rather, those who pray for the coming of the Lord (1 Cor 16:22) prefer a realistic politic of apocalypse rather than an ideological false politic.[177] Such a politic attempts, through conversion and preaching the gospel, to enact a politics not bound by the powers of sin and death as a means to anticipate their final defeat.

Third, in Paul's apocalyptic critique of Roman ideology, a way beyond both biopolitics and the politics of the new approach becomes evident. Elliott, like the new approach, recognizes that Paul's account of reality is far more accurate than modernity can construct. However, he argues that the powers that are so desirable to the materialists are directly confronted by the apocalyptic incursion of Christ. Paul's gospel does not need to be truncated by a materialist hermeneutic, but needs only to be unleashed in its full veracity on the depravity of biopolitics. This does not mean Paul cannot be oriented to materialist ends or that he cannot be friendly to materialist categories. Rather, it means confronting the ideology (*exousia*) of biopolitics, not with another ideology, but with the apocalyptic reality of God. This is a different kind of realism that pays close attention to God's gracious initiative in the cosmos. The new approach method denies the apocalyptic depiction of reality. Instead, Paul is used

174. Elliot, *Liberating Paul*, 195.

175. Elliot, *Liberating Paul*, 178. Emphasis mine.

176. Elliot, *Liberating Paul*, 25, 180.

177. Elliot, *Liberating Paul*, 180.

to sharpen their own ideological critique of biopolitical ideology. Such an argument is a "turtles all the way down" argument. Paul's apocalyptic provides a thick description of reality capable of enduring biopolitics. This new reality confronts ideology that leads to the "unselfing" of private interest. In light of God's revelation, a new reality emerges into which the believer must fit and cannot be captured for the purposes of the self. It calls the believing community to action in light of God's revelation as the new center of intimacy in the cosmos.

To claim that God is the new center of intimacy of the Christian life through God's invasion of the cosmos and God's own consummation of creation into the divine triune life is already a step away from the position proposed by the new approach. This does not mean that the new approach is fundamentally wrong in exploration of Paul. Quite the contrary—many themes are reflected in my own understanding of Paul's apocalyptic gospel (event, new community, and care for the victim). However, the God displayed in the new approach is mostly nonexistent in favor of certain strains of post-metaphysical materialism that serve to fill the void left by Paul's proclamation of God as an intimate center of the Christian life. Apocalyptic provides a very different account of reality, one akin to a classical understanding of metaphysics. In such an account, according to David Bentley Hart,

> [God] is the one reality in which all our existence, knowledge, and love subsist, from which they come and to which they go, and that therefore he is somehow present in even our simplest experience of the world, and is approachable by way of contemplative and moral refinement.[178]

The God Hart describes is the God of the classical theistic tradition. For many apocalyptic thinkers, such a connection between Paul and the classical tradition is an error.[179] However, Pauline apocalyptic makes certain claims about the very nature of the cosmos. Paul writes, "May I never boast of anything except the cross of our Lord Jesus Christ, by which the world has been crucified to me, and I to the world" (Gal 6:14, NRSV). Though this hardly could be a fully developed metaphysical system, it does make a metaphysical claim. "The point that apocalyptic makes," as Yoder argues, "is that people who bear crosses are working with the

---

178. Hart, *Experience of God*, 44.
179. Congdon, "Eschatologizing Apocalyptic," 132–36.

grain of the universe."[180] Such an account, coupled with Hart's analysis, suggests that in apocalyptic Paul presents readers with a "metaphysics of apocalypse."[181] It is the one who is crucified that is also the slaughtered Lamb who gives meaning to history because only the crucified can open the scroll of history (Rev 5:2–9).[182]

Therefore, the new approach not only gives an inadequate account of Paul's God, but of history, reality, and contingency. To claim that those who deal with crosses work with the grain of the universe "reconfigures" history and politics.[183] It does this in a way unthinkable to the new approach, namely from below. History must be *witnessed* from below and from the place of those who are slaughtered. It is the voices of the slaughtered who, in their plurality and difference, sing worthy is the slaughtered Lamb.[184] The voices of the slaughtered speak as those who have suffered. They communicate as in Pentecost, out of the tongue of their local speech, but this speech is local in dialect, and in its suffering and victimization. Since, as Yoder argues, "cross *and* resurrection" form the "shape of the cosmos," the gospel can embrace difference and particularity in the redemption of the cosmos.[185] This does not valorize suffering or propose a path of redemptive suffering. Rather, it is God's unique act of solidarity with the slaughtered calling the circumstances of history to judgement. Sovereignty and totalitarianism do not represent the powers by which the cosmos moves, but rather it is the crucified. Therefore, the metaphysics of apocalypse is summed up well by Yoder: "Jesus' acceptance of the cross . . . was an ontological decision, dictated by a truer picture of what the world *really is*."[186]

According to apocalyptic reality is the scene of God's *cruciform* sustaining and self-revealing presence in human lives amid fallen

180. Yoder, "Armaments and Eschatology," 58.

181. See Toole, *Waiting for Godot*, 216–18. See also Hiebert, *Architectonics of Hope*, 136–52.

182. Toole, *Waiting for Godot*, 218.

183. Toole, *Waiting for Godot*, 217.

184. Agamben uses this language of witness to describe his genealogical account of politics. However, it is precisely Agamben's failure to *see* from the place of the crucified, victimized, and slaughtered that limits him. Instead (as is the entire new approach) he is wed to ideological commitments that inhibit this seeing. Because Agamben is committed to a Western account of reality, the voices must be translated into a Western language. See chapter 3 of this book.

185. Yoder, *Politics of Jesus*, 160. Emphasis mine.

186. Yoder, "Are You the One," 211.

powers. Hart continues, "All things that exist receive their being continuously from [God], who is the infinite wellspring of all that is, *in whom* [to quote Paul] all things live and move and have their being."[187] This should be understood as cruciform in shape. Paul's apocalyptic gospel arises from the understanding that reality is not a flat amalgamation of material substances only accidently related to one another and to which material forces must fit. Rather, the crucified and resurrected Lord is the source of all goodness and the one who gives being to reality. Paul does not provide a better set of sense impressions over and against misused sense impressions, but rather unmasks the ill-intentions of fallen powers. Furthermore, Christ crucifies the whole cosmos of meaning established by these fallen powers.

I argue, then, that the apocalyptic theological picture of the cosmos, as a site of God's radical invasion, provides a more adequate account of reality into which political action can intelligibly arise than do the commitments of the new approach and their nihilistic revolution. The new approach, Milbank continues, "crucially recognizes . . . that human histories of apparent peace are really histories of hidden conflict and opposition," and this is correct.[188] Yet they mistake the materialist realities that they confront with their nihilistic hermeneutics. They "*ontologize* this prevailing circumstance" to their detriment.[189] Milbank points out that they should "instead insist on its contingency."[190] What is required is a new reality where "the cosmos is secretly such as to be hospitable to human harmony and to humanity living in harmony with the cosmos—that is to say, to (nondialectically) mediated differences."[191] This secret hospitality, which has been obscured by the powers of sin and death, is revealed to be the crucified and resurrected Lord, and the powers are, in fact, privations without sovereignty and with no ontology.[192] The ontological center of political life that enables harmonious correspondence with the neighbor is in the crucified and resurrected Lord revealed against the powers. This reality outside of the material order appropriately critiques the structures of sovereignty and totalitarianism.

---

187. Hart, *Experience of God*, 30.

188. Milbank, "Materialism and Transcendence," 423.

189. Milbank, "Materialism and Transcendence," 423.

190. Milbank, "Materialism and Transcendence," 423.

191. Milbank, "Materialism and Transcendence," 424.

192. See Yoder, *Politics of Jesus*, 134–61.

The preceding theological account of apocalyptic serves as the basis for a political rationality that takes shape in certain practices. Wesley states that, in order to develop habitual dispositions of the soul and heart, practices are required. As Benjamin understands, practices confront biopolitical, profane desires. The practices, and their connection to this narrative, will be further explained in chapters 3 and 4. If, as has been argued, Paul's scriptural writings are ontologically rooted in attesting to the self-presentation of the triune God, any political insight there within must arise from this ontology.

At the close of chapter 2, I have now cleared the Pauline apocalyptic ground in order to show how the just and loving gaze is the political activity most appropriate to the Pauline apocalyptic gospel. I argue for the just and loving gaze because it is the habitual disposition of the heart that does not rely on constructed, ideological descriptions of reality, but factual experiences of the neighbor. Apocalyptic clears the way for the just and loving gaze by offering both the common good and shared ends in which individuals must locate their public activity. This counteracts the biopolitical emphasis of modernity by providing a different vision of our neighbor. The humanity of the neighbor lies buried under technologies of the self. However, the *already* righteousness of God revealed in Christ and the *not yet* consummation of the cosmos gives an ability to locate individuals within a different narrative framework. This framework requires humanity be freed from bonds of unrighteousness. This will be the purpose of the final two chapters—to unpack the implications of Paul's apocalyptic as the tension between the *already* and the *not yet*, which takes shape in the just and loving gaze.

CONCLUSION

In conclusion, my purpose in this chapter has been to narrate what I believe to be the missing element in interpreting Paul. In place of the interpretation offered by the new approach, I have engaged in reading Paul as an apocalyptic theologian. This is the soil from which any political theology of Paul must grow. This means that, contrary to the new approach, I follow John Webster that the ontology of Scripture is its role in communicating the self-presentation of the triune God. Paul's apocalyptic gospel fills out the narrative question about what it means to say that God is real. In apocalyptic terms, God is real, Lord over the powers and

is the proper end of all action. The powers are those realities that shape
and form our moral presuppositions independent of God and the community. In order to deal with these powers, apocalyptic must have three
parts: Christ's past actions in the crucifixion and resurrection of Jesus as
an exhaustion of the sovereignty of the powers, the continual presence
of Christ in the community today in Christ's "at-handedness" in order
for the believer to not live according to sin and death, and the return of
Christ at the resurrection of the dead and the new creation when death
will be no more.

After settling on an apocalyptic interpretation of Paul, I unpacked
the main perspectives about Paul's apocalyptic in the twentieth century.
Apocalyptic is a slippery term that needs careful evaluation before it is
deployed. I reviewed the work of New Testament scholars Ernst Käsemann, Rudolf Bultmann, and J. Christiaan Beker. Through Käsemann
and Bultmann, a political understanding of the righteousness of God
is revealed, which provides a modern interpretation of apocalyptic that
confronts the new approach. Beker helps round out Käsemann's understanding of righteousness in the context of the coming triumph of
God, which completes the righteousness begun by God. These thinkers
struggle with whether apocalyptic means something present/*already*, or
something future/*not yet*.

These scholars offer important arguments for their positions, but
I find a mixture of them necessary for a full description of the Pauline
apocalyptic gospel. The *already* and the *not yet* must be held together, and
I argue this is by way of Wesley's hermeneutic of sanctification. Christ is
Lord over the powers now, which makes a new pattern of habituation
possible that doesn't include the powers. There must be a resurrection
of the dead. Paul's apocalyptic theology about the crucifixion and resurrection of Jesus makes sense only within an equally insistent theme
of the resurrection of the dead. Only a doctrine of the Trinity can hold
these two positions together because these theological foci are mutually
penetrative of one another and must be maintained despite the divide in
scholarship.

3

The Just and Loving Gaze of God with Us

Pauline Apocalyptic Politics of the Already

THE APOCALYPTIC PAUL MORE appropriately confronts the biopolitics of modernity than the new approach by proclaiming a new center of intimacy, which creates the possibility of a new political community. The new approach reads Paul as the proponent of a new social matrix built upon the community that arises from confessing Christ. However, Paul's theology is wed to an apocalyptic account of reality that proclaims the defeat of sinful fallen powers and a crucified sovereign. In this chapter, I draw from the political insights of the new approach to Paul only as it pertains to the subsequent social realities that arise from Paul's apocalyptic theology. I replace their exclusive materialism with the apocalyptic account of reality. In this chapter, I limit my study to the *already* of Paul's apocalyptic theology, which yields a new type of community not grounded in privately interested, self-sufficient individuality, but in the saving mystery of God. Apocalyptic articulates the common good as lacking in the new approach and even Arendt's own philosophy. The next chapter on Paul's apocalyptic *not yet* will furnish a vision of shared ends. Only by living in this apocalyptic ordering of the world can Paul truly confront modernity and its politics.

The chapter begins by defining the just and loving gaze and its importance for political action. This unfolds as an engagement with Arendt,

Iris Murdoch, and Agamben as exemplar of the new approach. For the new approach, a fundamental weakness exists in its inability to listen to the neighbor and victim. Arendt helpfully overcomes this in her emphasis on speech. However, without an account of why one should care for the neighbor and victim, speech cannot make an impact. The just and loving gaze, as described by Iris Murdoch, provides an account of why one should care about the speech and humanity of the neighbor. The just and loving gaze is an invitation into the reality of the good that requires individuals to "unself" from their private interests. Such an act leads to a new kind of politics of community where the common good and shared ends are found with others.

Since Murdoch's just and loving gaze is not, by her account, theologically focused, I must provide a brief theological translation of the just and loving gaze into Paul's apocalyptic theology. Utilizing Martyn's analysis of the antinomies of the old world versus the antinomies of Christ's incarnation and resurrection, I show that the just and loving gaze is a way of seeing reality. The reality now available in Christ is one that no longer divides the world according to harmful antinomies, such as circumcised and uncircumcised. This corresponds to biopolitical divisions of the world. The just and loving gaze is a type of realism not bound up with false consciousness and corresponds to the biofocal vision of apocalyptic, which is the ability to see the world in its sinful state, but also the new reality enacted by the invasion of Christ into the cosmos.

Following the new approach, I believe the community formed in the wake of Paul's apocalyptic confessions is a political response to modernity. The community is united around the confession Jesus is Lord, which is its common good. In turn, this begets certain practices. I will outline the practices of attention and remembrance at the Lord's Supper. Such practices will counteract biopolitical technologies of the self and the antinomic divisions of the world in modernity as a concrete practice of the just and loving gaze. Only as the community recognizes the common good in the apocalyptic *already* can these practices form a certain kind of political theology. I conclude with a brief Pauline political theology arising from this apocalyptic emphasis.

HANNAH ARENDT'S PARTICULAR POLITICS:
UNLEARNING PRIVATE INTERESTS[1]

Arendt's political philosophy provides a constructive alternative to private interests. In Arendt's experience, the influence of private interests impacted her daily life as a Jewish woman. Her response to private interests and the politics of self-sufficiency happens within an acceptance of her rejected Jewish identity. Arendt's particular form of identity politics reclaims her identity for the sake of speech and true public life. If one can speak and act in the public realm as a means to politically define one's life, then there can exist a politics free from private interests. I connect Arendt's biography, neglected Jewish writings, and political thought. I argue that this approach most accurately illuminates what Marie Louise Knott calls Arendt's politics of unlearning.[2] I utilize this metaphor in order to express that modern politics has taught humanity to think in very limited, ideological ways about politics. Arendt is not wed to any one position of political thought, but charts her own way. I find this crucially helpful because politics arises not first from private interest or sovereign bodies, but from the type of communities in which humans wish to live. Therefore, one must unlearn unjust forms of politics in order to learn new ones.

Arendt's political thought, through her Jewish identity, first unlearns anti-Semitism. Arendt's pathway to a political realm apart from anti-Semitism, or apart from the failures of work and labor, begins in her own life. Though Arendt's political philosophy does not create a specific Jewish political philosophy, her role as a Jewish woman serves to inform her engagement with politics. Commentator Ron Feldman writes,

> There is an essential link between [Arendt's] conception of Jewish history and her political theory: her view of the modern Jewish condition serves as an introduction to her political theory, while her political theory illuminates her interpretation of Jewish history.[3]

Arendt understands that, in the political realm, the person can only become a "self" when it unlearns how it has been put to use thus far. Only when the individual is free of external construction can there be a free

---

1. Biographical material adapted from Young-Bruehl, *Hannah Arendt.*
2. See Knott, *Unlearning with Hannah Arendt.*
3. Feldman, "Jew as Pariah," xlii.

public. She attempts to hold together the intrinsic worth of the individual along with the emphasis on the public realm, as delineated in chapter 1.

Arendt's identity was tied to being a German intellectual in the early twentieth century. In 1929, she completed her dissertation and began her research on anti-Semitism, but because of her ethnicity she was never allowed to "habilitate" (a professional academic procedure a German scholar must undergo in order to receive a professorship). In 1933, when Hitler came to power, Arendt fled to France and began assisting Jewish refugees. She would be stripped of her German citizenship in 1937, leaving her without means to travel due to her inability to obtain a visa. When Germany invaded France and began deporting Jews to concentration camps, Arendt escaped to the United States through an illegally obtained visa. It was then that she began to publish her work on the nature of totalitarianism and anti-Semitism. Confronted with this troubled history, Arendt learned that her German identity, her citizenship, could not save her.

As such, Arendt could not rely on rights and citizenship to secure her identity. She could no longer afford to doubt the givenness of her own identity in favor of the constructed, self-interested social realm. The German identity that formed the social space and social imagination of her environment subjected her to the private interests of the German population.[4] Anti-Semitism is biopolitical by dividing between appropriate and inappropriate German life. Arendt's political citizenship (i.e., German) was not stable enough to sustain her within the biopolitical antinomies present in the German *polis*. The symbolic universe—the German political realm—to which a German citizen could appeal in order to avoid violence was no longer available to her.

Arendt could no longer act out of the authority of her German identity because her continued existence as a Jew outweighed her German citizenship. Arendt's life was "bound-to-death" in light of labor's instrumental Jewishness.[5] She had only one choice: make the radical turn to her own Jewishness as a possible revolutionary identity, and reform it from its death-bound state at the hands of the Nazis. Nearing the end of her life, Arendt writes,

4. This idea of social imagination is largely taken from Taylor, *Modern Social Imaginaries*, 23–30.

5. This idea of "death-bound-subjectivity" is explored at length in JanMohamed, *Death-Bound-Subject*, 1–44.

> I have always regarded my Jewishness as one of the indisputable factual data of my life, and I have never had the wish to change or disclaim facts of this kind. There is such a thing as a basic gratitude for everything that is as it is; for what has been *given* and was not, could not be *made*.[6]

Arendt's Jewishness could not be made for her because it was not secured in the way that her German citizenship was. What *was* made for her was the German identity, and that identity had proven to be bankrupt. By reclaiming her Jewishness, Arendt was no longer epistemologically trapped by the complicated history of anti-Semitism. Rather, it served as a starting place for a new actions and new virtues. At the end of her life, this was her identity and the center of her existence.

It was from this position, a Jewish refugee without a country, that Arendt began her major political action. She understood that the solution to labor and work is a new type of action from within her own identity: speech. Speech is not an abstract notion, but the type of language that arises from the contingency of an individual to confront the world. When Arendt speaks out of her givenness (i.e., the Jew, the refugee, etc.), she would inhabit a new way of being-in-the-world and critique the public space created by labor and work.

> Those few refugees who insist upon telling the truth, even to the point of "indecency," get in exchange for their unpopularity one priceless advantage: history is no longer a closed book to them and politics is no longer the privilege of the Gentiles . . . Refugees driven from country to country represent the vanguard of their people—if they keep their identity.[7]

This is an act of speech, of a truth-telling that opens up the world to newness or, as Arendt calls it, natality. Speaking as a Jewish refugee helps Arendt craft a new future, one that all individuals can share. George Kateb writes this in summary of Arendt: "Speech is deliberation or discussion as part of the process of deciding some issue pertaining to the public good."[8] This is why speech exceeds the possibility of labor and work. It leaves something lasting, something memorable, and is freedom from the horror of private interests over the common good.[9]

6. Arendt, "Daughter of Our People," 392.

7. Arendt, "We Refugees," 274.

8. Kateb, "Political Action," 133.

9. Kateb, "Political Action," 133.

To be free, in Arendt's political thought, is a type of public life made possible by authentic political speech. Arendt recognizes that intrinsic to a free public space is the ability to speak and act among other people as equals. She writes, "A life without speech and without action . . . is literally dead to the world; it has ceased to be a human life because it is no longer lived among men."[10] Human life must be lived among other people in the political sphere. The importance of speech lies in "human plurality," which "has the twofold character of equality and distinction."[11] Naming equality and distinction as essential to human plurality and public space means that Arendt assumes a mutual recognition. Arendt's return to her Jewish identity names her distinction. Arendt's Jewish identity names her distinctive place in the community, which elevates speech, simultaneously elevates equality and distinction.

Arendt clarifies distinction by naming what it is not: otherness. Otherness is an abstract difference, while distinction is particular to human beings. As Arendt unlearns her constructed self, she claims her unique being as a Jewish refugee. It is from this place that she speaks: "Speech and action reveal this unique distinction."[12] As Arendt speaks, her listeners in equality cannot operate with private interests. In speech, Arendt names her identity as distinct from other humans. She writes, "only man can express this distinction and distinguish himself, and only he can communicate himself and not something."[13] Distinction and equality in speech not only name the type of individual who speaks, but how the world should change in relation to one's speech. It is clear that Arendt's life attempts to change the world of private interest. In her distinct Jewish speech to the public world, she names what has been excluded. This is a revolution of thought that disrupts the totalitarian hold of private interests. This is appropriately comparable to Agamben's remnant, which operates as an excess of the semantic codes of the world.[14] As she unlearns her constructed identity formed by private interest, she invites the public space of political community—the human plurality—to unlearn this as well. This is the only way to a genuinely free public space.

10. Arendt, *Human Condition*, 157.

11. Arendt, *Human Condition*, 175.

12. Arendt, *Human Condition*, 175.

13. Arendt, *Human Condition*, 175.

14. Agamben, *Time That Remains*, 56. See also Marquis, *Transient Apostle*, 19–20.

Arendt's emphasis on speech as the invitation to political unlearning resembles the task of political revolution. Speech is required for revolution because only in overthrow does the public unlearn politics of totalitarianism, private interests, etc. Arendt believes that the history of revolution must be read as a history of people reacting against private interests.

> The word "revolution" meant originally restoration, hence something which to us is its very opposite, is not a mere oddity of semantics. The revolutions of the seventeenth and eighteenth centuries, which to us appear to show all evidence of a new spirit, the spirit of the modern age, were intended to be restorations.[15]

In societies where private interests reign, it is the job of revolution to free people from those interests. This does not mean that Arendt promotes a singular revolution, as in Taubes, or a cycle of violence that moves history along, like we find in the philosophy of Hegel and Marx.[16] Quite the contrary—revolution is an action of the mind. Furthermore, Arendt is clear that revolution is, most importantly, about freedom and new beginnings. The political action of revolution is a public unlearning that frees people from private interest, restoring the dignity of the individual as equal in the public realm.

Revolution, unlearning, and speech couple nicely with Arendt's emphasis on natality, or the ability to start new. Action and speech form the ability for humans to present themselves as new, without having to be forever captive to past misdeed.[17] Arendt's political freedom must include this revolutionary spirit to make new. This revolution is tied to her world-affirming (as opposed to world-alienating) acceptance of identity, but it still maintains a modern ability to create out of the self. Freedom in the political realm includes freedom from determination by political authority and freedom for new political action.

Arendt's work correctly diagnoses modernity and provides a pathway out of the negative aspect of modernity's world-alienation and self-interest. Arendt still maintains certain elements of modernity. For example, Arendt maintains the importance of the will in modernity. Through the will, one can transcend to the political, public realm. Furthermore, the

---

15. Arendt, *On Revolution*, 33.

16. To see Arendt's distinction between violence and revolution, see Arendt, *On Revolution*, 24–25.

17. Arendt, *Human Condition*, 204.

will, through speech, makes the lasting element of politics memorable, such as constitutions and constitutional orders. The will arises, however, from the modern self. The self that speaks, in Arendt's philosophy, despite her emphasis on Jewish identity, is self-interested. Because the political is the place of lasting permanence and the source of true reality, it still moves away from the observable world as a source of meaning, and therefore implicitly becomes world-alienating in the process.

THE JUST AND LOVING GAZE

Arendt provides a politic of identity and speech embedded within a political community. However, she does not propose a communal affection and politics ordered toward the common good. Arendt cogently argues why identity is important but does not give a path toward how identity is celebrated and loved in community. I argue that Arendt correctly diagnoses the problem of modernity within private interests. However, the critique of private interests comes not through recognition of distinction, but by the loss of private interests through a love of the neighbor and the common good. This requires "unselfing": a death of the self-interested subject. Arendt sees the need to recognize identity and mutual speech, but she does not develop why speech *should* be heard. Arendt fails to argue for a political community that is capable of speech, one concerned with common good, love of neighbor, or general affection. She, like Badiou, slips into a political indifference where the subject must be dutifully alone in one's political action.

I turn to English philosopher and novelist Iris Murdoch to assist this lack in Arendt's otherwise helpful political insights. For Murdoch, it is not enough to recognize the neighbor; one must develop what she calls the just and loving gaze. In her words, "the just and loving gaze" is the "characteristic and proper mark of the active moral agent."[18] The just and loving gaze is a type of vision that best illustrates Arendt's epistemology of revolution, which determines not to see the other under-fetishizing inclinations but as they really are. Murdoch proposes the just and loving gaze as an understanding of the moral life beyond conceptual abstraction.

To illustrate a moral activity beyond abstraction, Murdoch utilizes an example of a Mother (M) and Daughter-in-law (D). At the outset, Murdoch proposes that M may not necessarily like D. Murdoch

18. Murdoch, *Sovereignty of the Good*, 33.

writes, "D is inclined to be pert and familiar, insufficiently ceremonious, brusque, sometimes positively rude, always tiresomely juvenile."[19] By trying to discern the actions of M toward D, Murdoch does not dwell abstractly, but attempts to address the typical problems of normal everyday people. Most individuals are possessed by a certain "fixed picture," as M appears to be imprisoned in her picture of D.[20] For our purposes, let's say that M possesses a set of particular private interests that harm her picture of D. However, Murdoch describes M as "intelligent and well-intentioned . . . capable of self-criticism, capable of giving careful and just *attention* to an object which confronts her."[21] This word "attention" is a very specific choice for Murdoch, which she borrows from philosopher Simone Weil. Attention, for Weil, is a religious concept. Weil writes, "Attention, taken to its highest degree, is the same thing as prayer."[22] Attention is a focus, namely a "mind [turned] toward the good."[23] This is true of M, according to Murdoch, because she is "moved by love [and] justice."[24] By being so moved, M is committing herself toward a certain type of progress, namely an intentional striving toward perfection, which is the perpetual task of seeing with the just and loving gaze.

The striving toward perfection, in Murdoch's philosophy, is a work of love. For Murdoch, love "shifts the center of the world from ourselves to another place."[25] It is a reaching outside of private interests and peer pressures that define how one should act. Love in this way is an occasion that inspires "'unselfing' wherein the lover learns to see, cherish, and respect what is not himself."[26] It is not just any object that can be loved highest of all in Murdoch's philosophy. Rather, it is the Good. Nothing short of a radical reorientation toward the Good can lead to the just and loving gaze. M gives proper attention to D, despite nagging misconceptions, because of a greater desire for the Good. In Murdoch's work, the Good is that which causes a desire for justice and love that will not settle with caricatures. This is what makes the Good so essential. In loving it,

19. Murdoch, *Sovereignty of the Good*, 16–17.

20. Murdoch, *Sovereignty of the Good*, 17.

21. Murdoch, *Sovereignty of the Good*, 17. Emphasis original.

22. Weil, *Gravity and Grace*, 170.

23. Weil, *Gravity and Grace*, 170.

24. Murdoch, *Sovereignty of the Good*, 18.

25. Murdoch, *Metaphysics as a Guide*, 17.

26. Murdoch, *Metaphysics as a Guide*, 17.

humans become good. The Platonic influence is evident in Murdoch's work because she places the Good as the highest object of love. Murdoch does not ascend to the ideal as the source of thought; rather, she is committed to the just and loving gaze turned upon individual realities in everyday life. Loving the Good has the effect, Murdoch writes, of causing a slow shift of attachments wherein *looking* (concentrating, attending, attentive discipline) is a source of divine (purified) energy."[27] Commitment to the Good causes the moral actor to lose the attachments that perpetuate false desires.

The innovation that Murdoch brings to this Platonic moral philosophy is that the same attention given to the Good becomes a reflex for how the individual sees a neighbor. Murdoch writes, "When M is just and loving she sees D as she really is."[28] M sees D clearly because of her commitment to the Good. Murdoch stresses that M, in her previous understanding of D, is trapped in a linguistic world that dominates her thinking. This is what she calls "the siege of the individual by concepts."[29] Here lies the difference between Murdoch and the new approach, as well as most of modern philosophy. Murdoch does not presuppose that the way out of such a dilemma is a new ethical schema or conceptual apparatus. Rather, it is actually giving attention to the real world found in front of the individual. In giving "attention" to D, M is counteracting the delusions about D she previously believed.[30]

Attention to the Good and to D is not a product of will. Murdoch insists the will cannot lead to a moral transformation. This is the issue she takes with modernity. See her critique of Kant and existentialism:

> The neo-Kantian existentialist "will" is a principle of pure movement. But how ill this describes what it is like for us to alter. Deliberately falling out of love is not a jump of the will, it is the acquiring of new objects of attention and thus of new energies as a result of refocusing.[31]

Goodness brings energies that motivate and attach the looking moral actor to new realities of goodness outside of previously held private

---

27. Murdoch, *Metaphysics as a Guide*, 25.

28. Murdoch, *Sovereignty of the Good*, 36.

29. Murdoch, *Sovereignty of the Good*, 31.

30. Murdoch, *Sovereignty of the Good*, 36.

31. Murdoch, *Sovereignty of the Good*, 54.

interests. Murdoch is clear: "pure will can usually achieve little."[32] But
how does one attend to the Good? Murdoch's answer lies in a religious
home.

Historically, Murdoch understands, loving God has been a powerful
source of goodness.[33] Attachment to God is powerful because it displaces
other attachments. If Murdoch were a theologian, the answer becomes
obvious, but she is not. Rather, she wants to utilize the historical means of
attention to God as a way to approach the Good. For Murdoch, the Good
is something unitary, true, just, and good that must be honestly reflected
upon.[34] Murdoch recommends that reflecting on the virtuous individual
leads to an understanding of the whole. For example, Murdoch asks what
courage is. She writes, "The best kind of courage (that which would make
a man act unselfishly in a concentration camp) is steadfast, calm, temper-
ate, intelligent, loving . . . suggest here . . . that reflection rightly tends to
unify the moral world, and that increasing moral sophistication reveals
increasing unity."[35] Murdoch interprets the bare factual realities we experience in the world in order to make judgments about the Good.

In order to see the Good, one must be committed to a type of realism, the conviction that reality can be identified. This is not altogether
different from the realism outlined by Elliot over the antiapocalyptic
political movements of first century Jews. Murdoch argues that realism
affords the individual the ability to "know what [is] real [rather] than to
be in a state of fantasy or illusion."[36] Since it is a freedom from illusion,
Murdoch's realism resists the false consciousness. Enabled by a freedom
from illusion, Murdoch engages in a type of ontological proof for the
Good, which she concludes is "an assertion of faith."[37] Murdoch is not
making a religious claim, but rather a claim about the type of posture
that is necessary to turn one's attention to the Good, which is ultimately
a transcendent, yet immanent, reality. In order to appreciate her Platonic,
antimodern view of transcendence, one must understand Murdoch's
definition of false transcendence: "False transcendence . . . [is] a transcendence which is in effect simply an exclusion, a relegation of the moral

32. Murdoch, *Sovereignty of the Good*, 54.
33. Murdoch, *Sovereignty of the Good*, 54–55.
34. Murdoch, *Sovereignty of the Good*, 55.
35. Murdoch, *Sovereignty of the Good*, 56.
36. Murdoch, *Sovereignty of the Good*, 62.
37. Murdoch, *Sovereignty of the Good*, 61.

to a shadowy existence in terms of emotive language, imperatives, behaviours [sic], patterns, attitudes."[38] The transcendent Good is something that reveals and inspires.

Murdoch, in order to describe this transcendent Good, appeals to art. This is a difficult process for Murdoch because it can lead to fantasy rather than reality. Art reveals Beauty much like goodness reveals the Good. However, the danger lies in the tendency of some artists, Murdoch writes, "to produce a picture whose purpose is the consolation and aggrandizement of its author and the projection of his personal obsessions and wishes."[39] Art of this kind is selfish and cannot reveal the Beautiful or the Good. The goal of art, as well as morality, according to Murdoch, must "silence and expel self, to contemplate and delineate nature with a clear eye."[40] Morality and art consist of constant "checking of selfishness in the interest of seeing the real . . . [and] how real things can be looked at and loved without being seized and used, without being appropriated into the greedy organism of the self."[41] Good art causes the individual to detach, to see a reality and love it for its own sake.[42] Therefore, "the authority of the Good," according to Murdoch, lies in the "ability to perceive what is true, which is automatically at the same time a suppression of self."[43] For Murdoch, the Good is found in the act of searching for reality.

The Good, then, is found in loving the real, but the Good is transcendent and escapes concrete definition.[44] Despite this elusiveness, the Good can be characterized. She writes, "We ordinarily conceive and apprehend goodness in terms of virtues which belong to a continuous fabric of being."[45] Goodness is found in and through virtues displayed. Take the example of courage. All virtues, like courage, present a unity of goodness. Discovering the Good is not unlike exhibiting fact. The Good is described, at least partially, in the recognizable goodness at the heart of virtuous conduct. Therefore, the Good is both transcendent in its sheer indescribability and immanent in its ability to be perceived within vir-

38. Murdoch, *Sovereignty of the Good*, 57.
39. Murdoch, *Sovereignty of the Good*, 63.
40. Murdoch, *Sovereignty of the Good*, 63.
41. Murdoch, *Sovereignty of the Good*, 63–64.
42. Murdoch, *Sovereignty of the Good*, 64.
43. Murdoch, *Sovereignty of the Good*, 64.
44. Murdoch, *Sovereignty of the Good*, 68.
45. Murdoch, *Sovereignty of the Good*, 29.

tue.[46] There is something admirable within virtue that can be recognized by all witnesses. The most illuminating example that Murdoch provides is the man who acts unselfishly in the concentration camp. This example reveals a person who, for no reason at all, acts completely against selfish interest. This impossible possibility reveals that "there is more than this."[47]

The action of the unselfish man in a concentration camp points beyond itself to that which is lovely and beautiful. There is more than just self-assertion of the will that leads to this type of behavior.[48] This revelation is a "spark of insight, something with, as it were, a metaphysical position but no metaphysical form."[49] The man who acts unselfishly in a concentration camp, then, is like good art. It is a real action, something that is seen in the world, just like art. Furthermore, it is the means by which Murdoch sees the Good. This man's unselfish behavior, like good art, is not a playful diversion, but the fundamental insight of the Good.[50] It is by interpreting the reality of one who is unselfish in the concentration camp that we come to know the Good. And it is by loving it that we mimic the virtues displayed in him. Thus, goodness and morality arise from a type of mysticism where one is drawn ever deeper into the Good as a means to be drawn outside of oneself. Murdoch does not offer any single, succinct definition, but it is clear she sees the Good, as Heather Widdows summarizes, "as an ever-present reality which draws one towards it."[51] It is only by attending to the real and one's attraction to the Good that we can be good.

The Good is what enables the just and loving gaze because it is "the serious attempt to look compassionately at human things which automatically suggests that 'there is more than this.'"[52] This takes us back to attention. Murdoch writes, "The direction of attention is, contrary to nature, outward, away from the self which reduces all to a false unity, towards the great surprising variety of the world, and the ability so to direct

46. Heather Widdows presents Murdoch as describing the Good in both a transcendent and immanent way. See Widdows, *Moral Vision of Iris Murdoch*, 72–75.

47. Murdoch, *Sovereignty of the Good*, 71.

48. Murdoch, *Sovereignty of the Good*, 71.

49. Murdoch, *Sovereignty of the Good*, 71.

50. Murdoch, *Sovereignty of the Good*, 71–72.

51. Widdows, *Moral Vision of Iris Murdoch*, 85.

52. Murdoch, *Sovereignty of the Good*, 71.

attention is love."[53] When starting in the goodness found while being attentive to virtues exterior to oneself, one finds the Good. The Good is that which draws us out of ourselves in order to love other visible realities. As we look with love upon the Good found in the man who acts unselfishly in the concentration camp, we also look with compassion upon the human realities in close proximity to us. It is a move of unselfishness by which we detach from ourselves and attend to the reality in front of us. Selflessness is learned in loving and searching for the Good.

For example, M loves D because she turns away from her captivity to her conceptual understanding of D and sees her as she really is. This is difficult, because humans are selfish. M could easily recede back into her selfish concepts of D, but, as Murdoch insists, M must keep attending to D, looking at D, and remaining in absolute attention to the situation.[54] This is not done out of a "strength of will but out of the quality of our usual attachments and with the kind of energy and discernment which we have available."[55] The Good inspires this kind of energy and attachment. Through the Good, energy is generated, but the Good also detaches us from ourselves and reattaches us to the world as it really is: the world decentered from the self. Therefore, the just and loving gaze is a practical exercise where one contemplates and loves the Good as a source of moral energy which includes a careful attention to the realities in the world as they are.[56]

The goal of the just and loving gaze is to love the Good and to love justly. Love and Good are not equal. Rather, "Good is the magnetic centre towards which love naturally moves."[57] The Good, by loving it, broadens our objects of love. However, there is a process to determine whether one loves the Good or not. Murdoch writes, "When true good is loved, even impurely or by accident, the quality of the love is automatically refined, and when the soul is turned towards Good the highest part of the soul is enlivened."[58] By loving the Good, according to Murdoch, humans become less selfish. "Love . . . even partially refined . . . is the energy and passion of the soul in its search for Good, the force that joins us to Good and joins

53. Murdoch, *Sovereignty of the Good*, 65.

54. Murdoch, *Sovereignty of the Good*, 89.

55. Murdoch, *Sovereignty of the Good*, 89.

56. Murdoch, *Sovereignty of the Good*, 99.

57. Murdoch, *Sovereignty of the Good*, 100.

58. Murdoch, *Sovereignty of the Good*, 100.

us to the world through Good."[59] The just and loving gaze is formed out of the love of the Good that joins itself to the world, without self-interest. This is how M loves D. Furthermore, it is the means by which humans can love and act in society.

Murdoch's just and loving gaze rounds out Arendt's politics of speech. Arendt suggests that speech is the height of political action. Murdoch completes Arendt's equation by showing the means by which speech can make a difference. Attention is also a type of listening. The just and loving gaze encourages the virtue of listening to the speech of others. This means that the neighbors, those to whom I must be attentive, interpret themselves for me. The just and loving gaze should include speech as an essential task of attention. To be attentive to, and look compassionately upon, a human reality is to allow speech. Speech contains the answer to this question: who are you?[60] Arendt writes,

> In acting and speaking, men show who they are, reveal actively their unique personal identities and thus make their appearance in the human world . . . This disclosure of 'who' in contradistinction to 'what' somebody is—his qualities, gifts, talents, and shortcomings, which he may display or hide—is implicit in everything somebody says and does.[61]

Arendt argues that hearing speech and learning who someone is only happens when we are not for or against, but rather with others (the concept of Mitsein). It is not about affection for the common good, but a passionless *being with* the neighbor in political community.

Murdoch challenges the indifferent nature of Arendt's politics. Arendt's position of being with humanity too easily collapses into indifference. Arendt proposes that the yield of speech and action is equality and distinction. Arendt's principle here is good, but it lacks the cohesion of the just and loving gaze. To this end, Murdoch writes,

> We have suffered a general loss of concepts, the loss of a moral and political vocabulary. We no longer use a spread-out substantial picture of the manifold virtues of man and society. We no longer see man against a background of values, of realities,

59. Murdoch, *Sovereignty of the Good*, 100.

60. Arendt, *Human Condition*, 178.

61. Arendt, *Human Condition*, 179.

which transcend him. We picture man as a brave, naked will surrounded by an easily comprehensible empirical world.[62]

Murdoch is attempting to maintain contingency of human beings set within the horizon of the Good against the backdrop of homogenized human identity and liberal self-assertion. She writes, "Contingency is destructive of fantasy and opens the way for imagination."[63] Murdoch's perspective is deeply critical of biopolitical antinomies, which are not attentive to contingency but operate out of pure fantasy of the neighbor. Contrary, the just and loving gaze sees and loves real people in their contingency according to an epistemology of revolution against fantasy. The ability for Murdoch to value contingency lies in the connection between fact and value. For Murdoch, one only comes to moral knowledge of the world through an entrenchment in the facts of the world. She writes, "Moral change comes from an *attention* to the world whose natural result is a decrease in egoism through an increased sense of the reality of, primarily of course other people, but also other things."[64] Only by paying attention to the "givenness of things," contingency, can one come to a full moral knowledge of it.[65]

The person who is just and loving is attentive to the contingent factual nature of a person or reality. The just and loving person listens for the sake of speech as an act of self-interpretation. This is necessary for the just and loving gaze because, in this act of attention, the real human is exposed in front of the one who sees justly and lovingly. Murdoch proposes a language of goodness that complements Arendt's emphasis on speech. Goodness is the necessary fabric against which we are attentive to the neighbor in the just and loving gaze and can hear speech. Speech then becomes a necessary feature of our political life because it is the necessary means of discovering fellow humans as they are. The Good enables attentive listeners; speech helps discover the Good. The political implications might be, as Rowan Williams suggests about the church, that it is less a matter of telling people who they are than "that the stranger has a gift and

---

62. Murdoch, "Against Dryness," 209.

63. Murdoch, "Against Dryness," 294.

64. Murdoch, *Metaphysics as a Guide*, 52. Emphasis original.

65. This is a reference to a similar description offered by novelist Marilynne Robinson. She writes, referencing William James, "that ideas should be tested in their playing out in the real world" (Robinson, *Givenness of Things*, 86).

a challenge that can change [the listener]."[66] The type of political community that engages in the just and loving gaze allows for fellow humans to change each other. It invites the contingency of the distinct individual into ourselves. Only when this happens do private interests fall away. In a community where virtue and goodness is fostered through the just and loving gaze, there need not be a competition between individuality and sociality; rather, there is true transformation and love that fosters a care for each other. A community that has not only learned to accept the stranger, but to love them, has learned a new politic without coercion and is a witness to politics of coercion.

In sum, the just and loving gaze is essential for a just politics. The just and loving gaze, for Murdoch, is a posture toward attending to the real and a way to deal compassionately with those around us. The just and loving gaze is a search for goodness in everyday experience. Embodied within a community like this is a politics of mutuality beyond the possibilities of private interests.

ANTINOMIES IN GALATIANS: THE APOCALYPTIC *ALREADY* AND THE JUST AND LOVING GAZE

Murdoch's just and loving gaze improves upon Arendt's political thought. I argue that Paul's apocalyptic theology improves upon Murdoch's just and loving gaze. The difficulty in Murdoch's position is that she does not offer a clear definition of the Good that must be loved. In Christian moral theology, God is the focus of our attention in love. I agree with Stanley Hauerwas that there is a muddle that prevents a simple translation of Murdoch into Christian theology.[67] However, the muddle can be answered through an interpretation of Paul's apocalyptic antinomies. The crucifixion of the cosmos in the apocalyptic invasion of Christ provides a new set of antinomies by which the Christian life is measured in the *already*.

It is unnecessary to divorce the *already* and the *not yet* from each other in the current debate of Paul's apocalyptic gospel. J. Louis Martyn writes that "apocalyptic is the heart of Paul's gospel."[68] Martyn clarifies what the apocalyptic *already* means in relation to Galatians' unique mes-

---

66. Williams, "Nobody Knows Who I Am," 289.

67. Hauerwas, "Murdochian Muddles," 190–208.

68. Martyn, "Apocalyptic Antinomies," 113.

sage. In Galatians, Paul finds himself combating, Martyn identifies, "the circumcising Teachers who are now among the Galatian congregations."[69] The Jew/gentile relation—the relationship between circumcised and uncircumcised—names a consistent problem in Paul's corpus. In Christ's incarnation, the good is Christ's lordship that crucifies these divisions of the world in order that a new community might arise. Paul writes to the Galatians:

> May I never boast of anything except the cross of our Lord Jesus Christ, by which the world has been crucified to me, and I to the world. For neither circumcision nor uncircumcision is anything; but a new creation is everything! (Gal 6:14–15, NRSV)

Paul describes the death of the cosmos, but not just any death of the cosmos. The cosmos is crucified, which is the way the cosmos *really is*. For Paul, the cosmos is rerouted through the crucified body of Christ. In the crucifixion, there is a negation of an old way of measuring according to the law and circumcision. Martyn argues the issue that Paul strikes out against is not just the law, but the pair of opposites themselves: circumcision and uncircumcision. This is, Martyn designates, an antinomy, an "expression by which the ancients referred (in many languages) to a pair of opposites so fundamental to the cosmos . . . as to make the cosmos what it is."[70] Therefore, the Pauline apocalyptic *already* (as opposed to the *not yet*) lies in eliminating the old antinomy—the circumcised and uncircumcised—and establishes a new antinomy, or as Paul describes, a new creation.

The typical antinomy is found in relation to the law. The division of circumcised and uncircumcised is in relation to the law. Agamben's work helps readers of Paul recognize that the law has been rendered inoperative in the messianic event. He writes, "With regard to this law that applies itself in disapplying itself, a corresponding gesture of faith ensues, applying itself in disapplying itself, rendering law inoperative while carrying it to its fulfillment."[71] The law under the sovereignty of death had become only that which divides according to Jew and non-Jew. Previously, the law was a means to righteousness, but under this alien sovereignty it has only led to unrighteousness. Therefore, the messianic revocation of the law performs a fulfillment of this righteousness outside of the log-

69. Martyn, "Apocalyptic Antinomies," 114.

70. Martyn, "Apocalyptic Antinomies," 115.

71. Agamben, *Time That Remains*, 107.

ics of such an antinomy. This division creates a new people Agamben terms a "remnant" under a new antinomy. Agamben argues that this new antinomy exists under messianic time, which serves as a suitable means to describe Martyn's new antinomy as the apocalyptic *already*. This is a consistent theme of the letter: to erase the way the antinomy becomes authoritative. For example, there is an opposition between sin and observance of the law (2:17–19), to be wrong and to be set right by observing the law (2:16, 21; 3:12), and to be dead and made alive by the law (3:21).[72]

In the crucifixion of the cosmos, these old antinomies disappear epistemologically. In light of the revelation of God, they do not operate in the moral and political life of disciples. Martyn said that the "fundamental structures are gone" that formerly made the cosmos intelligible.[73] In their place, a new antinomy arises. The remnant exceeds the former antinomy. Recalling another member of the new approach, Badiou correctly recognizes that the new event summons a new community in fidelity to the event, which displaces prior deployments of privilege. Even in his critique of antinomies found in the divisions created by the law, Paul does not suddenly privilege gentile discourses.[74]

In addition to this new unity and remnant, there is a new antinomy, one between flesh and Spirit. Paul writes,

> Live by the Spirit, I say, and do not gratify the desires of the flesh. For what the flesh desires is opposed to the Spirit, and what the Spirit desires is opposed to the flesh; for these are opposed to each other, to prevent you from doing what you want. (Gal 5:16–17, NRSV)

Paul details the various works of the flesh (5:19–21) versus the fruit of the Spirit (5:22–25). According to Martyn, "The Spirit and the Flesh are an oppositional pair that cause the world to be what it *now* actually is."[75] The apocalyptic antinomy described here in Galatians is the one described by Gorman. It is the Spirit of the Son that invades the cosmos for the sake of its liberation (Gal 4:6). The Spirit establishes the peace of Christ's invasion by bearing its fruit in the midst of the community.[76] Contrasting Galatians 5:12 with 5:22, Paul insists that living according

72. See Martyn, *Galatians*, 571.

73. Martyn, "Apocalyptic Antinomies," 118.

74. See 1 Cor 8–12.

75. Martyn, *Galatians*, 572.

76. Martyn, *Galatians*, 530.

to the Spirit results in "love, joy, peace, patience, kindness, generosity, faithfulness" (v. 22), whereas the life according to the flesh is a life where the community "bite[s] and devour[s] one another" (v. 15). Paul, in this new antinomy, is inviting his congregations to join in a certain way of judging the meaning of Christ.[77] As theologian Sarah Bachelard depicts, Paul shows his congregations that Christ has transcended the systems of goodness by which our lives formerly had meaning.[78] Instead of giving life meaning through a fleshy dichotomy between one's circumcision or uncircumcision, congregants must resist the flesh. Bachelard defines systems of goodness as "goodness over against badness, and [is] internally related to the construction of personal and group identities that are also defined over against others."[79] Life lived according to the flesh lives into this system where goodness is secured for the self against the neighbor. Congregants must live according to the fruit of the Spirit, the fruit born of Christ's invasion of the cosmos, which is a new framework of moral habituation enabled and enacted in the remnant for the sake of overcoming this type of moral practice.

Bachelard helps clarify the lived disposition of the fruits of the Spirit that encourages the just and loving gaze. Christ reveals the good in his crucifixion, the death of the old cosmos and its antinomies, and calls into question systems of goodness that perpetuate victimization. The fruit of the Holy Spirit is poured into our hearts, bringing the presence of the crucified Lord into our midst to enable us to do and say as Jesus commanded.[80] To follow such a command is to love the goodness revealed in the resurrection and see the new creation here and now beyond the antinomies of the old age. This leads to looking with compassion upon all human realities in order to, as Bachelard writes, "enact . . . justice for victims, forgiveness for victimizers, and participation for all ('divinization') in the trinitarian life of God."[81] The Spirit encourages a pattern already established in Christ: the just and loving gaze.

The flesh/Spirit antinomy and the new apocalyptic remnant are both, Martyn argues, motifs of the new creation brought about by

77. Bachelard, *Resurrection and Moral Imagination*, 34.

78. Bachelard, *Resurrection and Moral Imagination*, 44.

79. Bachelard, *Resurrection and Moral Imagination*, 4.

80. Bachelard, *Resurrection and Moral Imagination*, 45.

81. Bachelard, *Resurrection and Moral Imagination*, 45. (Bachelard is quoting the work of Brian Robinette.)

Christ's apocalyptic invasion of Christ.[82] According to Martyn, these are not "timeless first principles"; rather, they are born of "God's new creative act."[83] The new antinomy performed in the life of the remnant are events established after something final has occurred. Martyn notes that in Galatians there is a clear before and after in the acts of God, establishing a new reality in the cosmos.[84] The remnant lives in such a way that the life they know in creation has been established by "God's apocalypse of the crucified one," and fruitfully born in the life of the crucified's Spirit.[85]

Apocalyptic is not just the distant fulfillment of creation, but a time in which Christ has already set things right in the cosmos. Martyn concludes,

> It is the time after the apocalypse of faith of Christ (3:23–25), the time of things being set right by that faith, the time of the presence of the Spirit, and thus the time of the war of liberation commended by the Spirit. In a word, it is the time of the dawn of the new creations with its new antinomies. The result is a holistic vision, in scope categorically cosmic and emphatically apocalyptic.[86]

This is Paul's apocalyptic theology of the *already*. It does not exclude a future, final fulfillment. It would be too much of a radicalization to solely emphasize the *already* over and against the *not yet* because it is the war that must be completed. What Martyn does reveal is a thoroughly apocalyptic interpretation of Galatians that compliments the apocalyptic *not yet* provided by Beker and Käsemann.

Not only does the apocalyptic antinomy of Martyn complement Käsemann's and Beker's apocalyptic of the *not yet*, but it also compliments the just and loving gaze. If the remnant or new community lives according to the fruit born of the Spirit of the Son of God, then they see according to a new reality. As argued earlier by Yoder and Martyn, this is according to the crucified and resurrected Lord. Murdoch's just and loving gaze relies on a Spiritual reality that lies behind intelligible perceptions. As a Platonist, Murdoch argues this is the Good Beyond Being.[87]

82. Martyn, *Galatians*, 572.

83. Martyn, *Galatians*, 572.

84. Martyn, *Galatians*, 572.

85. Martyn, *Galatians*, 573.

86. Martyn, *Galatians*, 573.

87. See Plato, *Republic* VI, 509b8–10

Plato, as P. Travis Kroeker writes, "understands the moral drama of soul and society in terms of a theocentric cosmology where the 'Good beyond being' orders all reality toward its transcendent, harmonious, but also mysterious end."[88] Martyn's interpretation of Paul's theology centers on the cross. The cosmos is *crucified*, and thus former antinomies are put death in Christ revealing the truth of the cosmos and history. However, Paul's apocalyptic assumes that the cross is not understood alone, but along a trinitarian and no less transcendent power, namely the Spirit. As Kroeker continues, "The agent of this hidden power that reveals the hidden meaning of the cross is the divine Spirit 'of God' and 'from God.'"[89] Therefore, the person who is ordered toward this hidden spiritual reality is the one who lives according to fruits of the Spirit. The fruits themselves are most attuned to this invisible Spiritual reality.

The interplay between cross and Spirit is essential for Paul. Cross is the physical embodiment of God's wisdom in the world that makes foolish the things of the wise (1 Cor 1:27). However, it is the *pneumatikos* who is ordered by the cross. The means by which one becomes spiritually ordered is nothing less than a repossession. As Philip Ziegler writes,

> Paul's words bespeak a situation in which people are 'not their own masters' but are surrendered to, and dominated by, captivating powers . . . We should conceive of the Spirit's work as one of repossession, a second and salutary overpowering that translates one out of the thrall of idols and into the sphere of Christ's lordship.[90]

Only in this way can the believer, repossessed for the lordship of Christ, be "oriented by the divine Spirit toward the invisible (hidden and mysterious) divine wisdom" that is nonetheless embodied.[91] Furthermore, the embodiment of the spiritually oriented person lies with the fruits of the Spirit as opposed to the works of the flesh.

The works of the flesh are ordered toward private concerns that can fittingly be called private *interests*. Paul writes, "Now the works of the flesh are obvious: fornication, impurity, licentiousness, idolatry, sorcery, enmities, strife, jealousy, anger, quarrels, dissensions, factions, envy, drunkenness, carousing, and things like these" (Gal 5:19–21a, NRSV).

---

88. Kroeker, "War of the Lamb," 139.

89. Kroeker, "War of the Lamb," 141.

90. Ziegler, "Not Without the Spirit," 73.

91. Kroeker, "War of the Lamb," 142.

These words are permeated with private interests and that which would prevent equitable relationships with one's neighbor. These are activities under the sovereignty of death. Thus, they can never escape the political matrix of biopolitics. However, if the fruit of the Spirit is born of the invasion of Christ and reorients our love to joy and peace, then this is the path forward. Like Murdoch, Paul's fruit of the Spirit transcends all things since it comes from the life of God and is immanent in the life of the community. The community is called to a particular type of vision. Martyn writes,

> What lies exposed here is the bifocal vision of apocalyptic. Calling for emphasis is the fact that this vision has not robbed Paul of true realism. Exactly the contrary; it has given to him the ability to see simultaneously the continuing virus in Galatia and the antidote to that virus provided by God. *And* it has shown him which of these is the stronger . . . in the same bifocal vision Paul sees that the future, no less than the present, belongs to God's Christ.[92]

The just and loving gaze and the bifocal vision are one, not only in their realistic, revolutionary epistemology, but in their ability to see beyond sinful antinomies operating in the world. To celebrate the Good as the lordship of Christ over all creation in the presence of the Spirit with its fruits is to see the neighbor outside of biopolitical realities. This is dependent on a spiritual reality hidden from view, but unmasked in the cross. This biofocal vision of the just and loving gaze sees reality as it truly is in Christ. Much like the cosmos, the flesh has been "crucified" to the believer "with its passions and desires" (Gal 5:24, NRSV). This is the framework from which political actions of the community must emerge.

TROUBLING THE NEW APPROACH: AGAMBEN'S *MUSELMÄNNER*

Murdoch's just and loving gaze is a type of realism because it is attention to reality as it presents itself to the human. This is contrasted with the antirealism of the new approach. The political ontology of the new approach is a type of antirealism because it must *construct* an epistemic-ontological scheme through which all reality must filter. This is contrasted with the realism of the just and loving gaze of Arendt's emphasis on speech where

92. Martyn, *Galatians*, 103.

one must give attention to individual realities. The difference between realism and antirealism is the construction of a reality versus attention to reality as it confronts the individual.

Theologian Rowan Williams understands that the antirealism of the late modern period is hopelessly mistaken.[93] Contingency cannot be used as an instrument to express a universal truth *devoid* of contingency. It is impossible to come to specific relations between things and realities. We cannot, through isolated examples of truth and procedures contingent on certain conditions, propose a grand procedure of how everything comes together. Williams writes, "There are things we *come* to know, so that a certain attitude to the time-bound nature of our knowing is involved here."[94] This means that there are "contingently true propositions" that don't assimilate into such an antirealist perspective.[95]

Antirealism is ultimately the issue at stake in the new approach in that it proposes a grand ontological truth procedure that eliminates and discourages these irreducibly evident contingent realities that do not fit within a larger narrative. The chief example of this antirealist tendency of the new approach is found in Agamben's *homo sacer*. Agamben attempts a universal theory of victimhood into which all forms of victimization must fit devoid of certain contingent elements. The purpose of Agamben's interpretation of Paul is to critique law as that which removes the potentiality in people. To remove potentiality is to make an individual into something according to the will of sovereign power, namely to provide it with meaning. The *homo sacer* is the chief example of this power. In this person is displayed the power to kill with impunity and to turn an individual into bare life—no longer acting, but acted upon. Though the larger *Homo Sacer* series is dedicated to the development of this figure into which all victimhood must fit, Agamben utilizes a particular example in order to illustrate the effects of sovereign power: the *Muselmänner* in the Nazi death camps. Through his third volume in the *Homo Sacer* series, *The Remnants of Auschwitz*, Agamben shows firsthand witness accounts that the *Muselmänner* is the absolute example of bare life.[96]

The *Muselmänner* in German literally translates into "Muslim." In Arabic, the word "muslim" designates one who submits completely to

93. Williams, "Trinity and Ontology," 149.

94. Williams, "Trinity and Ontology," 149.

95. Williams, "Trinity and Ontology," 149.

96. See note page 141n184 of this work for more on Agamben's inadequate account of witness.

the will of God. Therefore, it has a theological origin. This is unintentional, as the subjects are overwhelmingly Jewish, and their status as *Muselmänner* does not signal a conversion of a religious nature. In Auschwitz, the *Muselmänner* "is instead defined by a loss of all will and conscientiousness."[97] This usually is the result of extreme malnourishment and exposure. Agamben describes the *Muselmänner* as one in which "the human being [is transformed] into a non-human."[98] The *Muselmänner* is the subject of absolute political power used to reduce a human to inhumanity. The *Muselmänner* has no will, dignity, or freedom. They are the walking dead, not alive or dead, inhuman. In Nazi politics of the death camp, Agamben quotes a holocaust survivor: "The *muselmänner* document[s] the total triumph of power over the human being."[99] For Agamben, the *homo sacer*, as exemplified by the *muselmänner*, is the reality of modern-day victimization. Political power in its sovereignty turns humanity into its bare form void of dignity and subjectivity. Agamben proposes that this is the state of modern politics: it produces bare life; i.e., the *homo sacer*. The *homo sacer* is the victim of sovereignty's forcible reduction of life to bare life. The *homo sacer* is the overarching political theory that guides Agamben's approach to politics.

Agamben's approach lacks the nuance to actually speak for all victims. Alexander Weheliye, a critic of Agamben, argues just this point. Victimization is not something that can be systematized through creating a universal structure of victimhood, which is Agamben's objective. The *homo sacer* is the conceptual figure that the *Muselmänner* must appeal to in order to articulate authentic victimization. Therefore, the *Muselmänner* must assimilate into the *homo sacer*. In short, the suffering of the *Muselmänner* is no longer under examination, but rather this human's authenticity to even be a figure of bare life. Alternatively, Weheliye believes that when one examines the actual narratives and speech of victims, something is learned that cannot be learned from Agamben's *homo sacer*. He writes, "the suffering voices exemplified by . . . the *muselmänner* should not be understood as fountains of authenticity but rather as instantiations of a radically different political imaginary that steers clear of reducing the subjectivity of the oppressed to bare life."[100] The tragedy

97. Agamben, *Remnant of Auschwitz*, 45.

98. Agamben, *Remnant of Auschwitz*, 52.

99. Agamben, *Remnant of Auschwitz*, 48.

100. Weheliye, *Habeas Viscus*, 126.

of Agamben's account is that the humanity of this victim is ignored. Agamben requires the established, ideological rhetoric of the *homo sacer* before he can listen to the *Muselmänner*. Agamben, by insisting on his conceptual vision, runs the risk of failing to see the suffering of the victim as *suffering*.

Such a failure to recognize the victims' suffering is Agamben's failure to recognize their speech and language. Speech and language are essential elements of a politics of the just and loving gaze. Such a breach must be explored. Agamben writes, "It is thus necessary that the impossibility of bearing *witness*, the 'lacuna,' that constitutes human language, collapses, giving way to a different impossibility of bearing witness—that which does not have language."[101] Agamben notes in interviews with those *Muselmänner* who survived the holocaust and those who witnessed the *Muselmänner* that the speech of the *Muselmänner* was not language at all. Rather, Agamben states that the *Muselmänner* has no language, but only babble.[102] Agamben reveals his antirealist sentiments at this point. His account of victimization rejects the language of victims as language. Weheliye argues that Agamben fails to take into account how the victims of sovereign violence narrate their own experience in language other than those recognized by Agamben. According to Weheliye, the language and speech of the *Muselmänner* cannot be assimilated into the *homo sacer*. Therefore, Agamben's error is that language, history, and interpretation of victimization all rely on his external metric, which perpetuates life that matters and life that does not. If language is discredited because it does not fit our late-modern categories, have we escaped biopolitics? As Weheliye understands, this makes bare life an inadequate global concept that attempts to explain oppression and victimization, especially racial oppression, and creates "hierarchical differentiation among human groups."[103]

The mode of discovery necessary to dismantle such a hierarchy requires the just and loving gaze directed toward the speech of another. This is the only way to take seriously the neighbor's "enfleshment," Weheliye argues.[104] Weheliye believes that the flesh is the form of embodiment that enables the articulation of contingency. This is the opulence of the flesh.

---

101. Agamben, *Remnants of Auschwitz*, 39. Emphasis mine.
102. Agamben, *Remnants of Auschwitz*, 37, 39.
103. Weheliye, *Habeas Viscus*, 128.
104. Weheliye, *Habeas Viscus*, 116.

Weheliye's purpose is to renegotiate the terms of what is deemed human and what is not. His work plunges the depth of slave narratives and the firsthand account of the experience of the oppressed. These narratives and accounts correct the approach offered by Agamben by making visible the things that he renders invisible or, to reverse Agamben's profound insight on Paul, to make operative that which he makes inoperative.[105] Practically, this means listening to "'cries and groans,' 'heart-rending shrieks,' 'the mechanical murmurs without content,' as language that does not rely on [already available] linguistic structures" in order to come to know their experience.[106] Rather than yielding to linguistic structures, like the *homo sacer*, these cries call the community to recognition of political violence and gesture toward a new form of politics arising from this place.[107] The just and loving gaze not only looks compassionately on these human realities, but also from these human realities. What emerges from these "hieroglyphics of the flesh"

> is transmitted to the succeeding generations of black subjects who have been "liberated" and granted body in the aftermath of de jure enslavement. The hieroglyphics of the flesh do not vanish once affixed to proper personhood (the body); rather they endure as a pesky potential vital to the maneuverings of "cultural seeing by skin color."[108]

These hieroglyphics affix a new power to the flesh, and a power outside the grasp of western metaphysics because it does not rely on its power. The issue in the antirealism of Western, modern politics is the failure to recognize all people—all victims—as human and the ways each narrates their suffering. The language of cries and murmurs is a summons to a different type of politics not mediated by Western, colonial ideologies, one which critiques and forms human communities that can confront biopolitical violence.

Agamben's struggle to hear the language of the *Muselmänner* is best described as the problem of validation.[109] Philosophically, this concept describes the desire to have a univocal language and village. Such an assimilation is biopolitical. Contrary to validation, the approach that is

---

105. Weheliye, *Habeas Viscus*, 38.

106. Weheliye, *Habeas Viscus*, 126.

107. Weheliye, *Habeas Viscus*, 126.

108. Weheliye, *Habeas Viscus*, 39.

109. Yoder, "On Not Being Ashamed," 285–86.

formed apocalyptically operates from a different location. The good news of apocalyptic is the "alternative to the epistemology of establishment, which seeks to adjust one's 'own' knowledge to the conditions of validity already dominating the wider culture."[110] Apocalyptic lives in exile of the necessity of validity. Agamben alludes to the importance of exile in his work, but it must be understood in its singular importance in relationship to its rejection of validation. Rather, apocalyptic "refutes" the necessity of validation through its "irreducible presence" and the particularity of a strange language proceeding from the mouth of a first-century Jewish man communicating "God with us."[111] Only through a rejection of validity, and thus biopolitics, can one find a politics of particularity suited for our times.

The Pauline answer to biopolitics lies in a politics of the just and loving gaze, where attention is crucial. Attention for apocalyptic politics again gives rise to the voices of the slaughtered in Revelation 5–7. Paul's apocalyptic theology can be understood in concert with these passages because, as Beker understands, the liturgy in Revelation might as well have been Paul's own liturgy.[112] The multiplicity of voices that sing and praise the slaughtered Lamb are defined by their very multiplicity (Rev 7:9). Added to this are the very "groans" of creation (Rom 8:22, NRSV) and varieties of flesh at the resurrection (1 Cor 15:37–41) presented by Paul. Taken together, the Pauline apocalyptic response to identity should be read within Weheliye's account. The voices that sing "Worthy is the Lamb, who was slain" (Rev 5:12, NRSV) sing outside the places of power. Their songs of praise are a kind of speech unintelligible from the historical loci of biopolitics because they reject the historical meaning assigned to them by such orders. Their shrieks and groans neither attest to the glory of redemptive suffering nor to a masochist acceptance of their lot, but are the melodious sounds of those who know power does not exist with "people who wear crowns."[113] In short, it is a realism by other means. The historically slaughtered know that praise of the slaughtered Lamb gestures toward a new and greater power that grants them power. It is within the plurality of this hymnody that a new politics not dependent on Western narratives of personhood begins to emerge.

---

110. Yoder, "On Not Being Ashamed," 295.

111. Yoder, "On Not Being Ashamed," 295.

112. Beker, *Paul's Apocalyptic Gospel*, 48.

113. Yoder, "Armaments and Eschatology," 58.

POLITICAL PRACTICE: PAUL'S MORAL EXHORTATIONS

The hymn of the slaughtered then provides the realism of the just and loving gaze to focus on what practices construct an apocalyptic politics. The theological importance of the just and loving gaze is crucial to understanding Paul's apocalyptic political theology. Reading Murdoch within Paul's apocalyptic gospel bears the fruit of combating the biopolitical systems and antirealism offered in the new approach. However, Paul's apocalyptic theology envisions practices of the just and loving gaze that confront these orders. Much like Benjamin, political orders must be confronted in practice. Paul's moral exhortations are grounded in Christ's apocalyptic saving event, which in turn constitutes the community and its life together. The means by which Paul confronts political orders are within the very life of the church. The political witness of the church lies in, as Christian ethicist Philip Turner writes, "how Christ forms a culture and how that 'Christianly' formed culture penetrates the wider culture."[114] The practices highlighted below reflect the apocalyptic *already* wherein Christ is already Lord over the powers, which restores God to the intimate center of human activity and confronts the biopolitical forms of sovereignty.

Remembering and the Eucharist: 1 Corinthians 10–12

The first passage is Paul's exhortation against the abuse of the Lord's Supper and the practice of remembrance in the Eucharist. Remembering is a crucial task of the church, according to Paul in his letters. Remembering, for Paul, is an aspect of communal discernment that answers the question "What should I do?" in light of the apocalyptic incursion of Christ into creation. It is out of the resources and confessions of the apocalyptic Christ that our moral convictions arise. It is clear through Paul that the person of Christ is not interested in providing moral principles for individuals to live by, but the creation of communities of discernment. A community able to discern through remembering can see and act with the just and loving gaze.

Paul's practice of remembering arises from Paul's confidence in the gospel. He writes to the Romans,

---

114. Turner, *Christian Ethics and the Church*, xviii.

> I myself feel confident about you, my brothers and sisters, that you yourselves are full of goodness, filled with all knowledge, and able to instruct one another. Nevertheless on some points I have written to you rather boldly by way of reminder, because of the grace given me by God to be a minister of Christ Jesus in the priestly service of the gospel of God. (15:14–16, NRSV)

Commentator Robert Jewett writes that here Paul attempts to remind the church to develop "commonly held beliefs in innovative ways that, if accepted, will move the Romans toward attitudes and actions that counter their current stance."[115] The belief that founded the community was the apocalyptic incursion of Christ into the cosmos to save humanity from the sovereign powers of sin and death. If Jewett's interpretation is correct, then this conviction is the one that will lead to moral change through practices arising from it. By way of reminder, the community is called back to its original witness for the sake of new moral judgements confronting the community.

Paul's moral exhortations to remembrance have implicit and explicit examples throughout his corpus. Most explicit is his exhortation over abuses of the Lord's Supper. At that time, the Lord's Supper served as a communal meal for the Corinthians. During the practice of this meal, we are told that some in the community abuse this meal by overindulging while others go hungry (1 Cor 11:21). The issue at stake is individuality over and against the neighbor. The gravity of this abuse is contrasted with the unity described in 1 Corinthians 10:16–17. This unity is read inside the unity of Israel, who, in the wilderness with Moses, "ate the same spiritual food, and all drank the same spiritual drink" (1 Cor 10:4). Historically, the unity of the Israelites is compromised by the worship of other deities and demons. False worship, not selfishness, is the issue in 1 Corinthians 10. Worship of the one true God establishes unity that binds the community together over and against other deities and demons. In 1 Corinthians 11, it is Christ whom the community worships, and it is of his body and blood they partake. This is how they become the body of Christ.

Remembrance in Paul's exhortation returns the community to proper worship of God. The Supper is performed "in remembrance" of Christ (1 Cor 11: 24–5) as a command of Christ. This is Paul's recounting and passing on of this practice as a reenactment of Christ's life, specifically of

---

115. Jewett, *Romans*, 905–6.

his betrayal and death. The specific act of remembrance surrounds the event of Christ's speaking to his disciples on the night of his betrayal. This recalls Christ's own classification of the elements of the supper as the "blood of the new covenant" (1 Cor 11:25). This remembrance of the new covenant established in the initial celebration of the meal signals two things First, the new covenant is, as Hans Conzelmann understands, both eschatological and apocalyptic.[116] Second, the new covenant is juxtaposed with Paul's description of the old covenant (2 Cor 3:14). Paul's use of new covenant here corresponds to Jeremiah 31:31. This is a new apocalyptic covenant that disrupts the old covenant. It is a new binding together that is signaled in this practice. The community, former to baptism, was separated by divisions of Jew/Greek, slave/free, etc. (1 Cor 12:13). Through the partaking of this meal, the community becomes "one body" (1 Cor 10:17; 12:13). In remembering Christ, the community unlearns a way of division that enabled overindulgence in the face of a member's hunger and learns a unity that is a continuation of table fellowship with the risen and exalted Lord, as perpetuated in the neighbor.

The practice of the Lord's Supper recognizes an apocalyptic trinitarian disruption of community. The practice is not done for its own sake; it finds meaning in the God who is proclaimed in the practice. Käsemann understands that there is a parallel between Christ and the Spirit in the practice of the sacraments. It is a function of unifying the body of Christ.[117] In the sacrament, "the exalted Lord conveys, along with his gift, participation in himself as the Giver, therefore the gift of the sacrament must also be *Pneuma*."[118] The presence of Christ manifest in the sacrament is a means toward freedom from the powers of sin and death exemplified in the community's failure to recognize its unity in the Supper. Käsemann explains that the sacrament is the site of a cosmic battle in which Christ, through the Spirit, is given to the believers for their transformation into a body.

Käsemann writes, "[humanity] finds redemption when the *pneuma* invades his earthly nature and recaptures him for the heavenly world."[119] This captures the point of Gorman's exegesis of Galatians 4. The cosmic trinitarian disruption in which the believer is returned to the Father, one

---

116. Conzelmann, *1 Corinthians*, 199–200.

117. Käsemann, "Pauline Doctrine," 113.

118. Käsemann, "Pauline Doctrine," 114. Emphasis original.

119. Käsemann, "Pauline Doctrine," 116.

Käsemann terms the "heavenly realm," is given a material expression. Paul does not envision the Spirit of Christ as a "disembodied force."[120] Rather, it manifests itself in the sacramental event, which is "the substance of resurrection corporeality and the dimension in which the Risen One exists."[121] Paul calls the Corinthians to the remembrance of this embodied reality as the opportunity to obey Christ.[122] In remembrance, ethicist Allen Verhey writes, Paul tells the story of Christ's death and institution of the Lord's Supper in order to "remedy . . . forgetfulness."[123] This story is *their* story. This story and its continual practice in the community is a constant rehearsal of something that demands a particular type of obedience.

The political and moral implications of remembrance are found in obedience to this reality practiced in the Eucharist. Theologian William Cavanaugh helps tease out the implications of remembering in the Eucharist:

> The word *anamnesis* (remembering) had the effect not so much of a memorial, as one would say kind words about the dead, but rather of performance. The emphasis is thus on the entire rite of the Eucharist as action, and not simply on the consecration of the elements . . . since the consecration turns the bread and wine into the body and blood of Christ, what the church does in the Eucharist must be what Christ did with his body and blood—offer them in sacrifice . . . since we are Christ's body performing His will, what we offered must be what he offered in the events on Calvary, His own body and blood.[124]

Cavanaugh summarizes the essential elements of Paul's moral exhortation on remembrance as a rehearsal of Christ's own apocalyptic incursion into the cosmos. In 1 Corinthians 10 and 12, Paul recalls the unity of the body of Christ for those who partake of the body of Christ and their sacrificial offering of themselves to God and each other. This unity is created for those freed for obedience from the sovereign powers of sin and death. However, in the center is a threat to this unity, factions that create divisions among believers. Such factions do not embody sacrificial love. Into this problem, Paul tells the story of Christ's betrayal and sacrificial death.

120. Käsemann, "Pauline Doctrine," 117.

121. Käsemann, "Pauline Doctrine," 118.

122. Käsemann, "Pauline Doctrine," 119.

123. Verhey, *Remembering Jesus*, 26.

124. Cavanaugh, *Torture and Eucharist*, 230.

If the Corinthians are the body of Christ, then they must, Cavanaugh stipulates, live sacrificially. What is not sacrificially minded is individuals going ahead with their meals where some become drunk and others go hungry (1 Cor 11:21).[125] The current state of the Corinthian congregation lies in selfish private interests, the opposite of sacrifice. By way of reminder, Paul shows the community that it is answerable to the body and blood (1 Cor 12:27). It is unworthy of the body and blood of Christ to treat members of the body unjustly and unlovingly. The Eucharist makes visible the members of the body of Christ, and in so doing condemns the maltreatment taking place in Corinth.

In the wake of the divisions among them, the community must be "re-membered" into the body of Christ.[126] Practicing the Eucharist achieves such an end and clarifies the politics of the Christian community. "Re-membering" is an incorporation of individuals back into the body of Christ. This incorporation is not an assimilation; there is still particularity in members of the church (1 Cor 12:14–20). Only when the body is re-membered can it serve and assist one another. The issue is the discrepancy between those who have and those who have nothing. The imagination of self-interestedness undoes the body of Christ.

In Paul's work, the Eucharist forms an imagination of a truly corporate polity that resists the present position of the Corinthian congregation. The practice of remembering in the Eucharist locates the neighbor inside of the body of Christ and against any private interest, such as hunger. Cavanaugh writes, "The emphasis [in the practice of Eucharist] is on the *externality* of the liturgy to individual bodies, the way it incorporates individuals into the body of Christ."[127] The Eucharist is a practice of the just and loving gaze. Through the Eucharist, the just and loving gaze finds a tangible rehearsal that resists all forms of "fragmenting discipline."[128] The Eucharist is not just a counter-epistemology, but is a "counter-discipline."[129] This is a counter-discipline wherein

> Christ's true body is enacted . . . by the incarnation of the church
> in the bodies of the poor. The true body of Christ is the suffering

125. One should also note the role drunkenness plays as a work of the flesh, which is directly opposed to the fruits of the Spirit embodied within the antinomy of the apocalyptic *already*.

126. Cavanaugh, *Torture and Eucharist*, 229.

127. Cavanaugh, *Torture and Eucharist*, 229.

128. Cavanaugh, *Torture and Eucharist*, 229.

129. Cavanaugh, *Torture and Eucharist*, 229.

body, the destitute body, the body which is tortured and sacrificed. The church is the body of Christ because it performs
an *anamnesis* of Christ's sacrifice, suffering in its own flesh the
affliction taken on by Christ. In the church's communities of
solidarity, the poor are fed by Christ but, insofar as they become
Christy's body, they also become food for others.[130]

A parallel between Yoder and Cavanaugh is apparent. Through attention the Corinthians are called to fix their gaze on the suffering and
the slaughtered. They fix their gaze not accidentally, but sacramentally.
The cross—nothing less than that which breaks Christ's body and sheds
his blood—is celebrated here. The grain of the bread is the grain of the
universe, and it is from here that the church will celebrate its power.
Therefore, the affluent Corinthians must be *for* the poor because they
work with the grains of the universe. Remembering unmasks those who
are most in need in the very concrete, material means they lack. In the
Corinthian community, those who overindulged were affluent. Certain
harmful antinomies still operated within the community. The possible
threat that the neighbor in the church poses to the hunger of the affluent
members must be discarded, because when they see the poor in their
midst, they recognize them as fellow members of the body of Christ in
need. Remembrance in the Eucharist, through its consistent practice,
focuses the congregation on the suffering death of Christ's poverty. They
are to remember Christ and, by extension, must also become poor with
those who already bear that burden.

     In conclusion, it is only by remembering Christ's poverty as their
own that they can see the poor in their midst with the just and loving
gaze. There is a connection between the gift received in the Eucharist
through the Spirit, meditation on the gift, and the vision it creates. The
church remembers in order to learn how private interests impact other
members in the body of Christ and the world.

Attention and Eating Idol Meat: Acts 10:9–16, 1 Corinthians 8–10, and Romans 14–15:13

Remembering in the practice of the Eucharist offers a concrete means to
practice the just and loving gaze, but it is not the only example of such
a discipline. Paul's discourse against idol meat builds upon memory as a

---

130. Cavanaugh, *Torture and Eucharist*, 229, 267.

practice of the *already* and the just and loving gaze. I propose that the political action embodied in Paul's moral exhortation against the consumption of idol meat is attention. Attention is political because it is a way of seeing the neighbor and their particularity without drawing the neighbor into an antinomy defined by the state (biopolitics), which is displaced by the apocalyptic incursion of Christ. I utilize this word "attention" as a specific reference to Murdoch's own use of the word as an appropriate way to describe the continued relevance of Paul's exhortation against the consumption of idol meat. Attention is a way to love the neighbor and engender a politic that can hear and instruct one another without coercion or exclusion. Idol meat offers an opportunity to discuss difference without collapsing into harmful antinomies.

The consumption of meat offered to idols is far removed from our cultural imagination, but in Paul's time it was a major concern. Could a Christian be a Christian and still eat the meat offered to an idol? The cause of concern was those who felt that partaking of the meat would be immoral because of its origin. There were others who contented all food is clean because of the newfound freedom in Christ through Christ's defeat of all idols. This allowed the consumption of meat offered to idols. The difference of opinion on this matter, along with the ubiquity of idol meat, caused division concerning correct conduct in the Christian community.

Paul's response to this issue in his first letter to the Corinthians and his letter to the Romans highlights what he believes is the central moral conviction of a Christian community: neighbor love and the maintaining of difference. In this instance, unlike other areas he addresses (i.e., sexual practice), Paul doesn't believe that there is a correct moral exhortation tied to either practice (i.e., to eat idol meat or not to eat idol meat). Rather, Paul creates the condition for difference to be maintained and moral stances relativized in the Corinthian and Roman churches. It was not one's position toward idol meat that mattered, but one's relationship to the other in his/her midst.

Acts 10:9–16

Before turning to the moral exhortation against the consumption of idol meat, it is important to locate Paul's text within another textual narrative: Peter's struggles with cleanliness in Acts 10. Acts presents a central theme of cleanliness and uncleanliness in the life of the apostle Peter. For Peter, the reversal of the kosher laws is nothing short of an apocalyptic disruption. This Petrine story establishes a base understanding of cleanliness to which Paul will directly and indirectly appeal. As such, the events of Acts 10 have an impact on Paul's own thought.

Acts 10:1–8 sets up the narrative necessary to understand Peter's vision. Cornelius, a gentile, hears a message from an angel of God. The message is for Cornelius to send for Simon Peter, who resided in Joppa at the time. This peculiar divine message to a non-Jewish figure is characteristic of the Acts narrative, which can be characterized as the opening of the Jewish story to the gentile world. Peter's vision in Acts 10:9–16 comes from a "heaven opened" (*ton ouranonaneogmenon*; Acts 10:11). New Testament scholar Carl Holiday understands this is not an accidental or minor detail. Holiday writes that an opened heaven "signals access to God's space," which is closely tied to apocalyptic events and visions.[131] An opened heaven, both to Peter and implied in the message to Cornelius, signifies the state in which humanity finds itself in relation to God. Due to Christ's apocalyptic invasion of the world, creatures have greater access to God. This is what precipitates the mission to the gentile world in which Peter and the apostles must engage. Openness to God is directed also to the fellow human, as evidenced in this vision's purpose to prepare Peter for ministry to the gentiles.

Peter's vision, within the context of the broader mission to the gentile world, is experienced in hunger and prayer. Theologian Willie Jennings writes of this moment of God's in-breaking:

> Now God comes. Peter will be the site of the in-breaking . . . the new order drops from the sky. God comes to Peter inside of Israel's first and deepest gesture—in the moment of prayer. God comes to Peter inside the creature's deepest truth—in the moment of his hunger. Prayer and hunger, hunger and prayer— these will be the pillars on which God will build the future of the creature.[132]

Jennings interprets this passage theologically with an eye toward the apocalyptic work in Christ. God meets the *creature* at the site of his/her own desires in order to call its attention to other creaturely realities. First, there is the desire for God in prayer, which is the first and most important desire of the creature. Second, God confronts Peter in his hunger. The

---

131. Holiday, *Acts*, 232.

132. Jennings, *Acts*, 105.

creature's hunger is the desire that names Peter *as* a creature. Both of these desires, according to Jennings, establish the basis that God is in the process of reorienting humanity at their most basic *creaturely* impulses.

God's appearance to Peter at the site of his desires is for the purpose of reorienting them to the divine mission to the gentiles. In verses 11–12, Peter is presented with a multitude of creatures. Peter is instructed to "kill and eat" (v. 13, NRSV), but he refuses due to the cleanliness of the creatures in question (v. 14b). It is here that God calls Peter to reorient his desires. Not only must he eat, but he must call good what God calls good. As he will see with Cornelius (vv. 17–23a), this classification is not just extended to animals, but also all people. As a creature who hungers, he is called to desire God and that which he formerly called unclean. This command to eat is in the form of radical intimacy with all of creation that harkens back to Genesis 1:24.[133] This is a disruptive continuity for Peter that joins him back to creation and to those human and nonhuman creatures around him. This invitation signals two important truths for the Lukan narrative.

First, it signals the act of eating practiced in the Eucharist. "Get up, Peter; kill and eat" (v. 13, NRSV) corresponds to, "This is my body, which is given for you" (Luke 22:19, NRSV). Broken body and shed blood, in both animal and Christ, here signals an ontological shift of all creation into the grains of the universe. Jennings takes this further: the command to kill and eat "grows out of . . . [Christ's] invitation to eat."[134] This recalls Paul's moral exhortation of remembrance for the sake of establishing unity in the body through eating offered in the moral/political act of memory. By eating, Peter enters into a new world of intimacy and unity made possible by Christ who takes on created flesh and recalls it to goodness.

Second, the invitation of the Spirit is realized in a concrete welcoming of two individuals together. Jennings writes, "The Spirit of God is on both sides, outside the door with the seekers and inside the door with the perplexed Peter."[135] Cornelius and Peter both receive messages from God, and it is the Spirit that speaks and brings these people together (Acts 10:19). God is changing the relational structures by which Cornelius and, especially, Peter come to define the world. To utilize the imagery

133. See Pervo, *Acts*, 269.

134. Jennings, *Acts*, 107.

135. Jennings, *Acts*, 108.

of Agamben, God makes inoperative former discourses of meaning in order to establish a remnant composed of those both inside and outside the door. Only when Peter can see the unclean as clean and the outside as inside can he truly see with the just and loving gaze. This aligns Peter with God's general bringing of the nations under the logic of the Spirit by bringing many tongues together (Acts 2). Jennings writes, "God is simply, beautifully interrupting conventional and normal structures of relating by mapping God's own relational logic across their bodies."[136] The inner trinitarian apocalyptic disruption of relationality, where God draws damaged sociality into Godself, establishes a new center of intimacy with God at its center. Only when Peter recognizes that God has called the gentile good can he participate in this new relational reality made possible by the Son and Spirit to draw us to the Father and make us all children of God.

Acts 10 shows us a God who draws humanity into Godself. This properly sets the context for Paul's moral exhortation for idol meat. We can assume the relevance of Acts for Paul's discourses in 1 Corinthians 8 and Romans 14 for two distinct reasons in addition to the role it plays in naming the intimate center of the community formed by God's new relational network. First, Paul seems to make a reference to this in Romans 14:14–20: "I know and am persuaded in the Lord Jesus that nothing is unclean in itself (v. 14a)."[137] In discussing the nature or appropriateness of consuming idol meat, though not the central issue in Paul's passage, it appears that Peter's vision at least plays a role in showing that nothing is unclean. Second, Paul rebukes Peter for seeming to fail to adhere to the truth of his vision to live into the just and loving gaze. In Galatians 2:11–14, Paul opposes Peter face to face because, as it is written in verse 11, "he stood self-condemned" (κατεγνωσμένος). Peter's condemnation is self-imposed, if one considers the testimony of Acts a credible witness against him. The central issue is that Peter still treats some as unclean (gentiles) and others as clean (Jews). Peter, at the behest of Paul, is reminded of the movement of the Spirit that is bringing these two groups together into one body, one remnant. The overall theme of the vision was so that Peter would not encourage or support this type of behavior. In fact, it appears that Peter has attempted to coerce gentiles into a Jewish lifestyle. The age that Peter embodies is not the age inaugurated by Christ.

---

136. Jennings, *Acts*, 109.

137. Pervo, *Acts*, 269.

It is for these reasons that Acts 10 frames Paul's moral discourse on idol meat, namely it deconstructs the former antinomies at the heart of the old cosmos and insists on that which is the grain of the universe. After the resurrection and ascension of Christ, his disciples engaged in a missionary effort to the gentiles in order to participate in the new order that God creates on earth. The themes and central convictions of Acts 10 are essential to the discourse on idol meat in Romans and 1 Corinthians. In Acts 10, Peter establishes the moral/political task of attention as central to the practices of the church, and Paul, through his own convictions and testimony to Peter's vision, follows suit. In his moral exhortations, we see Paul's intentional formation of a Christian community centered on intimacy with God and neighbor.

1 Corinthians 8

Paul's discussion in 1 Corinthians 8 of the moral issues of eating meat offered to idols in the Corinthian community begins by referencing the difference between knowing moral imperatives and communal love. Both involve moral formation, but only one aligns appropriately with the apocalyptic in-breaking of God. He writes, "Now concerning food sacrificed to idols; we know that 'all of us possess knowledge.' Knowledge puffs up, but love builds up" (1 Cor 8:1, NRSV). This is important because the goal is not to come to a common consensus (i.e., that Christ has robbed the idols of their power, all food is clean, etc.), but to set aside one's knowledge for the sake of the other and knowing Christ.[138] Paul affirms that knowing God outweighs other forms of knowing (1 Cor 8:4–6). Paul continues, "It is not everyone, however, that has this knowledge" (1 Cor 8:7a., NRSV). Some still live in the knowledge of idols in their moral conscience. Therefore, if they ate the meat they would, in their own conscience, sin (1 Cor 8:7b).

Paul does not say this to shame those he refers to as "the weak." Rather, he highlights this to prove a point about food altogether. "'Food will not bring us close to God.' We are no worse off if we do not eat, and no better if we do" (1 Cor 8:8). Food, among other things, is not the important thing in the community of Christ. Paul places "those . . . believers for whom Christ died" (1 Cor 8:11) at the center of communal concern. Food will not bring them closer to God, but the body of Christ will. The

---

138. See Horrell, *Solidarity and Difference*, 176.

center is not a universal standard of moral actions. It is the just treatment of specific individuals within the community itself. What matters is how actions impact others. Such a moral discernment process is the new rationality of the apocalyptic community of the Spirit.[139] If the community does something that causes one of these believers to suffer and sin, then the one sinned against is Christ (1 Cor 8:12). The knowledge of Christ and his crucifixion fulfills the promise of 1 Corinthians 2:2, placing this at the center of moral reasoning. The community's faithfulness is to those for whom Christ has died, and it is a corresponding faithfulness to Christ.

1 Corinthians 9

Continuing the argument about absolute regard for others in the community, Paul uses himself as an example. He writes, "Am I not free? Am I not an apostle? Have I not seen Jesus our Lord? Are you not my Work in the Lord? This is my defense to those who would examine me. Do we not have the right to our food and drink?" (1 Cor 9:1, 3, NRSV). Paul continues in this line of questioning (1 Cor 9:5–12a) in order to prove his right to certain material things (i.e., taking a wife, collecting a wage from the Corinthians, etc.). However, Paul engages in this rhetorical technique in order to prove that if the Corinthian "strong" think they have a right to certain material realities (i.e., eating meat) over and against the moral damage done to the weak, then Paul's rights to material realities (i.e., collecting a wage from his congregations) vastly outweighs their rights. In an indirect way, Paul is unmasking the limited ability rights (or private interests) have to preserve community. Paul uses this as a teaching moment in order to "make the gospel free of charge" (1 Cor 9:18). This only happens when one waves his or her own rights. Paul exerts none of his rights over those he preaches to, so that the gospel may not be encumbered. This is similar to what Paul sees at the heart of the meat offered to idols. If we require all to eat meat offered to idols, then the gospel is encumbered, and those with weak conscience caused to suffer. However, if the strong surrender their rights and don't eat meat, then the gospel is not encumbered, because the strong do not have any moral reservations about eating "clean" foods offered to idols.

139. New Testament scholar J. Louis Martyn writes, "It is life in the midst of the new-creation community, in which to know by the power of the cross is to know and to serve the neighbor who is in need" (Martyn, "Epistemology," 109).

Paul encourages the strong by his example. He writes, "For though I am free with respect to all, I have made myself a slave to all, so that I might win more of them" (1 Cor 9:19, NRSV). The purpose of one's actions lies in how they encourage and present the gospel to others, tying moral reflection to missionary effort.[140] This affirms Badiou's conviction of Paul's diagonal approach to a variety of subject positions. Paul moves diagonally through a variety of positions, not for the sake of privileging one over the other, but rather a universal affirmation that moves fluidly through all subjective dispositions in the community. The deployment of these terms of strong and weak are mere parodies that do not signal a hierarchy, but the mobilization of cultural antinomies against themselves. Accommodating behavior does not accommodate a privileged position, but always looks to those outside the hegemonic positions.

According to Paul, one's accommodating behavior reflects both the up-building of community members and the conversion of nonbelievers.[141] It is a new "law" (1 Cor 9:21), but a new law that operates in a totally new manner by not wedding itself to sovereignty. Rather, it exists in exile of sovereignty. The "weak" are among those who work with the grain of the universe. The new moral life does not appeal to a universal moral conscience, but a practice of christological attention to individuals in the community who are impacted by our actions.[142]

1 Corinthians 10

Paul summarizes his argument up until this point by alluding to the example of Israel in the wilderness, reaffirming his stance toward idolatry, which overlaps with his discussion on the sacraments (1 Cor 10:1–22). The strong allusion to pagan practices in this passage (10:1–22) is not a regression in his argument away from the freedom in Christ; rather, it affirms his prior stances on idolatry as a divisive, community-dividing practices. In verse 23, Paul picks up the moral thoughts behind abstaining from idol meat. He affirms the right to eat idol meat (i.e., "all things are lawful," 1 Cor 10:23) but continues that not all things should be practiced just because they can. There are certain practices (i.e., eating meat known to be offered to idols in the presence of those with weak conscience) that

---

140. This is a theme developed by Barram in *Mission and Moral Reflection*, 1–34.

141. Barram, *Mission and Moral Reflection*, 47–48.

142. Horrell, *Solidarity and Difference*, 182.

can tear down the community by allowing those with a weak conscience to stumble.

Still, Paul affirms that all things are clean according to the Lord (1 Cor 10:25). The only situation where it becomes problematic to partake of this meat is when "someone says to you, 'This has been offered in sacrifice'" (1 Cor 10:28, NRSV). In this instance, Paul urges abstinence from eating it. This is not for the believer's advantage, "but that of the other" (1 Cor 10:24b, NRSV). It is not for the conscience of the strong, but for the conscience of the weak. In the new age, formed by knowledge of Christ and his crucifixion, one is completely turned toward service to the other. To borrow from Martyn, "to know by the power of the cross is to know and to serve the neighbor who is in need."[143] This crucified restriction does not infringe on the believer's freedom in an absolute sense, in the way that certain things now become unclean—it is a practice toward other believers in love. All are still free in Christ, but one's freedom must be exercised cautiously. Paul concludes with this final thought:

> So, whether you eat or drink, or whatever you do, do everything for the glory of God. Give no offense to Jews or to Greeks or to the church of God, just as I try to please everyone in everything I do, not seeking my own advantage, but that of the many, so that they may be saved. (1 Cor 10:31–33, NRSV)

The whole matter at stake is that difference be maintained toward the health of a community and harmful exclusionary norms be discouraged so that the believer and nonbeliever may experience Christ. Weakness, then, is not a qualitative distinction that must be met with condescension. Rather, it is that which shames the strong (1 Cor 1:27). Therefore, Paul takes aim not only at sovereignty and those who wear crowns as the vantage point of the gospel, but affirms in practice the power from which the gospel itself proceeds, namely in other regard in conflict with self-assertion.

Paul relativizes the issue of meat offered to idols in order to locate the importance of regard for others as a central conviction of this new community. The Corinthian believers are Christians because of the supremacy of Christ, not because of universal moral consensus. Paul does not mean to say that the Corinthians can do as they please; rather, what binds them together is Christ, and one's moral formation must work

---

143. Martyn, "Epistemology," 109.

toward unity in Christ. Therefore, the material good of eating meat offered to idols is relativized for the sake of community love.

Romans 14–15:13

An addendum to Paul's exhortation on idol meat needs to be added by
way of Paul's continued discussion of the strong and weak in Romans 14.
As in 1 Corinthians, Paul does not commend either the strong or weak
over the other (Rom 14:1–6). Paul picks up themes from 1 Corinthians
by urging a christological vision of other believers rather than a universal
moral conscience (Rom 14:7–9).

In his letter to the Romans, Paul emphasizes not judging one another, reminding them that rights and private interests are secondary to
caring for and preserving the neighbor (Rom 14:10–16). He focuses, as
he does in 1 Corinthians, on idol meat because it illustrates Paul's moral
formation. He writes,

> If your brother or sister is being injured by what you eat, you
> are no longer walking in love. Do not let what you eat cause the
> ruin of one for whom Christ died. So do not let your good be
> spoken of as evil. For the kingdom of God is not food and drink
> but righteousness and peace and joy in the Holy Spirit. (Rom
> 14:15–17, NRSV)

Here again is a clear connection between the work of the Christ and the
Spirit. Here is the apocalyptic undoing of ancient antinomies in the replacing of antinomies, such as circumcision and uncircumcision, with
peace (Gal 6:14–16). Christ's death positively impacts and reveals the
neighbor for whom we should have concern. The individual we injure
(v. 15) is not just the neighbor, but is Christ by proximity. Paul claims
that this is what is at stake in injuring our neighbor. Furthermore, this
cadence of righteousness, peace, and joy in the Holy Spirit is juxtaposed
with food and drink as contradictory modes of the Christian life, much
like flesh and Spirit in Galatians 5. What holds the community together
is the Spirit of Christ working with believers toward their righteousness;
this is the presence of the new age in the community's midst. Biblical
scholar Robert Jewett comments that "The triad of 'righteousness and
peace and joy' . . . is used to describe the new life of the Christian congregation 'in [the] Holy Spirit,' in which love overcomes social distinctions

and barriers."[144] Jewett helps locate social distinctions and barriers within the antinomies of the old world. Paul, through this exhortation, invites the Romans to overcome the antinomies in concrete practice of the apocalyptic incursion of Christ. Commitment to Christ and those for whom he died, not food or drink, are the central mark of the community that confronts and exists in excess of these antinomies (Rom 14:18). This is what Christian moral formation looks like.

Paul does not propose a universal moral conscience, but a practice in light of one's pursuit of Christ in the community. Paul writes, "The faith that you have, have as your own conviction before God. Blessed are those who have no reason to condemn themselves because of what they approve" (Rom 14:22, NRSV). Paul continues his theme of conscience in moral formation. He argues that differences on matters such as food or drink must be affirmed and celebrated so individuals cannot be condemned in their own moral conscience. Even though all food is clean, "it is unclean for anyone who thinks it unclean" (Rom 14:14b). Individual moral choice must mind the impact on the neighbor so that true and genuine difference can be maintained for the sake of a loving community of Christ (Rom 14:15). Christ constitutes the absolute authority over the community. When discerning moral activity, it is Christ that must be remembered and attended to. Christ's relationship challenges all harmful antinomies that infringe and harm the neighbor in the community.

The Strong and Weak: An Apocalyptic Assessment

Now that the relevant texts have been explored, I venture a statement on the complex terms "strong" and "weak." For Paul, these terms have theological significance which become problematic when translated into late modernity. Strong and weak, for the late moderns, denote degrees of quality and strength of individuals. There is a great deal of condescension in such a distinction. Take for example, 1 Peter 3:7: "Husbands, in the same way, show consideration for your wives in your life together, paying honor to the woman as the *weaker* sex" (NRSV, Emphasis mine). This verse is paradigmatic for many modern interpreters that scripture is anti-egalitarian. For Paul, however, these terms function very differently.

To begin, it is clear that for Paul strong and weak are not on a continuum between obviously praiseworthy (i.e., strong) on the one hand

144. Jewett, *Romans*, 863.

and poor (i.e., weak) on the other. Rather, these function as competing moral consciences. In this way, as David Horrell has argued, Paul is open to a diversity of moral traditions (i.e., Jewish, gentile, etc.), while also "sharing ethical norms."[145] As argued, this shared ethical norm is other regard *in* Christ, which, when combined with shared worship *of* Christ, is the central bond of the community. Again, Paul opens up the Jewish story to embrace the gentiles. Therefore, these positions have to be read as two competing moral positions.

Paul uses strong and weak theologically in order to further bind the diverse Corinthians further together in Christ. The clarity of terms strong and weak comes through earlier in 1 Corinthians 1–2. It is precisely here that Paul is first dealing with divisions (strong and weak) and Christ's crucifixion in an attempt to bring them into an important theological conversation. To begin, Paul discusses the foolishness of the cross.

> For Jews demand signs and Greeks desire wisdom, but we proclaim Christ crucified, a stumbling block to Jews and foolishness to Gentiles, but to those who are the called, both Jews and Greeks, Christ the power of God and the wisdom of God. For God's foolishness is wiser than human wisdom, and God's weakness is stronger than human strength. (1 Cor 1:22–25, NRSV)

Paul assigns weakness and strength a cruciform meaning, thereby inverting the supposed late modern rejection of the strong/weak typology. Rather, God, who (to quote Philippians)

> though he was in the form of God,
> did not regard equality with God
> as something to be exploited,
> but emptied himself,
> taking the form of a slave,
> being born in human likeness.
> And being found in human form,
> he humbled himself
> and became obedient to the point of death—
> even death on a cross. (Phil 2:6–8, NRSV)

Combined with Paul's commitment to crucifixion in 1 Corinthians, it is clear that Paul means something other than valuing strong *over* weak qualitatively. Rather, *weak* contains power that *strong* lacks. Such a

145. Horrell, "Ten Years On," xxi.

recognition only comes by way of an apocalypse. Such a "metaphysics of apocalypse" does not simply invert the order of mastery (Nietzsche), but rather exists in exile from any system centered on an ontology of violence, biopolitics, and a universal moral conscience for the sake of mastery itself. This is a more radical critique of moral and political "value" than the new approach can attain. Instead, Paul crucifies the "strong" in order to become weak, which is a new form of power. To be clear, it is not power that asserts, coerces, and privatizes, but rather always that which graciously includes, patiently waits, and blissfully contingent. Paul identifies himself as one of the strong (Rom 14:14). However, Paul also vows to the Corinthians, "I decided to know nothing among you except Jesus Christ, and him crucified" (1 Cor 2:2, NRSV). Therefore, Paul's theological rendering of strong and weak recognizes that the strong must come under deep interrogation.

Weakness, though clearly associated with God's power, must be understood in its own context. To be clear, Paul's own description of strong and weak could be read as Kipling's "The White Man's Burden." The strong become the weak in order to liberate the weak, thus condescending and evacuating the weak's own moral capabilities. The crucifixion of the strong is, rather, a solidarity.[146] The reason for this move is rooted in the crucified moral ontology present in creation. As Paul makes clear in 1 Corinthians, the strong are characterized by human standards of nobility, power, and wisdom (1:26–27), but also those that claim their rights and privileges (9:1–14). Such is the case that the strong can be defined as self-sufficient individuals that exert their rights over others. As Horrell writes, "for Paul, 'right' practice can only be determined in relation to the context of human relationships in which one is enmeshed, the possible injury that one's actions may cause to others."[147] Any moral practice or habit that seeks lordship over another, as in the case of strong and weak, must experience the crucifixion of its moral subjectivity. The moral subjectivity of weakness is cruciform in shape and must regard the other as ones for whom Christ died (8:11). It is preferred that all exist as "weak" in reference to its surrounding culture and treat the neighbor with love and consideration. Only when all have surrendered their "self-sufficiency" and exist together in a perpetual state of other regard, which makes harm of others an essential epistemic consideration in mat-

146. This is one of the main two postures to understand Paul according to Horrell, *Solidarity and Difference*, 183–224.

147. Horrell, *Solidarity and Difference*, xx, 199.

ters of moral practice. The crucial distinction between strong and weak is between that which seeks to lord over and that which suffers with the ones who suffer. To be clear, in its christological context, weakness is not redemptive suffering, but solidarity in suffering.

Solidarity of the Pauline variety is one that imaginatively draws the community around tortured, slaughtered, and violated bodies as the site of new actions. As Horrell writes, "Paul devotes considerable space to articulating a kind of moral framework based on solidarity in Christ within which differences of opinion and practice on specific issues (such as food) can be encompassed."[148] Ironically, this matter of food is overcome, as illustrated in remembering, in another form of eating, namely the Eucharist. As womanist theologian M. Shawn Copeland writes,

> Our daily living out, and out of, the dangerous memory of the torture and abuse, death and resurrection of Jesus Christ constitutes us as his own body raised up and made visible in the world. As *his body*, we embrace with love and hope those who, in their bodies, are despised and marginalized, even as we embrace with love and forgiveness those whose sin spawn the conditions for the suffering and oppression of others.[149]

This forms a habit of "Eucharist solidarity" whereby Christians "pulse with new life."[150] Solidarity formed in this act of remembering "is a virtue, a practice of cognitive and bodily commitments oriented to meet the social consequences of Eucharist. We women and men strive to become what we have received and to do what we are being made."[151] Becoming weak "transvalues our values" in order to shape a new social imaginary centered around being with neighbors.[152] In short, "solidarity enfolds us, rather than dismiss[es] 'others,' we act in love; rather than refuse 'others,' we respond in acts of self-sacrifice—committing ourselves to the long labor of creation, to the enfleshment of freedom."[153] If there is a contemporary significance of such an ancient moral conundrum such as meat offered to idols, it is this.

148. Horrell, *Solidarity and Difference*, xx.

149. Copeland, *Enfleshing Freedom*, 126–27.

150. Copeland, *Enfleshing Freedom*, 127.

151. Copeland, *Enfleshing Freedom*, 127.

152. Copeland, *Enfleshing Freedom*, 127.

153. Copeland, *Enfleshing Freedom*, 128.

Paul's understanding of meat offered to idols and its associated moral practices is guided by a deeper knowledge of the supremacy of Christ. Both the strong and the weak have as their guiding source the supremacy of Christ, and their partaking or abstaining seeks that end. As a moral thinker, Paul evaluates in this passage what is the ultimate good of the community and places "those for whom Christ died" as critically important. There is a Christo-epistemic cypher at play in the moral reasoning of Paul. It is expressed best by something that Paul writes in his second letter to the Corinthians.

> From now on, therefore, we regard no one from a human point of view; even though we once knew Christ from a human point of view, we know him no longer that way. So if anyone is in Christ, there is a new creation: everything old has passed away; see everything has become new! (2 Cor 5:16–17, NRSV)

On the surface, it may appear that this would urge the eating of meat offered to idols. If everything is truly new, why cannot all believers reach a point of moral consensus on this issue? The key phrases are "regard no one from a human point of view" and "if anyone is in Christ, there is a new creation." Those in Christ are made new in the community of faith. These two apocalyptic statements endow the mind of the believer with a sense of the sacredness of those in our midst. In the former communities, there were communal antinomies based on historical, familial, and moral norms. The new creation involves a community where difference can exist. Even if this believer has a different moral position, that position is maintained in light of the saving power of Christ. They exercise abstinence from meat, not as signs of their continued subjection to idols, but as their freedom from it. The believer is free to eat or abstain from the consumption of idol meat. The apocalyptic power of Christ allows the community to see food and people within their appropriate positions. The freedom in Christ provides the context where both can be maintained in a community of the Holy Spirit. If the strong eat this meat in front of these weak, then they subject them back under the powers that caused them to stumble. However, Paul's congregations already think from the turn of the ages which realizes a community that resists the sovereignty of the powers of sin and death. The moral standard of the community is not in consensus about the manner in which this is played out, but that Christ has defeated the powers of sin and death and reclaimed the new believer as his own.

Paul provides us with four implications about the moral life in the defeat of the powers in the believer's apocalyptic context. First, knowledge of Christ and his crucifixion is the beginning of moral thinking that extends to those for whom Christ died. This is the common good. Second, regard for other believers is a central conviction because of the unity in Christ. The reason for this emphasis is that the community is not bound by a universal moral consensus, but by a love of Christ. Therefore, other believers present the opportunity to practice the love of Christ. Difference must be maintained in the community for the sake of Christ in order that this love might be continually practiced. Third, though moral reasoning takes place within a community, it also involves spiritual discernment. It involves understanding one's conscience about moral issues. Paul opens up the possibility for personal moral discernment to be local and correspond to one's engagement with the Spirit. Fourth, the freedom in Christ proclaimed in the new age is multilayered. The strong know their freedom is a freedom to eat, and the weak have the freedom not to eat meat. Both are free in their own context and both represent faithful practices of the gospel. Both the strong and weak have equal moral consciences. Yet even this freedom must be tempered by the first insight: regard for others. One's freedom must not be used in order to be a stumbling block (1 Cor 8:9) or for self-indulgence (Gal 5:13).

Attention: The One for Whom Christ Died

To conclude the discussion on Paul's moral exhortations, I wish to reflect on the mode of attention utilized in Paul's moral discourse on idol meat. Attention, an important aspect of the just and loving gaze, is evident in Paul's repeated emphasis on seeing the neighbor inside the crucified Jesus. To borrow from Simone Weil, an important philosopher to Murdoch's own position, "If we turn our mind toward the good, it is impossible that little by little the whole soul will not be attracted thereto in spite of itself."[154] For Paul, the good is found in Christ's death and resurrection. The just and loving gaze must first give undivided attention to Christ as the good. This renegotiates and transforms the believer, providing them with what Murdoch calls moral energies to do the good. Paul is less interested in a system of goodness or a universal moral conscience than an attentive consideration of the neighbor, the one for whom Christ died.

154. Weil, *Gravity and Grace*, 170.

Attention is a type of "unselfing" where the rights, interests, and persuasions of the individual give way to the needs of another. Paul's community struggled because the bonds that united Jewish and gentile bodies were strong and ancient with their own boundaries of belonging. Paul must persuade these communities not to abandon their particularity, but to open their particularity in service of another means of belonging. Theologian Willie Jennings helps describe how an entire network of moral conscience is guided through Christ crucified.

> If a world caught in the unrelenting exchange system of violence was to be overcome, then here was the very means God would use to overcome violence—by the introduction of a new reality of belonging that drew together different peoples into a way of life that intercepted ancient bonds and redrew them around the body of Jesus and in the power of the Spirit.[155]

The new family of God is those who love Christ and does the will of God.[156] Jennings continues, "He drew [these ancient bonds] to a new orientation, a new determination. The family must follow him. The one family must follow from him—flow from his life as its new source."[157] The source does not come exclusively from Jew or gentile, but by the opening of the Jewish story to include gentiles. The deeply held familial bonds must be the subject of "unselfing" by loving this new good, Christ's own body. In refusing to eat meat offered to idols, attention is given to Christ crucified and, by extension, those for whom Christ died. Martyn writes, "Those who recognize their life to be God's gift at the juncture of the ages recognize also that until they are completely and exclusively in the new age, their knowing by the Spirit can occur only in the form of knowing by the power of the cross."[158] As such, the attention is no longer on our own private interests, but on the neighbor, where the good is encountered and loved. It should be evident that attention to this good—Christ crucified as the grain of the universe—leads Paul to exhort what justice and love look like in this context and to whom they are directed. Only when the reality of the cosmos is recognized for what it is—the cross—can proper justice be determined. As such, language of rights and privilege are abandoned to exist in exile with those harmed by such logics. The cross sends

155. Jennings, *Christian Imagination*, 269.

156. Jennings, *Christian Imagination*, 263.

157. Jennings, *Christian Imagination*, 264.

158. Martyn, "Epistemology," 108.

the community into exile as a means of solidarity. This is how the community is attentive.

Attention follows the movement of the Spirit, which goes forth from the community and brings others into the community. Attention is shaped by the cross and is for others. The opening-up of the Jewish story by the Spirit to include the gentiles is a missionary posture. Attention to those who are brought in is a missionary vocation. The just and loving gaze is here in the new community because it makes the community capable of "unselfing" from its private interests.

In conclusion, attention to Christ opens up knowledge and love of the neighbor for whom Christ died. Attention to Christ, like in the Eucharist, means recognizing his poverty and his willful solidarity with the poor and with the suffering. Christ's death doesn't preserve privilege or private interest. This forces attention against private interest and toward the good of the neighbor. This is how Paul helps his communities practice the common good. The common good is that which does not cause injury. Speech and attention helps the community recognize what must be attended to. This is how the just and loving gaze assists moral reasoning: not by universal moral norms, but careful attention to the needs of the neighbor.

PAUL'S APOCALYPTIC POLITICAL THEOLOGY: THE *ALREADY*

Paul's apocalyptic theology is not an abstract doctrine, but the rationale that undergirds the life of the church. After exploring Arendt, Murdoch, and Paul's moral exhortations, I propose that it is the community that confronts powers, which often take shape in politics, through the power of Christ and the Spirit. Martyn writes, "The martial, cosmic dimension of Paul's apocalyptic applies, then, to the church and for that reason Paul can speak of the church itself both as God's new creation and as the apocalyptic community called to the front trenches in God's apocalyptic war against the powers of the present evil age."[159] The church enters the trenches concretely through practice in light of Christ's apocalyptic invasion of the cosmos. So, its practices of attention and remembrance are the means by which it understands itself in light of the fallen condition of the

159. Martyn, *Galatians*, 102.

powers. These practices resist the evil powers of the present age and, by extension, a firm resistance to biopolitics.

Sinful powers can be resisted materially through resisting certain "structurings" of the state. Obviously, this calls for a qualification because Paul himself calls the community to "be subject to governing authorities" (Rom 13:1). Having said that, the myth that Romans 13 gives a unilateral authority of the state to do what it pleases must be resisted. For example, what happens when the missionary effort comes up against the sovereign state's division, such as political theorist Carl Schmitt's distinction between friend and enemy?[160] Such a distinction is made by the sovereign because the sovereign determines the exception. This leads to the following question: Does the mission only extend to the ones called friends by the sovereign state or by God? Additionally, what if the state tortured members of the body of Christ as in Chile under Pinochet?[161] Is not the state claiming the member as its own and not Christ's? In this case, are those individuals still members of the body of Christ? Sovereignty, then, is a structuring of political communities against God's good intentions for the created order. This is the occasion for the mission of the church. As evidenced in the moral exhortations of Paul, sovereignty is resisted in communal practices. Paul's apocalyptic political theology resists powers through its missionary function among the nations, and it embodies a new body politic capable of witnessing to the nations.

Paul's apocalyptic political theology is a politics of mission. Theologian Nate Kerr understands that the formation of the church is an "*ecclesial* challenge to the powers."[162] It is a challenge because it is the human participation in the mission of God to defeat the powers. Kerr writes, "What emerges from within an apocalyptic perspective, then, is the requisite existence of a people who celebrate Christ's lordship by sharing in his mission, by being broken for the world as he was broken, by being poured out in sacrificial love for others."[163] This is Paul's mission (Gal 1:15–16). The conversion of the world, as witnessed in the gathering of a community to worship God, signals the sending of the *ecclesial* community into the world for its salvation. Kerr's central insight is that the apocalyptic community encounters the world in a liturgical praxis

160. Schmitt, *Concept of the Political*, 27–37.

161. This is a central feature of Cavanaugh's argument in *Torture and Eucharist*, 21–71.

162. Kerr, *Christ, History, and Apocalyptic*, 161. Emphasis original.

163. Kerr, *Christ, History, and Apocalyptic*, 16.

in which "the world (and thereby also the church) is *converted* by and to the subversive excess of God's coming Kingdom."[164] This does not make the church its own society or city. The church is *ecclesia*, and the mission makes the church. But what is this mission? Kerr writes,

> So mission, one might say, is the *form* in which Christ *gives* himself in the "historicity" of the Spirit: to be given over to the participation in the apocalyptic politics of Jesus, *through* whom our own historicity is opened to the excess of God's *agape*, we must have been given over, *in* the Spirit, to a work of love by which we are *bound* to the ongoing contingencies and singularities of history in their being "unhanded" by Christ to the reign of God's love. "Mission" thereby names the ongoing enactment of Jesus's non-territorial, subversive, apocalyptic historicity in the world.[165]

Mission is historically located and concretely embodied. Kerr does not describe in great detail specific practices of mission, but he names a few practices offered by John Howard Yoder. The "political novelty" of mission "is a community of those who serve instead of ruling, who suffer instead of inflicting suffering, whose fellowship crosses social lines instead of reinforcing them."[166] Mission is a way of receiving the neighbor into the community without forcing old communal antinomies.

Kerr's analysis of the missional nature of apocalyptic politics helps address the modern problematic addressed in Agamben and the new approach. The work of interpreting Paul apocalyptically opens up the possibility of missional politics. Unlike the new approach, Pauline apocalyptic operates from a different locus than modernity. Apocalyptic recognizes this not just at the limit of political authorities, but an actual war against the powers. Therefore, apocalyptic proposes both a new approach and a new world. Kerr writes that apocalyptic makes "concrete a world of life and action that the socio-political powers and principalities are themselves unable to imagine."[167] I propose that the missional politics of Pauline apocalyptic provides a viable alternative to both the biopolitical nature of modern politics and their recapitulated form of biopolitics, as noted in Agamben's use of the *muselmänner*.

164. Kerr, *Christ, History, and Apocalyptic*, 162. Emphasis original.

165. Kerr, *Christ, History, and Apocalyptic*, 174. Emphasis original.

166. Yoder, *Royal Priesthood*, 91. Quoted in Kerr, *Christ, History, and Apocalyptic*, 174.

167. Kerr, *Christ, History, and Apocalyptic*, 165.

A critique of biopolitics requires a practiced reception of the neighbors and strangers into a community by confronting the sovereign exception. Only by celebrating difference can it resist biopolitics. This is a liturgical confrontation with the sovereign exception by worshiping God alone. Liturgically, Christians live by the practices of its church discipline where prayer, praise, Scripture, and sacraments form a political imagination beyond what is deemed appropriate by political orders. Kerr wants to clarify this by stating that the liturgy of the church is not that of an already "given political identity."[168] Rather, liturgy and liturgical practice "is the 'apocalyptic ricochet,' we might say, of the 'inaugural rupture' that is Jesus Christ;" such practices bring the community to bodily repetition of the Spirit's own apocalyptic drawing.[169] The reception of the historicity of Christ in practice draws the community ever deeper into its own historicity by means of *practicing* the inaugural rupture in that historicity. Unlike the biopolitical structures of Western politics, an apocalyptic politic of mission is constantly broken open for the sake of those who have been discarded and placed outside.

The mission is a call to exist among those who have been deemed outside—not to bring them inside biopolitical structures, but rather for the sake of living in exile outside the biopolitical structures of the world, in relation to Agamben's insistence on validity and Weheliye's hieroglyphics of the flesh. Exile is important because it requires a new form of politics and language not dependent on dominate structures. Rather, as Yoder writes, "it seizes it, expropriates it, and uses it to say things that could previously not have been said in its prior language; nor could they have been said by anyone else using the wider world's language."[170] Exile is the place from which a new language can emerge. It does not require the semantic codes of the wider culture, but exists in excess of them. As such, the community in exile exists not as the abject zone of exclusion, but as alternative instantiations of politics absent from Western Man. The community does not reject the world, nor does it become quietist. It is a mission to the discarded for the sake of witness to and conversion of the nations. This is the difference between an apocalyptically formed *ecclesia* and the biopolitical imagination of modernity. The latter survives on a constant policing of the health of its citizens, necessarily excluding

168. Kerr, *Christ, History, and Apocalyptic*, 181.

169. Kerr, *Christ, History, and Apocalyptic*, 181.

170. Yoder, "On Not Being Ashamed," 296.

some in order to provide the most sterile environment for its citizens. The former is a center of intimacy around the body of Christ where its unity requires openness to those who are different, even if it threatens privileged positions. Furthermore, the church does not exclude the nations, but seeks to convert them to the mission of God. Only in this way is biopolitics confronted. Therefore, only a missionary politics can subvert the biopolitical tendencies of modernity through a full conversion of the nations trapped in biopolitical norms.

The conversion of the nations, central to Paul's politic, leads to a different understanding of government not bound by sovereignty. Despite the rejection of sovereignty, the notion of a worldly authority is not lost in apocalyptic theology. There is the potential to create just and loving political realities that last. This is suggested in Romans 13:1–7. Paul's purpose is not to uncritically endorse every authority. It is to claim that proper authority is found within God's good intentions for the created order. Proper authority is found within those who keep true justice.

In order to unpack the implications of this understanding of authorities, I utilize the political insights of Oliver O'Donovan. who argues that Jesus is the desire of the nations.[171] O'Donovan argues that God concretely works in human history for the purpose of God's own goodness and gives us clear insight into the theological understanding of politics.[172] God's gift to humanity is the human ability to participate in the authority of God. This requires an understanding of "the ontology of human freedom, action, and the good."[173] O'Donovan is not talking about the institutional structures that we typically associate with authority. Rather, he speaks of the reconciled and redeemed created order vindicated by Christ's resurrection.[174] We are not authorities, but we are given authority to do something. This authorization flows from God's lordship over all creation. It is from this understanding of the good of society revealed and redeemed in Christ's own lordship that a proper theological understanding of political authority can emerge.

In Christ's lordship, an uncontestable political identity emerges: Christ provides a political identity that "replaced all other political

---

171. O'Donovan, *Desire of the Nations*, 2.

172. O'Donovan, *Desire of the Nations*, 2.

173. O'Donovan, *Desire of the Nations*, 30.

174. See O'Donovan, *Resurrection and the Moral Order*, 31–52.

identities."[175] The authority that the church follows is Christ in every aspect of political life.[176] O'Donovan argues that Christ's lordship is only visible "in the life of the church."[177] The rule that the church experiences is not visible in the world in the way that it is visible in the church.[178]

O'Donovan is in agreement with what Martyn and Kerr state about the moral and political authority of the church. The struggle against the powers is waged by Christ and the community called by him. The political implications for the community in relation to "governing authorities" is what separates O'Donovan. O'Donovan writes, "Christ has conquered the rulers from below, by drawing their subjects out from under their authority."[179] Therefore, the rulers are now in need of the church in order to understand itself. O'Donovan writes,

> The ruler may belong within the Church, too, but not *qua* ruler. The essential element in the conversion of the ruling power is the change in its self-understanding and its manner of government to suit the dawning age of Christ's own rule. The church has to instruct it in the ways of the humble state.[180]

O'Donovan has more than a completely subversive model for the church. He interprets Christ's apocalyptic lordship over the powers to be celebrated by instructing the state who is coming to know this rule in a not-yet-visible way. O'Donovan still understands the need for mission as an apocalyptic gesture of the church. I believe that this arises from the church's practices whereby remembrance and attention embody a whole new politic that appears strange to the existing political authorities. It teaches the ruling authorities to unlearn their dependence on the sovereignty of sin and death, which is most acutely manifest in biopolitical structures.

The political theology of Paul is a politics of mission. Since the community repeats certain practices, it forms a particular type of missionary posture toward the world. Through remembrance and attention, the church celebrates the the new members being brought into the community by the work of the Spirit. This is why Acts is such a crucial narrative

175. O'Donovan, *Desire of the Nations*, 147.

176. O'Donovan, *Desire of the Nations*, 123.

177. O'Donovan, *Desire of the Nations*, 146.

178. O'Donovan, *Desire of the Nations*, 146.

179. O'Donovan, *Desire of the Nations*, 193.

180. O'Donovan, *Desire of the Nations*, 219.

for Paul's own theology. Through these practices, the church develops moral, political, and missionary postures. Since the church brings in the poor and the outcast, as evidenced in Paul's own exhortation on remembrance, it comes into conflict with the sovereign exception, which needs the poor and outcast in order to maintain its biopolitical foundations. The missional witness of the church exists in exile with these outcasts to witness to the state for its conversion. The nations, as the subject of conversion, can be reorganized around what the church is authorized to do by God alone, not having power of its own. The church does two things: it converts the nations and it instructs them in humility.

CONCLUSION

In conclusion, it is clear that Paul's politics is determined by the apocalyptic incursion of Christ and realized in the actions of the community who confesses that Jesus is Lord. Paul's political insight, as correctly suggested by the new approach, lies in the type of community formed by such a confession. However, they are wanting in their interpretation of Paul by implying that this confession is based on an antirealist conceptual apparatus, not on his particular practices. Only through these practices as outgrowths of his apocalyptic thought does the community exist in the concrete, not the abstraction. This community is a community of the just and loving gaze that engenders a politics of compassionate attention to the neighbor in light of one's love of God. The politics of this community is a witness to broader political authorities and a counter-discipline to their coercive politics by modeling how identity, truth, and communal instruction should take place. Such practices and confession yield a new moral ontology that offset that of the new approach.

Now that we have seen the common good illustrated in the apocalyptic *already*, we must see how the shared ends emerge in the *not yet*. Shared ends in the context of Paul's apocalyptic theology provides a tension in our understanding of the common good. Eschatologically, we do not fulfill history or our actions. Rather, our lives and actions are structured as such that they are brought to rest in the new creation. Therefore, the resurrection of the dead is the shared end of our political life and informs how we shape our missional, political responses to sovereignty.

4

Natality and the World to Come
Pauline Apocalyptic Politics of the Not Yet

THE PREVIOUS CHAPTER EXPLORED the relationship between the Pauline apocalyptic *already* and a possible political theology that resists biopolitical antinomies. It was concluded that the politic of the *already* relies on the apocalyptic incursion of Christ into creation, which leads to a newly found intimacy between humans and God. This reality is practiced in the presence of the community. In finding oneself addressed by the neighbor, one finds a new political imagination, one founded upon the just and loving gaze.

In this chapter, I argue that the *already* of Christ's invasion is fulfilled in the *not yet*. The common good reaches for shared ends, and for Christianity that shared end is the resurrection of the dead. For Paul, faithful Christian activity is not a means by which humans realize a new creation, else they collapse into the modern problematic of self-sufficiency. Rather, human actions are performed out of the agency of God who acts in history and brings history to completion. Since all creation finds its rest in the resurrection of the dead, one cannot hold private concerns in Paul's political theology. Distinctly Christian political action is for the sake of a shared, eschatological end. The *not yet* serves as an object of hope that gives a *telos* to political activities.

I begin my argument through a thick description of these shared ends in the resurrection of the dead through an exegetical engagement with Paul's famous eschatological text of 1 Corinthians 15. Such a description will orient Paul's political theology toward a shared eschatological end in the new creation, which utterly rejects private interests. The act that arises from the stress on new creation and resurrection is natality. Arendt describes natality as the act by which humans make new judgments. As humans are oriented toward shared ends in the resurrection of the dead, it requires an introspective "unselfing" that puts off past prejudices in favor of the world that is coming to pass. Natality is the political posture of the *not yet*.

Natality's proximity to the *not yet* also encourages the just and loving gaze. The just and loving gaze is not fixed until the new creation. Therefore, the just and loving gaze must consistently evaluate its moral prejudices in order to assure its ability to render appropriate love and justice to the neighbor. Through an analysis of the character John Ducane in Iris Murdoch's novel *The Nice and the Good*, I argue that when one fixes oneself upon the good, one is continually transformed according to its moral formation. Even though Ducane has not finally put off the fat ego by the end of the novel, it is clear that he is within the process of natality and the just and loving gaze.

Theologically, natality and the just and loving gaze require that private interest and self-sufficiency come undone. If natality and the just and loving gaze find their shared ends in the resurrection of the dead, then our agency relies on the agency of God. As such, the goal and tenure of our political life is ontologically grounded in the activity of God that culminates in the new creation. Though natality celebrates the coming kingdom of God, the finality of the resurrection of the dead gives a firm end to our actions.

The political posture of natality is practiced in the act of forgiveness. Like with the *already*, the *not yet* inspires certain practices that counter the tyranny of private interest and self-sufficiency. Such a practice prevents potential political violence. By forgiving instead of enacting violence, seeking reconciliation rather than attempting violent overthrow of the world, the Christian resists the tempting narratives of effectiveness and opts for faithfulness to the resurrection of the dead. Only by resisting narratives of effectiveness do private interests come undone.

THE RESURRECTION OF THE DEAD: PAUL'S
APOCALYPTIC THEOLOGY OF THE *NOT YET*

I begin with an exegesis of Paul's central eschatological teaching: the resurrection of the dead in 1 Corinthians 15. In this text, Paul unpacks the central themes of the *not yet* and the content of Christian hope: the resurrection of the dead. As such a content, it names the shared ends of the created. This is crucial because the resurrection of the dead answers the charge against the new approach that they are gnostic and they fail to recognize contingency. Paul highlights the goal and the meaning of history within that goal, which is the cross. Paul brings together that which the new approach tears apart. There is a meaning and purpose within history in which all creation is called to participate in its contingency and universal end for all creation. This text and the resurrection of the dead will be given a privileged place in our discussion of the *not yet*.

The meaning of the general resurrection of the dead lies within Christ's resurrection. Christ's resurrected body is a tradition in which Paul himself is a recipient. Much like the practice of the Eucharist in 1 Corinthians 11:23, Paul passes on the narrative of Christ's own resurrection (v. 3). The theme of Christ's death and resurrection is modified by the phrase "for our sins" (v. 3, NRSV).[1] This tradition is important for the whole of his argument, so he invokes it here in order to show that this is an established tradition (v. 3), rooted in the Jewish Scriptures (vv. 3–4), and attested to by a multitude of witnesses both living and dead, including Cephas, James, and even Paul himself (vv. 5–9). The culmination of this tradition results in the faith by which the Corinthians "have come to believe" (v. 11, NRSV).

The issue that is implicitly raised in this passage is not that this faith leads to salvation, but rather *how* this mystery leads to salvation. Paul connects the resurrection of Christ with the bodily resurrection of believers. Paul defies the Hellenism of the Corinthian congregation because they view with suspicion the state of a physically embodied life after death. Paul argues that Christ's own death and resurrection enables the resurrection of the believer. For Paul, this is an essential confession of faith. New Testament scholar Hans Conzelmann writes, "Paul does not have to prove the resurrection [of Christ] to Corinthian Christians because they do not doubt it."[2] Though Paul does not prove the resurrec-

1. See Fitzmyer, *First Corinthians*, 541.
2. Conzelmann, "On the Analysis," 23.

tion of Christ, he must prove the physicality of the general resurrection of the dead (vv. 12–49). The Corinthian congregation struggles because their Hellenistic convictions limit their ability to accept the goodness of material creation. This causes a stumbling block for three reasons.

First, the Hellenism of the day was suspicious of the future of the body in its physical state postmortem. Corinthian Hellenism most likely assumed the future of the soul. New Testament scholar Richard Hays notes that this particular skepticism persists into the early Christian period at the time of Justin Martyr.[3]

Second, it is quite possible that readers of Paul misconstrued the denial taking place among the Corinthians. The Corinthians might have wondered what *type* of body is raised (v. 35b). Joseph Fitzmyer understands that this is probably the proper question to ask because it clarifies the nature of the resurrection; is it a physical body or a spiritual body that is raised?[4] Paul clarifies what a spiritual body includes because, as Dale Martin states, the Corinthians were turned off by what they thought Paul understood as the resurrection: "the crass resuscitation of a corpse."[5]

Third, there is a question of the futurity of the resurrection.[6] Fitzmyer draws a parallel with 1 Corinthians 4:8: if the Corinthians are already rich, then why a future resurrection of the dead? Clearly this is the tension between the *already* and *not yet*. Though these stumbling blocks are the purpose of Paul's constructive exhortation, he does not explicitly state them until the middle of chapter 15. It is important to state these concerns as objects of concern for Paul's constructive approach.

These questions all center around one question: what kind of end can creation expect? Furthermore, what implications are drawn from this end? In order to answer these questions, I turn to Paul's narrative of the resurrection of Christ. Recapitulating the initial confession of verses 3–5, Paul writes, "if Christ has not been raised, then our proclamation has been in vain and your faith has been in vain" (v. 14). Christ's resurrection is so essential that without it, the Corinthians and Paul misrepresent God (v. 15). Paul makes a connection between Christ's resurrection and our own (vv. 16, 20–23) that will become a theme for the chapter. The connection is purely christological. Conzelmann writes that the resurrection of

3. Hays, *Interpretation*, 259.
4. Fitzmyer, *First Corinthians*, 560.
5. Martin, *Corinthian Body*, 123.
6. Fitzmyer, *First Corinthians*, 560.

the dead "is grounded in the fact that the resurrection itself is posited 'in Christ.' Christ is not the first to be raised, but is constitutive for our being raised: the dead will be made alive 'in him.'"[7] By placing his confidence in the creedal affirmation of verses 3–5, Paul does not speculate further than to state that those who die will be raised in Christ. The christological centrality of the general resurrection focuses Paul's discourse around the resurrection of Christ, which is not in doubt by the Corinthians.

If the dead are not raised, then Christ is not raised. If Christ is not raised, Michael Gorman writes, the consequences are "grave."[8] Believers are still in their sin (v. 17); believers who have died are gone permanently (v. 18); believers have endured much for what appears to be empty promises and, thus, are to be most pitied (v. 19); daily suffering of Christians and Paul himself are of no gain and absurd (vv. 30–32a); hedonism is logically the only lifestyle (v. 35b).[9] Gorman writes, "In other words, without the resurrection of the dead there is no reason for faith, hope, or love—the kind of love that endures suffering."[10] Paul understands the present lifestyle as an interpretive cypher for understanding the end of the Christian life. This end is manifest in Christ's own resurrection and assures the Corinthians of their own ends. Living in the tension between Christ's resurrection and their resurrection results in moral dispositions toward particular activity. Without Christ's resurrection, these actions are in vain because they lack true ends.

However, "Christ has been raised from the dead" (v. 20), so the opposite must be the case, according to Paul. The dead are not gone permanently, the Corinthians are not still in their sin, the promises are not empty, suffering is not without gain, and lifestyle is not bound to hedonism. An implicit argument emerges here. Paul does not suggest that the life Christ lived was for Christ alone. Christ invites believers into a new life made manifest in his resurrection in narrative continuity with his earthly life and ministry. As such, Christians are called to live according to this gospel where these promises are treated as true. This means that Christ is not the only life destined for resurrection—all life is. Paul recognizes that the life he asks the Corinthians to lead appears as foolishness to the outside world (1 Cor 1:27). Paul's list of consequences reveals

7. Conzelmann, *1 Corinthians*, 249.

8. Gorman, *Apostle of the Crucified Lord*, 279.

9. Gorman, *Apostle of the Crucified Lord*, 279.

10. Gorman, *Apostle of the Crucified Lord*, 279.

the impracticality in the life summoned by Christ's resurrection. Such an impractical means confronts a far greater hope that makes the Christian life possible.

The hope revealed in Christ's resurrection gives shape to the shared ends of creation through an activity synonymous with embracing death and cross. Richard Hays writes,

> Christians—in Paul's view—are called to a life of "embracing death," suffering through selfless service of others (cf. 10:33—11:1), not seeking their own advantage or pleasure. If there is no resurrection, this self-denying style of life makes no sense; those who follow the example of Jesus and Paul are chumps missing out on their fair share of life's rewards.[11]

Therefore, the call to embrace death—specifically the cross—reaches for an end coordinate to the one described by Paul in the resurrection. Only through *this* embrace that reaches for *this* end can believers embrace the grain of the universe. If Christ is not raised, then surely the Corinthians are missing out on something. These virtues exist for the sake of a pattern of faithfulness that find fulfillment in the new creation. Hays continues,

> Paul, along with the rest of the New Testament writers, believes that life in Christ is a source of great joy and peace and consolation in the present (see, e.g., Rom 5:1–5; 8:1–11; Gal. 5:22–23; Phil 4:4–7)—though he has said remarkably little about these themes in this particular letter to the Corinthians! His point here, however, is that the complex and fulfilling life of the Christian community has integrity only if it is premised on the truth and ordered toward the ultimate fulfillment of God's promises. If the *telos* (goal) of our life together in Christ is a mirage on an ever-receding horizon of time, then we are living an unhealthy self-deception—as Christianity's critics, ancient and modern, have charged. There is no authentic Christian faith without fervent eschatological hope, and there is no authentic eschatological hope without the resurrection of the dead.[12]

The resurrection of Christ presents believers with the ultimate end of their lives through a new pattern of habituation in the present. Their end is resurrection, which overpowers ends interior to the world alone. Paul, according to Hays, does not exclude the ends that are interior to the world. The Corinthians are called to self-sacrifice and selfless love. Such

11. Hays, *Interpretation*, 262.

12. Hays, *Interpretation*, 262.

a calling provides a way of being in the world, not captive to one worldly *telos*.

The way of being in the world now available resists the powers aligned under the sovereignty of sin and death. For our purposes, it is a way beyond the realm of private interest. Christ's resurrection establishes a habitus that resists death (or as Paul calls it, the enemy). Death for Paul, as New Testament scholar C. Kavin Rowe understands, is "the condition of our humanity and the power that reduces us to being dead."[13] Death is the final power to be defeated. In the cross and resurrection, death is defeated in the very person of Christ. In this way, Christ can be the New Adam. Paul writes, "For since death came through a human being, the resurrection of the dead has also come through a human being; for as all die in Adam, so all will be made alive in Christ" (vv. 21–22). The issue, as with all the powers, is the lack of visibility of Christ's lordship in the world. For example, believers still die. However, Christ is risen. Therefore, in the life of the church, as Paul established in verses 3–5, it is confessed that Christ has conquered death. This enables an apocalyptic community free from fear of death and captivity to the powers concretely manifest in private interest. There still remains a need to visibly liberate the cosmos from the enemy of death. To the question of futurity, then, Paul settles it by saying this has yet to happen.

The liberation of the cosmos from death comes through the trinitarian apocalyptic drawing of the cosmos, even death itself, into the very life of God. This is the text that Beker utilizes in order to shape his understanding of apocalyptic as a not-yet-realized apocalyptic in-breaking of the new creation into the old. Paul writes,

> Then comes the end, when he hands over the kingdom to God the Father, after he has destroyed every ruler and every authority and power. For he must reign until he has put all his enemies under his feet. The last enemy to be destroyed is death. For "God has put all things in subjection under his feet." But when it says, "All things are put in subjection," it is plain that this does not include the one who put all things in subjection under him. When all things are subjected to him, then the Son himself will also be subjected to the one who put all things in subjection under him, so that God may be all in all. (1 Cor 15:24–28, NRSV)

13. Rowe, *One True Life*, 99.

The "end" is the *telos* of creation. This is, as Conzelmann understands, traditional apocalyptic language.[14] In Christ, a kingdom has been given to Christ where he is enthroned over the powers.[15] At the end, the Son will come (παρουσία), and he will turn over the Kingdom to the Father. In the apocalyptic *already*, Christ receives lordship over the powers. This is the time of the Spirit and the life of the church, where Christians are called to confess Christ's lordship in the power of the Spirit. This is Christ's kingdom until every power is put under Christ's feet (vv. 24–25). At the end, death will be put under the feet of Christ and handed over to the Father to be destroyed. Father and Son work together for the mutual defeat of the enemy death.

The relationship between the Father and Son becomes complicated when Paul claims that Christ is then subjected to Father. Richard Hays writes that it would appear that "it is impossible to avoid the impression that Paul is operating with what would later come to be called a subordinationist Christology."[16] However, another reading is possible. It lies in the constructively loose reference to Psalm 110:1b (NRSV), "Sit and my right hand until I make your enemies your footstool," and in Psalm 8:6 (NRSV), "You have given them dominion over the works of your hands; you have put all things under their feet." Paul references these Psalms in passing in verses 25–28. These passages from the Psalms refer to God's ability to make an emissary on earth to enact God's rule. It would appear that Christ is this emissary, but New Testament scholar Wesley Hill contends that this is missing Paul's intention in summoning these Psalms.[17] Hill's reading of 1 Corinthians 15:25–28 suggests that we read Christ as taking the place of God in the Psalms. One must first recognize that Paul

14. Conzelmann, *1 Corinthians*, 270.

15. Conzelmann, *1 Corinthians*, 270.

16. Hays, *Interpretation*, 266.

17. Hill, *Paul and the Trinity*, 120–33.

reads these texts as a monotheist, but with christological stipulations.[18] According to Hill, Christ is the active agent putting enemies under God's feet.[19] Therefore, to "hand over" (v. 24) and to "destroy" (v. 26) are both actions of Christ for the sake of making God all in all.

The activity of Christ is complicated and nuanced in Paul's reference to Father and Son in this passage. It is written, "When all things are subjected to him [Christ], then the Son himself will also be subjected to the one who put all things in subjection under him so that God may be all in all" (v. 28, NRSV). Christ places himself in subjection to the one called God the Father who is the one who put all things in subjection under Christ. Hill understands verse 28 to be understood alongside verse 24, that Christ's handing over to the Father must be understood in the context of the Son's subjection to God. These texts belong together as a means of expanding our understanding of God inside the relationship between Father and Son explored in this passage. Hill writes, "The Son is not who he is as the one who subjects himself to the Father without the Father."[20] The handing over and subjection are not separate, but inside of Paul's monotheism. The eschatological relationship between Father and Son determines and clarifies Paul's language. Hill writes,

> God's eschatologically ultimate identity is inseparable from that of Christ as his Son; God is, in a real way, *determined* as the God who is all in all by the Son's glorification of him as such. The titles 'Father' and 'Son' thus serve a dual, complementary purpose: to bind God and Christ together in a relationship of

18. I am aware of Agamben's argument that the modern understanding of "sovereignty" is trinitarian. God the Father establishes a rule in God the Son. The two orders are distinct but "economic" in their relation. This is the distinction between throne (the Father) and governing (the Son). The former is substantiated in the latter, and the latter obtains its direction from the former. This leads to much of modernity's political ailments, such as Adam Smith's invisible hand. See Agamben, *Kingdom and the Glory*, 68–105. Agamben's error lies in a failure to account for Paul's apocalyptic expectation. Käsemann writes, "Expectation of an imminent *Parousia* thus ceases to be meaningful [when] everything which [one] apocalyptically still hopes for has already been realized" (Käsemann, "On the Subject," 131). The expectation of God's coming consummation of the cosmos resists the ontological basis of such modern orders. The immediacy of expectation prevents the metaphysical claim from carrying weight. Kroeker writes, "If one is to speak of an economy of glory, therefore, it must be related to the ignominious death of the Messiah crucified by all forms of worldly authority—religious, political, economic, cultural" (Kroeker, "Introduction," 6).

19. Hill, *Paul and the Trinity*, 127.

20. Hill, *Paul and the Trinity*, 129.

mutuality whereby each of their distinct identities is inextricable from the other's, but also able to distinguish them as irreducibly particular actors or agents on the eschatological stage.[21]

The Father and Son work toward the same ends (*telos*): the defeat of death and the establishment of God's existence as all in all. The new creation that is distinguished from the kingdom of Christ is characterized by the radical intimacy created by the mutual activity between Father and Son. This passage speaks about how God is in Christ, reconciling the world to Godself (2 Cor 5:19). God destroys death by drawing it deeply inside the triune life so that death is not free from God's presence within it. Thus, God might be all in all.

In order to understand how God will be all in all, it is necessary to understand the bodies that are raised. Paul writes, "So it is with the resurrection of the dead. What is sown is perishable. It is sown in dishonor; it is raised in glory. It is sown in weakness; it is raised in power. It is sown in a physical body, it is raised a spiritual body. If there is a physical body, there is also a spiritual body" (vv. 42–44, NRSV). Dale Martin suggests that, in this passage, Paul makes a hierarchy of bodily substances.[22] It would be a mistake to read this passage, Martin argues, and think of this body as immaterial in any way.[23] He writes,

> When Paul says that the resurrected body will be a pneumatic [spiritual] body rather than simply a psychic body or flesh-and-blood body, he is saying that the immortal and incorruptible part of the human body will be resurrected—or, to put it more accurately, that the body will be raised, constituted (due to divine transformation) only by its immortal and incorruptible aspects, without its corruptible and corrupting aspects such as sarx [flesh].[24]

The flesh is a cosmic substance that represents the power of sin and death in the human body, and the illumination of its presence by no means disparages the body. However, Martin does argue that though there is no disparity, there is hierarchy in that only the imperishable survives. According to Martin, Paul is defending Jewish apocalyptic understanding of the resurrection, but he does so by "redefining *soma* to such an

21. Hill, *Paul and the Trinity*, 129–30.

22. Martin, *Corinthian Body*, 128.

23. Martin, *Corinthian Body*, 128.

24. Martin, *Corinthian Body*, 128.

extent that it would probably have made the doctrine unrecognizable to many less educated Christians."[25] In the resurrection, Martin continues, the "body is stripped of flesh, blood and soul (*psyche*); it has nothing of the earth in it at all, being composed entirely of the celestial substance of *pneuma*."[26] Paul does not reject the physiological/spiritual hierarchy, but redefines it in order to place the body in a higher place.

Despite this defense of Paul's redefinition of the body in the register of its potential immortality, it still fails to grapple with the true scandal of Paul's description of the resurrected body. Martin's description of the resurrected body makes sense of the cultural, linguistic context of the Corinthian congregations and helps clarify Paul's statement that "flesh and blood cannot inherit the kingdom of God, nor does perishable inherit the imperishable" (v. 50b, NRSV). This is neither the only, nor the most persuasive, interpretation. New Testament scholar Andy Johnson understands that 1 Corinthians 15 should be read within the context of 1 Corinthians 2:14–15.[27] There, Paul writes,

> Those who are unspiritual do not receive the gifts of God's Spirit, for they are foolishness to them, and they are unable to understand them because they are spiritually discerned. Those who are spiritual discern all things, and they are themselves subject to no one else's scrutiny. (NRSV)

Johnson recognizes that this is the only other place in the letter where Paul contrasts spiritual and unspiritual.[28] In 1 Corinthians 2, Paul appears to be referencing epistemology, for the known spiritual things are folly to the unspiritual (v. 14). The difference between spiritual and unspiritual lies in the transformation by the Spirit of the life of the believer. It is not a matter of the body moving up the scale of being, but the Spirit's permeation of the body to the point of transformation. Johnson writes, "the distinction between [spiritual and unspiritual] has been enacted by the Spirit who effects a transformation whereby the epistemological categories of the *psychikos* person are changed in such a way that s/he becomes a *pneumatikos* person."[29] The Spirit marks the essential difference

---

25. Martin, *Corinthian Body*, 129.

26. Martin, *Corinthian Body*, 129.

27. Johnson, "Turning the World Upside Down," 291–309.

28. Johnson, "Turning the World Upside Down," 292, 294.

29. Johnson, "Turning the World Upside Down," 294.

between knowing in this age and knowing in the age to come (i.e., the new creation enabled by the Spirit).

Building on this insight, Johnson points out that this change in the order of knowing corresponds to the change of physical reality brought about by the future *parousia* of Christ.[30] Therefore, 1 Corinthians 3:14 should be read as an unpacking of this new reality made possible in Christ through the power of the Spirit as first evidenced in the epistemological shift in 1 Corinthians 2 and completed in 1 Corinthians 15.[31] Paul's letter should be read as a "two-fold movement of God's invasion of the cosmos in that he rhetorically brackets what he says with a beginning discourse on the cross (1:18–2:16) and an ending discourse on the resurrection (15:1–58)."[32] The letter consistently places the congregation within the new reality brought about by Christ through crucifixion, resurrection, ascension, and coming consummation.[33] The letter ends with a fulfillment of Paul's proposed form of life, as exemplified in the cross and in the resurrected body. The shift to talking about a new body must resonate with the new knowledge imparted by the Spirit in order to form a particular kind of communal life. Johnson writes,

> Paul uses the adjectives [unspiritual] and [spiritual] in 1 Corinthians 2 to distinguish a way of knowing characteristic of "this age" from a way of knowing characteristic of the "new creation." We will see that in 1 Corinthians 15 Paul uses the same two adjectives in a corresponding way in the context of ontology, i.e., to distinguish between a body characteristic of "this age" and a body that will be truly changed by the Spirit to make it appropriate for the "new creation" at its consummation.[34]

Johnson summarizes the connection between the *already* and the *not yet*. The purpose of the *already* lies in the communication of the new creation in the now, and the *not yet* is the consummation of creation into the new creation.

Johnson agrees with Martin that the question occasioning the chapter is, at least in part, the ability of the body to participate in the world

---

30. Johnson, "Turning the World Upside Down," 294–95.

31. Johnson, "Turning the World Upside Down," 295.

32. Johnson, "Turning the World Upside Down," 295.

33. This was the argument I made in chapter 3.

34. Johnson, "Turning the World Upside Down," 296.

to come.[35] However, Johnson differs in his interpretation of Paul on the body's relationship to the spiritual in the afterlife. Martin emphasizes a Pauline shift in the substance of the human body up the hierarchy of materiality. Johnson proposes that Paul provides continuity between the preresurrection body and the body raised.

Though quickly clarifying that there is a disruptive element to this continuity, Johnson argues that the continuity is illustrated in the set antinomy established in verses 42–44. Johnson argues that this is a rhetorical device utilized "not to accommodate [the cosmological assumptions of his audience] but to begin turning them upside down."[36] Paul is performing a similar function as he is depicted in Acts 17 turning the Hellenistic mindset on its head. In verse 42, Paul contrasts σπείρεται ἐν φθορᾷ (sown in corruption) with ἐγείρεται ἐν ἀφθαρσίᾳ (raised in noncorruptibility) as a means to show the antithetical relationship between what is sown and raised.[37] This pattern sets up an expectation in Paul's audience in order to show the continuity of the *body* being sown and raised by emphasizing *how* it is sown and raised. Johnson notes that the specific pattern of words Paul uses to describe what is sown—perishable, weakness, dishonorable—is σάρξ (sarx/flesh). The fleshy realities are contrasted with the spiritual realities: imperishable, glory, power. Presumably, Paul's audience would have expected Paul to continue this pattern in verse 44. Rather than opposing πνευματικὸν (spiritual) with σάρξ, Paul contrasts it with ψυχικόν (physical), which Johnson notes is not the opposite of spiritual in the Greek hierarchy. This "disrupts" Paul's display of antitheses that characterize earlier verses by maintaining a continuity in the *body* we have now with the resurrected body.

The purpose of setting up this continuity between the body ψυχικόν with the body πνευματικὸν is in order to pick up the distinguishing factor between this age and the age to come. Paul uses 1 Corinthians 2 to describe the apocalyptic epistemological distinction between those who *know* by this age and those who *know* by the new creation. In 1 Corinthians 15, Johnson argues that Paul is referring to the ontology of the body itself.[38] The distinction between this age and the new creation is not that

35. Johnson, "Turning the World Upside Down," 297.

36. Johnson, "Turning the World Upside Down," 299.

37. Johnson, "Turning the World Upside Down," 300.

38. Johnson, "Turning the World Upside Down," 301.

the former is the fleshy, sinful state and the latter spiritual.[39] Rather, all Paul intends is that the physical body marked by perishability is appropriate for the present, and that the πνευματικὸν body is "a human body that has been truly changed by the Spirit to make it appropriate for the 'new creation' at its consummation."[40] Thus, the physical body will be incorporated into the consummation of the world that is the new creation by means of the Spirit and is in continuity with the present body.

The main distinguishing mark between the body of this age and the new creation is a *temporal* one. The body is marked by what it knows of the creation now but will in the coming reign of God be so permeated and transformed by the Spirit that it will be called πνευματικὸν. The work of the Spirit implied here by Paul, through Johnson's comparison with 1 Corinthians 2, should be read in concert with the *perichoretic* dance of the triune God. In verses 20–28, Paul speaks of the synchronous movements between the Father and Son to subject all things to the very Godhead itself. The Son destroys death by giving it over to the Father so that all enemies must be subjected to the very life of God. This is true even in the body. Theologian David Bentley Hart summarizes Paul well:

> In the age to come, the "psychical body," the "ensouled" or "animal" way of life, will be replaced by a "spiritual body," beyond the reach of death—though, again, conventional translations usually obscure this by speaking of the former, vaguely, as a "natural body."[41]

God being all in all and defeating death is both experienced in the body. The Son subjects the entire cosmos under himself and places it under the feet of the Father. This takes place through Christ's own defeat of the powers evidenced in his resurrection. The defeat will come through the Spirit's own taking of the body beyond the reach of such powers. The Spirit's movement must be read mimicking the synchronism between Father and Son. The Son destroys death in the world, but the Spirit transforms the body to match the reality now coming to pass. In equal senses, the Son and Spirit draw creation into the very life of the Godhead.

This eschatological *telos* in the life of the Godhead positions human life outside private interest by placing hope and fulfillment beyond its own capabilities. The gift of the resurrection of the dead suggests that our

---

39. Johnson, "Turning the World Upside Down," 301.

40. Johnson, "Turning the World Upside Down," 302.

41. Hart, "Everything You Know," para. 7.

own private moorings over the world ultimately must give way to God's total consummation of the cosmos. The apocalyptic in-breaking of God names the *telos* of creaturely life, which reorients any immanent, private *telos* within the world: "My beloved, be steadfast, immovable, always excelling in the work of the Lord, because you know that in the Lord your labor is not in vain" (v. 58, NRSV). The end toward which moral action works is the resurrected body. However, it is not an end that is achievable by private means. Rather, "in the twinkling of the eye" all will be changed (vv. 51–52, NRSV). Paul uses traditional apocalyptic language in order to describe the interruptive nature of the resurrection of the body (v. 52). This means that the *telos* of the world interrupts human doing and breaks in upon the private interests of humanity. In a traditional understanding *telos*, one perfects their own work. However, the resurrection interrupts all work in order to draw it into God's perfected life. It is not a matter of achieving the legitimate ends of our actions or lives; it is that our ends meet us in the new creation.

The importance of recognizing our ends within an eschatological *telos* lies in a theological understanding of virtue. For example, justice should be understood eschatologically in order to preserve it against a capture by the powers through private interests. Take, for example, Beker's own analysis of the event of martyrdom as eschatologically intelligible. According to Beker, justice for martyrs and the avenging of their blood (Rev 6:10) requires an eschatological fulfillment of creation.

Such a fulfillment is illustrated well in Augustine's description of martyrdom in the *City of God*. Augustine's two-city typology must be understood eschatologically. According to Augustine, Christians exist on earth as pilgrims. As pilgrims, the Christian is called, as Paul writes, to present her body as a "living sacrifice" (Rom 12:1, NRSV). Augustine writes on sacrifice, "true sacrifice, then, is every act done in order that we might cling to God in holy fellowship, that is, every act which is referred to the final good in which we can be truly blessed."[42] To be a pilgrim is to cling in sacrifice to God and thus to witness in faith to God's eschatological reign. Such a witness often can take the shape of martyrdom. As Augustine continues, "In giving their witness they endured the world's fiercest hostility and cruelty, and they overcame the world not by fighting back but by dying."[43] The martyrs understand true justice because

42. Augustine, *City of God* X.6.
43. Augustine, *City of God* XXII.9.

they, as P. Travis Kroeker writes, refuse to "grasp prematurely, through faithless violence, the gift that God offers fully only eschatologically."[44] Justice, according to the blood of the martyr, is not found in fallen violent power. Power does not exist merely in the fallen propensity to coercion and violence, but exists here with those who bear crosses in the grain of the universe. Justice, then, is a gift *fully* given in the eschatological reign of Christ and now only liturgically enacted through faithful discipleship to Christ.

Therefore, one must crucify any form of justice that does not conform to this eschatological pilgrimage that resists the violence of this age. Rather, it must conform to the patient reign of Christ. As Augustine rightly asks, how do we come to an understanding of this justice? How is it enacted in patience? Augustine shows that perceiving justice is unlike perceiving other realities. He writes, "I am perceiving something that is present to me, and it is present to me even if I am not what I perceive, and many will agree with me when they hear me."[45] Thus, justice cannot be known as other material realities, it must be known, much like the martyr, in patient self-giving. The ability for a broad recognition of justice is essential. It is by cleaving to justice—that can be known through patience and self-giving—that it is beheld "in order to be formed by it and become just minds." Only by this can we

> "knowingly and deliberately in life and in conduct [give] each [human] what is [their] own," but . . . now living justly and conducting themselves justly by giving each [person] what is [their] own, in order to *owe no [one] anything but to love one another.* (Rom 13:8)[46]

Augustine here refers to an ancient definition of justice as rendering to each what is due to them. For Augustine, the internal recognition of what is due another is bound in the command to love one's neighbor. Once justice is clarified, it should be lovingly enacted in the world, which most concretely takes the shape of loving the neighbor.

Therefore, loving the neighbor is how one lives justly. Augustine argues that humanity loves this justice in the person of Christ, who loves his neighbor perfectly and thus God.[47] As he writes, "True love then is

44. Kroeker, "Messianic Political Ethic," 150.
45. Augustine, *Trinity* VIII.9.
46. Augustine, *Trinity* VIII.9.
47. Augustine, *Trinity* VIII.9–10.

that we should live justly by cleaving to the truth, and so for the love of [humanity] by which we wish them to live justly we should despise all mortal things."[48] In apocalyptic terms, believers are asked to lovingly give themselves to their neighbor in full knowledge that the world (i.e., the mortal thing) is passing away. Believers are encouraged, in Pauline terms, to owe nothing but love. This is justice. This is how believers overcome the fiercest violence of this world. By lovingly giving oneself to God in Jesus Christ, to one's neighbor, and to the world, true justice is enacted and violent forms of pseudo-justice (i.e., that which is passing away) resisted.

This type of just love peaceably encounters violence, which means justice might require martyrdom for the sake of the pilgrimage toward eschatological fulfillment. Only when the new creation is taken seriously for ethical reflection can the Christian form of justice emerge. As Augustine suggests, the meaning of our actions find intelligibility in a *telos* not restricted to the influence of the present world order. Loving one's neighbor, one could say, does not establish a community of power, but of weakness, and it is somehow this posture that is more authentic to its eschatological fulfillment.[49] Christian activity is faithful to God's coming eschatological fulfillment by recognizing the form of this world's violence, not by grasping at it, but by giving itself away in loving service to that which is passing away. This is only intelligible in light of an eschatological fulfillment. Those who fall victim to this violence and the world that is passing away, both the martyr and the victim, will be given bodies that cannot be parted by death.[50] By resisting the powers of death in loving service to this world, they gain victory over it. The resurrection of the dead is the answer to the question posed in Revelation 10:6, "When will our blood be avenged?" (NRSV). Thus, justice, like all actions, takes the form of a concrete activity (loving the neighbor) in order to witness to another end (eschatological fulfillment).

I wish to briefly clarify the posture toward the end of the world that also gives justice to victims of violence of the powers. This includes not just the martyrs in faith, but all who experience the violence of the powers that dominate this age. I believe that this is the most provocative and important claim arising from God's exclusive agency to bring about the end of the world. A justice that loves the neighbor and witnesses

48. Augustine, *Trinity* VIII.10.

49. Augustine, *City of God* X.6.

50. Augustine, *City of God* XXII.26.

to eschatological fulfillment means a just end for all victims. As Philip Ziegler writes,

> Final divine judgment puts things to rights *for the sake of an unhindered future for creaturely life*. Identical in substance with the saving work of Christ, its essence is positive and generative: God judges to save and fulfill. And the eternal life to which it gives rise is shorn of all that would threaten, truncate, and undermine true life with and for God, a life founded ultimately beyond the entire "dissolution of the world of evil."[51]

The generous and saving work of the eschaton is for the sake of an unhindered creaturely life. Furthermore, if this unhindered creaturely reality is the fulfillment of the justice that loves neighbors sacrificially, then these neighbors taken as a result of violent powers are also held in this generous love. This is a life beyond death and beyond the very conditions that lead to victimization. If the eschaton and final judgement is just and for the purpose of unhindered creaturely life, then a *not yet* hope must consider these victims too.

The internal logic of 1 Corinthians 15 and Augustine presents a differing view of ends and history. If justice is only understood eschatologically, then our views of universal maxims and progress come undone. Compare the apocalyptic *parousia* of the resurrection of the dead with Hegel's own view of history:

> History in general is therefore the development of Spirit in *Time*, as Nature is the development of the Idea in *Space*. If then we cast a glance over the World's-History generally we see a vast picture of changes and transactions; of infinitely manifold forms of peoples, states, individuals, in unresting succession. Everything that can enter into and interest the soul of man—all our sensibility to *goodness, beauty, and greatness*—is called into play. On every hand aims are adopted and pursued, which we recognize, whose accomplishment we desire—we hope and fear for them.[52]

The Spirit that develops in time is a progress that humanity makes through ever greater movements toward greatness and beauty. This view of history involves humanity's ability to achieve its own ends and justice. The best this can do is a perpetual revolution and the worst defines, as Nietzsche

51. Ziegler, "Final Triumph of Grace," 103. Emphasis original.
52. Hegel, *Philosophy of History*, 72. Emphasis original.

suggests, "Right . . . with the victorious: they represent the progress of mankind [and a]ttempt to prove the dominion of morality by means of history."[53] However, when viewed apocalyptically God meets humanity with its holy end. Ultimately either elements of Hegel's view of history—prevalent in contemporary philosophy and the new approach—is erroneous for Paul. The apocalyptic Paul is far more radical in his understanding of history. History is the site of God's incarnational inbreaking which sets history on its course, only to be broken into again—not in order to destroy it, but consummate it. Justice, mercy, goodness, and the like meet humanity and is practiced now in eschatological expectation. History is not told from the place of the victorious, but from the crucified, and it is from there that it will find its fulfillment.

Due to this peculiar posture toward our end, the Christian life is wrought with actions unintelligible to surrounding cultures, actions such as suffering and selfless service to others (1 Cor 10:33—11:1) and facing the beasts (1 Cor 15:30–32). If this is true, the Christian moral life must be dominated by hope. Richard Hays writes,

> The resurrection of the dead serves as a warrant validating not only Christian preaching but also "the work of the Lord" more generally; everything that we do stands under the sign of Christ's resurrection, and all our actions are given worth and meaning. *The resurrection is the necessary foundation for faithful action in the world.* Therefore, the Corinthians are urged to remain "steadfast, immovable" in holding the faith and putting it into action . . . Those who affirm the truth of Christ's resurrection will be given the moral confidence to live in a way that shows that their hope is not in vain.[54]

Christians are not called to master the world, but to live in such a way that clearly resembles faithfulness to the bodies they will receive. The phrase "εἶτα τὸ τέλος (end) ὅταν παραδιδῷ," traditionally translated "then comes the end" (15:24, NRSV), could instead read "and then comes rest." Only in the resurrected body does the believer cease to labor. Rest and labor serve as suitable terms to describe the *poesis* and release of the moral life. Laboring does not yield the new creation or make all things new. Rather, laboring struggles against the sovereignty of sin and death for the purpose of faithful response to the revelation of the new creation

53. Nietzsche, *Will to Power*, §415.

54. Hays, *Interpretation*, 277. Emphasis original.

within the old aeon (1 Cor 2:14–15), which is the fulfillment of our moral responsiveness to the revelation of God in the *already*. What is required is a repetition, a constant rediscovery of the newness of life in action that can be repeated without becoming stale.

Facing the Sovereign: Novelty and Eschaton

The question of hope and newness is essential to the faithful political witness of Christian congregations. Only by an ability to practice faithful, moral activity can the church avoid the constant temptation to novelty. As Augustine illustrates with justice, so it is with all political activity. Developing Augustine's insights on this point is crucial for a full picture of Paul's political theology. By novelty, I mean political fanaticism, which attempts to make the world "new" again by a certain framework of moral responsiveness contrary to the means by which God makes all things new. An example of this type of novelty is evident in Timothy Snyder's research into the National Socialism of World War II Germany. Snyder notes that there was a concentrated effort to rewrite the very nature of statehood in order to serve the evil purposes of Adolf Hitler and his followers.[55] Time and again, Snyder notes, German citizens were asked to ignore international and traditional principles of jurisprudence for the sake of advancing the "flow" of German power.[56] In fact, the law was made an instrument for the purpose of the Aryan race. Snyder quotes Hitler's personal lawyer in saying, "'The law is what serves the race, and lawlessness is what hurts the race.' Nonracist norms were simply the work of the Jews, 'who instinctively saw in jurisprudence the best possibility to carry out their own racial work.'"[57] The weakening of law was for the sake of bringing Germany to an end so that the Reich could emerge. As understood by both Agamben and Schmitt, this weakening lead to the sovereign establishment of exceptional, lawless zones (i.e., concentration camps), and to the combining of SS with traditional police, whose policies were directed against German citizens.[58] Snyder writes, "only beyond Germany could the exception truly become the rule . . . because only beyond Germany could normal political life be obliterated and a *new* ethos

55. Snyder, *Black Earth*, 144–45.
56. Snyder, *Black Earth*, 144.
57. Snyder, *Black Earth*, 145.
58. Snyder, *Black Earth*, 146.

of nihilistic power be created."[59] Snyder appeals to the very definition of sovereignty proposed to Schmitt—the deciding of the exception—in order to locate the ends envisioned by Germany. The issues of sovereignty and ends raised by Snyder are instructive for Christians facing political claims to novelty.

Hitler and others were quite effective in inspiring a people to abandon law and concern for their neighbors for the sake of a new political reality centered in the private interests of the German *ein Volk*. Like in modern biopolitics, private interests form a political community centered around preserving life against those labeled as living death. The death camps, SS, and new laws and policies mobilized the threat of death, the power of death itself, against individuals for the sake of preserving private interests of the German people. Death as power united the German people under a sovereignty greater than Hitler. Death, therefore, is a power that attempts to constantly reinvent itself.

The new that was celebrated by Hitler's lawyers and legal apologists is resisted in the resurrection of the dead because it does not preserve private interests mobilized under the sovereignty of death, as the resurrection is a creation-wide consummation. The creation groans, awaiting fulfillment (Rom 8:22–24). In 1 Corinthians 15:39–41, Paul alludes to the variety of flesh confronted in the resurrected life. The resurrected life, in that it is an embodied life, must have creation in order to sustain that bodily life. The continuity in the resurrected and preresurrected body lies in the embodied state. Therefore, all creation is subject to the resurrection of the dead. Since the resurrection of the dead consummates all of creation, then our own private concerns are not of ultimate concern for God. An event such as the resurrection of the dead is so large and creation-wide that it cannot respect the interests of a private few and a lonely sovereign. The resurrection of Christ, the future bodily resurrection, and the creation-wide consummation signaled in both becomes the shared ends of Christian political life.

The labor of Christianity confronts the power of death in its ever-novel appearances throughout time by relying on the *telos* of the resurrection of the dead. Christian actions are grounded in the hope for a new creation. This hope is reborn and strengthens the Christian moral life in every new encounter with the power of death manifest in the world. Christian hope is the "ableness" that refuses the trap of the sovereignty

---

59. Snyder, *Black Earth*, 146. Emphasis mine.

of sin and death. Paul writes in 2 Corinthians, "We do not lose heart. Even though our outer nature is wasting away, our inner nature is being renewed day by day" (4:16, NRSV). To be renewed is a state of stubborn hope where the Christian moral life is able to perform a different political imagination that lives within the *not yet*. Christian moral, political action needs hope in order to perform new actions as it confronts the continued presence of the sovereignty of sin and death.

POLITICS AT THE END OF HISTORY: NATALITY, THE JUST AND LOVING GAZE, AND ESCHATOLOGY

In order to combat the continued presence of death, one must be able to make new moral judgments and perform new actions in the face of the new forms of death. Politically, this necessity is best exemplified in Hannah Arendt's emphasis on natality. Arendt's natality is "the new beginning inherent in birth . . . [and] inherent in all human activities."[60] In short, natality serves as a basic reminder that humanity is always capable of new judgments, new activities, and a new life not bound by past misdeeds. In a religious sense, natality is new birth or being born again. All action, according to Arendt, is "ontologically rooted" in this fact.[61] This potentiality for newness and spontaneity is a type of political and moral grace. As such, natality suggests that human political activity always gestures toward the future for new ways of being peaceable. It is a being toward that which is new. Such a political posture couples nicely with the theological hope in the resurrection of the dead. Both the resurrection of the dead and natality suggest that a genuinely new beginning lies ahead. Therefore, natality contains an inner political rationality that corresponds to the work of the *not yet*.

Natality as a "being toward new," much like the creation-wide scope of the resurrection, presumes plurality. Plurality is "the fact that men, not Man, live on the earth and inhabit the world."[62] In a world of private interest, plurality is the concrete reminder of the inclusive nature of political. Plurality is the broad affirming of particularity among others not in competition. Arendt's very notion of speech and action lies in this concept of natality. In politics, humans speak and act with other people in a free,

60. Arendt, *Human Condition*, 9.

61. Arendt, *Human Condition*, 9.

62. Arendt, *Human Condition*, 7.

unhindered way. Insofar as actions have this potentiality to emerge, they possess the possibility of newness. Arendt writes, "If action as beginning corresponds to the fact of birth, if it is the actualization of the human condition of natality, then speech corresponds to the fact of distinctness and is the actualization of the human condition of plurality, that is, of living as a distinct and unique being among equals."[63] Freedom lies in this ability to act and speak among equals in a manner that corresponds to one's own distinctiveness and existence and offers the potentiality for newness.

Natality mirrors the moral convictions of the resurrection of the dead and helps articulate the continual work of the just and loving gaze, which requires an eschatological outlook. Much like Wesley, Murdoch's philosophy insists on the continual forming work of perfection, a gradual move into goodness. That being said, Murdoch lacks Christian convictions of the eschaton and her treatment of the just and loving gaze lacks a narrative of eschatological fulfillment. The just and loving gaze recognizes that one's judgments and prejudices are not fixed. Much like in the example of Mother (M) and Daughter-in-Law (D), the just and loving gaze models a posture of self-criticism, careful and just attention, and the ability to look again at situations previously thought to be understood.[64] An ability to reevaluate the values one previously assigned to a reality is required in order that one's moral and political life does not devolve into caricature. The great insight here is that moral activity is not finally fixed. I contend that this is also how Paul understands eschatological hope. It is the continual unselfish reevaluation of our moral prejudice in light of the new creation. The implication is that, at the eschaton, moral judgments will finally be fixed. A theological interpretation of natality in the just and loving gaze is a constant reevaluation of one's moral prejudice.

Murdoch's best text for interpreting the just and loving gaze inside of Arendt's natality is her novel *The Nice and the Good*. This work examines, though not intentionally, the theme of natality in the moral life. I propose that this most clearly appears in the main character John Ducane and his romantic exploits, as displayed in the novel. Romantic relationship in Murdoch's work serves to best illustrate the moral life. She writes, "A love relationship can . . . prompt a process of 'unselfing' wherein the lover

63. Arendt, *Human Condition*, 178.

64. Murdoch, *Sovereignty of the Good*, 17.

learns to see, and cherish and respect, what is not himself."[65] This process is not something momentary and finalized. It is a lifelong practice at "innumerable points . . . at which we have to detach ourselves, to change our orientation, to redirect our desire and refresh and purify our energy, to keep looking in the right direction: to attend upon the grace that comes through faith."[66] Murdoch helps her readers see that the work of the just and loving gaze requires perpetual work on behalf of the agent in order to purify its energy to make new judgments as prejudices are unmasked.

The character of John Ducane is a legal advisor to the British government who is asked to investigate the suicide of a fellow civil servant. Though this thriller element of the novel is provoking for the moral life, it is John's relationships that most illuminate the moral life. In the novel, John is portrayed as an intelligent, well-intentioned man who suffers from being too nice. Murdoch, who was working on "The Idea of Perfection" while writing *The Nice and the Good*, utilizes similar language in describing Ducane as she does her example M. Contrary to M, John fails at key points to "unself" in a way that is befitting of the just and loving gaze.

John's moral weakness is most clearly displayed in his love life. At the beginning of the novel, John finds himself attempting to end an affair with an art teacher named Jessica Bird. It is clear that John has misgivings about this relationship. She is younger than John and, as became clear over the course of his affair, "not his kind of thing."[67] John begins the relationship with Jessica, as it appears, out of a sexual desire for her. She is foreign to him because of her youth and lack of intellectual curiosity, which puzzles Ducane.[68] Since he is an intelligent, reflective man, John realized over time the inappropriateness of this relationship. They were able to make each other happy, but not permanently. He notes that "his nervous uncertain sensuality needed some sophisticated intellectual encouragement, a certain kind of play, which Jessica was unable to provide."[69] Though this seems obviously selfish of John, it arises from a reflective element of his personality. It was clear to John that he was using Jessica in an unjust manner. To "keep" her with no intention of marriage

65. Murdoch, *Metaphysics as a Guide*, 17.

66. Murdoch, *Metaphysics as a Guide*, 25.

67. Murdoch, *Nice and the Good*, 26.

68. Murdoch, *Nice and the Good*, 26.

69. Murdoch, *Nice and the Good*, 26.

or care for her was wrong, and his objectification of her was not befitting of his typical moral activity. John knew the relationship could not continue.

Despite this knowledge, John could not outright end the affair. This was not because he failed to address the issue, but because of his apparent unease with confrontation. He failed to end the affair because of his unwillingness to cause Jessica to suffer and his need to be well thought of.[70] What John actually loves when he loves Jessica is not the good, but himself. John's need to be thought of well has not yet subsided, and John has yet to make a new—natal—judgment. The seed of such a judgment is present, but he has failed to orient himself to this good end. He fails to truly love the good, only loving his own public perception of himself. Despite this failure, it is clear that John would like to be free in order to pursue a platonic relationship with his friend, Kate Gray, which he pursues despite his remaining attachment to Jessica.

The relationship with Kate Gray is entirely different from the relationship with Jessica. The biggest difference is that "Kate was very married."[71] Kate's husband is John's superior, Octavian Gray. John even frequently visits their house in the country. John prefers his relationship with Kate due to her joy, happiness, and generosity, not because of a stronger sexual attraction.[72] There is something about Kate that enables Ducane to rid himself of loneliness.[73] By loving Kate, John loves generosity, joy, etc.[74] The good that John loves in Kate is a beauty that attracts John to her. Despite these advantages, the relationship often seems to exceed the platonic nature of their friendship. Ultimately, Kate does not move John beyond his own selfish interest or his need to be well thought of. The question of having such a morally ambiguous relationship with Kate is fraught with jealousy and mistrust. The relationship becomes uncertain when a letter appears, detailing the nature of John's relationship with Jessica, from an opponent of John. Kate decides to leave John in order to free him to be with Jessica, not knowing that Jessica has done the same for Kate.[75]

---

70. Murdoch, *Nice and the Good*, 315.

71. Murdoch, *Nice and the Good*, 26.

72. Murdoch, *Nice and the Good*, 25.

73. Murdoch, *Nice and the Good*, 50.

74. Murdoch, *Nice and the Good*, 30.

75. Murdoch, *Nice and the Good*, 270–74, 326–29.

At this point it is worth noting the change and new judgments John undergoes in his shift of love from Jessica to Kate John begins to love, not carnal desires or selfishness, but generosity and kindness. It is his feeling of dissatisfaction with his relationship with Jessica that leads to his desire of these virtues, which leads to his recognition that he is mistreating Jessica. The attractiveness of the good leads John away from a harmful relationship with Jessica toward the good in Kate. John is in search of goodness. He seeks the good instead of selfish ambition. Yet, he does not come to love the good unselfishly, as is evident in his relationship with Kate. Despite this failure, the presence of hope is distinguishable in the pages of the novel. John has come to hope for a better life and has slowly, albeit imperfectly, begun subtly making new shifts in his behavior. These troubled relationships lead John on a journey toward the good, in which he constantly finds himself renegotiating and refreshing his moral prejudices.

John's search for goodness in his love for these women works itself out in a very particular way. One incident illustrates this very well. One day, Pierce Clothier, the son of John's lifelong friend Mary Clothier, swims into a small cave with the intention to drown himself. John swims in as the hero but finds himself trapped along with Pierce, presumably to drown with him. Yet again, his need to be well thought of leads him into trouble, and this time it may cost him his life. This causes him to reflect on the whole of his life: love, the investigation, his own grasp of the good. While trapped, he wonders, if this is the end, what will his life amounted to? "How tawdry and small it has all been. He saw himself now as a little rat, a busy little scurrying rat seeking out its own little advantages and comforts. To live easily, to have cozy familiar pleasures, to be well thought of."[76] In other words, being well thought of is not the Good and cannot satisfy. This event pushes him into a yet-unexamined depth of his own life. The process of learning to love and "unself" has culminated in John's new judgment. He decides, "if I ever get out of here I will be no man's judge . . . not to judge, not to be superior, not to exercise power, not to seek, seek, seek. To love and to reconcile and to forgive, only this matters. All power is sin and all law is frailty. Love is the only justice. Forgiveness, reconciliation, not law."[77] In a mode of selflessness, John finds a new way

---

76. Murdoch, *Nice and the Good*, 315.

77. Murdoch, *Nice and the Good*, 315.

of being in the world, through goodness. The journey of John Ducane has led to an inspiration of new activity and judgments.

The way that John's experience in the cave operates is strangely familiar to the Myth of the Cave in Plato's *Republic*. For Plato, the Good is that by which we gain vision of all reality.[78] It is a type of light that illuminates reality among others in the dark.[79] In the cave, John experiences a similar revelation of what is ultimately worth doing and a means of being in the world. John discovers that love is justice, and one must forgive and reconcile. Goodness, as discovered in the cave, is anticipated by John's long and jagged relationships. But even there, he realizes that he is not loving them well; only when he "unselfs" does he learn that his relationships with Jessica and Kate are unloving. John's paralysis of needing to be thought well of finally abates. Much like the relationship between M and D, John "unselfs" and abandons his private interests in favor of his ever-growing understanding of the Good.

John Ducane escapes the cave and finally acts on his new judgements by abandoning his relationships with Jessica and Kate. Due to his experience in the cave, he concludes his investigation and retires from civic duty. It is clear that John is more convinced of the Good than the need to be well thought of. Upon completing the investigation of the suicide, he decides to have the man most directly involved with the crime reconcile with his wife rather than turn him over to the proper authorities. This is to fulfill the Platonic liberation of others from the cave, namely to lead others into a better way of being. A leap is made by John where the new, natal judgements of the nature of the Good is both seen and practiced. John's experience in the cave provides him with purifying moral energy to commit to new actions. Only through the potential of natality are these new practices available.

Understood in the context of the just and loving gaze, John Ducane has experienced natality. Though it is not clear if he finally puts off the relentless ego, it is clear that he has made sufficient judgements that lead him away from the need to be well thought of. In his moral life, John is not captive to repeat the immoral cycle of his past moral judgment. He now exhibits the need to continually pursue new judgements. Like death, the fat, relentless ego will reinvent itself. Natality is an essential mark of the just and loving gaze because it is a lifelong practice where, Murdoch

78. Plato, *Republic*, 199.

79. Plato, *Republic*, 214.

writes, at "innumerable points we have to detach ourselves, to change our orientation, to redirect our desire and refresh and purify our energy, to keep looking in the right direction: to attend upon the grace that comes through faith."[80] The nature of being human includes private interests; these interests are fluid in nature and constantly shift as a result of new experiences. However, in order for the moral life to be considered good, one must not be bound by past prejudices. John's moral discovery of ever-greater love is a journey into the Good, which calls for ever-greater acts of "unselfing," culminating in his excursion into the cave. Only when following John from the beginning of the narrative to this moment is the Good in view.

In addition to its centrality to the just and loving gaze, Arendt's natality gives a political orientation for Paul's apocalyptic theology of the *not yet*. Theologian John Webster translates natality into a theological register by locating the newness of human action/agency within the action of God. The action of God is twofold according to Webster, namely God's reconciliation of reality and the eschatological fulfillment of God. Locating human action in the tension between reconciliation and fulfillment requires humanity's orientation to a particular *telos*, one which brings our actions to completion in the context of God's already-present saving activity. Therefore, natality is present in Christian moral and political activity, persisting—as Augustine understands—despite remaining unfulfilled. One must constantly reevaluate and persist in the activity most appropriate to the apocalyptic coming of God.

Webster claims that human lives are "converted" realities.[81] The apocalyptic ontological ground of our agency lies in our freedom from sinful antinomies. Our political life requires our rebirth and our natality. To say that human agency is a converted reality is to claim that human lives involve the "exclusion of certain ways of understanding the continuity of the self."[82] Rather, there is an apocalyptic break that disrupts the basic form of the self that comes before conversion. Webster writes, "The convertedness of human life is 'undirivable' from all that has gone before, our account of it has to talk of divine agency as its cause."[83] Moral and political agency within the ontological ground of conversion means that,

---

80. Murdoch, *Metaphysics as a Guide*, 25.

81. Webster, "Eschatology, Ontology, and Human Action," 5.

82. Webster, "Eschatology, Ontology, and Human Action," 5.

83. Webster, "Eschatology, Ontology, and Human Action," 5.

through the apocalyptic in-breaking of God, God reorders the cosmos to new ends and common good.[84] According to Webster, as in the fundamental convictions of Pauline apocalyptic, divine agency exercises the will of God through the incarnation, death, resurrection, and ascension of Christ. This activity "is . . . not the realization of latent human possibilities, but a *gift*, realized by an external agency which destroys and makes alive."[85] Webster is resisting the modern self's tendency toward mastery and sovereignty. Paul's apocalyptic prioritizes the history of Christ, albeit in our own historicity, as the context of all future human activity.[86]

The contextualization of human action *within* the action of God yields a certain set of "ontological categories" for human agency.[87] Taken this way, human action is eschatological, meaning that human agency is "oriented toward 'the new,' towards that which the creation *becomes* by virtue of the regenerative action of God in Christ through the power of the Spirit."[88] To give the regenerate human life priority in human action indicates that humans are not fundamentally defined by what they were, but what they eventually become.[89]

Webster acknowledges the Pauline tone of the ontological priority of God's activity in human life. Christ calls life into being (Rom 4:17); Christ is raised from the dead (Rom 8:11); and believers are considered dead to sin and alive to Christ (Rom 6:11) as Christ is the source of our redemption, righteousness, etc. (1 Cor 1:30). "It is no longer I who live but Christ who lives in me" (Gal 2:20).[90] One passage, 2 Corinthians 5:17 (NRSV), is most central to Webster's analysis: "So if anyone is in Christ, there is a new creation: everything old has passed away; see, everything has become new." Webster is interpreting this passage in light of the *already* of Christ's redemptive action. *Already* in the regenerative, reconciliatory activity of God's creation becomes new. Webster argues that this divine activity is identified as the new creation and, as such, must be treated as new.[91]

84. Webster, "Eschatology, Ontology, and Human Action," 6.
85. Webster, "Eschatology, Ontology, and Human Action," 6.
86. Webster, "Eschatology, Ontology, and Human Action," 6.
87. Webster, "Eschatology, Ontology, and Human Action," 4.
88. Webster, "Eschatology, Ontology, and Human Action," 4. Emphasis original.
89. Webster, "Eschatology, Ontology, and Human Action," 6.
90. Webster, "Eschatology, Ontology, and Human Action," 6–7.
91. Webster, "Eschatology, Ontology, and Human Action," 9.

Despite its newness, this natality is not a static reality but is caught within the power of God's continued creative, regenerative, and redemptive action. Historical realities, humanity, and creation find their history inside their movement in Jesus Christ.[92] There is a *not yet* element of this history that is a consistent pulling toward an eschatological future. The eschatological future is constitutive of human agency now. Webster is clear that we become other than what we are and that our agency is secondary to God's activity. This does not mean that we are passive. Passivity must be rejected in light of the "emergence of creative, imaginative patterns of human action which, in their human limitation, correspond to but do not in any way realise[*sic*] God's redrawing of the boundaries of human existence."[93] Actions are distinct possibilities that arise from the newness of Christ's apocalyptic invasion of the cosmos and point to the fulfillment of the cosmos.

The natality associated with the new reality in Christ—a new pattern of habituation in light of the incarnation, death, and resurrection—is coupled with the eschatological that is the account of the end of all things. Webster recognizes that his work on the newness of regenerated reality is insufficient if it does not consider its eschatological end, one that is truly worthy of being called the last things. Here, my analysis of 1 Corinthians and Webster converge. Eschatological fulfillment of action must be maintained, as Webster argues, in order "to prevent the first, more subjective, aspect from expanding to become the totality of what is said about eschatological humanity."[94] In Webster's view, this regenerated humanity in its reconciled state

> needs to be supported on more than simply the rather narrow base of convertedness, which, however important it may be and however thoroughly it may pervade a Christian ontology of the human, cannot provide the whole scope . . . What is required is an understanding of destiny sufficiently sturdy and expansive to resist being collapsed into the psychological or ethical dramas of self-hood. And so a dogmatic account of converted human identity will be closely related to an account of the ends of creation.[95]

---

92. Webster, "Eschatology, Ontology, and Human Action," 10.
93. Webster, "Eschatology, Ontology, and Human Action," 11.
94. Webster, "Eschatology and Anthropology," 265.
95. Webster, "Eschatology and Anthropology," 265.

Therefore, any fully eschatological account of political theology and general humanity must possess this *not yet* character that includes the fulfillment of the created order.

The task, then, is to describe the eschatological *not yet* in a way that does not "sidestep the exigencies of . . . culture . . . but so as to be able to address them with the right kind of Christian specificity, determination and hope."[96] This is the Pauline task, as well. This is an "exegetical and dogmatic" task, which fulfills humanity not by realization of its own actions, but by God's fulfillment inaugurated in Christ. Webster offers a theological description of teleology. Webster acknowledges the troubled reception of teleology in our late-modern context and does not dismiss the rejection of it. Webster recognizes the political totalizing narratives of history often found in modern thought. These accounts seize upon teleology for more sinister purposes, constructing a teleology that seeks "to possess and control the outcomes of human history."[97] This structuring of history only leads to the "homogenization and singularization" of history and people.[98]

Webster argues that the late moderns are correct to deride this use of biopolitical teleology. However, he does not abandon teleology for the sake of locating humanity beyond such harmful finite teleological endeavors. He argues that we do not, in explaining the eschatological, "abandon teleology, but . . . specify its character with right kind of Christian precision."[99] By precision, Webster means a coherent christological center to its eschatological appropriation of teleology, or the apocalyptic christological center of teleology. Webster argues that eschatology is "the forward expansion of the name of Jesus," in that it is concerned with "the reality indicated *by* the name of Jesus."[100] This center cannot be laid aside unless we abandon less fruitful endeavors, like the "immanent teleologies of human history" that dominate the movements of history.[101] Only this offsets biopolitics. If less fruitful endeavors dominate Christian

96. Webster, "Eschatology and Anthropology," 267.

97. Webster, "Eschatology and Anthropology," 274.

98. Webster, "Eschatology and Anthropology," 274.

99. Webster, "Eschatology and Anthropology," 274.

100. Webster, "Eschatology and Anthropology," 274–75. Emphasis added.

101. Webster, "Eschatology and Anthropology," 275.

eschatology, then Jesus "becomes a mere ornament in what is, in effect, a theory of temporality or an ideology of human achievement."[102]

Christian eschatology distances itself from ideology by means of promise. Promise is the eschatological importance of faith. Theologian Robert W. Jenson writes,

> Faith as my act is that I give up my attained self in order to receive myself from the Coming One who just as such undoes all security. But when I try to *perform* this act, I of course achieve the opposite, for I necessarily do it within my project of self-securing, even if in this case religiously . . . Only a proclamatory word spoken to me can free me from myself, a word that *so challenges me to live from God's future rather than my own possessed life that such eschatological existence is the only possibility open in the moment of hearing,* that in the event of this word the future of God, and so indeed God himself, *happens* to me.[103]

Jenson helps describe how eschatology is natality. By receiving one's identity from the future, one lives within a persistent expectancy. Even though one performs particular activities consistently—serving the poor, seeking justice, etc.—it is always new as it receives this imperative and identity from the futurity of God. The eschatological is a natality continually meeting the Christian in identity.

Eschatology, Webster argues, "cannot be replaced by an act of intellectual or spiritual or political possession of the object of hope."[104] Christian apocalyptic eschatology, which is simultaneously political theology, is an echo of the Pauline prayer: "Our Lord, come!" (1 Cor 16:22b, NRSV). Webster argues that such a central conviction yields three implications for Christian moral and political life.

> First, it gives expression to the personal specificity of Christian eschatology. Jesus is our hope: come Lord *Jesus.* Jesus is not an emblematic figure in a larger historical canvas; he *is* the future. Second, in praying that he may come, Christian speech indicates that Jesus is not to be handled as an available object, something or someone to hand. As the one who will come, he is other than an object or figure within the horizon of the world. Third, we *pray* that he may come; that is, we look for the action of another, we implore him to take the initiative, to act in an affair

102. Webster, "Eschatology and Anthropology," 275.
103. Jenson, *Systematic Theology,* 167. Emphasis added.
104. Webster, "Eschatology and Anthropology," 275.

where we cannot act. Here, in other words, Christian speech is other than some sort of apparatus for controlling destiny; it is supplication.[105]

The eschatological supplication is quite clear in political speech: humility is required in acting. Christian moral and political action toward the neighbor and powers must reflect this nature of supplication. To know, despite one's actions, that the goodness of the world is not fulfilled by those actions requires abandoning the pretext of modern self-sufficiency and our own private interests. The pattern of moral responsiveness is determined by what Christ has done and is a posture of supplication in which they will be fulfilled by Christ.

The supplication to pray "Our Lord, come!" (1 Cor 16:22b, NRSV) anticipates a set of moral activities to participate with him at the site of his coming return, which is the fulfillment of the work he began. Jenson assists in clarifying the implications of Webster's point by arguing that the narrative of Christ's life identifies "the eschaton that in fact is proclaimed."[106] This is the connection between the *already* and the *not yet*. Christ came to "cure the sick, raise the dead, cleanse the lepers, cast out demons" (Matt 10:8, NRSV). The narrative continuity between the *already* and the *not yet* lies in the apocalyptic invasion of Christ. This is the central narrative that names what is continuous with the old into the now and what will be. It is not enough to be unconditionally open to the future. One must be open to a specific future named by the content of his life, death, and resurrection.[107] Jenson writes,

> Jesus the Christ, in his full historical reality of birth, life, death, and resurrection, is the Word of God in that he is the identity of the future opened by the Word of God. He is the Word of God in that he is the narrative content of the proclamation that, because it poses eschatological possibility, is the Word of God. He is the Word of God because he is the narrative content of the word-event that is the Word of God.[108]

Jenson's description of the eschaton fits within a christological confession. What we see in the event of Christ's apocalyptic invasion will be fulfilled for all creation. To be sure, Christ is Lord over the powers now

---

105. Webster, "Eschatology and Anthropology," 276.

106. Jenson, *Systematic Theology*, 170.

107. Jenson, *Systematic Theology*, 170–71.

108. Jenson, *Systematic Theology*, 171.

and, as such, presents humanity with a new course of actions that participate in Christ's lordship. In the end, this lordship will be revealed publicly to all of creation in a new and visible way. Paul writes, "For now we see in a mirror, dimly, but then we will see face to face. Now I know only in part; then I will know full, even as I have been fully known" (1 Cor 13:12, NRSV). Now we walk by faith. In the eschaton, we will walk by sight (2 Cor 5:7).

The emphasis on walking by faith, as it relates to seeing in the eschaton, is a matter of understanding the ends of our action and their present natal potential. This is Webster's position. He writes, "The Christian is now empowered by the Spirit to act in anticipation of the final coming of the Son of God, in which the creative purpose of the Father will reach its ultimate goal."[109] One must recognize how deeply critical this is of the biopolitical appeal to private interest. In biopolitics, the ends of actions are located toward their approximate ends in sterilizing culture. The apocalyptic, eschatological hope in which Christians find their ontological ground can resist such ends because it resists antinomous teleological constructions of the world. Eschatology encourages and sustains moral actions, despite an inability to personally achieve such an end. It is always an action of supplication in which action itself reaches *toward* its final goal.

The eschatological end of all things is also, as Oliver O'Donovan argues, the end of all actions.[110] Paul writes, "Then comes the end" (1 Cor 15:24, NRSV). This passage could alternatively be translated "then comes rest." O'Donovan helpfully places the eschatological emphasis of the ends of action within the context of rest. O'Donovan writes, "Nothing 'rests' unless it has striven, labored, or exerted itself."[111] The metaphor of rest serves as the proper understanding of teleology proposed by Webster. In resting, one finds the proper fulfillment of action. Rest achieves this in two distinct ways: rest *from* one's actions, and rest *in* the end of all things.[112] Rest *from* is the rest from labor and effort, "withdrawing from it . . . Rest is the entropy of life."[113] This is a striving into the good, a working in and toward the work that will be fulfilled. This is a work that

---

109. Webster, "Eschatology and Anthropology," 285.

110. O'Donovan, *Entering into Rest*, 37–40.

111. O'Donovan, *Entering into Rest*, 30.

112. O'Donovan, *Entering into Rest*, 30.

113. O'Donovan, *Entering into Rest*, 30.

can never be completed by humans alone, but it is something for which they must, nevertheless, strive. To find rest *in* means resting in what is accomplished.[114] As an eschatological end, it is not an end the individual accomplishes, but an end accomplished by God. The actions arising from the present moral responsiveness in the Spirit envisions an end that will be realized in the eschaton.

This situates our understanding of moral actions in a very specific way. O'Donovan notes that the good we pursue "is not the goods we pursue; it is not even the goods 'for us'; it is the way in which those goods offer themselves, in combination or separately, as possibilities to be realized in our lives."[115] O'Donovan does not mean the fruits of our labor as we achieve them. Rather, fruit is realized *into* our lives. This does not promote a moral quietism, but activity that is motivated by the action of Christ and finds its rest in the world to come.

The connection between eschatological, moral activity and natality lies in the narrative continuity between what has been accomplished in Christ and what will be fulfilled in his return. Moral activity for Christians identify the patterns made available by Christ's incarnation, death, and resurrection. These actions are not done in order to identify an effective means of bringing the kingdom near, but as a faithful mode of responsiveness that is often counterintuitive to established codes of moral responsiveness. It appears, especially in Paul, that the patterns of moral responsiveness offered by the double apocalyptic move require hope in order to be sustained. One can only gather from this that to be a Christian is to walk a virtuous path, wherein discouragement is indeed common and another path is much more tempting. This is the difference between faithfulness and unfaithfulness. Natality is essential to the Christian because one must see the new reality that will be realized in the eschaton for one's pattern of discipleship to be maintained.

Natality, Hope, and Paul: 1 Thessalonians 3:6–13

Webster's dogmatic translation of natality is acutely exemplified in 1 Thessalonians 3:6–13. Though Webster acknowledges his deep indebtedness to Paul's own theology, natality still requires an exegetical analysis to illustrate the continuity between Arendt's political philosophy and Paul's

114. O'Donovan, *Entering into Rest*, 30.

115. O'Donovan, *Entering into Rest*, 40.

apocalyptic theology. The important connection between natality and Paul's apocalyptic is hope and expectancy. Both in Paul and Arendt, humans should expect and hope for newness. This expectation gives moral energy to the activities of the community. The loss of hope means the loss of natality, which is determinantal to the moral and political life of the Christian community.

New Testament scholar Alexandra Brown summarizes the theological context of 1 Thessalonians 3:6–13.

> The hope whose fulfillment is promised—God's liberation of the enslaved cosmos—has already, in effect, been cosmically accomplished in the events of the first advent, the cross and resurrection of Jesus. And yet the future parousia remains the locus of human hope in the present; it is the promise of final liberation from hostile powers that continue, despite their *actual* defeat at the cross, to hold sway over human affairs. Lacking a firm expectation of the future parousia, believers are liable to the loss of hope, courage, and conviction that threatens the embattled existence of those "upon whom the ends of the ages have come" (1 Cor. 10:11).[116]

As Brown notes, a loss of hope can be detrimental to the life of faith and love. However, this is precisely the situation in which Paul finds the Thessalonian congregation. The Thessalonians suffer from a loss of heart directly related to their own persecution in which Paul shares (1 Thess 2:17—3:5). It is clear that the congregation has unexpectedly lost people (1 Thess 4:13). These deaths could be unexpected due to the amount of time presupposed until the Lord's return, or from violent persecution.[117] Either way, it is clear that this was cause for a loss of hope.

The loss of hope in 1 Thessalonians 3:6 is evident in Paul's relay of Timothy's report from the Thessalonian congregation. Paul commends the congregation on their great "faith and love." Such a description should be read in concert with Paul's admonition of the theological virtues of faith, hope, and love in 1 Corinthians 13:13. Paul's rhetorical use of the coming of the Lord is a means to encourage their faith and love (1 Thess 3:13; 4:13–18). Paul masterfully draws the goodness of the Thessalonians and their lost loved ones into the "image of the Lord's own future coming."[118] Paul's purpose, other than consolation for lost loved ones, is

116. Brown, "Paul and the Parousia," 50. Emphasis original.

117. See Boring, *1 & II Thessalonians*, 157–58.

118. Brown, "Paul and the Parousia," 50.

to encourage the Thessalonians to "stand firm" (3:8, NRSV) in their faith and to strengthen them (3:13) in love. The source of moral agency to continue in this life is the hope of Christ's return. A life of faithfulness and love, apparently, is not self-sustaining, but needs the continued animation that is found in anticipating and hoping for Christ's return.

This passage in 1 Thessalonians illustrates the Pauline, apocalyptic importance of natality. In Paul's understanding, the constancy of approaching faithful and loving actions with newness and vigor is necessary to the point where converts learn how to please God "more and more" (4:1, NRSV) in their repetition of love and faith. The language of gradual expansion of one's moral behavior matches the newness into which the believer grows. Paul argues that this growth comes to fulfillment by the Lord's coming. Paul's prayer, "may he so strengthen your hearts in holiness that you may be blameless before our God and Father at the coming of our Lord Jesus with all his saints" (3:13, NRSV), suggests that hope and natality arise from the fact that God's work is yet to be completed in the lives of the Thessalonians. Love and faith are not virtues for the sake of perfecting an inner piety. They are actions done in prayerful supplication for God to continually strengthen believers. Through prayer, one finds a newness each day in performing acts pleasing to God, which is coordinate to the newness that can only be realized at Christ's apocalyptic coming. An antithesis to hope and natality is discouragement; Christ's followers lose the vision of the eventual fulfillment of their actions by Christ's return.

Natality is the political posture of the *not yet*. Only through natality can violent cycles be escaped and new judgments formed without requiring past (sometimes biopolitical) prejudices. This is necessary for the just and loving because only by continually breaking cycles of selfishness can one embrace goodness. Natality serves as a useful explanatory tool toward how Paul's apocalyptic theology is political. The basic conviction of 1 Corinthians 15 is that the resurrected body is the fulfillment of the preresurrected body and the moral and political life. Our actions take the form of supplication by always reaching toward their fulfillment in God's activity. Actions are natal in this way because they continually confront new manifestations of sovereignty. As is evidenced in 1 Thessalonians, the newness is not always different action. Actions always take the form of faith and love, but their natality happens in ever-different situations as hope drives them along.

Political Practices: 2 Corinthians, Reconciliation, and Forgiveness

Natality names the political posture of the *not yet*, but a specific practice must orient our discussion in order to confront and unseat biopolitical realities. Focusing natality—the apocalyptic *not yet*—and the just and loving gaze on a practice shows the coherence of the argument that an eschatological end resists private interests, enables the just and loving gaze, and always requires vigilant hope. This practice must also complement those of remembrance and attention of the *already* that draw the community into an intimacy with the triune God It also provides a coherent means to embody natality. The practice must be distinct in its apocalyptic appeal to the *not yet* but familiar in its conjunction with the *already*. Such a practice is forgiveness. Forgiveness is a practice of receiving a new creation from God and participating in God's reconciliation of the entire cosmos.

In Paul's second letter to the Corinthians, forgiveness serves as the conduit of natality in Christ and enables new judgements about the neighbor for the just and loving gaze. Paul alludes to his own need of forgiveness in order to repent from his former life, enabling a new life of apostolic ministry (2 Cor 4:1). Paul also affirms the need to forgive those in the congregation who have done wrong (2:5–11). These practices are bound within the "ministry of reconciliation" (5:18) given to believers as a means to participate within Christ's reconciliation of the whole world into the life of God (5:19). The reconciliation of the whole world to God is an eschatological movement, which culminates in the new creation (5:1–10). The practice of forgiveness serves as a necessary component to the practices of the *already* by establishing a community with the central posture of reconciliation and patience that rehearses in their communal life the broader drawing of the cosmos into the life of the triune God. By remembering and showing attention, believers recognize their failure to be faithful and need for mercy and consolation (2:7, 4:1). By being forgiven and offering forgiveness, the community finds the presence of natality—new judgments and new paths forward in the moral and political life not bound to cycles of violence. These lead to a concentrated political activity that is less violent, forgiving instead of retaliating. In each case, the theme of new creation makes the vast applicability of forgiveness cohere.

One of the contexts of 2 Corinthians is Paul's defense of his own ministry. According to theologian Laurie Brink, some in the Corinthian congregation believe that Paul's former persecution of Christians casts doubts on his apostolic authority.[119] This is the context into which Paul speaks in the opening of chapter 4. He writes, "it is by God's mercy we do not lose heart. We have renounced the shameful things that one hides; we refuse to practice cunning or to falsify God's word; but by the open statement of the truth we commend ourselves to the conscience of everyone in the sight of God" (2 Cor 4:1–2, NRSV). The gospel that Paul preaches is not a gospel of "personal accomplishment."[120] His ministry is based on his reception of a revelation (apocalypse) of God (Gal 1:12). By placing his ministry within the context of the mercy of God, Paul shows it is not the adequacy of the apostle that matters, but the one from whom mercy has been received. In Webster's terms, the ontological ground of Christian agency is in God's activity of mercy. Natality proves to be the essential Paul, for without it he would have no authority because of his former life. Paul writes, "not that we are competent of ourselves to claim anything as coming from us; our competence to be ministers of a new covenant, not of letter but of spirit; for the letter kills, but the Spirit gives life" (2 Cor 3:5–6, NRSV).

The context of God's mercy is fully developed in Paul's rhetoric of a new creation. Paul's former life and persecution is depicted as a sin against Christ (Acts 9:4). It is clear that Paul offends God in his actions. For reconciliation to occur in Greco-Roman epistle writing, Brink understands, there is a clear example "of how one is to repair the relationship in the context of an epistle."[121] The established method was an act of contrition by the offending party, request for forgiveness, and an appeal to friendship.[122] However, Paul turns this logic on its head. It is the offended party that reaches out for the sake of reconciliation. Brink writes, "God, as the offended party, initiates the reconciliation, 'not counting their trespasses against them' (5:19), even though humanity continued in sin (Rom. 5:8) and remained hostile to God (Rom. 5:10)."[123] Paul argues that God has made reparation in Christ's death (2 Cor 5:14–15). Through this reparation, Christ no longer counts trespasses against the offending

---

119. See Brink, "From Wrongdoer to New Creation," 303.

120. Furnish, *II Corinthians*, 245.

121. Brink, "From Wrongdoer to New Creation," 306.

122. Brink, "From Wrongdoer to New Creation," 306.

123. Brink, "From Wrongdoer to New Creation," 306.

party (v. 19). Paul is the beneficiary of divine forgiveness, which not only forgives but also becomes a "new creation" (v. 17).

The use of "new creation" here needs a brief unpacking. The phrase appears to suggest the new heaven and new earth. However, to forgo the present significance of this phrase for Paul would be to undercut a crucial aspect of his *already* apocalyptic gospel. Paul can say with confidence, "If anyone is in Christ, there is a new creation" (2 Cor 5:17a, NRSV). This is a present victory wherein the old antinomies have passed away. In what sense can we also talk about the new creation as a new heaven and a new earth? Charles Wesley's hymn "Love Divine, All Love Excelling" grasps how Paul can maintain this tension.

> Finish then thy new creation,
> Pure and sinless let us be,
> Let us see thy great salvation,
> Perfectly restor'd in thee;
> Chang'd from glory into glory,
> Till in heaven we take our place,
> Till we cast our crowns before thee,
> Lost in wonder, love, and praise![124]

Wesley's doxological summary illustrates the harmony between the *already* and the *not yet*. The new creation is now and available to those in Christ, but it still requires God's act of fulfillment. The new creation must be fulfilled and finished. This is not an activity of our doing; it is God's activity. Humanity can only live and act by means of supplication, which resembles one lost in wonder, love, and praise. Much like the distinction between the resurrected and the preresurrected body, the former will bring the latter to completion by finishing the work begun in Christ's own resurrection.

Paul's rhetoric of new creation reasserts his position of apostolic authority set apart from his past misdeeds. It displays his offer of forgiveness to an offender in the congregation. Paul has previously written to the Corinthians as a means of emergency advice on how to handle the offender.[125] The offender is portrayed as having offended Paul, but the resolution by the community resulted in Paul's favor.[126] It is not just Paul

---

124. Wesley, "Hymn 9," 12.

125. See Matera, *II Corinthians*, 61.

126. Matera, *II Corinthians*, 61.

who is wronged by the offender's actions, but the whole community. Paul, in this passage, prefigures himself in the offender by making the offender the subject of divine mercy.

Paul's call to forgiveness should still be read within the context of the formula of epistolary forgiveness, specifically as an appeal to friendship. In Paul's example of his own enmity with God, he shows that God has forgiven him through Christ. Brink writes, "Without reparations or punishment, Paul, the former persecutor, was reconciled by God's grace through Christ's death."[127] Through this reconciliation with God, Paul is drawn ever deeper into a new creation of friendship with God. It is this new friendship to which Paul is inviting the Corinthians to participate. Paul writes, "So now instead you should forgive and console him, so that he may not be overwhelmed by excessive sorrow. So I urge you to reaffirm your love for him" (1 Cor 2:7–8, NRSV). The community has already punished this offender. He has offered conciliating measures in order to offer penance for his wrongdoing. Therefore, Paul's encouragement to forgive and console this offender is for the sake of reaffirming their love (ἀγάπην) for the offender. It is curious that Paul, if really arguing for friendship, uses ἀγάπη instead of φιλία, which traditionally refers to love denoted by friendship. The reason lies in Paul's larger argument about his own reconciliation and the Corinthian reconciliation to God. In this case, ἀγάπη refers to the type of love that God shows Paul and the Corinthians, one in which God is not "counting their trespasses against them" (5:19). Despite the "pain" (2:5), the Corinthians are called to act in such a selfless way devoid of private interests.

Though most of Paul's exhortations concerning forgiveness are couched in God's unmerited offer of reconciliation with humanity, communal judgement is essential. It is clear that the Corinthians have already punished this offender, and that he has been punished for his wrongs by submitting himself. The penance of the offender is probable since the weight of the implemented or impending punishment is causing him to "be overwhelmed by excessive sorrow" (2:7). Paul's understanding of his own forgiveness involves the offended party, Christ, to offer reconciliation without reparations. Paul calls the Corinthians to the type of love that Paul himself experienced from Christ. He also allows the congregation to impose a particular punishment on the offending party for the sake of penance. This punishment is not divorced from forgiveness; it is

127. Brink, "From Wrongdoer to New Creation," 307.

essential to it. Forgiveness, in the Pauline sense, can include a communal prescription of reconciliation or penance that makes the situation right. There will be times that the community will forgive and reconcile without punishment, but in either case, the community cannot fail the rubric of love and ultimate forgiveness and reconciliation.

Such a posture of love, forgiveness, and reconciliation in the community is the ministry of reconciliation (5:18). The ministry of reconciliation must exist inside Paul's early emphasis on the "ministry of justness [δικαιοσύνης]" (3:9) and is contrasted with the "ministry of condemnation" (3:9). The activity of the ministry of reconciliation arises from Christ's reconciliation of the world to God (5:18). It is a ministry, a partnering, with God for the sake of divine mission in the world. Paul alludes to this when he urges the Corinthians to "persuade others" of the gospel. Frank Matera writes, "The work of 'persuading' is an integral aspect of preaching the gospel. By [Paul's] apostolic preaching he tries to bring people to the gospel by persuading them of its truth (cf. Acts 13:43; 18:4; 26:28, where the verb is used in this way)."[128] Paul's persuasion is not just a verbal, rhetorical technique. It is a way of living in social space. Robert Schreiter writes that, in Paul's example, a "whole new way of reckoning is being introduced. As a result, the law court or the negotiation room is no longer the model for reconciliation; it is, rather, a social space where things are made utterly new."[129]

The brand new social space signals the apocalyptic, eschatological nature of forgiveness and reconciliation. The context in which Paul demands that the Corinthians "be reconciled" (5:20) is that "in Christ God was reconciling the world to himself" (5:19). The Greek in this statement can be misleading. On the surface, the English translation suggests a past completed action. However, the Greek, θεὸς (God) ἦν (was) ἐν (in) Χριστῷ (Christ) καταλλάσσων (reconciling), is not oriented to a past, completed event. Rather, ἐν is the imperfect tense of εἰμί (to be) and signals the ongoing, uncompleted nature of God's reconciling work. Friedrich Büchel writes in the *Theological Dictionary of the New Testament*:

> "Our" reconciliation is concluded, and Paul can speak of it in the aorist (R. 5:9, 10 [11]; 2 C. 5:18). But this is not so with the reconciliation of the world. The phrase ἦν καταλλάσσων in 2 C. 5:19 does not denote a concluded work: "He was present to

128. Matera, *II Corinthians*, 130–31.

129. Schreiter, "St. Paul's Vision," 727.

reconcile the world to Himself"; when and where this work will
be concluded is not brought under consideration in 2 C. 5:19–
20 . . . [Rather it has] begun in the cross of Christ, and . . . [is] in
the course of fulfillment.[130]

Büchel's description of reconciliation as *not yet* fulfilled describes the
apocalyptic expectation of the fulfillment of the world and the ontological foundation of human reconciliation. Webster states that human action is not self-fulfilling, but brought to completion by God. Here, the
specific example of forgiveness and reconciliation is clear. Christians do
not seek reconciliation and forgiveness for the purpose of bringing to
consummation God's kingdom, but because it is the liturgical act of the
church that prays "Our Lord, come!" (1 Cor 16:22, NRSV). According to
Wesley's hymnody, it is a cry for God to "finish then thy new creation."
In so doing, it is an apocalyptic expectation of the final reconciliation of
all creation.

The final cry enabled by forgiveness for the apocalyptic reconciliation of all creation into the life of God also serves as a means to encourage natality in Christian political practices. As stated above, natality
helps prevent political action from becoming bound to past misdeeds.
In a world where the sovereignty of sin and death still operate, even after
their defeat by Christ, misunderstandings and missteps inevitably occur.
Believers sin against God and neighbor. Forgiveness enables natality by
preventing these missteps from fully consuming our political activity.
Forgiveness is practiced for the sake of persuading the world of the validity of the gospel of God's continued reconciliation between the world
and the Godself, as well as showing the importance of a more-peaceful
political reality practiced in the church.

Forgiveness enables natality, which enables peaceful politics. Natality is one of the most unique aspects of Arendt's political thought.[131]
Arendt recognizes the importance of forgiveness in natality. Forgiveness
allows humans to be free from past actions and to be unrestrained from
future actions. Arendt writes,

> Without being forgiven, released from the consequences of
> what we have done, our capacity to act would, as it were, be
> confined to one single deed from which we could never recover;
> we would remain the victims of its consequences forever, not

---

130. Büchel, "καταλλάσσων," 257.

131. Arendt, *Human Condition*, 232–35.

unlike the sorcerer's apprentice who lacked the magic formula to break the spell.[132]

Forgiveness is an act of natality because of its unpredictability and its ability to end cycles of violence and retribution. It is new because it *acts* natally in situations bound by repetitive cycles of violence. Arendt continues,

> Forgiveness is the exact opposite of vengeance, which acts in the form of re-acting against an original trespassing, whereby far from putting an end to the consequences of the first misdeed, everybody remains bound to the processes . . . in other words, [forgiveness] is the only reaction which does not re-act but acts anew and unexpectedly, unconditioned by the act which provoked it and therefore freeing from its consequences both the one who forgives and the one who is forgiven.[133]

If we are capable, as Arendt suggests, of making correct judgments after being freed from the bonds of private interests and biopolitics, then our judgments can be surprising and new. Being caught in the process of violence is much like being caught in a docile body doomed only to react out of a certain authority or expected outcome. Arendt believes that forgiving actually frees individuals from the process of biopolitics. This begins the process of doing the radical, revolutionary, and unexpected thing. This forms new judgments about the reality of the world and new prejudices free from the process of biopolitics. This is the promise of natality. It is natality that Arendt found in her life as she located her identity as a Jewish woman. It leaves open the possibility that we are not doomed to repeat history, but can genuinely break the bonds of bad judgments on our way to freedom.

Arendt does not have theological interests in mind, but her political commitments provide a helpful insight for theological translation. Theologian Brent Waters sees the opportunity that Arendt gives to theology. Waters, in a Pauline vein, recognizes the story of incarnation, crucifixion, and resurrection as a constitutive realization of creaturely life in creation and, consequently, sets patterns of hope and worship for Christian communities' discernment of political and moral action.[134] In light of this

132. Arendt, *Human Condition*, 237.

133. Arendt, *Human Condition*, 240–41.

134. Waters, "Incarnation," 5–21.

drama of salvation, forgiveness emerges as a central practice to the community discerning its place among other political entities.

Forgiveness helps maintain familial, political, and social ties.[135] Forgiveness deals with the bare fact that past deeds cannot be undone.[136] Waters states that "forgiveness is the remedy for the irreversibility of deeds and acts."[137] This being the case, forgiveness is an indispensable political practice, because a failure to forgive would

> prevent any meaningful human action, especially political action, because individuals and associations would be frozen by the unintended consequences of [past] acts. Forgiveness . . . [is] thereby predicated upon the central reality of plurality: political community is not a static whole, but a dynamic amalgamation of different individuals and associations pursuing their respective and changing interest.[138]

Here, Waters describes the transient and unpredictable nature of political community. In a community of changing interests and culture, one must have the ability to forgive in order to avoid a constricting political life. Waters points out, Arendt's emphasis on forgiveness arises from what she sees as the central role of forgiveness in Jesus. According to Waters, Arendt's interpretation of Jesus's prescription of forgiveness has the potential to renew and transform political relationships where natal, and possibly better, actions emerge.[139] Specifically, Waters argues that forgiveness can "ameliorate" more destructive alternatives.[140] For example, vengeance is a more certain way to deal with wrongs committed than the uncertain act of forgiving and of promise-making (an act both Arendt and Waters argue is necessarily bound up with forgiveness). However, forgiveness is the only way to free "political ordering" from the destructive fate of endless cycles of vengeance.[141]

That being said, Waters does recognize, via Arendt, the alternative to forgiveness, namely punishment. Waters is skeptical of the preeminence

135. Waters, "Incarnation," 22.
136. Waters, "Incarnation," 22.
137. Waters, "Incarnation," 23.
138. Waters, "Incarnation," 23.
139. Waters, "Incarnation," 24.
140. Waters, "Incarnation," 24.
141. Waters, "Incarnation," 24.

of punishment insofar as it excludes the possibility of forgiveness.[142] Instead of slipping into a cycle of punishment that enacts a form of "final vengeance," a relationship where forgiveness and punishment exist in fluidity is essential to "a practice of governance stemming from discourse about the common good."[143]

Despite the attractiveness of Arendt's position, it suffers, according to Waters, in two main areas. First, Arendt's emphasis on forgiveness places too little emphasis on judgment, confession, and repentance. In Waters's critique, "punishment *is* an enacted judgement."[144] A judgment is necessary in order to determine the way and degree to which one's action has wrongly impacted an individual or community.[145] For example, in Paul's second letter to the Corinthians, the offender has wronged the community and has been punished for this wrong. This can only be possible in light of a judgment from Paul or the community. Paul has made a judgement that this person has caused pain for both himself and the congregation (2 Cor 2:5, NRSV). Without this judgment, Paul's admonition would make little sense.

A Theological Excursus on Judgement: The Judge Judged in Our Place

Waters's emphasis on judgement is central to Paul's apocalyptic, political theology. Judgement and Final Judgement both require a judge. The judge, in most situations yielding forgiveness, is the human who forgives instead of punishes. Forgiving is a judgement in two senses: someone is found to be at fault, and the one offering forgiveness does not to pursue vengeance. Judgment and forgiveness are incendiary to the highest degree because they radically disrupt cycles of violence. The audacity of the judgement to forgive arises from an apocalyptic disruption of all judgements as it proceeds from, as Karl Barth explains, the Judge being judged in our place.

For Barth, Christ comes to humanity and judges as one who proceeds into a "Far Country."[146] As Barth writes, "In being gracious to [hu-

---

142. Waters, "Incarnation," 25.

143. Waters, "Incarnation," 26.

144. Waters, "Incarnation," 27.

145. Waters, "Incarnation," 26.

146. See Barth, *CD* IV.1 §59.1.

manity (*mensch*)] in Jesus Christ, He also goes into the far country, into the evil society of this being which is not God and against God."[147] The procession of God into the far country is an apocalyptic incursion and invasion into a world held captive by sinful powers. This world professes sovereignty unto itself and apart from God. As Barth writes, "The whole world finds its supreme unity and determination against God in looking for justification from itself and not from God."[148] Here judgement enacts cycles of violence because it judges reflexively upon itself. These sovereign judgements are not upheld by peaceful acts of forgiveness, but must be maintained by greater and greater acts of violence. These postures must perpetuate attitudes of self-justification. Sovereignty alone wishes to hold up the good as its private possession. This is the essence of the sovereign equation, namely to decide the exception. The exception is good based on a logic internal to sovereignty, itself apart from God. Therefore, two things are required for a truly theological account of judgement. First, judgement must not slip into the sovereign equation. Second, the world in this sovereign condition must be judged.

Barth's theology of judgement provides an important layer to the theology of judgement assumed in the act of forgiveness, because not only does Christ judge, but he is also judged. The judgement laid on Christ is a judgement laid on humanity. As Barth writes, "What took place is that the Son of God fulfilled the righteous judgement on us [humans] by Himself taking our place as [human] and in our place undergoing the judgement under which we had passed . . . He judged, and it was the Judge who was judged, who let Himself be judged."[149] Barth signals two key aspects of judgement that leads to atonement and the judgement of worldly authorities.

First, Barth signals a judgement that leads to atonement. Barth writes,

> this judgement of God, this justification by God which comes to [humanity], is something which has taken place concretely in Jesus Christ. It had to take place in Him because in His person as the Son of the Father He is Himself both very God electing and creating [human] and very [human] elected by God and as such ordained from all eternity to fulfill all the righteousness of God. It could take place in Him, because as very God and

147. Barth, *CD* IV.1 §59.1.
148. Barth, *CD* IV.1 §59.2.
149. Barth, *CD* IV.1 §59.2.

very [human] He was competent and qualified to accomplish and suffer the contest between God and [humanity], to be both the Judge and the judged in this conflict.[150]

Judgement, as Barth understands, happens internal to God's own self here in the second person of the Trinity. Furthermore, the internality is made external in history in the person of Jesus Christ.[151] As Barth writes,

> It could take place only in Him because only He as this one person could be both subject and object in this history, uniting the antithesis of it in Himself; Himself the full end which is made in it; and Himself also the new beginning which is made in it; and both in the place and therefore in the name of all other [humans], for them and in their favour. It took place in him in that He as the true Son of God became true [human], and in this unity of His person became the Judge of all other [humans]: their Judge as the One who was judged in their place—delivered up in His death, and reinstated in His resurrection from the dead. As it has taken place in Jesus Christ this is the justification of sinful [humanity].[152]

This judgement—which is simultaneously internal to God and external in history among the witnesses of the New Testament—condemns that which seeks its own justification and sovereignty. Christ alone judges humanity. In so doing, Christ as Judge takes away humanity's self-sufficient, private judgements. Christ judges and *is* judged. He takes the full weight of human judgement and exhausts it. This takes justification and atonement firmly out of the hands of human authority and sovereignty. This judgement is entirely extrinsic to human control.

By making judgement and justification external to human control, it is impossible for humans on their own merit to judge good from evil. We are, as Barth clarifies, "displaced from the office of judgement" because we "can never know by reflections about ourselves in the light of a standard of good and evil which we have freely chosen or discovered" if we are good.[153] Thus, humans cannot occupy the place of sovereign knowledge or the sovereign equation. Christ not only radically invades and displaces, but "compromises" this private "stronghold" and "destroys

---

150. Barth, *CD* IV.1 §61.2.

151. See Jones, "Barth and Anselm," 279.

152. Barth, *CD* IV.1 §61.2.

153. Barth, *CD* IV.1 §59.2.

it."[154] The apocalyptic singularity of the gospel of redemption in Christ's incarnation, displaces any claim to sovereignty or private interests.

Second, the fact that Christ is judged calls to mind the scene of Jesus before Pilate. Here the Judge is judged by worldly power. This underscores Christ's humanity. "Because He was a [human] like us, He was able to be judged like us."[155] By allowing himself to be judged, Christ "allows the world and humanity to take part in the history of the inner life of His Godhead, in the movement in which from and to all eternity He is Father, Son and Holy Spirit, and therefore the one true God."[156] In Christ's submission to earthly powers, he allows humanity a spot in the event of redemption as they are participating in the powers of sin and death. Christ was crucified under Pontius Pilate, as it is stated in the creed, but he did so without needing human ratification of the event. Therefore, in no way does redemption become the object of private interests. The fact that the event of redemption is so internal to the Godhead and external within history in the person of Jesus Christ robs private interests of its power. Therefore, judgement—specifically political judgement and judgement that leads to forgiveness—must be routed through this one who is judged at the hands of earthly authority.

Since judgement is rerouted through this Judge, then judgement that leads to forgiveness takes on the character of a "shared mercy" between God and humanity.[157] Humans are merciful because they have been shown mercy. This account of judgement is liberating. Barth writes,

> It is a terrible thing to know good and evil if only in this ostensible and ineffective way, and to have to live with this doubtful knowledge. It agrees quite simply with what is written in Gen. 2:17, that if we eat of this tree we must die. We are all in process of dying from this office of judge which we have arrogated to ourselves. It is, therefore, a liberation that has come to pass in Jesus Christ that we are deposed and dismissed from this office because He has come to exercise it in our place . . . Jesus Christ is Judge. The matter is taken out of my hands. And that means liberation. A great anxiety is lifted, the greatest of all.[158]

154. Barth, *CD* IV.1 §59.2.

155. Barth, *CD* IV.1 §59.2.

156. Barth, *CD* IV.1 §59.2.

157. This is a direct appeal to Jon Coutts's work on Barth's theological account of forgiveness. See Coutts, *Shared Mercy*, 27–94.

158. Barth, *CD* IV.1 §59.2.

Liberation in modernity means that the self-sufficient, privately inter-ested human is displaced. Furthermore, since Christ judges from the place of one who is judged, it calls into question the very ground from which we judge. Humanity "wants to be [their] own and [their] neigh-bour's judge."[159] Humanity wants to be good over and against the neigh-bor. They desire systems of goodness, but Christ's own judgement frees humanity from the safety of systems of goodness and instead calls them to God's goodness. Barth makes clear "that the one who exalts himself as judge will be abased, that he can only fall into the judgement which will come upon himself."[160] To those embedded in cycles of violence where vengeance begets vengeance, a judge who opens up their vision to see where they stand in judgment leads them to *new* judgements. The threat of judgement against those who exalt themselves presses against private interests. In short, the one who judges recognizes that they are not alone in their judgements. They too are judged. Therefore, judgement is a risk because, as Dietrich Bonhoeffer shows, we no longer have immediate access to our neighbor.[161] Everything is rerouted through the Judge. In-dividuals either stand as Pilate or with the Judge judged in their place. Forgiveness can replace vengeance because humans are forgiven instead of subjected to violence. This is the essential basis of judgement that leads to forgiveness, Christians are called to mercy because mercy has been given. A failure to do this will result in stricter judgement from the Judge. This motivates new judgements against cycles of vengeance.

Though one has much to fear from a failure to be merciful, one has great reasons to hope. Barth writes, "That means, therefore, in fear before the Judge on whose good and redemptive will I can already count, whose decision I can look forward to with trust whatever it may be, in whose hands I can know that my own case and that of others is at least safe."[162] Humanity can afford not to act in violence because it trusts that God's consummating activity far exceeds our human capabilities for resolu-tion. This does not mean that one must continually submit to abuse and violence, but rather a mere recognition that our activity is open to God's own mercy. The judgement made in forgiveness not only recognizes a wrong committed, but the orientation toward which forgiving a wrong

159. Barth, *CD* IV.1 §59.2.

160. Barth, *CD* IV.1 §59.2.

161. Bonhoeffer, *Discipleship*, 97–99.

162. Barth, *CD* IV.1 §59.2.

proceeds. God's mercy proceeds to a time and place when all things will be made natal (Rev 21:5).

Natality, then, is essential to the judgement that leads to forgiving. As Arendt understands, forgiveness breaks cycles and allows for new actions to take place, unencumbered by past misdeeds. Therefore, judgement is wed to natality in its ability to participate in the newness seen in the new creation by making *new* judgements through the vision offered by the Judge. As Barth writes, "It is as the One who carries His cross to Golgotha that He comes to judge the living and the dead."[163] As such, judgment is an expression of both an apocalyptic politic and the just and loving gaze. In recognizing human solidarity with judges of the world, humans recognize Christ in even the ones they judge and the ones by which they are judged. This recognition opens up forgiving, generous activity. Christ's sovereignty cannot be abstracted from his status as crucified Messiah and coming judge.[164] Christ's disruption of sovereignty as the crucified is apocalyptic to the highest degree. This sovereignty negates all other claims to sovereignty. Here the grain of the universe is recognized in crosses and motivates all judgements. Only by enacting judgements in perpetual mercy does forgiveness emerge as a practice of natality.

Forgiveness: Confession and Repentance

Waters insists that in order for forgiveness to perform natal actions, confession and repentance—in addition to judgement—is required in the face of the ever-present hegemony of private interests. In the absence "of confession and repentance (or their equivalents) on the part of the individual who committed the wrong, forgiveness simply diminishes or negates justice."[165] This returns to the earlier emphasis that only that which can be judged and punished can be forgiven. Waters foresees that to commute or pardon a person who has expressed no remorse or recognition of the crime would make any promise the wrongdoer might promise "vacuous."[166] Waters asks, "How does he amend his life in reaction

---

163. Barth, *CD* IV.1 §59.2.
164. Barth, *CD* IV.1 §59.2.
165. Waters, "Incarnation," 26.
166. Waters, "Incarnation," 26.

to an act that he neither confesses nor repents?"[167] To show remorse in the moral life, one must confess, repent, and amend. Life is not a closed system capable of mastery. The need for confession and repentance provides a helpful corrective to private interest. To confess and repent recognizes one's fallibility in relation to another. Private interest that leads to self-sufficiency lacks the ability to recognize harm done to another because no common goods or shared ends are recognized. When these are recognized, then one is no longer operating with private interest. By confessing and repenting, the ego of the will (driven by private interests) acknowledges the inability to be self-sufficient and confronts the vanity of private interest. If there is no confession and no repentance, the corrective amendment to one's action that is a requirement of a just order is absent.

Arendt's account of forgiveness does not adequately deal with unintended consequences of past activity. Waters utilizes the example of the generational impact that radical and religious groups have on a larger civil community.[168] Arendt's position presumes that the civil community asks forgiveness and the group accepts it.[169] However, this presents a twofold problem. First, many of the groups or communities that committed the original offense have died before a confession or repentance can be offered. This is a problem because the dead cannot offer and receive forgiveness. Second, there is a problem of authority to forgive. If forgiveness is a duty, as Arendt suggests, then is it not true that the descendants of an oppressed group bear the duty to forgive and show mercy?[170] Questions such as: the duty of a continually oppressed group to show mercy to their oppressor, the continuity of governance, and what type of promises can realistically be made by a former oppressor should be asked of Arendt's account of forgiveness. Furthermore, such questions lay bare the weaknesses in Arendt's account of forgiveness.[171] Waters writes, "The best Arendt can offer are promises based on forgetfulness rather than forgiveness."[172] There is no true change and natality in this practice of forgiveness, according to Waters.

167. Waters, "Incarnation," 26–27.

168. Waters, "Incarnation," 27.

169. Waters, "Incarnation," 27.

170. Waters, "Incarnation," 28.

171. Waters, "Incarnation," 28.

172. Waters, "Incarnation," 28.

The reason for the lack of true change in Arendt's proposed method of forgiveness, according to Waters, is her transmutation of Jesus's teaching "into a Kantian host emphasizing the centrality will."[173] Waters writes in a Pauline vein:

> Jesus's teaching on forgiveness contains both imperative and teleological elements that are lost in Arendt's transplantation into a Kantian political body . . . The exaltation of Christ initiates a new rule for the ordering of creation in this time between the times . . . In respect to political ordering, the civil community exercises judgment, punishment, and forgiveness not because it possesses the necessary will and power to do so, but because it has been authorized by Christ to perform these functions in obedience to his rule to which it is subject.[174]

Waters indirectly summarizes Paul's apocalyptic exhortation on forgiveness and reconciliation in 2 Corinthians. Therefore, the Pauline emphasis on reconciliation realizes natality because it reorients political life according to "the *telos* of Christ."[175] As stated in the exegesis of 1 Corinthians 15, the *telos* of Christ is the future parousia and the resurrection of the dead that reorients any *telos* immanent in the world. The activity of forgiveness is determined by the reality, Webster argues, of God's bringing to fulfillment of human action. Waters concludes, "The purpose of forgiveness, therefore, is not to undo (or forget) what was done in the past, but to restore, forge together, and reorient broken social and political associations toward their proper *telos* in Christ where, in the fullness of time, the past is redeemed."[176] Waters helpfully interprets Paul's ministry of reconciliation along with natality in our moral and political life. Forgiveness provides a means to live natality, in spite of cycles of violence. The natality of forgiveness practices an apocalyptic *telos*, and puts off private interest. A community of forgiveness is capable of a new political reality fulfilled by the parousia of God. Forgiveness is not the means by which we make the kingdom come or create a utopian order, but it is a faithful political means to be in the world that participates in the reality that is yet to come.

173. Waters, "Incarnation," 29.
174. Waters, "Incarnation," 29.
175. Waters, "Incarnation," 30.
176. Waters, "Incarnation," 31.

The importance of forgiveness in political theology provides a peaceful politics that is also a genuinely new (natality) way of being in the world. A further example of this pertains to victimization. Here, I will limit my study to the individual as one faces an unrepentant oppressor. This is problematic. Forgiveness can provide a means to overcome a constructed caricature of the individual in the face of the oppressor. Victims are not vacuous sites of bare life. Agamben argues, however, that modern politics eliminates the subjectivity of the victim. However, I argue that forgiveness provides a means to recuperate their subjectivity. This is not the only means through which subjectivity is recuperated, but it certainly presents an opportunity for the victim to escape a caricature of personal existence. This gives a more positive capability to victims than Agamben's narrative allows. In fact, forgiveness places the subjectivity as central to the act itself. As I elaborate on this, I argue that reclaimed subjectivity must meet four requirements. The first will extend beyond Waters's analysis, while the second, third, and fourth will elaborate on Waters's analysis.

First, forgiveness must be an empowering act that is an exercise of victimized subjectivity. As already stated, forgiveness is a gift of God offered to humanity. Despite this gift, which is to be taken up and practiced by believers, one could interpret the forgiveness offered by the victim as the willingness to place subjectivity back under the one who originally victimized. Forgiveness seems only to open up the possibility to future victimization, especially if we understand forgiveness in the context laid out by Waters. It encourages the past wrongs committed on the victim. This is not Christian forgiveness. Christian forgiveness must, as Bonhoeffer famously wrote, resist the "justification of sin but not the sinner."[177] However, forgiveness does not accept anything less than confession, repentance, and contrition. One can forgive without accepting further violence. Rather, Christian forgiveness means exercising subjectivity. Philosopher Kelly Oliver understands that "Forgiveness is not about the colonizers, the oppressors, the dominant groups, or heirs to power; rather, it is about restoring that definitive feature of subjectivity—forgiveness—to the victims."[178] In forgiving, the victim claims the action of "I forgive" and, by claiming this activity, the victim is not reduced to bare life. This is a moral activity in which the victim is not acted upon, but

177. Bonhoeffer, *Discipleship*, 43.

178. Oliver, *Colonization of Psychic Space*, 191.

acts in response to violence. Oliver writes, "To begin to imagine forgiving the unforgivable requires the restoration of the oppressed person's agency and ability to take the position of 'I forgive.'"[179] Forgiveness is always a possibility that assists victims in regaining the exercise of his or her subjective faculties.

Second, through the act of forgiveness, the subjectivity of the victim is transformed. Theologian Herbert McCabe writes, "Our forgiving others is the work of God's forgiveness in us."[180] Much like Paul's moral exhortation, when the victim forgives as a means to participate in the future parousia of God, one experiences a change of disposition. It is a work of God "by which we become, for example, forgiving instead of vengeful."[181] This must be expressed carefully, especially with the historical persistence of racial violence, because the point is not that the anger of the victim is misplaced, or the transformation of the victim's subjectivity is a process of amnesia. Here we should return to Waters's careful analysis of forgiveness as a reorientation of political space. It is clear that Waters does not see forgiveness as an alternative to punishment. Rather, they "anticipate and are tempered by God's final acts of judgment, punishment, and forgiveness, but God's redemptive economy is also at work in the penultimate affairs of civil community."[182] This locates forgiveness beyond abstract practice that ignores the lived subjectivity of the victim. Forgiveness is something that correctly takes place within the divine economy and works concretely inside the one who forgives, as well as within the community.

Third, Christian forgiveness must avoid forgiving for the sake of inverting the order of mastery. If forgiveness, as exercising subjectivity, is only a power play in order to gain power over one's former oppressors, then it is a colloquial way to become master. This must be carefully articulated because what is not being proposed is a stabilizing of current structures of power. Rather, the structures of power that create victims must be destroyed through the activity of forgiveness, judgment, and punishment. If forgiveness is just a way to create new structures of victimization, then it is not interested in justice. Philosopher Rey Chow suggests such a critique. Chow draws on the character Lee Shin-ae in

---

179. Oliver, *Colonization of Psychic Space*, 192.

180. McCabe, "Forgiveness of God," 123.

181. McCabe, "Forgiveness of God," 123.

182. Waters, "Incarnation," 30.

the movie *Secret Sunshine*.[183] A recent widow and Christian convert, she visits the prison of her son's killer in hopes of forgiving him. However, upon finding the killer, the murderer explains how God has forgiven him, and her presence was the affirmation of that forgiveness. She then leaves, deeply grieved. Chow writes, "Much more than the loss of her husband and even the loss of her son, the murderer's words devastate Shin-ae."[184] What Chow illustrates is the dissatisfaction with forgiveness that seeks the gaining of mastery over one's oppressor. For Shin-ae, forgiveness was her way of winning the game of oppression. Chow writes,

> by dramatizing the moral hierarchy involved in forgiveness as nothing more than a psychological supposition premised on the desire for empowerment and superiority over the adversary—in a nutshell, the desire to win—*Secret Sunshine* has put its finger on what is perhaps the most ideologically charged aspect of the Christian enterprise.[185]

Chow charges Christian forgiveness as a way of winning over one's oppressor, which is merely another cycle of violence and not the just and loving gaze.

Finally, I want to extend Waters's analysis with the work of Margaret Farley. Waters and Farley do not contradict one another but instead are complementary. Waters understands that forgiveness anticipates, and is tempered by, God's final forgiveness at the *parousia*. Forgiveness, then, relativizes penultimate civil constructions centered on vengeance. Farley argues that forgiveness of the wrongdoer must take place in order that "the sacredness at the heart of the human" can be affirmed.[186] By refusing to enact vengeance upon the wrongdoer, the one offering forgiveness preserves "the same sacredness that crimes against humanity aims to destroy."[187] The humanity of our bodies is anticipated and tempered by the bodies we will have in the *parousia* of God. Vengeance, Waters understands, can be more effective, but forgiveness anticipates the *parousia*. Therefore, practicing forgiveness as described by Farley also anticipates and affirms humanity in this way.

183. Chow, "I Insist," 107–31.

184. Chow, "I Insist," 110.

185. Chow, "I Insist," 119.

186. Farley, "Forgiveness," 327.

187. Farley, "Forgiveness," 327.

Forgiveness, because of its ability to affirm the goodness of humanity, is a necessary practice of the just and loving gaze. In order to sustain the just and loving gaze, as Ducane found, one must be open to new judgments. In order to fully inhabit new judgments, one must seek forgiveness and repent of old prejudices and habits. Ducane eloquently realizes that all that is left is "to love and to reconcile and to forgive, only this matters."[188] Not only is this a new judgment for Ducane, but it is also a new practice that will then enable the possibility of new judgments in the future. The remorse and repentance required by forgiveness is a mode of "unselfing." It is a mode of submission to the judgment of the offended party for the purpose of reconciliation. To forgive is a means to seek the good in others, even if, for the sake of humanity, the offender seeks to destroy. In forgiving or seeking forgiveness, the just and loving gaze is required.

To summarize, forgiveness is the particular practice of the *not yet* that brings together Paul's apocalyptic, natality, and the just and loving gaze. Forgiveness ontologically locates our agency in the coming reconciliation of the cosmos. By forgiving, believers participate in the future consummation of the cosmos. Forgiveness, then, also practices natality. Arendt argues that only by forgiving can individuals commit new actions. Vengeance and retribution only repeat certain actions that maintain cycles of violence. To this end, forgiveness is also essential for the just and loving gaze. Only by forgiving can individuals, like Ducane, form new judgments. Furthermore, only by forgiving can one give careful attention to human realities that unmask the humanity struck by wrongdoing. Forgiveness ties these three elements together and has the added bonus of giving a political theology appropriate to victims that recuperates subjectivity in a way unimagined by Agamben. Forgiveness provides the political practice of the *not yet*, like with attention and remembrance in the *already* before it that forms the political rationality of Paul's apocalyptic theology.

PAUL'S APOCALYPTIC POLITICAL THEOLOGY: *NOT YET*

The practice of forgiveness gives a political rationality that rests in the ability of God to bring to completion our moral activity. Chief among the

188. Murdoch, *Nice and the Good*, 315.

reasons for the centrality of forgiveness is that it creates the disposition of patience, which is how Christians are actively engaged in the world. This was the tactic of the early church. As Alan Kreider writes, "The Christians believed that God is patient and that Jesus visibly embodied patience. And they concluded that they, trusting in God, should be patient—not controlling events, not anxious or in a hurry, and never using force to achieve their ends."[189] However, patience is misleading. Patience cannot mean inactivity. Rather, with the prophet Isaiah, it means

> but those who *wait* for the Lord shall renew their strength,
>
> they shall mount up with wings like eagles,
>
> they shall run and not be weary,
>
> they shall walk and not faint. (Isa 40:31, NRSV)

As such, the political rationality centered on patience resists the two equally problematic political alternatives of "insurrection and quietism."[190] The political rationality of the *not yet* resists violent overthrow, but is also engaged in concrete political activity. The political activity of the *not yet* arises from an openness to allow God to finish God's new creation, rather than Christians trying to finish it themselves.

Christian political rationality is not measured by completion of our own moral activity, but by patient faithfulness to the coming reign of God. Paul's words to the Philippians helps shape the type of operating imagination of the church as they await Christ's coming.

> Not that I have obtained this or have already reached the goal; but I press on to make it my own, because Christ Jesus has made me his own. Beloved, I do not consider that I have made it my own; but this one thing I do: forgetting what lies behind and straining forward to what lies ahead . . . For many live as enemies of the cross of Christ; I have often told you of them, and now I tell you with tears. Their end is destruction; their god is the belly; and their glory is in their shame; their minds are set upon earthly things. But our citizenship is in heaven, and it is from there that we are expecting a Savior, the Lord Jesus Christ. He will transform the body of our humiliation that it may be conformed to the body of his glory, by the power that also enables him to make all things subject to himself. (Phil 3:12–13, 18–21, NRSV)

189. Kreider, *Patient Ferment*, 2.

190. Yoder, *Politics of Jesus*, 36.

The echo of 1 Corinthians 15 is evident here in Philippians. Paul connects the resurrection of the dead with the command to live according the cross of Christ. The activity in which we press toward the goal of resurrection is a particular activity shaped by the cross of Christ that expects fulfillment at the final parousia of Christ. This apocalyptic expectation is shaped by the gift of our political citizenship, or as John Reumann translates, "our governing civil association."[191] This citizenship comes from heaven where Christ is (1 Cor 15:47) and from where he will come again (Phil 3:21b). Rather than trying to create an empire of earthly rule, our citizenship, which strives for the cross of Christ, comes from another location, where, Paul states, we hope to "attain the resurrection from the dead" (Phil 3:11, NRSV).

The role of citizenship illustrated in Philippians emerges as a particular vocation of the political community formed by the *not yet*. The activity of the *not yet* includes a recasting of social space free from private interest. Liberalism attempts a definition of citizenship where citizenship is guaranteed based on contract, individual freedom, and rights. These liberties are codified with the biopolitical technologies that grant life to citizens as evident and exemplified in Arendt's life of her seized citizenship as a Jewish woman in Nazi Germany. Heavenly citizenship resists this violent form of citizenship and emphasizes the gift of the coming reign of God. As such, heavenly citizenship resists the biopolitical. Therefore, it is the imagery of the citizenry in the *not yet* that can recuperate a sense of the sociality undone in both liberalism and biopolitics.

An example of how heavenly citizenship resists biopolitics lies in the political theology of jurist Carl Schmitt. Schmitt is the figure who influences Agamben, Taubes, and, either by direct appropriation or reaction, all political theology of the new approach to Paul. The issue is Schmitt's construction of the sovereign. Sovereignty, in Schmitt's political theology, is a juridical authorization to decide the exception.[192] As Schmitt writes, "What characterizes an exception is principally unlimited authority, which means the suspension of the entire existing order."[193] This applies to the one who acts outside the authority of the law and the one who is acted upon, namely the one for whom the law is no longer a protection

---

191. Reumann, *Philippians*, 566, 597.

192. Schmitt, *Political Theology*, 5.

193. Schmitt, *Political Theology* 12.

(i.e., the *homo sacer*). Schmitt serves as an example of potential biopoliti-cal citizenship against which Paul's theology must react.

The historical context of Schmitt's theorization of sovereignty is the chaos of the Weimar republic. In his mind, the issue central to this chaos was the liberal democratic policies that he believed crippled the government and immobilized any type of activity. Steven Ostovich summarizes the type of liberal politics Schmitt rejected as "framed in terms of contractual agreements among these individuals, and political legitimacy in terms of legality."[194] Schmitt rejected all of this because it reduced politics to a pluralistic enterprise. Ostovich continues, "Liberal individualism entails pluralism, and pluralism undermines politics and potentially destroys the state."[195] The reason that this was so detrimental to politics, according to Schmitt, is that it reduced politics to one activity among others in the human experience.[196] For Schmitt, politics was the definitive activity necessary for human self-realization—the realization of the self and its interests rather than a mere pluralism.

For Schmitt, sovereignty overcomes the pluralism of liberal democ-racy by dramatically reconfiguring the political. The sovereign decides the exception. For Schmitt, such an exception lies in distinction between friend and enemy, which forms the basis of all politics.[197] In this way, Schmitt's political theology serves as a possible interpretation of Paul's description in Philippians 3 of those "enemies" of the cross of Christ. For Schmitt, and likely for Paul, citizenship serves as a rubric against which the "enemies" of the cross are determined. This distinction is essential for a politic of sovereignty that decides the exception, the enemy. In order to understand the necessity of this function in the sovereign, we must recall that, for Schmitt, "All significant concepts of the modern theory of the state are secularized theological concepts."[198] The distinction between friend and enemy is an apocalyptic designation akin to the designation between God and the devil.[199] According to Schmitt, in politics this signi-fies a distinction between two ways that do not reach a synthesis.[200] This

194. Ostovich, "Carl Schmitt," 56.

195. Ostovich, "Carl Schmitt," 56.

196. Ostovich, "Carl Schmitt," 56–57.

197. Schmitt, *Concept of the Political*, 16, 26.

198. Schmitt, *Political Theology*, 36.

199. Schmitt, *Political Theology*, 55.

200. Schmitt, *Political Theology*, 55.

cannot be underemphasized in Schmitt's analysis. The apocalyptic *not yet* is served as a warrant to distinguish that which is finally acceptable and finally not. One must place this within its historical context as the way that Schmitt rewrites the legal apparatus of his nation. That being said, Schmitt does not wish to demonize the enemy. The enemy does not literally embody the forces of darkness. They only pose a threat to the order of the state. Therefore, since there is no pluralization, there is only one way to be political and to be a citizen, according to Schmitt. All else is the enemy.

The chaos created by the continued presence of the enemy in the political sphere, the plural nature of politics, must be overcome by the sovereign. For Schmitt, the sovereign was legally represented by the dictator.[201] Schmitt believes that Paul's apocalyptic theology of the *not yet* serves as a means to understand the dictator. The dictator is the Pauline *katechon*, or restrainer.[202] In 2 Thessalonians 2:1–12, Paul refers to the vocation of the *katechon* as the one who represses the lawless one. Jacob Taubes offers a full definition of the *katechon's* activity: a "retainer [*der Aufhalter*] that holds down the chaos that pushes up from below."[203] In Schmitt's mind, the *katechon* displays the activity of those awaiting the parousia, namely to repress chaos. The dictator as *katechon* restrains and holds in check the chaos that might overtake the world. For Schmitt, the chaos was liberalism and the dictator was the *katechon*. The dictator serves a purpose to repress, by any means necessary, this chaos. Taubes summarizes Schmitt's political theology:

> Schmitt's interest was in only one thing: that the party, that the chaos not rise to the top, that the state remain. No matter what the price. This is difficult for theologians and philosophers to follow, but as far as the jurist is concerned, as long as it is possible to find even one juridical form by whatever hairsplitting ingenuity, this must absolutely be done, for otherwise the chaos reigns.[204]

As a jurist, Schmitt is simply giving legal authorization to fulfill this secular interpretation of a theological vocation, which is the problem.

---

201. Schmitt, *Political Theology*, 51–52.

202. Ostovich, "Carl Schmitt," 62–62.

203. Taubes, *Political Theology of Paul*, 103.

204. Taubes, *Political Theology of Paul*, 103.

Schmitt argued for the reconstituting of Germany unfettered from its legal restraint. According to historian Timothy Snyder, "Schmitt believed that the German understanding of the law had to be purged of the Jewish 'infection,' by which he meant principles that blocked conclusions such as his own."[205] The connection between Schmitt, biopolitics, and private interests is clear. The Jewish people were the enemies that must be repressed and removed from public space in order to preserve life for the greatest number. The continuation of the liberal constitution, for Schmitt, served only Jewish interest. The sovereign must suspend the constitutional order for the sake of repressing Jewish chaos and protecting private interests. The Jewish people were the site of the exception, the enemy, and chaotic liberalism all tied up in one. It represented the reason for declaring the state of emergency and named the people who ceased to find protection under the law.

Sovereignty and exception, in the work of Carl Schmitt, are important for two main reasons. First, they illustrate a theological use of Paul's apocalyptic theology of the *not yet* for the sake of political ends. It located a theological rendering of statehood whereby law is suspended for the effective oppressing of the chaos in his present context. Second, it gives a context to understanding Paul's use of citizenship. In Schmitt's political theology, citizenship is read over and against "enemies" of God.

Arendt helps readers of Schmitt recognize the failure of this political theology in the context of her German citizenship. These two insights help us locate a clear object of critique in order to discern faithful political action of the *not yet* and what it means to be citizens of the heavenly realm. Schmitt's political theology cannot divest the public sphere of private interests. Schmitt's political theology, as a possible interpretation of Philippians, must be rejected. Instead, the political theology of the *not yet* present in Philippians 3 is coordinate to the apocalyptic agency as displayed in Webster. The "governing civic association" is a faithful form of political life only fulfilled in the new creation.

In order to unpack the political implications of Paul's apocalyptic theology, we must reevaluate Paul's intentions by deploying the distinction between heavenly citizenship and enemies of the cross. On the surface, it appears that Paul makes a similar distinction between friends and enemies, according to Carl Schmitt. However, read in concert with 1 Corinthians, Paul's pronouncement mirrors his use of crucifixion. The

205. Snyder, *Black Earth*, 145.

enemies of the cross, therefore, are those who operate under the power of this world. The powers of this age seek satisfaction and pleasure in what they can accomplish and realize. The crucifixion brackets the type of wisdom that is properly called the wisdom of God while excluding other competing wisdoms as foolishness (1 Cor 1–2). The distinction between spiritual and unspiritual made by Andy Johnson applies here; those who see spiritually (πνευματικὸν, 1 Cor 2:15) see according to the cross. Richard Hays argues these "are called to a life of 'embracing death,' suffering through selfless service of others (cf. 10:33—11:1), not seeking their own advantage or pleasure."[206] The enemies of the cross are those who oppose the way of the cross. According to Jenson, the cross serves as the narrative continuity between the *already* and the *not yet*. The enemies of the cross are also enemies of the fulfillment yet to come.

The enemies of the cross seek a conflicting end from the *not yet* of Paul's apocalyptic theology, one more in line with private interest. Rather than denying their own pleasure, the enemies of the cross seek it, for their god is "the belly" and their "glory" is "shame" (Phil 3:19, NRSV). The enemies of the cross pose an apocalyptic problem for Paul because they reach for a different *not yet* telos. Enemies do not operate with a proper understanding of the fulfillment of their actions, and would have desired the promised destiny described by Paul in Philippians 3:12b and 15. John Ruemann proposes that they must "have thought they had already realized" their goal.[207] The issue is that of worship. Ruemann continues, "A false object of worship goes with wrong notions of glory normally expected at the End."[208] The muddled ability to realize the end goal of their actions in lives of self-fulfilling, privately interested pleasure and the false worship of God is problematic because it causes an antithesis between competing ways of life with those who profess citizenship in the heavenly realm.

Paul contrasts the enemies of the cross with the citizens of heaven. Paul uses the word πολίτευμα (*politeuma*, "citizenship," NRSV) in order to distinguish the activity of heaven, namely the reality of the not-yet, from the πολίτευμα of the enemies of the cross.[209] Paul is not talking about a governmental association that guarantees rights and privileges to

206. Hays, *Interpretation*, 262.
207. Reumann, *Philippians*, 595.
208. Reumann, *Philippians*, 595.
209. Reumann, *Philippians*, 597.

its adherents, as is common in modern descriptions of citizenship, but an activity that operates out of a specific agency. In short, πολίτευμα signals different worlds.[210] The described agency arises from the "power" that will glorify the body in a way not tied to self-fulfilling pleasures (Phil 3:19b, 21b). Citizenship, therefore, is not guaranteed by the state in this Pauline understanding. Rather, it is guaranteed and fulfilled in God's actions. By placing Philippians in continuity with 1 Corinthians, citizens are the ones who have been given the revelation of God by the Spirit in order to see by the coming Reign of God (1 Cor 2:6–15).

The redefinition of apocalyptic citizenship as agency mirrors the cruciform interpretation offered by theologian and ethicist Luke Bretherton. This definition builds on Paul's apocalyptic theology and offers a helpful political translation in light of Schmitt's wanting political theology. Bretherton, in his book *Resurrecting Democracy*, acknowledges the loss of coherent language about citizenship, which is essential for a truly democratic community. The issue that Bretherton has with modern forms of citizenship, as with Arendt, is that it takes an over-confident legalism. Legalism ties citizenship to the specific place of the nation-state and loses its way. Bretherton writes, "Constructions of place other than the nation-state enable different ways of performing citizenship."[211] The error in exclusively locating citizenship in such legal terms is that it falsely locates citizenship as a function of the state. Rather, citizenship is concerned with community organizing. This narrative of citizenship reconstructs "a political and moral rationality . . . which . . . is a way of discerning goods in common and a vision of the good life through which 'we, the people' come to decide how to live."[212] By locating citizenship in a place other than the nation-state, common goods and shared ends emerge in excess of the legal structures that normally guarantee citizenship. By locating citizenship in a not-yet-fulfilled *politeuma*, shared ends can be celebrated and acted upon. Citizenship is a type of rationality that, though considering life in the nation-state, is not relegated to the state alone. Rather, citizenship is a faithful form of sociality in the public sphere.

The political rationality of heavenly citizenship lies in a crucified sociality of lifting up humble states of human existence in order to reveal the glory that state-centered citizenship can never recognize. This new

---

210. Reumann, *Philippians*, 597.

211. Bretherton, *Resurrecting Democracy*, 4.

212. Bretherton, *Resurrecting Democracy*, 5.

rationality emerges from the way Paul interprets the activity of the incarnation (Phil 2:6–11) and the way the body is renewed in the new creation (Phil 3:21). Paul writes, "He will transform the body of our humiliation that it may be conformed to the body of his glory, by the power that also enables him to make all things subject to himself" (Phil 3:21, NRSV). The power that will make all things new reveals a goodness of humanity in a way unforeseen by legal modes of citizenship. That which is humble, much in the same manner as Mary's Magnificat (Luke 1:46–55), is made high. An imperative is made in light of this indicative. The good of the political rationality of a heavenly citizenship is the good for which the legal and economic structures have forcibly made low. The cruciform nature of this citizenship places at its center the humility of Christ's solidarity with the poor and lowly to the point of crucifixion.

Heavenly citizenship includes a very particular understanding of the common good. Womanist theologian Emilie Townes argues that this has always been difficult in political communities. Townes argues that this is because the common good that would inform citizenship is obscured by "fantastic hegemonic imagination."[213] She writes, "Fantastic hegemonic imagination uses a politicized sense of history and memory to create and shape *its* worldview. It sets in motion whirlwinds of images used in the cultural production of evil. These images have an enormous impact on how we understand the world, as well as others and ourselves in that world."[214] Fantastic hegemonic imagination prevents common good or, in Pauline terms, the cruciform, heavenly citizenship. The fantastic hegemonic imagination settles for "lives that are caricatured or pillaged so that the imagination that creates the fantastic can control the world in its own image."[215] This imagination is more akin to enemies of the cross, those who utilize created things for the sake of their own fulfillment. It is not a cruciform citizenship which has at its heart a political rationality that considers the humble, abused, and the lowly for the glorification of their bodies. Townes suggests that a Christian framework can serve a political function toward the formation of a common good. She argues that in order to do this, the common good must be expressed "not in terms of how the state sees it but in terms of how we understand it from our

213. Townes, *Womanist Ethics*, 21.

214. Townes, *Womanist Ethics*, 21.

215. Townes, *Womanist Ethics*, 21.

various religious worldviews and realize that we will not always agree."[216] The common good in heavenly citizenship takes as its subject the glory of the body and those, as with the *already*, for whom Christ died.

The common good for cruciform, heavenly citizenship is the just and loving gaze. The political rationality—heavenly citizenship—of the just and loving gaze loves the oppressed neighbor for the sake of the heavenly realm. Though it is the crucifixion that unmasks the central importance of the poor and the oppressed, it is the eschatological fulfillment that makes working against the ever-increasing systemic apparatus of poverty in our world hopeful. The good that is sought in heavenly citizenship mirrors the glorification all will experience in the heavenly realm. As all work, all expect the fulfillment of it there. The actions must not be an actionless quietism. Townes stipulates that "We need to bring the poor to the center of our questions and our options and our decision-making—not theoretically, but concretely."[217] The just and loving gaze sees beyond the caricatures of those impoverished, instead looking toward the humanity at the heart of the oppressed. It is for these that we act.

A concrete mode of political rationality that embodies heavenly citizenship is to offer a sense of home to our neighbors. This supports Bretherton's argument that the nation-state may not be the primary place to understand a political rationality that encourages civic life centered on the common good. Harvard sociologist Matthew Desmond has written, "Civic life too begins at home, allowing us to plant roots and take ownership in a spirit of solidarity and generosity."[218] Desmond continues, "Working on behalf of the common good is the engine of democracy, vital to our communities, cities, states—and, ultimately, the nation . . . [Vital communities'] foundation is the home."[219] Desmond is most concerned with eviction. In his argument, eviction upsets this communal, political rationality by removing a stable sense of home. The resulting reality of eviction is increasing concentrations of poverty, which correspond to an increase in violence in these areas of poverty.[220] This impacts the jobs and educational opportunities for the families evicted.[221] Removing neigh-

---

216. Townes, *Womanist Ethics*, 137.

217. Townes, *Womanist Ethics*, 137.

218. Desmond, *Evicted*, 294.

219. Desmond, *Evicted*, 294.

220. Desmond, *Evicted*, 297–298.

221. Desmond, *Evicted*, 298.

bors from a community has the added impact of destroying social cohesion. Desmond writes, "Eviction can unravel the fabric of a community, helping to ensure that neighbors remain strangers and that their collective capacity to combat crime and promote civic engagement remains untapped."[222] Working on giving poorer neighbors a real sense of home is an essential task for a heavenly citizenship.

A concrete means of exercising this political rationality of the *not yet* requires work on behalf of our poor neighbors facing eviction. This particularly takes shape in confronting the types of economic practices that lead to mass evictions. According to Desmond, the issue central to mass evictions lies in the unequal treatment of the poor by landlords. Desmond argues that landlords overcharge the impoverished simply because they can.[223] Desmond is quick to point out that this "exploitation does not mean haranguing landlords as greedy or heartless."[224] In a market-based economic system, Desmond asks, "Would any of us price an apartment at half of what it could fetch or simply forgive and forget losing thousands of dollars when the rent checks didn't arrive?"[225]

Appealing to this human urge helps place landlords within an understandable framework for moral imagination. However, citizens of heaven are called to a different political rationality. It is one grounded within the wisdom of the cross as contrary to those enemies of the cross, whose God is the "belly." This does not mean that landlords should be discouraged from making "a modest rate of return" on their properties.[226] Rather, it means resisting the unjust economic practices that target the poor for the sake of making a spectacular amount of money off the poor.[227] Housing should be approached as a "human-capital investment" for the sake of creating communities and neighborhoods of contributors.[228] In other words, housing as capital investment increases a sense of stability where better paying work becomes not only possible, but probable. Desmond writes,

---

222. Desmond, *Evicted*, 298.

223. Desmond, *Evicted*, 311.

224. Desmond, *Evicted*, 307.

225. Desmond, *Evicted*, 307.

226. Desmond, *Evicted*, 311.

227. Desmond, *Evicted*, 307.

228. Desmond, *Evicted*, 310.

> Families crushed by the high cost of housing cannot afford
> vocational training or extra schooling that would allow them
> to acquire new skills; and many cannot stay in one place long
> enough to hold down the same job . . . A stable home would
> extend to them the opportunity to realize [the dream of better
> contributing work].[229]

Making a capital investment in poorer neighborhoods allows for the possibility of finding better work. It creates conditions for neighbors to contribute and exchange in society in ways that exploitation and eviction discourage. Brent Waters writes, "Charity or assistance will often be needed to help raise the poor to a subsistence level, but it is exchange that will enable them to sustain and improve their material well-being."[230]

The political rationality of stability and work arises from an understanding of human flourishing. As Paul is clear in Philippians 3, the human body's end is flourishing. He writes, "He will transform the body of our humiliation that it may be conformed to the body of his glory, by the power that also enables him to make all things subject to himself" (v. 21, NRSV). The body of glory represents a clear *telos* for the body as one meant for a flourishing that surpasses the present state. There is a coordinate way that the human body is created for flourishing in the present creation, as well.[231] Working to loosen neighbors from unjust bonds of exploitation and eviction correlate to the loosening of the bonds of humiliation on the body. The creation of a sense of home among neighbors mirrors the home of the new creation, where bodies will flourish and find their *telos*. Laboring in our present neighborhoods for just landlords and expressing the church's option for the poor is a difficult task that may only impact small, incremental changes in the world while costing much, thereby resisting the narratives of effectiveness.[232] Faithful political citizenship of the heavenly order is one committed to exerting pressure on those systemic orders that oppress and bind bodies for the purpose of change. The patterns of faithful political rationality arise from this understanding of the justice present in the glorification and flourishing of the human body in the *not yet*.

To live in such a way for the poor is to live an exilic existence, whereby God calls the community to seek the good of the city. This call is to follow

229. Desmond, *Evicted*, 310.

230. Waters, *Just Capitalism*, 110.

231. See Waters, *Just Capitalism*, 111.

232. See Bedford, "Little Moves Against Destructiveness," 157–81.

the urging of Jeremiah to the exilic Israel: "But seek the welfare [*shalom*] of the city where I have sent you into exile, and pray to the Lord on its behalf, for in its welfare [*shalom*] you will find your welfare [*shalom*]" (Jer 29:7, NRSV). To seek the *shalom* of the city, John Howard Yoder writes, is to "address to the wider society, including the state, and to the persons exercising power within it, the invitation, as good news, to participate, in their own best interest, in the cosmic meaning of the sovereignty of their risen Lord."[233] Jeremiah's command is a call to live the gospel in such a way that the nations who do not confess Jesus as Lord can attest to his lordship. For example, the preferential option for the poor, in this light, is for the good of the city—a good that lives in the excess of God's mission to the world. It is a good that reminds the city that justice is based on the just treatment of all its inhabitants. Living out the preferential option for the poor is a call to the city to recognize the goodness of God. Yoder continues, "The challenge to the faith community should not be to dilute or filter or translate its witness, so that the 'public' community can handle it without believing, but so to purify and clarify and exemplify it that the world can perceive it to be good news without having to learn a foreign language."[234] The task of the Christian community lies in a positive political relation to the world for its betterment.

The issue needing to be addressed in light of this *shalom* on behalf of the city is the just treatment of enemies. In Schmitt's view, it would be easier to suppress the enemies of the sovereign. Sovereignty is a biopolitical trap and a false eschatology. This could include, in the case of eviction, forcibly seizing the land of all landowners for the sake of establishing cheaper housing and attacking policy-makers and politicians for complicity with landlords. This trend would continue until the entire world was labeled as the "enemy." The danger in acting violently toward the enemy lies in the latent possibility to continually find new enemies as a means to unify the community. The violent suppression of enemies only leads to an unjust desire to control the wheel of history. This posture is fundamentally a human desire but is thoroughly antiapocalyptic. The goal of faithful Christian action is faithfulness, not actions that would lead to the control of history, which, in essence, is unfaithful.

This distinction between faithful and unfaithful political actions of the Christian community is the difference between faithfulness and

233. Yoder, "Introduction," 5.
234. Yoder, "Firstfruits," 24.

effectiveness. Yoder best teases out this difference by describing Christianity's historical obsession with the meaning and direction of history.[235] When Christians become exclusively obsessed with immanent procedures of history, then the difference between Schmitt and Philippians 3 is lost. When this happens, our ethical concern "is to make things move in the right direction."[236] This desire shapes the political and moral activity in such a way that the goodness or end of an action is no longer in view, only "what effects it will cause."[237] Effectiveness in moving history toward the right direction is the highest political end.[238] When effectiveness becomes the highest political end, then the common good is no longer a primary end. Instead, Christianity becomes obsessed with its ability to achieve its own ends apart from God. For example, Waters argues that vengeance is a far more certain and effective mode of political action to bring about certain ends than is forgiveness. However, it is the latter that Christians are called to enact. This is problematic because when effectiveness is your highest aim, Yoder writes, "it is justified to sacrifice to this one 'cause' other subordinate values, including the life and welfare of one's self, one's neighbor, and (of course!) of the enemy."[239] No longer is an action performed in anticipation of the end. It becomes an attempt to fulfill one's vision of history.

In order to illustrate the specific vacuity of effectiveness and the way that it changes the nature of Christian confession and activity, I return to Timothy Snyder's read of Nazi Germany and the Christian church.

> Hitler learned to be politic [sic], using the energy of German resentment to further his own extraordinary ambitions. He exploited the broad German consensus in favor of revising the European political order, even though his own goal was to destroy it. He presented himself as a determined advocate of national self-determination, even though he did not actually believe in national rights. Likewise, he learned to soften his presentation of the Jewish menace. He no longer said in public that Christianity was as Jewish as Bolshevism. German Christians would be allowed to modify their doctrine rather than be forced to abandon it, as they were drawn into the larger struggle that would

235. Yoder, *Politics of Jesus*, 228.
236. Yoder, *Politics of Jesus*, 228.
237. Yoder, *Politics of Jesus*, 228.
238. Yoder, *Politics of Jesus*, 228.
239. Yoder, *Politics of Jesus*, 229.

drain it of all meaning. To Hitler, his fellow Germans were of interest only insofar as they could be rallied to join a mindless war for future racial prosperity. In other words, Germans [including German Christians] were disappointingly frivolous as they pursued their petty preoccupations of the Weimar Republic . . . Hitler could hardly tell them that, and he did not.[240]

Snyder's provocative interpretation of Nazi Germany reveals the temptation embedded in the political activity of the church. The temptation is always for Christianity to modify its positions in order to not appear petty. For example, the German church modifies its confessions during Nazi Germany in order to serve the purposes of the Nazi regime. Hitler's vision prompts these changes, though it is clear they are already embedded within the society. The German church sacrifices subordinate values for the sake of effectiveness in controlling history's movements by relativizing the doctrinal standards, which formerly guided its political life.

This doctrinal standard should be understood as a loss of an apocalyptic expectation of God's coming reign. When this hope is lost, the context and temperament of our political ordering is also lost. Paul's emphasis on not being found to labor in vain (1 Cor 15:58) or appearing before the judgment seat to account for one's deeds (2 Cor 5:10) are both apocalyptic statements. They are apocalyptic because laboring and judgment presume a particular type of activity of faithfulness. The apocalyptic nature of these actions is judged as faithful or not. It is in the new creation that their appropriate end is fulfilled. This shows that the political organization of the church is not for the sake of fulfilling any particular historical purpose of its own making; rather, it is a purposive, faithful accountability to the reality that is only understood as "coming."

To live in such a way that the pattern between faithful and effective actions are manifest is to seek the good of the city. However, this reality is not interested in overthrowing the city. It is to exit in a middle way. Nate Kerr writes,

> To "seek the peace of the city" in a foreign land is not then to sanctify its given structures and polities, but rather to live in that city by way of positive relation that which is in *excess* of it, namely, that "'higher' or 'future' city of peace" by which the liberation not only of Zion but also of *all* the nations is to come . . . It is to live relative to and in subversion of the given mechanisms of political power by way of that mode of action which is uniquely

240. Snyder, *Black Earth*, 33.

receptive to the peace of that eschatological city which occurs always in excess of so-called "politics" as such.[241]

Thus we have reached the key political rationality of the *not yet*: excess. The future fulfillment of creation and human agency is always in the mode of excess. It is not dependent upon the mechanisms and structures of the given in order to understand its political activity. This is the vocation of the remnant in Agamben's antihegemonic philosophy. The peace of the fallen city is sought by means of subversion of the systemic structures reorienting them toward this heavenly goal for the sake of the good of the city and its citizens.

The task of an apocalyptic politics of the *not yet* is to step out of the role of God in bringing history to an end. It is to cease to use the moral yardstick of effectiveness. This includes the ecclesial separation from the political authorities when its confessions are in danger of being compromised. The task of just and loving gaze in the time that remains is to always reconcile ourselves to the coming reign of God. It is an introspective task of continually evaluating whether we seek our own version of history or, with the rest of the community, participate in the cry "come." The ability to resist death and to "unself" from the possessive private interest is embracing this different mode of time. The just and loving gaze, to use the imagery of J. Louis Martyn, is to look at the world with the bifocal vision of apocalyptic.[242] It is to see the world as it already is, in all of its sin and horror, but it is also to see the world under the lordship of Christ and the coming transformation of the cosmos. This prevents the community from the seduction of powers alien to this new coming kingdom.

CONCLUSION

In conclusion, the apocalyptic political theology of the *not yet* is driven by the hope for the future consummation of the world. The future consummation of the world is the resurrection of the body and the drawing of all creation into the life of the triune God. In this context, our moral and political agency lies in the fulfilling of our actions in the eschaton rather than in our own power and ability. In this regard, the *not yet* complements the political activity of the *already*. The actions of the *already*—attention and remembrance—need what Hannah Arendt calls

241. Kerr, *Christ, History, and Apocalyptic*, 185.

242. Martyn, *Galatians*, 103.

"natality." Natality is the ability for actions to be new, not trapped in old judgments and habits. Only through natality does one remember well and remain lovingly attentive. The main practice of the *not yet* is forgiveness. When new judgments and habits emerge, the need to repent from old ones must occur. Without forgiveness, we can never fully escape destructive cycles of vengeance and see with the just and loving gaze. As is the practice of the *already*, so is the political theology of the *already*; it is complimented by the *not yet*. In order to properly instruct the nations, Christianity must avoid the temptation to act unjustly or immorally. This is illustrated in Philippians 3, where our governing political allegiance is located in a distinct rationality rather than the Schmittian temptation to suppress the chaos. This is the temptation to control the course of history and use effectiveness as a moral yardstick. Such practices are incongruent with the life of the crucified, which is the form of the eschaton. Therefore, Christian apocalyptic political theology is a mode of activity within the time that remains.

Conclusion

On Being a (Political) Disciple of the Crucified Nazarene

THE QUESTION "WHY DO so many contemporary philosophers take up the apostle Paul as a source for a new political philosophy?" prompted this study. According to these philosophers, Paul displaces certain hegemonic and biopolitical structures in modernity. These structures arise from private interests and biopolitical apparatuses, as narrated by Arendt and Foucault. The apparatuses are able to divide the populace based on private desire for life and work for the purpose of creating antinomies that establish desirable and undesirable life. Paul, even as an ancient figure, provides the means to address these harmful biopolitical antinomies and resists the temptation to slide back into certain ontological divisions of the world. In order to do this, Paul must be placed inside the materialist hermeneutic of these figures.

Such a hermeneutic provides a fruitful political discussion, but must be approached with caution. This caution begat my secondary question in response to the figures of the new approach to Paul: Does a materialist approach finally escape the traps of the biopolitical order? I argued that it did not. Ultimately, there is a harmonious depth to reality that is missed when such a hermeneutic is deployed, a depth already available in Paul. This leaves the new approach in a paradoxical position; they enthusiastically embrace Paul's account of reality, then immediately reject him because of his confessions about God. If one is to confront the biopolitical structures of modernity, then one must appeal to a harmonious order where biopolitical antinomies are not operative. This is an order that forms people in a particular path of neighborly love instead of reifying biopolitical antinomies. Therefore, I turned to Paul's apocalyptic gospel as a possible alternative to a purely materialist philosophy. The value of Pauline apocalyptic lies in its natural correspondence to the theology of Paul and the way Paul might critique hegemonic political orders. Apocalyptic undoes biopolitical antinomies because it reclaims the goodness of all created order. Rather than "ontologizing" the errant political order, apocalyptic suggests that the world is subject to alien powers of sin and death. Paul's apocalyptic gospel proclaims that in Christ's incarnation, God has invaded the cosmos for the sake of freeing the created order from these powers, enabling the *summum bonum*. This includes the political authorities that often find themselves swayed and seduced by fallen powers.

The powers are coordinate to the malformative nature of biopolitics. The fallen powers for Paul are those powers that fundamentally reorient human desire toward less productive ends. Therefore, the sovereignty of death reveals itself to be the power to make humans disappear, the power to reign over and claim bodies for another sovereignty, and binds humanity to types of deeds that are taken up in technologies of the self. All of these factors lead to a formation of the political order bound to an alien sovereignty that must be overcome.

The powers of sin and death are confronted by Christ in Paul's apocalyptic gospel. This is the reality that replaces the materialist depiction offered by the new approach. Christ defeats the powers of sin and overcomes the sovereignty of death. In Christ's invasion into the cosmos, he exhausts this foreign power in his life, death, resurrection, and ascension in his own body. In this way, Christ is already Lord over the powers. However, there is a yet-to-be-completed defeat of death in the lives of believers. Historically, this has been the distinction between the *already* and the *not yet* in Paul's apocalyptic theology. This distinction allowed me the opportunity to reflect upon and adjudicate the past and present condition of Paul's apocalyptic theology in the academy. The academic study of Paul's apocalyptic vacillates between the *already* and the *not yet*. Currently, it is proposed that one must choose one or the other as *the* apocalyptic Paul. However, I argued that a marriage between the two can be a fruitful endeavor. In the *already*, Christ defeats the powers of sin and death by placing the triune Lord as the new center of intimacy in the cosmos. This encourages faithful activities that live into this new ontological shift in reality. In the *not yet*, Christ fulfills the activities established in the *already*. If the triune Lord is the new center of intimacy in the cosmos, then the *not yet* realizes that intimacy by drawing creation further into

Godself. Therefore, the *already* and *not yet* complement each other in the task of resisting biopolitical orders.

The strength of biopolitics lies in its ability to divide the world according to inside/outside and friend/enemy distinctions. Its ability to have this antinomy becomes so fundamental that it is taken up in the life of the individual, namely in technologies of the self. This entails an epistemological stance that divides the world according to biopolitical standards, allowing for the will of the sovereign to be diffused into the masses. For biopolitics, there is a clear inside and outside. If these biopolitical antinomies are to be overcome, it must be at the point where the will of the sovereign is practiced in the lives of the masses. A new practice at the site of the internalized biopolitical antinomies must offset the technologies of the self. A new reality, Christ's invasion of the cosmos, achieves a new way to see the world in excess of the biopolitical order.

I argue that the vision created by the apocalyptic invasion of Christ is the just and loving gaze. Biopolitics divides the world according to the living and the dead. The gaze of biopolitics must perpetuate certain private interests that are coordinate with the sovereign will. This fundamentally challenges any appreciation of neighbors for their own sake. It only funnels them through private interests—is this person an avenue toward life or death? The just and loving gaze, as offered by Murdoch, performs a different function. It requires an "unselfing" in which one's private interests are set aside so as to make just and loving interaction possible with neighbors. The just and loving gaze requires the moral agent to interact with and come to know the neighbors in their own particularity and to love them in that particularity. Only from this place can the moral agent ask what justice and love our neighbors require.

The just and loving gaze exceeds the capabilities of the new approach to counter biopolitics. Hannah Arendt's emphasis on speech showed that a positive political response to private interest must place speaking and hearing as an essential political task. A people capable of speech and listening is already outside the rationality of biopolitics. However, Arendt does not give an avenue toward which speech can be heard. Why should the moral agent care about the speech of neighbor? I argued that the just and loving gaze creates the inward and outward dispositions that make hearing the speech of another possible. Such political activity brings down biopolitical structures by refusing to allow them to define another for us. By listening to another's speech, the moral agent acknowledges the indebtedness to another for a proper understanding of the common good.

The just and loving gaze is preferable to the new approach. I high-lighted this in Agamben's attempt to see the *Muselmänner* beyond the biopolitical realm. I argued that the issue with Agamben's approach is the failure to actually account for the speech and contingency of this very particular victim. The inability of Agamben to do this lies in the residue of a materialistic account of reality, which is at the heart of the new approach. This tendency lays within a modern propensity to create a categorical matrix to understand contingent realities. Though Agamben's position is accommodating, he fails to reckon with his deep indebtedness to a Eurocentric subjectivity, which ultimately distracts from his central aim. Agamben and the rest of the new approach offer many antibiopo-litical insights, but they cannot finally overcome biopolitical seizure of contingency. This is because the categorical seizing of experience can be co-opted by the same biopolitical structures they wish to overcome. Therefore, the just and loving gaze subverts this tendency by seeking and loving the contingency of the neighbor.

If the just and loving gaze is the proper expression of the political response to biopolitics, then some translation into Pauline apocalyptic must occur. Murdoch, though friendly to Christian theology, is opposed to confessional theology. However, her openness to theological categories leads to a helpful reinterpretation of her work. If the categorical seizing of experience by Agamben is the gaze enabled by the materialist view of reality, then the just and loving gaze is enabled by the apocalyptic inva-sion of Christ.

The apocalyptic invasion of Christ enables the just and loving gaze in the tension between the *already* and the *not yet*. In the *already*, the just and loving gaze is the vision enabled by the elimination of the harmful antinomies of the old cosmos, such as circumcised versus uncircumcised. Living in the new community, enabled by the crucifixion of the old world, means no longer applying the antinomies of the old world.

Within the theological vision created by the apocalyptic *already* is a certain set of practices. For Paul, it is never enough to see—one must also practice this vision. I proposed two practices of the *already* Paul utilized in order to make the just and loving gaze a lived reality. First, there was memory. In communal memory, the Pauline communities engaged in a moral imagination of present life within the context of the tradition passed to them. This was lived through the partaking of the Eucharist. By par-ticipating in the Eucharist, believers are asked to remember Christ's death and practice the Eucharist as a means to reevaluate one's relationships in the community. The antinomy at play in the abuses of the Eucharist (1 Cor 11) operate as a harmful division between those who have nothing and those who are drunk. This must be overcome in concrete practice. The practice of remembering places the poor at the center of concern and overcomes this division within the life of the church. Second, Paul offers the practice of attention. In Paul's moral discourses against the consumption of idol meat, he ties one's attention to Christ's crucifixion as that which positively impacts those weak in his congregations. Attention means looking at the harm certain actions may inflict upon another. This requires knowing the neighbor in a way that understands the justice and love required. This directly connects Paul's moral exhortations with the just and loving gaze, for it, too, is a type of attention.

The political theology arising from the *already* and the just and loving gaze is, then, a politics of mission. The community, while practicing its internal discernment of attention and remembrance, partners with the mission of God in the world. The mission of the church is to convert the nations, stand in solidarity with the poor, and seek the good of the nation. Recognizing that authorities can assist in limiting the violence and evil in the world, the church also instructs and embodies proper authority to the nations. As such, the just and loving gaze is a politics of seeking the good.

The just and loving gaze is a practice in the *already* but always exists within the tension of the *not yet*. All actions reach their end, not by our abilities but by God's ability. It is through God's resurrection of the dead that our actions are brought to an end. The just and loving gaze must always be open to new judgments. The work of the believer is always reaching toward an eschatological end and is always natal. As such, the just and loving gaze requires the practice of forgiveness and reconciliation as a means to reevaluate prejudice. If believers suffer the need to reevaluate prejudices, then the harm those prejudices caused must be the subject of forgiveness and reconciliation. Without forgiveness and reconciliation, the community is subject to neverending cycles of violence. Forgiveness breaks this cycle and, in light of God's place as the intimate center of our communal love, restores the community's ability to see with the just and loving gaze.

The political theology arising from the just and loving gaze in this tension is always a resistance to the narrative of effectiveness. Paul's language of both the resurrection of the dead and the heavenly citizenship reveals a political activity geared toward a not-yet-visible polity, except in the life of the church. The just and loving gaze, as embodied in the life of the community, is one that resists being effective toward the *telos* of earthly political bodies, which might lead the community from the ultimate *telos* in God's being all in all. For example, the community glorifies the bodies of the lowly rather than dominating them for their own immanent gain, which may cause the community to fall back into biopolitical orders of the world.

This study was an exercise in theopolitical thinking, utilizing the apostle Paul and a variety of nontheistic philosophical voices. The project has a variety of implications for a variety of fields. Despite this fact, my primary intention lies in suggesting certain reflections for future political theology. I offer five brief conclusions that arise from the guiding argument of this work.

1. Political theology should helpfully employ the insights of nontheistic philosophers, but they cannot replace the effort of theological reflection. I utilized many philosophers (Agamben, Badiou, Arendt, Murdoch, etc.) in order to help me critique biopolitical orders and to read Paul into modern political philosophy. This was very fruitful for two main reasons. First, it gives political theologians helpful conceptual tools to confront modern political regimes. The epistemological conceit of modernity forces us to acknowledge that theology's most important historical figures don't have biopolitics as their main aim. Therefore, some translation must occur, and certain figures who actively engage biopolitics help toward the end of this translation. Second, contemporary philosophy has rediscovered Paul. This should be encouraged. Paul is rediscovered and is presented as a figure who can answer even our contemporary political aliments.

Despite this advantage, it cannot replace the work of theological reflection, specifically Scriptural reflection. Though the new approach utilizes a figure of Scripture, their deployment of Paul is in a different vernacular. I do not object to the modern philosophical use of Paul that seeks an answer to the contemporary malaise of politics. My objection is that Paul is a tool to clarify *their* systems. The reverse must take place. In Scripture lies sanctified speech. The language of Scripture is the speech to which *our* speech must appeal. The interior rationality of Scripture, specifically the gospel, must guide political speech, even if it is in conversation with nontheistic philosophy.

2. Political theology must remain apocalyptic. Paul's theology is both revelatory to the lordship of Christ and hopeful that God will do more. The *already* character of Paul's apocalyptic theology eliminates cosmic

antinomies from which the biopolitical antinomies arise. Because Christians are already under the lordship of Christ, they cannot operate under these antinomies anymore. Instead, they live with the meaning found in the grains of the universe. This is a fundamental Christian political activity. However, there is a persistent hope that guides and tempers the enthusiasm of the *already*: the *not yet*. In such a hope, Christians recognize they are not fit to choose the ends toward which history should be steered. Such a realization prevents much immorality. When Christians confess that God will ultimately bring history to an end, it absolves them of the need to do so.

3. Political theology must give up the concept of sovereignty and recover a robust language of the common good. Schmitt illustrates, with critique from Agamben and Taubes, that this is a problematic concept. The close alliance between biopolitics and sin in their antinomous ordering of the world is evident in their appeal to sovereignty in place of God's sovereignty. The use of political theology as justification for an earthly ruler to decide the exception must come to an end. In its place, a theological articulation of authority must emerge with the correct Christian clarity.

4. The church community is formed and shaped in order to confront any political order it finds itself under. The church's political reflection is always relative to its time and place. However, the church is summoned together by the inauguration of Christ's lordship. Under this lordship, Christians are committed to the repetitive task of a complex life together. This life together is funded in a unified confession and by practices of hospitality and love, built on the rationality of that confession. The practices shape and form the community in a particular way of being in public. The community's witness and interior life confronts wider political culture, regardless of time.

The rise of sovereignty is a result of private interest. The way around this is a robust account of the common good. The common good enables a political life capable of sustaining many narratives for the purpose of working toward shared ends. Thus, the neighbor is not available to me for my personal use, but is the one with whom I partner on the road to the common good. The sovereign decision, which is made possible by my own assent to biopolitical structures, is satisfied in late modernity to sterilize society. This has an adverse impact on the poor and powerless. The common good is beatitude. The common good is the reality that humans work for the sake of both personal beatitude and that of the neighbor's.

5. The just and loving gaze informed by Pauline apocalyptic is an appropriate path beyond biopolitics. Biopolitics fails in its inequitable division of the world. In order to overcome its inequitable divisions of the world, one must see the particularity of neighbors, treat them justly, and understand that their humanity is essential to the determination of the common good. The just and loving gaze, as preferable not only to biopolitics but also in the new approach, is able to achieve all three. By experiencing factual data of the neighbor as a means to know and love the good, one learns about the particularity of the neighbor. The moral agent can then learn the justice and love due the neighbor through the factual data one gleans by experiencing and engaging the neighbor, not through false consciousness. This is a collaborative effort not dependent on an abstract "ism" applied to the neighbor, but is dependent upon placing oneself at the feet of the neighbor. This collaboration leads to the common good.

In conclusion, politics has always been a difficult activity for Christians to engage faithfully. The vexed legacy of Christendom, Christian participation in German National Socialism, and other moral atrocities committed by Christians are unfortunate reminders of the risks they take by entering into political arenas. However, with the revitalized discussion of Paul's political theology and the coordinate rise in the theological academy of Paul's apocalyptic theology, an opportunity arises to begin again. The church is the community caught in the praise of the crucified, resurrected, ascended one it calls Lord, and this praise is a witness to the realities to which she binds herself. The church's confession of salvation, the blessed Trinity, and its many gifts construct the identity by which she is understood. As such, she is responsible to live a life in light of these realities and one not motivated by the antinomies of the former world. She must feel free to, as the angels say, "fear not" (Luke 2:10, NRSV). The church does not fear that its life somehow becomes antiquated with the changing times, but persists in a stubborn faithfulness to God, from whom she receives her gifts. Faithfulness is a fidelity to the crucified Nazarene and to the gifts and promises of God's kingdom, which will have no end. In light of this, the church can hope instead of fear. For the church, there is not a qualitative difference between political faithfulness and doxology.

Bibliography

Agamben, Giorgio. *The Coming Community.* Translated by Michael Hardt. Minneapolis: University of Minnesota Press, 1993.

———. *The Highest Poverty: Monastic Rules and Form-of-Life.* Translated by Adam Kotsko. Stanford: Stanford University Press, 2013.

———. *Homo Sacer: Sovereign Power and Bare Life.* Translated by Daniel Heller-Roazen. Stanford: Stanford University Press, 1995.

———. *The Kingdom and the Glory: For a Theological Genealogy of Economy and Government.* Translated by Lorenzo Chiesa with Matteo Mandarini. Stanford: Stanford University Press, 2011.

———. *Potentialities: Collected Essays in Philosophy.* Translated by Daniel Heller-Roazen. Stanford: Stanford University Press, 1999.

———. *The Remnant of Auschwitz: The Witness and the Archive.* Translated by Daniel Heller-Roazen. New York: Zone, 2002.

———. *The Time That Remains: A Commentary on the Letter to the Romans.* Translated by Patricia Dailey. Stanford: Stanford University Press, 2005.

Althusser, Louis. "Ideology and Ideological State Apparatuses. Notes towards an Investigation." In *Mapping Ideology,* edited by Slavoj Žižek, 100–140. New York: Verso, 1994.

Aquinas, Thomas. *Summa Theologica.* Translated by the Fathers of the English Dominican Province. South Bend: Ave Maria, 1948.

Arendt, Hannah. "A Daughter of Our People: A Response to Gershom Scholem." In *The Portable Hannah Arendt,* edited by Peter Baehr, 391–96. New York: Penguin, 2003.

———. *The Human Condition.* 2nd ed. Chicago: Chicago University Press, 1998.

———. "Introduction *into* Politics." *The Promise of Politics,* edited by Jerome Kohn, 93–200. New York: Shocken, 2005.

———. *The Jewish Writings.* Edited by Jerome Kohn and Ron Feldman. New York: Shocken, 2007.

———. *The Life of the Mind.* 2 vols. New York: Harcourt, 1997.

———. *On Revolution.* New York: Penguin, 2006.

———. *The Origins of Totalitarianism.* New York: Harvest, 1968.

———. "Socrates." In *The Promise of Politics,* edited by Jerome Kohn, 5–39. New York: Shocken, 2005.

———. "We Refugees." In *The Jewish Writings,* edited by Jerome Kohn and Ron Feldman, 264–74. New York: Shocken, 2007.

Aristotle. *Nicomachean Ethics*. Translated by Robert Bartlett and Susan Collins. Chicago: University of Chicago Press, 2012.

Augustine. *City of God (De Civitas Dei) I/6*. Edited by Boniface Ramsey. Translated by William Ramsey. The Works of Saint Augustine: A Translation for the 21st Century. New York: New City, 2013.

————. *The Trinity (De Trinitate) I/5*. Edited by John E. Rotelle. Translated by Edmund Hill. The Works of Saint Augustine: A Translation for the 21st Century. New York: New City, 1991.

Bachelard, Sarah. *Resurrection and Moral Imagination*. Burlington: Ashgate, 2014.

Badiou, Alain. *Logics of Worlds: Being and Event II*. Translated by Alberto Toscano. New York: Bloomsbury Academic, 2013.

————. *Metapolitics*. Translated by Jason Barker. New York: Verso, 2005.

————. *Saint Paul: The Foundation of Universalism*. Translated by Ray Brassier. Stanford: Stanford University Press, 2003.

————. "What Is It to Live?" In *Biopolitics: A Reader*, edited by Timothy Campbell and Adam Sitze, 412–20. Durham: Duke University Press, 2013.

Balthasar, Hans Urs von. "Characteristics of Christianity." In *Explorations in Theology Vol. 1: The Word Made Flesh*, 161–80. San Francisco: Ignatius, 1989.

Barclay, John G. M. "Apocalyptic Allegiance and Divestment in the World." In *Paul and the Apocalyptic Imagination*, edited by Ben C. Blackwell et al., 257–74. Minneapolis: Fortress, 2016.

Barram, Michael. *Mission and Moral Reflection in Paul*. New York: Lang, 2006.

Barth, Karl. *Church Dogmatics, Study Edition 19: Doctrine of Creation III.4, §52–54*. Translated by T. F. Torrance and G. W. Bromiley. New York: T. & T. Clark, 2009.

————. *Church Dogmatics, Study Edition 21: Doctrine of Creation IV.1, §57–59*. Translated by T. F. Torrance and G. W. Bromiley. New York: T. & T. Clark, 2009.

————. *Church Dogmatics, Study Edition 23: Doctrine of Creation IV.1, §61–63*. Translated by T. F. Torrance and G. W. Bromiley. New York: T. & T. Clark, 2009.

————. *The Epistle to the Romans*. Translated by Edwyn Hoskyns. 6th ed. New York: Oxford University Press, 1965.

————. "October 18, 1914." In *A Unique Time of God: Karl Barth's WWI Sermons*, translated and edited by William Klempa, 145–54. Louisville: Wesminster John Knox, 2016.

————. *Theological Existence To-Day!: (A Plea for Theological Freedom)*. Translated by R. Birch Hoyle. Eugene, OR: Wipf & Stock, 1993.

Bedford, Nancy. "Little Moves Against Destructiveness: Theology and the Practice of Discernment." In *Practicing Theology: Beliefs and Practices in Christian Life*, edited by Miroslav Volf and Dorothy C. Bass, 157–84. Grand Rapids: Eerdmans, 2002.

Beker, J. Christian. *Paul the Apostle: The Triumph of God in Life and Thought*. Minneapolis: Fortress, 1980.

————. *Paul's Apocalyptic Gospel: The Coming Triumph of God*. Minneapolis: Fortress, 1982.

Bell, Daniel M., Jr. *Diviniations: Theopolitics in an Age of Terror*. Eugene, OR: Cascade, 2017.

Benjamin, Walter. "Critique of Violence." In *Reflections: Essays, Aphorisms, Autobiographical Writings*, edited by Peter Demetz and translated by Edmund Jephcott, 277–300. New York: Schocken, 200.

———. "Theologico-Political Fragment." In *Reflections: Essays, Aphorisms, Autobiographical Writings*, edited by Peter Demetz and translated by Edmund Jephcott, 312–13. New York: Schocken, 2007.

———. "Theses on the Philosophy of History." In *Illuminations: Essays and Reflections*, edited by Hannah Arendt and translated by Harry Zohn, 253–64. New York: Schocken, 2007.

Boer, Martinus C. de. "Paul's Mythologizing Program in Romans 5–8." In *Apocalyptic Paul: Cosmos and Anthropos in Romans 5–8*, edited by Beverly Roberts Gaventa, 1–20. Waco: Baylor University Press, 2013.

Bonhoeffer, Dietrich. *Creation and Fall: A Theological Exposition of Genesis 1–3*. Edited by John W. de Gruchy. Translated by Douglas Stephen Bax. Minneapolis: Fortress, 1997.

———. *Discipleship*. Edited by Geffrey B. Kelly and John D. Godsey. Translated by Barbara Green and Reinhard Krauss. Minneapolis: Fortress, 2003.

Boring, M. Eugene. *1 & II Thessalonians: A Commentary*. The New Testament Library. Louisville: Westminster John Knox, 2015.

Bretherton, Luke. *Resurrecting Democracy: Faith, Citizenship, and the Politics of a Common Life*. New York: Cambridge University Press, 2015.

Brink, O. P. Laurie. "From Wrongdoer to New Creation: Reconciliation in 2 Corinthians." *Interpretation: A Journal of Bible and Theology* 71.3 (2017) 298–309.

Brown, Alexandra. "Paul and the Parousia." In *The Return of Jesus in Early Christianity*, edited by John T. Carroll, 47–76. Peabody: Hendrickson, 2000.

Büchel, Friedrich. "καταλλάσσων." In *Theological Dictionary of the New Testament: Volume I*, edited by Gerhard Kittel and translated by Geoffrey W. Bromiley, 254–58. Grand Rapids: Eerdmans, 2006.

Bultmann, Rudolf. "The Christian Hope and the Problem of Demythologizing." *The Expository Times* 65.8 (1954) 228–30.

———. "New Testament and Mythology." In *New Testament & Mythology: And Other Basic Writings*, translated by Schubert M. Ogden, 1–44. Philadelphia: Fortress, 1984.

———. "On the Problem of Demythologizing." In *New Testament & Mythology: And Other Basic Writings*, translated by Schubert M. Ogden, 155–64. Philadelphia: Fortress, 1984.

———. "The Problem of Ethics in Paul." In *Understanding Paul's Ethics: Twentieth Century Approaches*, edited by Brian Rosner and translated by Christoph Stenschke, 195–216. Grand Rapids: Eerdmans, 1995.

———. *Theology of the New Testament*. Translated by Robert Morgan. 2 vols. Waco: Baylor University Press, 2007.

Butler, Judith. "Can One Lead a Good Life in a Bad Life?" *Radical Philosophy* 176 (November/December 2012) 9–18.

Castelli, Elizabeth. "The Philosopher's Paul in the Frame of the Global: Some Reflections." *South Atlantic Quarterly* 109 (2010) 653–76.

Cavanaugh, William T. "Are Corporations People?" In *Field Hospital: The Church's Engagement with a Wounded World*, 13–31. Grand Rapids: Eerdmans, 2016.

———. "The Mystical and the Real." In *Field Hospital: The Church's Engagement with a Wounded World*, 99–120. Grand Rapids: Eerdmans, 2016.

———. *Torture and Eucharist: Theology, Politics, and the Body of Christ*. Malden: Blackwell, 1998.

Chow, Rey. "'I Insist on the Christian Dimension': On Forgiveness . . . and the Outside of the Human." In *Entanglements, or Transmedial Thinking about Capture*, 107–32. Durham: Duke University Press, 2012.

Chua, Amy. *Political Tribes: Group Instinct and the Fate of Nations.* New York: Penguin, 2018.

Congdon, David. "Bonhoeffer and Bultmann: Toward an Apocalyptic Rapprochement." *International Journal of Systematic Theology* 15.2 (2013) 172–95.

———. "Eschatologizing Apocalyptic: An Assessment of the Present Conversation on Pauline Apocalyptic." In *Apocalyptic and the Future of Theology: With and Beyond J. Louis Martyn*, edited by Joshua B. Davis and Douglas Harink, 118–36. Eugene, OR: Cascade, 2012.

———. *The God Who Saves: A Dogmatic Sketch.* Eugene, OR: Cascade, 2016.

———. *The Mission of Demythologizing: Rudolf Bultmann's Dialectical Theology.* Minneapolis: Fortress, 2015.

Conzelmann, Hans. *1 Corinthians: A Commentary. Hermenia: A Critical and Historical Commentary on the Bible.* Translated by James Leitch. Edited by Geolge MacRae. Minneapolis: Fortress, 1975.

———. "On the Analysis of the Confessional Formula in I Corinthians 15:2–5." *Interpretation: A Journal of Bible and Theology* 201 (1996) 15–25.

Copeland, M. Shawn. *Enfleshing Freedom: Body, Race, and Being.* Minneapolis: Fortress, 2010.

Cosgrove, Charles. *Appealing to Scripture in Moral Debate: Five Hermeneutical Rules.* Grand Rapids: Eerdmans, 2002.

Coutts, Jon. *A Shared Mercy: Karl Barth on Forgiveness and the Church.* Downers Grove: InterVarsity, 2016.

Cullman, Oscar. *Christ and Time.* Philadelphia: Westminster, 1964.

Davis, Creston, et al. *Paul's New Moment: Continental Philosophy and the Future of Christian Theology.* Grand Rapids: Brazos, 2010.

———. "Introduction." In *Paul's New Moment: Continental Philosophy and the Future of Christian Theology*, 1–20. Grand Rapids: Brazos, 2010.

Desmond, Matthew. *Evicted: Poverty and Profit in the American City.* New York: Broadway, 2016.

Eagleton, Terry. *Ideology: An Introduction.* Updated edition. New York: Verso, 2007.

———. *Materialism.* New Haven: Yale University Press, 2016.

Elliot, Neil. "Creation, Cosmos, and Conflict in Romans 8–9." *Apocalyptic Paul: Cosmos and Anthropos in Romans 5–8*, edited by Beverly Roberts Gaventa, 131–56. Waco: Baylor University Press, 2013.

———. *Liberating Paul: The Justice of God and the Politics of the Apostle.* Minneapolis: Fortress, 2006.

Farley, Margret. "Forgiveness in the Service of Justice and Love." *Changing the Questions: Explorations in Christian Ethics*, edited by Jamie L. Manson, 319–42. New York: Orbis, 2015.

Feldman, Ron. "The Jew as Pariah: The Case of Hannah Arendt (1906–1975)." In *The Jewish Writings*, edited by Jerome Kohn and Ron Feldman, xli–lxxvi. New York: Shocken, 2007.

Fitzmyer, Joseph A. *First Corinthians: A New Translation with Introduction and Commentary.* The Anchor Yale Bible Commentary. New Haven: Yale University Press, 2008.

Foucault, Michel. *The Birth of Biopolitics: Lectures at the College De France 1978–1979*. Edited by Michel Senellart. Translated by Graham Burchell. New York: Picador, 2004.

———. *The Birth of the Clinic: An Archaeology of Medical Perception*. Translated by A. M. Sheridan. New York: Vintage, 1994.

———. *Discipline and Punish: The Birth of the Prison*. Translated by Alan Sheridan. New York: Vintage, 1977.

———. Foucault, Michel. *The Order of Things: An Archaeology of the Human Sciences*. New York: Vintage, 1971.

———. *Society Must Be Defended: Lectures at the College De France 1975–1976*. Edited by Mauro Bertani and Alessandro Fontana. Translated by David Macey. New York: Picador, 2003.

Frick, Peter. "Paul in the Grip of Continental Philosophers: What is at Stake?" In *Paul in the Grip of Philosophers*, edited by Peter Frick, 1–15. Minneapolis: Fortress, 2013.

Furnish, Victor Paul. *II Corinthians: Translation with Introduction, Notes, and Commentary*. The Anchor Yale Bible Commentary. New York: Doubleday, 1984.

———. *Theology and Ethics in Paul: New Testament Library*. Louisville: Westminster John Knox, 2009.

Gaventa, Beverly Roberts. *Our Mother Saint Paul*. Lousiville: Westminster John Knox, 2007.

Gorman, Michael. "The Apocalyptic New Covenant and the Shape of Life in the Spirit according to Galatians." In *Paul and the Apocalyptic Imagination*, edited by Ben C. Blackwell, John K. Goodrich, and Jason Maston, 317–38. Minneapolis: Fortress, 2016.

———. *Apostle of the Crucified Lord: A Theological Introduction to Paul and His Letters*. Grand Rapids: Eerdmans, 2004.

Hallward, Peter. "Badiou's Ontology." In *Badiou: A Subject to Truth*, 82–106. Minneapolis: University of Minnesota Press, 2003.

———. "Generic or Specific?" In *Badiou: A Subject to Truth*, 271–91. Minneapolis: University of Minnesota Press, 2003.

Harink, Douglas, ed. "From Apocalypse to Philosophy—and Back." In *Paul, Philosophy and the Theopolitical Vision: Critical Engagements with Agamben, Badiou, Žižek and Others*, 1–12. Eugene, OR: Cascade, 2010.

———. *Paul, Philosophy and the Theopolitical Vision: Critical Engagements with Agamben, Badiou, Žižek and Others*. Eugene, OR: Cascade, 2010.

Hart, David Bentley. *The Beauty of the Infinite: The Aesthetics of Christian Truth*. Grand Rapids: Eerdmans, 2004.

———. "Everything You Know about the Gospel of Paul is Likely Wrong." *Aeon*, January 8, 2018. https://aeon.co/ideas/the-gospels-of-paul-dont-say-what-you-think-they-say.

———. *The Experience of God: Being, Consciousness, Bliss*. New Haven: Yale University Press, 2013.

Hartwich, Wolf-Daniel, et al. "Afterword." In *The Political Theology of Paul*, translated by Dana Hollander, 115–42. Stanford: Stanford University Press, 2004.

Hauerwas, Stanley. "Murdochian Muddles: Can We Get Through Them If God Does Not Exist?" In *Iris Murdoch and the Search for Human Goodness*, edited by Maria Antonaccio and William Schweiker, 190–208. Chicago: University of Chicago Press, 1996.

Hays, Richard B. *Interpretation: A Bible Commentary for Teaching and Preaching: First Corinthians.* Louisville: John Knox Press, 1997.

Hegel, G. W. F. *Lectures on the Philosophy of History.* Translated by J. Sibree. Mineola: Dover, 1956.

Hiebert, Kyle Gingrich. *The Architectonics of Hope: Violence, Apocalyptic, and the Transformation of Political Theology.* Eugene, OR: Cascade, 2017.

Hill, Wesley. *Paul and the Trinity: Persons, Relations, and the Pauline Letters.* Grand Rapids: Eerdmans, 2015.

Holiday, Carl L. *Acts: A Commentary. The New Testament Library.* Louisville: Westminster John Knox, 2016.

Horrell, David G. *Solidarity and Difference: A Contemporary Reading of Paul's Ethics.* New York: T. & T. Clark, 2005.

———. "Solidarity and Difference: Ten Years On." In *Solidarity and Difference: A Contemporary Reading of Paul's Ethics,* xix–xl. 2nd ed. New York: T. & T. Clark, 2016.

Jacobs, Harriet. *Incidents in the Life of a Slave Girl.* New York: Penguin, 2000.

JanMohamed, Abdul R. *The Death-Bound-Subject: Richard Wright's Archaeology of Death.* Durham: Duke University Press, 2005.

Jennings, Willie. *Belief: A Theological Commentary on the Bible: Acts.* Louisville: Westminster John Knox, 2017.

———. *The Christian Imagination: Theology and the Origins of Race.* New Haven: Yale University Press, 2010.

Jenson, Robert W. *Systematic Theology, Vol. 1: The Triune God.* New York: Oxford University Press, 1997.

Jewett, Robert. *Romans: Hermenia, A Critical and Historical Commentary on the Bible.* Edited by Eldon Jay Epp. Minneapolis: Fortress, 2007.

Johnson, Andrew. "Turning the World Upside Down in 1 Corinthians 15: Apocalyptic Epistemology, the Resurrected Body and the New Creation." *Evangelical Quarterly* 75.4 (2003) 291–309.

Jones, Paul Dafydd. "Barth and Anselm: God, Christ and the Atonement." *International Journal of Systematic Theology* 12.3 (2010) 257–82.

Käsemann, Ernst. "The Beginnings of Christian Theology." In *New Testament Questions of Today: Study Edition,* translated by W. J. Montague, 82–107. London: SCM, 1969.

———. *Commentary on Romans.* Translated by Geoffrey Bromiley. Grand Rapids: Eerdmans, 1980.

———. "Healing the Possessed." In *On Being a Disciple of the Crucified Nazarene: Unpublished Lectures and Sermons,* edited by Rudolf Landau with Wolfgang Kraus and translated by Roy A. Harrisville, 195–205. Grand Rapids: Eerdmans, 2010.

———. "New Testament Questions of Today." In *New Testament Questions of Today: Study Edition,* translated by W. J. Montague, 1–22. London: SCM, 1969.

———. *On Being a Disciple of the Crucified Nazarene: Unpublished Lectures and Sermons.* Grand Rapids: Eerdmans, 2010.

———. "On the Subject of Primitive Christian Apocalyptic." In *New Testament Questions of Today: Study Edition,* translated by W. J. Montague, 82–107. London: SCM, 1969.

———. "The Pauline Doctrine of the Lord's Supper." In *Essays on New Testament Themes,* translated by W. J. Montague, 108–35. London: SCM, 1960.

———. "The Righteousness of God in an Unrighteous World." In *On Being a Disciple of the Crucified Nazarene: Unpublished Lectures and Sermons*, edited by Rudolf Landau with Wolfgang Kraus and translated by Roy A. Harrisville, 181–94. Grand Rapids: Eerdmans, 2010.

———. "'The Righteousness of God' in Paul." In *New Testament Questions of Today: Study Edition*, translated by W. J. Montague, 168–82. London: SCM, 1969.

Kateb, George. "Political Action." In *The Cambridge Companion to Hannah Arendt*, edited by Dana Villa, 130–50. New York: Cambridge University Press, 2001.

Kerr, Nathan R. *Christ, History, and Apocalyptic: The Politics of Christian Mission.* Eugene, OR: Cascade, 2009.

Knott, Marie Louise. *Unlearning with Hannah Arendt.* Translated by David Dollenmayer. New York: Other Press, 2015.

Kreider, Alan. *The Patient Ferment of the Early Church: The Improbable Rise of Christianity in the Roman Empire.* Grand Rapids: Baker, 2016.

Kroeker, P. Travis. "Introduction." In *Messianic Political Theology and Diaspora Ethics: Essays in Exile*, 1–14. Eugene, OR: Cascade, 2017.

———. "Is a Messianic Political Ethic Possible? Yoder Critically Considered." In *Messianic Political Theology and Diaspora Ethics: Essays in Exile*, 144–72. Eugene, OR: Cascade, 2017.

———. "Living 'As If Not?': Messianic Becoming or the Practice of Nihilism?" In *Messianic Political Theology and Diaspora Ethics: Essays in Exile*, 15–33. Eugene, OR: Cascade, 2017.

———. "Messianic Ethics and Diaspora Communities: Upholding the Secular Theologically from Below." In *Messianic Political Theology and Diaspora Ethics: Essays in Exile*, 64–82. Eugene, OR: Cascade, 2017.

———. "The War of the Lamb: Postmodernity and Yoder's Eschatological Genealogy of Morals." In *Messianic Political Theology and Diaspora Ethics: Essays in Exile*, 130–43. Eugene, OR: Cascade, 2017.

Lackey, Michael. "Killing God, Liberating the 'Subject': Nietzsche and Post-God Freedom." *Journal of the History of Ideas* 60.4 (1999) 737–54.

Lee, Gregory. "Republics and Their Loves: Rereading *City of God* 19." *Modern Theology* 27 (2011) 553–81.

Lemke, Thomas. *Bio-Politics: An Advanced Introduction.* Translated by Eric Frederick Trump. New York: New York University Press, 2011.

Lowe, Lisa. *The Intimacies of Four Continents.* Durham: Duke University Press, 2015.

Lubac, Henri de. *A Brief Catechesis on Nature and Grace.* Translated by Brother Richard Arnandez. San Francisco: Ignatius, 1984.

Maddox, Randy. *Responsible Grace: John Wesley's Practical Theology.* Nashville: Abingdon, 1994.

Marquis, Timothy Luckritz. *Transient Apostle: Paul, Travel, and the Rhetoric of Empire.* New Haven: Yale University Press, 2013.

Martin, Dale. *The Corinthian Body.* New Haven: Yale University Press, 1995.

Martyn, J. Louis. "Apocalyptic Antinomies." In *Theological Issues in the Letters of Paul*, edited by John Barclay et al., 111–24. New York: T. & T. Clark, 1997.

———. "Epistemology at the Turn of the Ages." In *Theological Issues in the Letters of Paul*, edited by John Barclay et al., 89–110. New York: T. & T. Clark, 1997.

———. *Galatians.* Anchor Bible 33. New York: Doubleday, 1997.

————. "Review of *Paul the Apostle: The Triumph of God in Life and Thought*, by J. Christiaan Beker." *Word and World* 2 (1982) 194–98. http://wordandworld. luthersem.edu/issues.aspx?article_id=2827.

Matera, Frank. *II Corinthians: A Commentary. The New Testament Library*. Louisville: Westminster John Knox, 2003.

McCabe, Herbert. "The Forgiveness of God." In *God, Christ and Us*, edited by Brian Davies, 119–24. New York: Continuum, 2005.

Milbank, John. "Can Morality Be Christian?" In *The Word Made Strange: Theology, Language, Culture*, 219–32. Malden: Blackwell, 1997.

————. "Materialism and Transcendence." In *Theology and the Political: The New Debate*, edited by Creston Davis et al., 393–426. Durham: Duke University Press, 2005.

Milbank, John, and Adrian Pabst. *The Politics of Virtue: Post-Liberalism and the Human Future*. New York: Rowman & Littlefield, 2016.

Montesquieu, Jean-Jacques. "The Spirit of Laws." In *Great Books of the Western World*, edited by Robert Maynard Hutchins, 38:1–315. Chicago: Encyclopedia Britannica, 1952.

Morse, Christopher. *The Difference Heaven Makes: Rehearing the Gospel as News*. New York: T. & T. Clark, 2010.

Murdoch, Iris. "Against Dryness." In *Existentialists and Mystics: Essays on Philosophy and Literature*, edited by Peter Conradi, 287–96. New York: Penguin, 1999.

————. *Metaphysics as a Guide to Morals*. New York: Penguin, 1993.

————. *The Nice and the Good*. New York: Penguin, 1968.

————. *The Sovereignty of the Good*. New York: Routledge, 1970.

Nietzsche, Friedrich. "Thus Spake Zarathustra." In *The Portable Nietzsche*, edited by Walter Kaufmann and translated by Walter Kaufmann, 103–49. New York: Penguin, 1954.

————. *The Will to Power*. Edited by Walter Kaufmann. Translated by Walter Kaufmann and R. J. Hollingdale. New York: Vintage, 1967.

Norris, Christopher. "Event." In *The Badiou Dictionary*, edited by Steven Corcoran, 115–20. Edinburgh: Edinburgh University Press, 2015.

O'Donovan, Oliver. *The Desire of the Nations: Rediscovering the Roots of Political Theology*. New York: Cambridge University Press, 1996.

————. *Entering into Rest: Ethics as Theology, Vol. 3*. Grand Rapids: Eerdmans, 2017.

————. *Resurrection and the Moral Order: An Outline for Evangelical Ethics*. 2nd ed. Grand Rapids: Eerdmans, 1994.

Oliver, Kelly. *The Colonization of Psychic Space: A Psychoanalytic Social Theory of Oppression*. Minneapolis: University of Minnesota Press, 2004.

Ostovich, Steven. "Carl Schmitt, Political Theology, and Eschatology." *KronoScope* 7 (2008) 49–66.

Pervo, Richard I. *Acts: A Commentary. Hermeneia: A Critical and Historical Commentary on the Bible*. Edited by Harold Attridge. Minneapolis: Fortress, 2009.

Pickstock, Catherine. *After Writing: On the Liturgical Consummation of Philosophy*. Malden: Blackwell, 1998.

Plato. *The Republic*. Translated by C. D. C. Reeve. Indianapolis: Hackett, 2004.

Poettcker, Grant. "The Messiahs Quiet Approach: Walter Benjamin's Messianic Politics." In *Paul, Philosophy and the Theopolitical Vision: Critical Engagements with Agamben, Badiou, Žižek and Others*, edited by Douglas Harink, 90–118. Eugene, OR: Cascade, 2010.

Rad, Gerhard von. *Genesis: A Commentary*. Translated by John H. Marks. Philadelphia: Westminster, 1956.

Rawls, John. *Political Liberalism*. Expanded edition. New York: Columbia University Press, 2005.

Robinson, Marilynne. *The Givenness of Things: Essays*. New York: Farrar, Straus, & Giroux, 2015.

Rowe, C. Kavin. *One True Life: The Stoics and Early Christians as Rival Traditions*. New Haven: Yale University Press, 2016.

Reumann, John. *Philippians: A New Translation with Introduction and Commentary*. Anchor Bible 33B. New Haven: Yale University Press, 2008.

Salzani, Carlos. "Coming Community." In *The Agamben Dictionary*, edited by Alex Murray and Jessica Whyte, 44–46. Edinburgh: Edinburgh University Press, 2011.

Schmitt, Carl. *The Concept of the Political. Expanded Edition*. Translated by George Schwab. Chicago: University of Chicago Press, 2007.

———. *Political Theology: Four Chapters on the Concept of Sovereignty*. Translated by George Schwab. Chicago: Chicago University Press, 1985.

Schreiter, Robert. "St. Paul's Vision of Reconciliation." *Origins* 38.46 (2009) 725–32.

Scruton, Roger. *Fools, Frauds, and Firebrands: Thinkers of the New Left*. New York: Bloomsbury, 2015.

Snyder, Timothy. *Black Earth: Holocaust as History and Warning*. New York: Duggan, 2015.

Storck, Thomas. *From Christendom to Americanism and Beyond: The Long, Jagged Trail to a Postmodern Void*. Kettering: Angelico, 2015.

Taubes, Jacob. *Occidential Eschatology*. Translated by David Ratmoko. Stanford: Stanford University Press, 2009.

———. *The Political Theology of Paul*. Translated by Dana Hollander. Stanford: Stanford University Press, 2004.

Taylor, Charles. *Modern Social Imaginaries*. Durham: Duke University Press, 2004.

Toole, David. *Waiting for Godot in Sarajevo: Theological Reflections on Nihilism, Tragedy, and Apocalypse*. Boulder: Westview, 1998.

Townes, Emilie M. *Womanist Ethics and the Cultural Production of Evil*. New York: Palgrave MacMillan, 2006.

Turner, Philip. *Christian Ethics and the Church: Ecclesial Foundations for Moral Thought and Practice*. Grand Rapids: Baker, 2015.

Verhey, Allen. *Remembering Jesus: Christian Community, Scripture, and the Moral Life*. Grand Rapids: Eerdmans, 2002.

Waters, Brent. "The Incarnation and the Christian Moral Life." In *Christology and Ethics*, edited by F. LeRon Shults and Brent Waters, 5–31. Grand Rapids: Eerdmans, 2010.

———. *Just Capitalism: A Christian Ethic of Economic Globalization*. Louisville: Westminster John Knox, 2016.

Webster, John. "Eschatology and Anthropology." In *Word and Church: Essays in Christian Dogmatics*, 263–86. New York: T. & T. Clark, 2016.

———. "Eschatology, Ontology, and Human Action." *Toronto Journal of Theology* 7.1 (Spring 1991) 4–18.

———. "God's Perfect Life." http://henrycenter.tiu.edu/resource/gods-perfect-life/.

————. *Holy Scripture: A Dogmatic Sketch.* New York: Cambridge University Press, 2003.

Weheliye, Alexander G. *Habeas Viscus: Racializing Assemblages, Biopolitics, and Black Feminist Theories of the Human.* Durham: Duke University Press, 2014.

Weil, Simone. *Gravity and Grace.* Translated by Arthur Wills. Lincoln: University of Nebraska Press, 1997.

Welborn, L. L. "Jacob Taubes – Paulinist, Messianist." In *Paul in the Grip of Philosophers,* edited by Peter Frick, 69–90. Minneapolis: Fortress, 2013.

Wesley, Charles. "Hymn 9." In *Hymns for Those that Seek and Those that have Redemption in the Blood of Jesus Christ,* edited by Randy L. Maddox, 11–12. London: Strahan, 1747. http://divinity.duke.edu/sites/divinity.duke.edu/files/documents/cswt/44_Redemption_Hymns_%281747%29_mod.pdf.

Wesley, John. "The Circumcision of the Heart." In *John Wesley's Sermons: An Anthology,* edited by Albert C. Outler and Richard P. Heitzenrater, 23–32. Nashville: Abingdon, 1991.

————. "The General Spread of the Gospel." In *The Works of John Wesley: Sermons Vol. II.34–70,* edited by Albert Outler, 485–99. Nashville: Abingdon, 1985.

————. "The New Creation." In *John Wesley's Sermons: An Anthology,* edited by Albert C. Outler and Richard P. Heitzenrater, 493–500. Nashville: Abingdon, 1991.

————. "On God's Vineyard." *The Works of John Wesley: Vol. VII.* Grand Rapids: Baker, 1996.

Widdows, Heather. *The Moral Vision of Iris Murdoch.* New York: Ashgate, 2005.

Williams, Rowan. *Lost Icons: Reflections on Cultural Bereavement.* Edinburgh: T. & T. Clark, 2000.

————. "Nobody Knows Who I Am Till Judgement Morning." *On Christian Theology,* 276–89. Malden: Blackwell, 2000.

————. "Politics and the Soul: Reading the City of God." *On Augustine,* 107–30. New York: Bloomsbury, 2016.

————. "Trinity and Ontology." *On Christian Theology,* 148–66. Malden: Blackwell, 2000.

Wink, Walter. *Naming the Powers: The Language of Power in the New Testament.* Philadelphia: Fortress, 1984.

Yoder, John Howard. "Are You the One to Come." In *For the Nations: Essays Evangelical and Public,* 199–220. Eugene, OR: Wipf & Stock, 1997.

————. "Armaments and Eschatology." *Studies in Christian Ethics* 1.1 (1988) 43–61.

————. "Firstfruits: The Paradigmatic Public Role of God's People." In *For the Nations: Essays Evangelical and Public,* 15–36. Eugene, OR: Wipf & Stock, 1997.

————. "Introduction." In *For the Nations: Essays Evangelical and Public,* 1–14. Eugene, OR: Wipf & Stock, 1997.

————. "On Not Being Ashamed of the Gospel: Particularity, Pluralism, and Validation." *Faith and Philosophy: Journal of the Society of Christian Philosophers* 9.3 (1992) 285–300.

————. *The Politics of Jesus: Vicit Agnus Noster.* 2nd ed. Grand Rapids: Eerdmans, 1994.

————. *The Royal Priesthood: Essays Ecclesiastical and Ecumenical.* Edited by Michael G. Cartwright. Scottsdale: Harold, 1994.

Young-Bruehl, Elizabeth. *Hannah Arendt: For Love of the World.* 2nd ed. New Haven: Yale University Press, 2004.

Ziegler, Philip G. "The Final Triumph of Grace: The Enmity of Death and Judgement unto Life." In *Militant Grace: The Apocalyptic Turn and the Future of Christian Theology*, 97–110. Grand Rapids: Baker, 2018.

———. *Militant Grace: The Apocalyptic Turn and the Future of Christian Theology*. Grand Rapids: Baker, 2018.

———. "Not Without the Spirit: The Eschatological Spirit at the Origin of the Faith." In *Militant Grace: The Apocalyptic Turn and the Future of Christian Theology*, 71–80. Grand Rapids: Baker, 2018.

Žižek, Slavoj. *Absolute Recoil: Towards a New Foundation of Dialectical Materialism*. London: Verso, 2014.

———. "The Spectre of Ideology." *Mapping Ideology*, 1–33. New York: Verso, 1994.

Index